THE MOVIE INDUSTRY BOOK

(How Others Made And Lost Money In The Movie Industry)

This is Volume 5 of the books in The Entertainment Industry Series

Johnny Minus & William Storm Hale

Special Articles by Guest Authors

7 Arts Press

HOLLYWOOD, CALIFORNIA 90028, U.S.A.

THE MOVIE INDUSTRY BOOK

(HOW OTHERS MADE AND LOST MONEY IN THE MOVIE INDUSTRY)
(HOW WELL WILL YOU DO?)

"Every man who knows how to read has it in his power to magnify himself, to multiply the ways in which he exists, to make his life full, significant, interesting."

- Aldous Huxley

This book was printed and manufactured in the United State of America

Library of Congress No.

This is a first edition limited to 1000 copies.

This is Copy No.

Standard Book Number 0911370-05-6.

The address of Seven Arts Press, Inc. is 6605 Hollywood Boulevard,
Suite 215
Hollywood, California 90028
Telephone: (213) Hollywood 9-1095

To readers: If you would like to be put on our THE ENTERTAINMENT INDUSTRY SERIES mailing list, please let us know.

DEDICATION

This book is dedicated to the millions of dollars lost by our sources of information, to the millions of dollars made by our sources of information, and to the motion pictures to be made by readers of this tome.

ACKNOWLEDGEMENTS

Richard Bernstein
Leslie Kovacs
Hans Richter
Sam Arkoff
Clu Gulager
Corey Allen
Marvin Miller
Reta Chandler
Jack Sattinger
Sam Zagon
Gordon Stulberg
William Hines
Jack Shapiro
Nora Alexis
Don Rico
NABET
Dee Carter
Barry J. Guggenheim
Peter Heiser
Andre' Stojka
Irwin Zucker
Steven M. Leon

Rene Hall
Peter Sorel
Joe Yore
John Ashley
Fay Spain
Myron Griffin
Nancy Bacon
Type-A-Syst
Gunther Schiff
Don Carle Gillette
Kim Fowley
Pat Miller
Joe Hallock
Jimmy O'Neill
Joan Cooper
Dootsie Williams
Pacific Title & Art Studio
General Film Laboratories
Larry Rosenblum
Tammy Marihugh
Mama Cat
Bob Maurice
Richard Basmajian
George George

ABOUT THE AUTHORS

The name of Johnny Minus and William Storm Hale are pseudonyms.

PREFACE

This book is designed to be read by businessmen who are in and who wish to be in the movie industry, by cinema students who wish to be financially rewarded instead of just thanked when they work on spec, by attorneys who wish some background knowledge before they tell their clients "You are taking a risk," by cinema course teachers who have been dodging their students' business questions, by lay readers who want to learn why so many stars who invest in their own pictures are so broke, by stars who want to learn the same answers.

Professionals who know their area of the movie industry may learn a lot about other areas. For example, producers may believe they are getting short-changed by distributors, but they may not know the activities of distributors well enough to spot the jokers in the distributor's contracts and business activities. This book will supply some of that needed knowledge.

The forms and contracts in this book are educational tools; they may be considered in preparing your own contracts. They should not be followed blindly.

Contracts tend to change with (a) the time, (b) the area, (c) the bargaining power of the parties, (d) the attorneys, (e) the law, (f) new ideas, (g) new technology.

Topics covered include steps in putting together a movie package, copyright, censorship, limited partnerships, Uniform Commercial Code, obscenity, working forms for producers and distributors, short contracts and long contracts, book reviews and magazine reviews.

It is our hope that you will use the education provided by this book to have a more financially rewarding experience in the motion picture industry.

JOHNNY MINUS

WILLIAM STORM HALE

HOLLYWOOD, CALIFORNIA

F O R E W O R D

As a publicist, writer, and producer of motion pictures,
I have known many a man who spent decades at various production
jobs in the motion picture industry, who finally rached the top
as producer of motion pictures, only to find that - no matter
how many hit pictures he may have made - it took only one picture
to ruin him financially, as well, as in some instances, emotionally
and mentally.

I have seen professional and businessmen knowingly risk
"extra money," money to play with, money that might otherwise
have been spent pursuing some other pleasure, back a motion
picture with their "extra money" and with their credit.

I have asked men to back me and my motion picture and
television projects. Some backers have been fascinated by the
glamor; others have treated their activities as a hobby. I
have always wanted a book available for backers so that they
could make their decision to "get in" or "stay out" intelligently.

You are lucky that this book now exists.

Richard Bernstein

Hollywood, California

v

THE MOVIE INDUSTRY BOOK

TABLE OF CONTENTS

PART I

PUTTING A PICTURE TOGETHER

THE MOVIE INDUSTRY BOOK

TABLE OF CONTENTS

PART II

BOOKS

PART III

MAGAZINES

THE MOVIE INDUSTRY BOOK

TABLE OF CONTENTS

PART IV

PARTNERSHIPS

PART V

DISTRIBUTION PRACTICES

PART VI

CENSORSHIP

THE MOVIE INDUSTRY BOOK

TABLE OF CONTENTS

PART VII

LABORATORY AGREEMENT

PART VIII

PRODUCER-DISTRIBUTOR AGREEMENT

PART IX

COPYRIGHT

PART X

UNIFORM COMMERCIAL CODE

PART XI
LONG CONTRACTS

THE MOVIE INDUSTRY BOOK

TABLE OF CONTENTS

PART XII

SHORT FORMS & CONTRACTS

THE MOVIE INDUSTRY BOOK

TABLE OF CONTENTS

PART XIII

SUPERSTITION

PART I

H E ' S   O V E R   2 1

This part of the book is a teaser. Before this part
is read, the reader may be enthusiastic about immediately producing a picture, and "letting financial matters take care of
themselves."

At the end of this part, the reader may wonder how
anybody with any financial sense can back movies. But don't
worry; there are additional parts of this book.

INTRODUCTORY CHAPTER

There are two ways for persons and companies in the entertainment industry to make money: (1) From customers; (2) From investors, creditors and suppliers.

Producers of motion pictures sometimes make money from (1) Customers (distributors); often make money only from (2) Investors, creditors, and suppliers.

Distributors of motion pictures sometimes make money from (1) Customers (exhibitors); often keep money rightfully belonging to (2) Investors, creditors, and suppliers (the producers).

Exhibitors of motion pictures sometimes make money from (1) Customers (movie goers); often keep money rightfully belonging to (2) Investors, creditors, and suppliers (the distributors).

Hundreds of motion pictures have been produced by producers and businessmen who have not known what they were doing in their business dealings.

Producers and financial backers of pictures have lost their lifesavings because the papers they innocently, ignorantly signed to get the movie on the way turned up to haunt them in later years.

This is a business book for businessmen, a thought-provoking source for students, a mine of statutory, case, and form information for lawyers, a source of information designed for the business, motion picture and reference shelves of libraries.

Should producers lend copies of this book to businessmen? No. Producers should get businessmen to buy their own copies.

Will some businessmen be scared to invest after they read this book? Yes, some will be scared. But others, who **may** be more scared of the unknown than of dangers they have been warned about, may decide to invest.

Is this book wholly accurate? Of course not. What book is?

William Storm Hale

Hollywood, California

February 6, 1970

THE WORD - THREE MISQUOTES

"In the beginning was the Word . . ."

JOHN I:1.

"In the beginning of every movie project is a word, an idea, a story outline, a screen treatment, a first-draft script, a series of revisions, a shooting script."

Curtis Sanders, *Writer.*

"In the beginning of every motion picture is a word - a producer saying, 'OK.' Until then, there are lots of very talented people - on the unemployment line."

Richard Bernstein, *Producer.*

<u>S U C K E R</u>

"Credulity is the man's weakness, but the child's strength."

      Lamb, *Witches and Other Night Fears.*

"There's a sucker born every minute."

      Phineas Taylor Barnum.

"Hello, Sucker!"

      Texas Guinan, *(Greeting to night club patron).*

"Hello, Sucker!"

      Producer, *(Under his breath, addressing potential investor).*

"Hello, Sucker!"

      Distributor, *(Under his breath, addressing producer with picture project).*

"Hello, Sucker!"

      . . . .

THE PRODUCER AND THE BUSINESSMAN

Act I - Years Ago

A businessman told another: "A producer told me that he made his last picture for $100,000. He sold it outright to a distributor for $150,000. The picture is grossing millions at the box office.

"The producer wants to make another picture and he is letting me invest $10,000 at this time. This time the producer plans not to sell the picture outright. This time he plans to lease it to the distributor on a percentage basis; that way, the production company will make millions and the investors will get their money back many times over."

Businessman #2: "Don't invest."

Act II - One Year Later

Businessman #1 to Businessman #2: "I gave the producer $10,000 and he typed out a half-page agreement stating that he would pay me 10% interest in four months and I would get 10% of the profits of the picture. The agreement was so simple that I signed without showing it to my lawyer.

"The producer used my $10,000 to live on and to pay his office expenses. I did not want him to do that. I wanted him to hold the $10,000 until he had raised the $100,000 budget of the picture.

"The producer did not pay me 10% interest at the end of

four months. In fact, he has paid me nothing."

"The principal photography is over. The producer says he needs additional financing for the music. Creditors are harassing the producer. I don't want to sue for my money because I'm afraid the creditors will close in."

Businessman #2: "I told you not to invest."

Act III - Another Year Later

Businessman # 1 to Businessman #2: "I'm in real trouble. That simple half-page agreement between the producer and me is so vague and indefinite that I'm having trouble in court. If I loaned the producer the $10,000, then I charged him too much interest. If I became a partner with the producer with my $10,000, then I may be liable with the producer for the unpaid debts incurred in the production of the picture."

Businessman #2: "Can't you say you were only a limited partner?"

Businessman #1: "No. Limited partnership protection for limited partners is available in this state only if the certificate of limited partnership is properly recorded. Our simple half-page agreement was not recorded."

Businessman #2: "I told you not to invest."

Act IV - Another Year Later

Businessman #1 to Businessman #2:   "Am I glad I home-
steaded my home! The bank which loaned money to the producer
took all the money I had in my savings account and checking
account in one of the bank's branches. Now the bank has notified me to pay them at least $10,000 by next week or they will
sue me."

Businessman #2:   "Why did the bank do that?"

Businessman #1:   "A few years ago the producer told me
he was going to the bank to talk about a loan for the picture,
and the producer said I had a good business head so he wanted
me to come along. At the bank, the banker gave the producer a
lot of contracts totaling over fifty pages to read. They concerned instructions between the producer and the distributor,
and the distributor and the laboratory. The producer told the
banker that the producer trusted the banker and the producer
signed the contracts.

"Then the banker gave me a simple half-page guarantee
agreement to sign; it was so simple that I did not take it to
my lawyer to read; so I signed it. . . .

"The picture is not doing as well at the box office as
we hoped, according to the distributor. The bank loan was not
repaid within the two years after the loan. The bank then

collected under the terms of the guarantee from me; one of the terms of the guarantee was that the bank could take my money which I had in any of the bank's branches. So the bank took my money.

"But the money they took was not enough to repay the loan in full. Now the bank wants an additional $10,000 by next week and wants a system of payments for the rest."

Businessman #2: "I told you not to invest."

Act V - Another Year Later

Businessman #1 to Businessman #2: "Can you give me a job? I lost everything."

Businessman #2: "How did you lose everything?"

Businessman #1: "The producer was very good to me while he was preparing the picture; he wanted me to learn as much as I could so that I would be of more use in his next project. The producer took me to the film laboratory which processed the footage as it was shot and then made the prints for distribution. I don't remember signing anything, but the film lab had my signature on a guarantee.

"For a long time the film lab waited for the distributor to pay them. Every year the distributor's accounting statement to the producer would show that the distributor ordered another $1000 worth of prints. Now, I think that no prints were ordered, and that this was a way for the distributor to bribe the laboratory to stay in line. But, finally, the film laboratory decided to sue, and they are suing not only for the initial work and the prints made when the picture was actively released, but also for the $1000 each for the last few years.

"The lab won its lawsuit against the producer and me, and others whom the producer had suckered the way he suckered me. And that's not all."

Businessman #2: "There's more?"

Businessman #1: "Yes. Some creditors of the producer sued me as a supposedly silent, but not limited, partner. The creditors showed the court that I had been with the producer since the beginning of his business activities concerning the picture, that I had attended business conferences, that I had guaranteed the bank loan and the lab bill, and the court held me liable as a general partner. Since the producer skipped town, the burden of paying all debts falls on me.

"I can't stay in business because creditors keep attaching my assets or keep throwing in a keeper.

"Can you give me a job?"

Businessman #2: "Why should I give a job to a man whose wages are always going to be attached? Anyway, I told you not to invest."

Act VI - Yesterday

Businessman #2 to Businessman #1: "You look fine. What are you doing these days?"

Businessman #1: "I'm doing well. I'm a producer. Do

you want to invest in my next picture?"

        ((The story you have just read is incomplete. We
failed to tell what the unions of the drunken actor and the
pregnant actress did. Maybe we'll be able to get to them later
in the book.))

"HE'S OVER 21"

Toward the end of this book is a bibliography of books, both hard cover and paperback, which contain business information.

The producer who deals with potential investors, money lenders, and guarantors has many problems. His goal is to get money. To do so he must present the facts and his hopes that the picture will make a lot of money for all concerned.

Frequently, the hopes of the producer are better than actual events. Investors fail to receive expected proceeds, and scream to the producer and to others.

The investor with some of the business knowledge available in books and trade publications can better understand delays, whether a producer's words are meant as representations of fact or puffs and optimistic hopes.

The potential investors can also decide whether to invest in the business of the producer (producer's weekly salary, office overhead, etc.) or only in pre-production of specific projects (options, treatments, scripts), or only in production of the picture (actual shooting and post-shooting).

The potential money men can make better decisions if they know the business better.

Also, if potential money men understand systems

involving distributors' accountings (the distributor gets his
share, then more, then the remainder), the potential money men
can better understand contracts offered by distributors.

In the absence of such understanding, businessmen
may be too lazy to read the "standard" (joke; there is no such
thing) contract offered by distributors. The lazy businessmen may sign what they do not understand. And, in accordance
with the philosophy of too many distributors, such businessmen deserve to be plucked. ("He's over 21. He did not have
to sign.")

CREDITS

THE HOLLYWOOD REPORTER, a leading trade publication, has offices at 6715 Sunset Boulevard, Hollywood, California 90028. Daily issues sell for 15 cents each; an annual subscription costs $30.00.

Every Friday *THE HOLLYWOOD REPORTER* devotes several pages to "Feature Film Production." On Friday, November 29, 1969, listed among other pictures was "Soldier Blue."

This picture has been selected at random to illustrate credits. Nothing else in this book concerns "Soldier Blue."

SOLDIER BLUE

(Listed with other pictures under the heading of AVCO-EMBASSY).

Katzka-Loeb Productions shooting in Mexico.

Cast:	Candice Bergen
	Peter Strauss
	Donald Pleasance
	John Anderson
	Alph Elson
Producer:	Harold Loeb
Director:	Ralph Nelson
Associate Producer:	Bill Gilmore
Assistant:	Terry Morse, Jr.
Production Manager:	Antonio Guerrero Tello
Photography:	Arthur Omitz
Art Director:	Frank Arrigo
Film Editor:	Alex Beaton
Sound:	Barry Thomas
Unit Publicist:	Axel Madsen

Why are these credits listed here? We wish to introduce a few of the occupations which must be considered by a producer of a motion picture.

THE TALENT MAN AND THE MONEY MAN

"When I first started producing motion pictures, there would be two key men - one who knew talent and one who knew money.

"The <u>talent man</u> would have had experience doing or supervising some of the following: writer, director, assistant to producer, photographer, editor, agent, personal manager, actor, publicist, producer; it was important that he knew how to bring in the finished picture within budget.

"The <u>money man</u> would have to be able to impress the money sources (investors, banks, laboratories, deferral takers) that each would not only get his money back, but would get ample profits, dividends, interest, etc. Often the money man would be a business manager or a lawyer.

"Both the <u>talent man</u> and the <u>money man</u> often get producer credit on the screen - the talent man as 'producer' and the money man as 'executive producer,' as 'co-producer,' or as 'associate producer.' Frequently, the <u>talent man</u> and the <u>money man</u> share evenly the amount in the budget set aside for the 'producer.'

Richard Bernstein, Producer.

MONEY SOURCES

"What is money? We can better understand its definition
if we consider what money will do for us. It has three main functions. First, money is a means of payment or a medium of exchange.
Second, it is a storage of purchasing power. Third, it is a standard of value."

*Pugh, CALIFORNIA REAL ESTATE FINANCE, Page 20, Prentice-
Hall, 1966.*

"It is unquestionably true that the economy of the United
States is a credit economy. Thus, the usual situation, except
for inexpensive personal purchase, is for purchases or investments
to be made possible only by the buyer or investor borrowing a
considerable percentage of the sale price of an item or of the
amount to be invested. Banks are the most significant general
source of credit available to individuals, institutions, and
business establishments. . . . their major loan activities involve personal and commercial loans. Emphasis upon these loans
is logical since banks are normally established to serve such
borrowers."

*Pugh, CALIFORNIA REAL ESTATE FINANCE, Page 5, Prentice-
Hall, 1966.*

Money sources are: (1) Investors; (2) Lenders.

"Whilst that for which all virtue now is sold,
  And almost every vice, - almighty gold."

Ben Johnson, EPISTLE TO ELIZABETH, COUNTESS OF RUTLAND.

ONE-MAN MOVIE - JOE YORE

(Part I - Talent)

"I had an idea concerning a movie about a hippie who had lots of "love" for everybody, but no respect for anything or anybody.

"I imagined the story of happy loving Hippie, Hippie Meets Groovie, Hippie Kills Groovie (thus losing Groovie), Hippie Commits Suicide (thus getting Groovie).

"I imagined each scene, the setting, the sound, and had everything in my mind before putting anything on paper.

"I wrote the first draft of the script, broke it down into locations, and prepared a shooting schedule.

"I obtained permission to use each location: bank, liquor store, park, beach. I shot many scenes at home and in my parking lot.

"I did some talent scouting, found the girl to play 'Groovie,' found other actors and actresses to play parts.

"I produced, directed, and starred as 'Hippie.' I was production manager, director of photography, film editor, and script supervisor.

"I wrote and recorded the music, sound effects, dialog, and combined the sound tracks.

"I previewed the motion picture, listened to audience reaction, tightened some parts of the picture, and shot some additional minutes."

(Part II - Money)

"Money was a problem. I had savings. A relative loaned me money. I had credit with companies which rented equipment, such as cameras, lights. I exchanged labor (mine) by working for the cameraman, editing-equipment suppliers, for a man who had credit with a recording studio, and I did not have to pay cash for these items. I worked for pay for others to get money for film. I settled an accident case, and received enough money to complete my movie. Various people cooperated for friendship reasons or to get exposure.

"People told me that I could not make a 'one-man' movie of feature length.

"People were wrong.

"I made a one-man movie.

"But I think that for bigger motion pictures where highly talented persons are on salary and every technical sound, lighting, or camera mistake can cost a fortune, I would use professional men for each task. And to finance these professional motion pictures, I would seek banks in the business of lending money on motion picture productions, investors and guarantors who have sufficient available money for motion picture projects."

(Mr. Yore is a television and motion picture actor, composer, and recording artist-editor.)

ONE-MAN MOVIE

THE STILL PHOTOGRAPHER

A free-lance still photographer-writer thought of a story idea for one of the magazines which regularly accepted his picture stories. The magazine liked the idea, approved it, commissioned the photographer to shoot the story.

The photographer found models, lights, proper cameras, directed the action, shot the still photographs for the magazine story.

Then the photographer took out his professional movie camera, used the same models and lights, directed the action, and shot one-tenth of his ten-episode movie.

His pay from the magazine covered all expenses for selling, models, lights, cameras, development of the still shots, development of his movie footage.

It required a year before he shot ten episodes in that manner, but finally it was complete.

This picture was commercial.

(This story has been presented to illustrate how one man was producer (talent man and money man), talent (director, cameraman, writer), and financier.

THIRTEEN RULES FOR THE PRODUCER

OR

HOW TO SUCCEED WITHOUT TALENT

1.   Study to look tremendously important.

2.   Speak with great assurance - sticking closely, however, to generally accepted facts.

3.   Avoid arguments, but, if challenged, fire an irrelevant question at your antagonist and intently polish your glasses while he tries to answer. As an alternative, hum under your breath while examining your fingernails.

4.   Contrive to mingle with important people.

5.   Before talking with a man you wish to impress, ferret out his remedies for current problems, then advocate them strongly.

6.   Listen while others wrangle, then pluck out a platitude and defend it righteously.

7.   When asked a question by a subordinate, give him a "Have you lost your mind?" stare until he glances down, then paraphrase the question back to him.

8.   Acquire a capable stooge, but keep him in the background.

9.   In offering to perform a service, imply your complete familiarity.

10.   Arrange to be the clearing house for all complaints.

It encourages the thought that you are in control and enables you to keep the stooge in his place.

11. Never acknowledge thanks for your attention -- this will implant subconscious obligation in the mind of your victim.

12. Carry yourself in the grand manner. Refer to your associates as "some of the boys in our office." Discourage light conversation that might bridge the gap between boss and man.

13. Walk swiftly from place to place as if engrossed in affairs of great moment. Keep your office door closed. Interview by appointment only. Give orders by memoranda. Remember, you are a *BIG SHOT*, and you don't give a damn who knows it!

ROCK FESTIVALS

The 1969 Rock Festival near Woodstock, N.Y. is reputed to have been attended by over 200,000 people; the 1969 Rock Festival at the Altamont Speedway in Alameda County, California is reputed to have been attended by over 300,000.

The information in the following paragraphs is based on an *INCIDENT REPORT, Sheriff's Office, San Luis Obispo.*

The Altamont audiences by their mass were causing inter-state highways to be closed and near-riot conditions to exist. The Alameda County Sheriff's Office maintained a Command Post at the Altamont Freeway. Helicopter operations were maintained during daylight hours.

The sheriff's office received reports of two accidental deaths, one homicide, and numerous incidents of drug-overdose patients being admitted to local hospitals. The accidental deaths in the area of the "Rock Festival" were attributed to drug intoxication. The homicide was believed to have been com-mitted by a member of the Hell's Angels Motocycle Club.

Three unattended births were reported.

Indiscriminate use and sale of narcotics, alcoholic beverages and various sexual activities had been observed by officers in observation helicopters. Policing within the area was contracted to an Oakland Security Patrol and the Hell's

Angels Motorcycle Club. Several deaths were attributed to drug
hallucination. The death of an eighteen-year-old male was attributed to an unidentified member of the Hell's Angels, allegedly in self-defense. Two tactical squads of shotgun-armed
officers were necessary to merely enter the compound and remove the victim's body. The body had been moved throughout the
concert area by intoxicated individuals for several hours before
the Sheriff's Office was notified of the slaying. . . . Ranch
fences, etc. had been torn down to use as firewood and property
owners had been subjected to massive intimidation by transient
trespassers.

        . . . A maximum number of thirty tactical officers and
commanders was maintained at the Command Post at all times.
Additional personnel could only be obtained by airlift or by
walking approximately six miles. All routes of vehicular traffic were closed by massive traffic jams.

        Intelligence reports, films and photographs were made
by police officials.

        * * *

        Now, back to New York's festival near Woodstock. Over
150,000 feet of film were shot in a few days. About one year
of editing followed. The film may be(come) the most successful
documentary.

        Since part of the Americana of Woodstock is the speed,
nudity, obscene dialogue, it will be interesting to see what the
ignorance-maintaining pressure groups do in connection with this
film.

HOW TO MAKE MONEY IN MOTION PICTURES

WITHOUT SUING

By

Woodrow Olivetti

(NOTE: Woodrow Olivetti is a well-known producer-writer of about a couple of dozen motion pictures, which have been released by internationally-known major distributors. His films have starred some of the top box office names in motion pictures, have been directed by famous directors, photographed by Academy Award-winning cameramen. Woodrow Olivetti is a pseudonym, since this gentleman feels that using his real name might impair his status in the motion picture industry.)

To start off, movie investors should know that only 2 out of 500 independent films are sold to major studio distributors at an immediate profit. Usually, the studio gets the picture on a releasing deal, and pays the producer back out of money earned. The producer also pays 35% or more for distribution fees, repays the distributor for the prints and about $10,000 for pressbooks and possibly $50,000 for advertising.

One afternoon, a distributor's secretary called him on the intercom and told him that a young producer was asking to see him. For the fourth time he told his secretary that he was too busy to see the producer. The producer heard his answer on the intercom, stepped past the secretary, opened the door to

the executive's office, walked to his desk. The executive was

flabbergasted.

"You've got some gall!" he said.

The young producer, wild-eyed, reached into his pocket,

drew out a revolver, pointed it at the executive and said,

"You've been using my money for four years now and I've lost

everything, because my personal cash has been tied up in my

picture; so I decided to blow your brains out!"

The executive blanched and clicked on the intercom and

told his secretary to call his partner. The partner came in and

the young producer held him at gunpoint, too.

"What do you want?" asked the partner.

"I want my profits and my money back," the producer re-

plied, "my film has been in profit two years."

The distributor is very important. He sells the pro-

ducer's film world-wide for a fee and handles the delivery of

prints and advertising material to theatres all over the world.

What the young producer said was true in word, but the

company's trickery in report sheets, showed that he owed them

about $20,000 before the film broke even, as the movie industry

says.

Report sheets explain the amount of money the film takes

in. "Break even," is the amount of money a film must make to

pay its investors back and go into profit.

Both partners thought it a little foolhardy to bring up their report sheets so they agreed to buy the producer's ownership. They paid him $30,000 profit and his investment back, and gave him $20,000 for the rest of his percentage of the film. Despite the fact that the producer came in at gunpoint, they decided not to call the police and they hushed up the whole thing because of fear of scandal.

Distribution or releasing company "cheating" is as common as the cold. Companies bill the big money-making pictures for the charges that really belong to the flop films owned by the distributors. This is hard to prove, because the independent producer's report sheet received by the producer from the distributor is just one sheet, and does not go into detail as to whom charges are paid, but just gives a lump sum of money paid out.

One producer, who made a $400,000 film, looked at his report sheet and saw that the film was charged $98,000 "miscellaneous" by the distributor. He has been trying for two years to get the distributor to explain what the charges were. So far, he hasn't gotten a definite maybe on anything.

The distributor is like the cool-looking blonde, who is being ogled by a wolf. They both feel that if you ignore someone, they will go away.

However, this isn't true. One major distributorship, that releases independent films, has settled 24 law suits in the last two years, and has another 27 unsettled. Because of this state of affairs, each distribution company has its own staff of lawyers, in some cases two to three, in other cases more.

In writing this article, I feel that I can do a service to the prospective investor, the would-be independent producer, writer or director.

In any business, any person, who has a chance to make or lose money, likes to keep the chance of losing down to almost nothing. In Hollywood, Diogenes could walk around with his lamp for an eternity without finding an honest releasing company.

A lawyer for a major studio told me, "Sure we owe you all that money, and it's all profit, but we can't pay you because we used your money to pay other bills."

Distributors tell the producer what quality they want in a film, what stars, what director and approve the screen play. Once the film is completed, it is given to the distributor for distribution.

However, no studio tells a producer anything once they have his film. The average distribution contract ties up the motion picture for years, gives the distributor most of the money from TV and has options for renewal every seven years.

Despite distribution "cheating," it will probabl many years before the average independent produce guarantees for the return of his investment, which enforced against distributors in court. Like gamblers, the would-be millionaires of film-making do not believe that distributors "steal" from the majority of independent producers, and publicize the few they don't steal from.

When it comes to suing, only one out of 100 lawsuits started by producers against distributors are not settled out of court. One major settled 40 lawsuits out of court and paid off the producers or the production company that sued. Suits bring more suits and bad publicity.

60% of the money used to produce independent pictures is obtained from sources outside the motion picture industry, from banks, loan companies and financiers.

It is money from successful men in other industries, who want to "take a flyer" at making money in motion pictures because they hear of the big money that is made in films.

One investor, who invested $400,000 a few years back, just got back $70,000 and was told that was all that he would recoup. He lost $330,000. His film was so bad that he and his associates were told that it would go right on TV with no release in theatres. He made it without a release because no distributor liked the project.

A top producer made an all-star $650,000 picture for a major national distributor. After it was in distribution for three years and the picture grossed twice its budget, the producer was told that, "if you live to be 100, you might see some profit money." Not too many people live to be 100, and not too many independent producers get to see "profit money" although distributors boast that they do.

Let's assume you are an investor in one of my films, "Star Bright." I have a distribution contract that guarantees me 80% of the cost of "Star Bright" in 18 months. I take this to a bank and the bank, based on the distribution contract, loans my company 60% of the money for the film. Next comes deferments, which are delayed money payments taken by stars, directors, producers, and writers. These are part of my other 40%. The rest of the 40% is "second money" or "risk money." It is guaranteed back to the investor by nobody. The investor stands to make money only if the distributor distributes the film profitably.

Many producers barely get their deferments and personal money back because the national distributor takes all the money, fills his report sheet with a load of charges, and then informs the producer that he had too many prints, that they had to pay too much for advertising, and had some "bad breaks."

A boyish, middle-aged star took a large deferment and a percentage in an independent film that grossed about $3,000,000. He was delighted with all the publicity about the success of the film. After two years of waiting for his percentage of profits, he called the distributor - who told him " were all publicity, and we didn't do that well."

He was astonished after an audit, which c

to find that the film did gross $3,000,000. The distributor
still insists on settling out of court; the actor agreed to
settle for $83,000. The distributor countered with $43,000.
They have not settled.

At a theatre owners' convention, the president of a
major company admitted to me that "some independents" got hurt
and that all the major distributors were trying to work out a
way to assure independents a profit for a good film.

It doesn't take much of an imagination to realize that
two high-budget independent films that do not pay off within 18
months of their release can ruin the independent producer for
many years.

I learned that a distributor made $300,000 distributing
an independent producer's film, but the producer almost lost
his home because he had used it as collateral for his risk money.

A lawyer told me, "When a producer makes a film for release by _____ distributing company, he should start suing the
first day of shooting.

However, a hit picture can be a short cut to fame. A
star took a deferment and starred in a gangster story. The film
was a runaway hit and changed the man's career. Five years later,
he admitted to me that he had never received "much money" from
the film that made him famous. But due to his reputation from
that film, he made money starring in other films.

However, there is a small and private circle of

independent film producers who make a profit on their films.
What is their secret? Simple; they make their films in partnerships or co-productions with the distributor. In this way,
in order for the distributor to get his money back, he has to
"bail out" the independent producer.

Releasing company "cheating" has been a big factor in
runaway productions. It sent some producers to Europe. The
fact that many financial backers in the U.S. have lost money on
independent films, and are discouraged, has led a lot of independent producers to go to Europe - where they can share in the
money subsidies, get co-financing, and also get a "fair shake"
in distribution in other parts of the world, through European
distributors.

Surprisingly enough, there is always a steady flow of
young independent producers, who sign with major national distributors despite the pitfalls. They are awe-struck by suc-
cesses such as "Bonnie and Clyde."

The same fate faces the writer, whether he is the novelist whose book is filmed, or the screen writer who takes "part
cash and part deferment." Chances are that they will see only
the cash and may never see the deferment, unless the distributor feels he should give a particular producer a square count.

One producer had $45,000 due in deferments. He finally
decided to sue. The average top motion picture attorney charges
$75 an hour at his office, $100 if he has to go to court.

There is one point, however, that is consoling: most companies settle out of court. Why? Because they sell stock, and adverse publicity can hurt them. Most of all, they settle because they are guilty.

There is almost nothing more exciting than shooting a motion picture; but there is something else that is just as exciting, and that's getting your money back plus a profit.

After a great many films, and a great many lawsuits, one independent producer has come up with what he considers an ideal modus operandi.

"Remember," he says, "Order is Heaven's first law - and so it is with motion pictures. A motion picture must be put together and then filmed systematically."

The first step is the word, getting the story down on paper and then into screen play form. Then a star has to be found to play in it, a box office name.

The star must work for part of his normal salary, plus a deferment (delayed payment), which means that he will get a part of his salary when the film goes into profit. In order to take a deferment, an agent usually insists that his star also own an interest or percentage in the picture.

The star of this producer was a $45,000-a-picture star. He took $25,000 in cash, a deferment of $20,000 for 18 months, and 10% of the picture. That means he actually owned no part of the picture, but owned 10% of its profits.

It is the star that he gets who inspires the top director to work with the producer. He now has a name star, the top director, and himself - the producer - so he approaches the national distributor.

If the distributor finds the project interesting, he will: (a) give the producer a guarantee; (b) give him a contract which can be taken to a bank that will lend money to the producer on the strength of the distributor's guarantee.

After that comes the leading lady. She has to be a talented and attractive young woman. One of the greatest difficulties in film-making is getting a feminine lead to be approved by your top male star. It is easier to have a female name star approve a male lead, than a male approve a female lead. Nobody knows why.

The screenplay is important. It is the director's blueprint and also the cameraman's pattern. Details are important. If a script shows every detail, no matter how small it is, then shooting of the film will be both cheaper and simpler. (A name script writer gets $10,000 or more for the script).

A script has to be flexible so that, if the director gets a good idea while the film is shooting, it can be incorporated without upsetting what has gone before on the screen, or what will follow.

When writing a script, some writers make mental notes of how long each shot will look on the screen. Young directors today use weird closeups, but one thing is sure: the closeup is a life saver; it gives any film its shock value. It is a "neutral" shot, that can be fitted in almost anywhere. It excites the audience.

The director's job is to get the story on the screen so that it entertains. A "talky" film can be very dull. Most directors avoid too much talk by using a lot of action, fights, and sex.

An audience likes a film that tells a story. They get interested in a story and watch the film. It takes a talented director to make simple words sound good and have the actors look good on the screen.

Cities and places where a film is shot are very important. Human beings present different personalities at different times. A sexpot in one film can play a virgin in another film.

Fritz Lang, who made the classic "Fury" with the late Spencer Tracy, said, "On the screen everything must be clearer, more simple and really more interesting than things in real life."

With experience in making films, a producer learns that realism comes with editing, script, camera work and acting. And, of course, direction.

The director composes the scenes, so that they have the proper emotional effect on the audience. It is up to him to determine the visual qualities of a situation.

In some scenes, the pictorial value is more important than any words.

The rarest film today is the comedy. A good comedy makes money. A comedy must have two ingredients: it must deal with funny situations, and it must be fast-paced.

There is a fine line between comedy and tragedy. Charles Chaplin and Buster Keaton proved that over and over again in their films, that people laugh at tragedy.

As time goes on, there seem to be fewer and fewer good comedians.

The story is the thing in producing a film. It introduces the characters in the motion picture and the situations in which the characters find themselves, and the problems they get into. It acts as a connecting thread between all the action in the film.

Another popular film is the horror film. However, because there have been so many, today's horror film has to have "fresh new grotesque situations," that will shock audiences.

Bela Lugosi made millions for studios, and died leaving a modest estate.

Motion pictures entertain the whole world. They tell on the big screen, sorrow, joy, excitement, fear, and every other kind of emotion.

A film's title is important. It is the title that

draws people into the theatre. Once in the theatre, the customer
is attracted by the screen titles, which get his attention and
keep it.

Once a producer has finished filming, he starts editing
and sound editing. Then the music is put to the film. When
the film is completed, he "sneak previews" the film about five
times in five different cities. This helps him find the "dull"
spot.

The film is then delivered to the distributor. This is
the "moment of truth." This is when the independent producer
has to watch his step.

An independent producer's basic "deal" today can be very
simple. He may demand 80% financing for his films, or an 80%
guarantee which he can take to a bank; he comes up with another
20% from investors. Once he has completed the film, he delivers
it to the distributor, who then takes over the bank loan, and
his risk money from the investors. He has obtained his screen
writer's fee and his producer's fee. He also gets 10% of the
profits, if there are any.

In the past I never used to audit a distributor; today,
I audit every six months. I demand a list of all advertising
and in what magazines and newspapers they appeared, and what
the cost was. I demand to know how many film prints are made;
the average print costs $250. One of my films has 250 prints.
Multiply $250 by 250 and you have $62,500.

To avoid another pitfall, I have my attorney draw up
the contracts with the distributor's attorney. This gives me
additional protection. I know if I sue later, my attorney
understands the contract.

Stars with percentages are a problem. Their careers
go up and down like yo-yos. When they are "slipping," or
"falling," or whatever you want to call it, they think of where
they can get money. They suddenly remember the percentage or
delayed payment, and they go after the producer like the hounds
after the hare. I have the distributor assume all deferments.

A great producer-director made a million-dollar comedy.
The comedy grossed 5 million, but the distributor had the
"crying towel" out and told him that "the film would break even
in another year."

The producer-director attached the company's assets,
got to their books and sued. He was awarded $2,000,000 for
his percentage of the profits. Distributors lie, they wait to
go to court. They feel that the longer they can stall, the
more time they have use of "your money."

It is a sick way to think, but this is a sick, sick
world and a lot of people, not only in show business, think the
same way.

I once signed with a major distributor as an independent,
and said to my attorney, "I think that they should pay me in
gold." I may not be wrong.

James Coburn, who is a big name today, after a career of 10 years of being another face told me, "I'm a household face now; they know me."

I was at a major studio, when Rod Steiger played Al Capone. He became the Capone character and, today, he is one of the greatest stars in films. That hit film had a big part in aiding him to acquire his present stature.

The late Humphrey Bogart once said about deferments, "Not for me; I take the money and run."

However, when John Huston and Sam Spiegel came along with an independent production, "The African Queen," in which Bogie co-starred with Katherine Hepburn, he changed his mind and he made a bundle of money.

Why? Because "The African Queen" was like today's "Bonnie and Clyde." How can a distributor tell a producer who has a film that is playing all over the world with lines around the theatre that it isn't making money? It's pretty difficult for honest people.

However, the sharp producer - and the investor, too - watches the distributor. He looks out for "fictitious costs," "prints" that don't exist except on the report sheets, and that old devil, "miscellaneous."

Today, creative producers try to have a little more interest in what's being done with a picture that they have made. They want the money due them and they don't indulge the distributor.

A few years back, a distributor owed a producer a lot of money. The distributor told the producer that he would like to buy the producer out and to own the film. The producer agreed. The next day, the distributor verbally told the producer's attorney that the film was $35,000 in profit and that the producer had a $15,000 deferment. He agreed to pay the producer $50,000 to own the film. The producer sold out. Two years later, the producer learned that the distributor's report sheets were three months behind and that when the distributor bought out the producer the film was really $80,000 in profit and that the distributor had made an additional $30,000 off the producer the day the producer signed his sale contract.

To show you what a great conscience the distributor had, I met him at a party and told him that I knew of his little duplicity. He smiled and said, "The producer was over 21."

In Hollywood, to these robber barons, if you are over 21, it means that they can steal your wife, sell your children, hock your home, steal your money, cheat you, smear you, and you're supposed to giggle and smile like a court jester and say, "Wheeeeeee!"

A young motion picture star-producer recently died broke. His tearful wife went to an attorney to sue a distributor who was releasing her husband's most successful film.

The attorney contacted the distributor and told him the

widow was destitute.

The president of the distribution firm smirked, "Tell her that we can't do anything till his estate goes through probate."

"She's broke," the attorney repeated.

The benevolent executive smiled, "So are a lot of people."

The widow is still suing.

An attorney told me a story about this releasing company, "When you sue them, you just get exercise."

The company has a way of ducking court, by having its executives play "musical airplanes." When a court date approaches, they petition the court for an extension because one of the key witnesses has to leave the country.

One producer had waited five years for his day in court. When he got to court, he had a heart attack in the corridor. He died the next day; now his widow is suing. The distributor has never offered to settle.

A now-deceased robber baron distributor, known affectionately as "The Fortieth Thief," once said, "Screw them all but six and save them for the pall bearers."

When he died, they had a hard time getting six pall bearers. He had screwed more than his share, I guess.

Very important is the foreign revenue on a film, both theatrically and TV. The distributor reports that last, but the alert investor and producer make sure what countries have been sold for what price and when they will collect the money or if they have already collected the money.

A distributor sold a film of mine with a major star to 45 countries in one week and collected money from all of them; they put it on my report sheet six months later.

When I called it to their attention, they called it "an oversight." Oversights for independent producers are very popular and you can find them all over; they're like rabbits.

I had a good friend who made some of the greatest gangster films ever made. He had made some money, but admitted that "the distributors made 75% more." He was very broke. One day he raced into my office; he was going to be arrested for a $150 bad check. I loaned him the money to cover it.

He went to Europe and was gone two years. He came back with a great money-making movie. He owned 50% of it, and a French company owned 50%. The distributor was taking 35% distribution. The guy was making money hand over fist for the first time in his life. He sent me the $150 he'd borrowed and called me from New York.

"We'll celebrate; we'll have dinner together next week. I'll be 43 Friday," he enthused.

He never made it; he died the day before his birthday; but it was, to my mind, a moral victory. He died on the way to the bank.

However, distribution companies have their "inner circle" jungle battles, and a man who is president today can be locked outside the studio tomorrow.

Being "kicked out" or "fired" can be a very big handicap in Hollywood. One top distribution executive did not work for 10 years after he was removed as the head of a big distribution company. He just sat in a big office in Beverly Hills and played solitaire.

"I hope that I die every day, but I'm still here," he once told friends.

It's that important to some people, this mad rat race that grinds up hopes and dreams, consumes people, grinds up their personalities, slashes their marriages, jades them until they are beautiful, unemotional "plastic people."

A late producer-writer-director-actor once said, "What is love? It's when you look in the mirror and you see something that you like."

In Hollywood, Faith, Hope and Charity can only be the names of three swinging big-busted starlets who are looking for that "big break."

So, if you're going to be a producer, remember what I have written.

THE   STAR

We keep trying to get our producer along the way to producing *THE JOE YORE STORY*, also known as *WHO IS JOE YORE?*

Our valiant producer has found a story idea, has promoted the screen writer into writing a screen play (thus violating union regulations against writing on spec ("spec" for speculation).

The next step for the producer is to find a box office star.

The star should be right for the picture and for the budget. For example, a producer who wants to bring in a picture for under a million dollars can forget about the stars whose salary per picture is more than $250,000.

One producer had an idea. He could shoot a picture in 10 working days for $100,000 plus the cost of the star. The producer was able to raise $300,000 with which to shoot the picture. This would allow him to pay a super star $100,000 weekly for 2 weeks for the remaining $200,000. However, the producer was unable to get any star worth $100,000 weekly to appear in his picture. A superstar wants to protect his image with a multi-million production, which also stars other box office attractions.

The star must be right for the picture. Certain stars

of Westerns were draws in Westerns, only, but were not draws in any other type of picture.

The star must not be wrong for a picture. Generally, boxing pictures do not star any actor who has already appeared in a starring role as a boxer.

The producer must sell a lot of persons on the idea of making the picture. After the picture is made, a lot of people connected with distribution and promotion must be sold on the idea of pushing the picture and showing the picture.

Most of the people along the road to the theatre are middle aged (31-99) by movie-goers' (15-30 years) standards. Thus, the star must qualify two ways - he must be known to the ticket buyers and must be known to the middle aged group.

The super stars (Elizabeth Taylor, Burt Lancaster, Ingrid Bergmann, Richard Burton, Charlie Brown) are known to the middle-aged crowd (the director, the distributor, the distributor's branch personnel, the newspaper columnists, the exhibitors).

But are they known to the readers of *TEEN SCREEN*? *TEEN SCREEN* never mentions the super stars. Those super stars are older than the parents of the kids who read *TEEN SCREEN*.

But the middle aged crowd knows of the super stars; so the middle aged crowd backs the super stars.

Most of the middle agers are employees. They may be fired for making mistakes. So they must always have alibis ready for each mistake. What's a better alibi for having

guessed wrong than that the picture contained super stars?

The middle-agers recognize that it is important to get

a picture distributed, promoted and exhibited. For that, a

middle-aged star is desirable.

It is also desirable to get a box office attraction

who will bring in the customers and a specified admission price.

A record industry hit artist may serve that purpose.

John Wayne was supported by Fabian in one picture, by Frankie

Avalon in another, by Rick Nelson in a third, by Glen Campbell

in a fourth, by Johnny Crawford in a fifth.

Often a recording artist is so eager to do a picture

and develop the motion picture aspect of his career that he

will make himself available for less than he could get making

live appearances in concerts and dances.

Once a producer has selected the male and female lead

stars, the younger male and female stars, the producer must

prepare a list of alternatives.

The producer may want to do a Western starring John

Wayne. The first distributor with whom the producer deals may

want William Holden in the lead. The banker may see Rock Hud-

son in the role. The producer must know whether John Wayne,

William Holden, Rock Hudson are available and what the probable

price of each would be.

How much of the budget is left for the female star?

Should she be a box office star, or is it merely desirable that she be known by name to the youth audience through her television shows, former shows, or old movies?

How does the producer go about trying to get his stars?

The producer, as a last resort, could try to work through the agent of the star. The producer can find the agent by looking up the Academy of Motion Picture Arts and Sciences' *Academy Players Directory* issued three times annually. Or the producer can call up SAG (Screen Actors Guild).

While this is routine, it is dangerous. The successful agent is a first-class salesman. He will try to get the highest possible price for his client. It will be he who can decide how to report the producer's interest to the star.

Generally, stars are hungry. Stars eat three or four or more times a day. But they are burdened by installment payments for house(s), car(s), ex-wife or wives, American Express, Diners Club, etc.

Generally, male stars are unemployed most of the year (more than 26 weeks out of every year).

Record industry stars often make live-performance appearances only on week-ends. Thus, they have time on week days to make movies.

Female leading women work even less than leading men, except for the super stars.

All this availability and pressure means that if a

star does not work for the producer during the time the film is
shot, the star won't be working at all during those weeks.

The star knows this. He wants the work, and does not
want to lose it. The star is afraid that the agent will blow
the deal by demanding too much money.

The star generally is not as good a bargainer as his
agent is. The star may use the agent as a buffer. The star
and the agent working together can assist a producer, if they
both like the project. Many agents have become producers.

The producer cannot afford to sign a contract with the
star until after the whole package (backers, lenders, distributor) has been arranged. What is needed by the producer is a
non-legally-binding commitment by the star. "If I'm available,
I will work on the following terms: . . . ."

Once an old-time producer was trying to sucker a would-
be producer into a co-production deal. The old-timer wanted to
get a star to sign a contract so that it could be taken to the
bank and the distributor. The star's agent insisted that the
contracting producer would have to pay the star $150,000 to
make a movie, and insisted on a definite starting date with the
$150,000 to be paid whether or not the movie was made. The old-
time producer told the would-be producer to set up a shell corporation with absolutely no assets; the shell corporation would
then offer the $150,000 contract to the star. If the star
signed, the shell corporation could then show the contract to

the star. If the star signed, the shell corporation could then
show the contract to the distributor and the bank. If the
shell corporation was able to make the picture, then it would
be able to pay the star the $150,000. If the shell corpora-
tion should be unable to make the movie, then the star would be
able to sue only the empty shell corporation for violating the
contract; and it was doubtful that the star would waste attorney's fees to sue a corporation without assets.

The would-be producer almost fell for the old timer's
trick. The would-be producer did not know that, if he tried
the shell corporation game, the star's agent would probably insist on a personal guarantee from the would-be producer. Nor
did the would-be producer know that courts sometimes "pierce
the corporate veil," and hold stockholders of empty corporations
liable for corporation debts. The would-be producer vaguely
felt that it was wrong to trick a star into signing a contract
promising a definite starting date when there was no definite
date, and therefore the would-be producer did not start on the
path suggested by the old-time producer.

Many stars and featured actors have their minimum price,
which may be daily, weekly, or per picture. The price may vary
according to the median worked for (e.g., $1750 weekly for TV;
$3000 weekly for movies), according to the studio (e.g., $2000
weekly for Disney; $3000 weekly for MGM), according to the
budget of the picture (less for a lower-budget picture; more

for a higher-budget picture), according to location (less in Hollywood; more on location), less cash if a profit-sharing plan or co-production credit is offered), less cash but more cash-and-deferment if a deferment is offered, less if the work is supposed to start sooner than later (when it <u>might</u> inter-fere with a better job), less if the agent is afraid he will lose the star as client if the work is not accepted.

In other words, the minimum price is generally so ad-justable as to be more of an excuse for the actor's not working ("MGM refused to pay my minimum price."), more of an agent's bargaining device ("Even Universal pays my client more than you are offering."), more of a producer's boast ("Star works for me for only $24,995 weekly instead of his usual price because he likes me."), than a <u>real</u> minimum price.

The minimum, minimum, minimum (3) price is union scale. The minimum, minimum (2) price is scale plus 10% so that the agent can get the 10% as commission. The minimum (1) price of an actor has kept many an actor unemployed. Agent to actor: "You have been working for $300 per day; from now on you don't accept a job paying less than $500 per day." The actor agrees. Since he is known to be a $300 value, nobody pays $500 for the $300 value, and the actor stays unemployed. On the other hand, the minimum price plus reasons causing producers to pay ever more, have raised the prices of many actors and stars to very high amounts. In some cases, stars have overpriced themselves

so high that they did not work until they lowered their prices
to within reason.

The emergence for middle-aged (30-99 years) character
actors into stars (Lee Van Cleef, Lee Marvin, James Coburn) illustrates the abilities of actors' prices to be raised and
raised. The paths of many stars from box office attractions to
lead players to featured players to bits (courteously called
"cameos") illustrates men sensible enough to keep working in
their chosen professions (and kind enough to their fans to let
the fans see the stars once in a while), rather than sticking
to a former (now unobtainable) minimum price.

Many new producers are mightily impressed by old-time
producers, who have many credits. The old timers profess to
be able to reach many stars. This may or may not be true. Many
stars will never again work for a producer, who has burned them
once.

Part of the pleasure that new producers have is the
star game. The newcomer and the oldtimer sit back, and say,
"Who will be star in this picture?" The newcomer gets a feeling
of mighty power in his daydream position of starring his own
idols.

Sooner or later the producer must be able to say to the
bank and the distributor, "For the male lead, I spoke to _____'s
agent, who said that _____ would work for $_____ and he
was available from July 1 to September 10."

Then, for each lead part, the producer must have a verbal <u>non-binding</u> commitment.

Why non-binding? The only way for a producer to bind a star is with a contract which also binds the producer to pay money. And unless the picture is made, the producer is often in no position to pay money.

Since the producer is not willing to bind himself, the producer can't reasonably expect the star to bind himself.

Also, generally, the producer does not have to worry. The star will probably be unemployed and available when principal photography starts.

If the star balks at the last minute, he can be replaced.

Sometimes producers are accused of promising a greater star to backers and then making the picture with a lesser star. Producers should be careful not to promise backers that the $500,000 picture will star James Garner, Doris Day, John Wayne, and the ghost of Marilyn Monroe. On the other hand, backers must realize that producers are quite willing to spend as much money as backers promise in conversation, but are partially limited by the cash amounts backers finally contribute, (and by the pyramiding allowed by the cash).

Sometimes the producer and the stars will negotiate contracts, draw up the complete negotiated contracts, and then not sign the contracts with the understanding that they will be signed if and when the producer has made all arrangements (lab, bank, distributor).

This enables the producer to then go to the lab, the bank, the distributor, director, backers, etc., and tell them that the star is willing.

THE DIRECTOR

The producer will be asked by the lab, bank, distributor, etc., "Who is your director?"

The producer will say: "I can get A, who has directed 50 pictures of the kind we plan to make." (Reaction: But is he up-to-date?). "I can get B, who has been working regularly in television for three years and knows how to work fast." (Reaction: But does he know movie quality factors?). "I can get C, who won a prize at the _____ Festival." (Reaction: But is he commercial?).

The producer may say, "I can get D, who is used to directing the biggest stars. D is willing to direct our lower budget picture at 1/4 his former fee." (Reaction: Why is D not working for his former fee? Can't he get it any more? Did he make flops?).

The director from television offers a producer several theoretical advantages. He is used to working quickly, to getting a lot of usable film each day. He is used to getting paid at television rates. He has had a lot of time to think of artistic contributions he would make on his first motion picture. He is used to being a co-operative employee of a factory.

The old timer director may offer name value to the producer when the director and his better credits are mentioned to the lab, banker, backers, etc.

        The better directors at all salary levels are quite likely to be employed when the producer is finally able to shoot the picture. Therefore, the producer should obtain a list of directors to be approved in advance by the banker and the distributor.

R E S U M E

JOE YORE

SAG - AFTRA

HAIR. . . . . . BROWN - WAVY
EYES . . . . . HAZEL
WEIGHT . . . . 140 lbs.
AGE 26
COMPLEXION . . Tan*

Hippie, sportsman,
Service man, pimp, cab
Driver, waiter, desk
clerk, bell hop, cowpoke,
jail inmate, garageman,
cook, reporter, sports car
driver, bartender, dancer,
bar scene, medic, Indian,
clerk, bum.

*Joe can pass for many different
nationalities.

"A Good Character or Leading
Man" - (ON THE UPRISE).

TV   "Camp Runamuck" "Day In Court" "Johnny Carson Show"
                  CBS Playhouse
Motion Pictures - "Funny Girl" "Psychout" "Hell Breed" "Diary Of
                     A Hippie"
Modeling -   Thompson Clothing - Cleveland, Ohio
                  30 magazines for December release.

Extra   -   "Via Las Vegas" "What a Way To Go" "Greatest Story
                  Ever Told"

Commercials -   Texaco Educational Film

Stage   -   HOME OF THE BRAVE, BYE, BYE, BIRDIE, SPINSTER DINNER,
                  WEST SIDE STORY

Books   -   Reviews on me: TEEN SCREEN, MUSIC INDUSTRY BOOK
                  RECORD INDUSTRY BOOK, MOVIE INDUSTRY BOOK

Address: 6605 Hollywood Blvd., Suite 215, Hollywood, Calif.90028

Telephone: 662-4529

Sports: Swimming, bowling, waterskiing, boxing, mountain hiking,
                  football, pool, dancing (all), sailing, riding, singer
                  (had several records released)

Coaching: Raikin Ben-Ari, Jim Kirkwood (Hollywood Center) UCLA -
                  Production.

Talents: Actor, Artist, Singer, Writer.

THE ACTOR'S ACTOR

By

JOE YORE

He was always too tall for the short,
or too short for the tall.

He was always too ugly for the handsome,
or the handsomest man you saw.

For he never did look like the character
the producer wanted that day.

But he never did hunger; acting was
food in his blood to stay.

The Earth was his stage, and
in Life he played the part.

The Oscar was his soul,
Emmy and Tony, his heart.

He touched the hems of heaven,
cried with song.

He swam the fires of Hell,
and laughed with wrong.

Where once muscle carved the solid body
he once bare,

Now wrinkles help to lighten
the silver in his hair.

He played Life's role
but his own he could not save.

He watched the shadows fall slowly
upon his grave:

The Actor's Actor.

THE LABORATORY

For a minute, please try on the shoes of a laboratory. You are in business. You have made a lot of profit operating your business, but you have been forced to plow back most of your profit into new equipment. Each year your accounts receivable rise, but so do your bad debts.

A producer comes to you and asks whether you will do the lab work on his next picture. You happily agree to do so.

The producer next asks for credit. You know that the producer is so broke that he shares his 15¢ *HOLLYWOOD REPORTER* with four other producers. Each one of the five has to buy the trade paper on his respective day of the week.

But you also know that the producer may soon put together a business which will spend $1,000,000 within a thirty-day period, and you want the lab work. So you agree to give him credit.

You prepare papers for the producer to sign. In one paper, the producing corporation, the producer personally, and some of the moneymen backing the picture promise to pay the lab bill in thirty months if the distributor has not paid it earlier.

You know that your overhead is high, and that your direct costs of processing the picture are less than half of what you charge. Let's assume, for sake of example, that your costs

are 50¢ of your billing dollar ($1.00). The interest rates you
charge are based on the billing dollar - let's say 10% per year,
or 10¢ for the first year. Thus, your interest, 10¢, is actually
20% of your cost of 50¢. 20% is not a bad interest rate.

Actually, you can feel fairly certain that you will
never be paid a penny by the distributor on the credit you are
giving on the production. The distributor may pay only himself
and costs of distribution. If the bank is lucky, the distributor will pay the bank (which gets paid before the laboratory's
production costs.

Thus, the lab can count on being in the collection
business in three years. It will be trying to collect against
the production corporation, the producer, and the moneymen who
signed the guarantee.

The lawsuit will point out the clause in the lab credit
agreement in which the defendants (producer, etc.) agreed to
pay plaintiff's attorney's fees in the amount the court judges
reasonable. The court might judge a 10%-20% fee reasonable.

You, as the lab, are doing well with your money.

But, you have another trick up your sleeve. As part of
your agreement, you insisted that you get the print business.
Making prints is not part of the cost of production, but is
part of the costs of distribution. The distributor orders the
prints, and pays for the prints. (Later on the distributor
monkeys around with the costs and the producer winds up

reimbursing the distributor).

The lab may make enough profit on the prints to cover all of the lab's expenses in the production. This is especially so when the lab bills the distributor for many more prints than the lab produces. (The distributor has his own reasons for not objecting).

Thus the lab often makes money on the whole job (production expenses, distribution expenses) as soon as it is paid by the distributor; any money it later receives from the moneymen-guarantors on the original lab bill is just that much more profit.

Why do distributors go along with labs' overcharging for prints? The distributor has little choice; he owes the labs too much. Distributors also make pictures and most of them turn out to be money losers. The producer-distributors save money by having the lab charge an independent producer's picture for prints actually made for the producer-distributor's product.

You, as the lab, have the choice of incorrectly charging the independent producer and thus getting paid, or of charging the producer-distributor and thus not getting paid. Which do you choose?

The producer may suspect all of this chicanery the very first time he deals with the lab on a new movie project (possibly because the lab has already stung the producer).

But does that mean the producer will not deal with the lab again? No!

The producer makes his living by producing pictures. If he produces a picture, he will get a fee. If he does not produce a picture, he will not get a fee. Therefore, the producer will do whatever is required in order to get his picture project going.

What is required is that the production company, the producer, and the moneymen sign the credit agreement furnished to them by the lovable lab.

The lab also helps finance films, providing "second position" money, which is money that comes after the producer's bank loan. Usually, if the producer is successful and his films have paid off, the distributor will provide him with an 80% guarantee, which he can bank. The lab, to help both the distributor and the producer, will loan up to 20% of a film's cost.

T H E   B A N K

The movie banker knows one thing: Movies are lousy security.

The movie banker wants to make money for the bank. Banks make money by lending money and then collecting money loaned out, plus interest.

Good loans mean good borrowers. Good borrowers are people and companies who will repay the loan if the movie bombs. Good borrowers furnish collateral for exceeding the total of the loan (stocks, bonds). Good borrowers have high and stable income (doctors, dentists, lawyers).

So the loan is made based on the collateral and the borrowers.

Does the movie banker concern himself with scripts, stars, directors, distributors, lab agreements; track record of the producer, details of production?

Sure, why not? It's lots of fun. It's also a good cover and a necessary beginning to what really matters - the collateral and the borrowers.

The movie banker wants a lot of paperwork.

The bank wants to own or have the equivalent of a first mortgage (here called a "security interest") in everything possible, from copyrights to negative to prints.

The bank wants the distributor to guarantee the loan, or at least to promise to pay the bank out of the producer's share. The bank does not trust the producer to pay the bank in the event the distributor should happen to pay the producer directly.

The bank wants all givers of credit (lab, studio in which the film is shot, stars and writer and director who give deferments) to agree in writing that the bank gets paid first.

The bank wants the production company to borrow the money, and wants as guarantors the producer, individually, and as many moneymen as possible.

Readers of this book may be disappointed - so far I have not mentioned crookedness. All right, I will.

The producer can tell the moneyman that the bank will not make the loan unless the bank officer who has power to approve the loan is slipped $3,000 under the table. The moneyman is afraid of being caught giving a bribe. The moneyman gives the $3,000 to the producer. The producer pockets the money.

The bank loan is due and payable two years after it is made. The bank officer has the power to renew it for a year. The producer tells the moneyman that the bank officer will renew the loan if he is slipped $3,000 under the table. The moneyman does not want to make the crooked payoff, so he gives the producer the $3,000. The producer pockets the $3,000.

Possibly there may be two different loans, one similar

to a construction loan (to make the movie), and one similar to a pick-up loan (when the distributor accepts the completed picture.) The first loan is riskier, since the picture may never be made. The second loan may be guaranteed by the distributor, and the interest rate may be less than for the first loan.

THE DISTRIBUTOR

Sometimes producers try to make a picture without first getting a commitment from a distributor.

These producers are fair game for distributors.

A few of these no-release pictures are bought outright by distributors at a profit to the producers and all persons backing the picture.

Most of these no-release pictures are rejected by distributors. They are rejected as "unreleasable" because distributors cannot make money distributing these pictures.

They are rejected also because distributors know the pressures on producers of such pictures. Loans made to the producer by lenders and the lab steadily near the due date. The lab is usually in "first" or "second" position, and can foreclose on the picture. The lab can also sue the moneymen backing the film.

After a while the moneymen are mentally willing to write off their total cash investment in the picture, but they don't want to pay the lab bill.

The lab finds a distributor willing to pay off the lab bill. Everyone except the lab is wiped out. Thereafter, the lab makes its profit by making prints at the expense of the distributor.

Or, the producer may find a small distributor willing to distribute the picture. The small distributor makes a minimum number of prints (possibly 25). The distributor then peddles these 25 prints at a time to chains needing "B" pictures in each of about 30 cities. Having done this, the distributors have made their profits the easy way, have paid for the prints and a few trade ads, and lose interest in the pictures. The tiny distributors often have neither the men nor the power to get adequate distribution throughout the United States or foreign countries. It is possible for money to be left over for the producer, if the distributor is not careful.

For the above and other reasons (such as insistence by the lab and the bank), the producer tries to line up a distributor.

The distributor needs product to distribute. The distributor has high overhead which can handle many pictures each year with only slight direct cost increases per picture. The distributor would like to have commercial product, product on which he can make money quickly.

The distributor wants a producer with good credits, a director with good credits, stars and featured actors and actresses with good credits. The distributor wants the picture for free, without having to pay any creditors of the production.

Sometimes the distributor guarantees to the bank that,

if the picture goes over budget, the distributor will advance the funds to complete the picture. Usually a producer pays cash to a financial organization for this. It is called "a completion bond."

The bank often will not lend money to the production company unless the distributor guarantees that the loan will be repaid 24 months after the loan is made (or 18 months after it is released, whichever is sooner).

The guarantee by the distributor used to mean something; it used to mean the distributor would try to pay the bank.

But the distributors learned that they had little reason to pay even the bank. The unpaid bank had the theoretical contractual right to pull the film and to have it distributed by somebody else. But why should the bank bother to do so? The second distributor was unlikely to do a better job than the first. The first had probably skimmed the cream by making the easiest sales during the initial two years.

Some banks even bother to sue defaulting distributors on their guarantees. This did not bother the distributors. True, the distributors had to pay 7% interest. But the value of money to the hard-pressed distributors was more like 25% per year, so a mere 7% interest was easy to bear.

That's why, after a while, banks paid less attention to script, stars, director, producer, distributor, and more to the moneymen who would bank the movie with their credit.

The distributor knows that he must sell theatres on the idea of playing the picture. Theatres want to pack in customers. Theatres have learned that good pictures increase box offices not only while the good pictures are played, but also for the week thereafter. Similarly, bad pictures hurt the box office during the following week.

The distributor wants to be able to sell the forthcoming picture to theatres. A picture is good or bad according to one criterion - does it make money for the party doing the judging?

Theoretically, the single most important element in a movie is the story. The distributor must have the ability to visualize the story from the screenplay. The distributor may know what he looks for in a screenplay (Western: enter hero, fist fight within 7 minutes, horses, cattle, other moving animals within next 7 minutes, unavailable heroine, a killing, another fist fight, some victory for the villain, deadly danger, a thrilling-killing resolution). (Love story: Boy meets girl; boy loses girl; somebody gets girl). (Family film: One widower, one widow, one young adult, one early teenager, one sub-teenager, one dog or cat, one unusual pet, one foreign accent as love interest for the young adult, any location, mix well, happy romantic ending).

The distributor knows that the exhibitor's first question will be, "How's the film doing in theatres like mine?"

The answer to that is, "Very well. We did tremendous business in _____." There usually is one place where business was better than elsewhere.

The exhibitor will ask the distributor, "Who's in it?" The exhibitor knows he needs star names. One Western movie starred Mitchum-Ladd-McCrea. (Jim Mitchum, Alana Ladd, Jody McCrea).

Therefore, the distributor wants star names in the movie. The producer lists his preferred cast, and then adds "or equivalent." The producer may list the star with whom he has been speaking (for example, Chuck Connors) and will add, "or equivalent." The distributor and producer then argue which stars would serve as "equivalents." (Q: John Wayne? A: Yes.) (Q: Audie Murphy? A: OK for Westerns only.) (Q: Jack Lord? A: What pictures has he starred in?) (Jerry Capehart? Who's he?)

The distributor and the producer then agree that the female star available and willing to play the female lead is satisfactory. (Distributor: "But will Susannah York work for the amount in your budget?" Producer: "She wouldn't for anybody else. But I did her a favor when she started her career.") Next problem: Who is "equivalent"? (Q: Jane Fonda? A: Yes.) (Q: Doris Day? A: She does not have the right image.) (Q: Elizabeth Taylor? A: She costs more than the whole budget of the picture.)

The distributor wants approval of the director, the budget, and as a practical matter of many more items. The distributor has a say-so about the shooting schedule, about the day principal photography is supposed to start, and end.

The distributor may, with or without the contractual right to do so, veto any of the proposed persons whom the producer wants to work on the movie, including cameraman, editor, providers of music, etc.

The producer may have theoretical freedom of control of the production; but the producer knows that an unenthusiastic distributor can kill a picture financially.

Distributors frequently leave producers alone to a great extent during the planning and production of a picture for one simple reason - usually the youngster representing the distributor knows even less than the youngster representing the producer.

The distributor may have one man whose sole job is knowing about each censorship board and its dislikes. The distributor wants to be able to cut a picture quickly and easily to adjust for each important board.

For example, if one board will try to hurt every film with nudity, the distributor wants to be able to delete the nude scenes without hurting the picture, and without making the deletion obvious.

Another black/white conscious censor may object only

to blacks and whites getting along (a) if they are of different
sexes, or (b) if they are school children, or (c) if they are
equal, or (d) etc.

The distributor may have suggestions concerning the
censorship problem. A producer may not be willing to scrap a
$25,000 sequence after it has been shot; but he may be willing
to make adjustments before shooting. Also the producer may
wish to study the story line during the dangerous sequence, and
may decide to shoot two versions, one for the entertainment
market and one for the ignorance makers' market.

The producer may be able to check his projects against
the marketing experience of the distributor. "Do you think the
public will want to see a film about a Caucasian fisherman's
son and an upper middle class Nisei girl?"

The distributor will test the producer's idea by his
wife, asking branch managers and salesmen, exhibitors, his
teenage relatives, and other producers. "Would you see a
story about three American soldiers who train a little, fight
a little, picnic with the native girls, are caught in a dangerous situation, and bravely save themselves, each other, and
their whole company?"

The distributor wants to avoid losing money. He knows
(1) that even though an expense dollar may eventually be
charged to the producer's share of receipts, (2) the expense
dollar first comes out of the distributor's pockets and

(3)   there must be receipts before there can be allocation of receipts.

The distributor must advance money for prints, press-book, advertising, publicity, selling.

One movie producer who decided to distribute his picture himself made only two prints, and made back every penny in the project with just those two prints. Then, from additional receipts, he made additional prints. Thus his initial cost of distribution was under $1000 for everything (prints, ads, freight, telephone).

On the other hand, it is not too difficult for a distributor to spend a million dollars in distribution within 30 days in order to hit countrywide coverage at the same time (400 prints cover half the U.S. at Christmas time, the other half during the one-week school vacation around February 1.)

Simultaneous ads in *LIFE*, *LOOK*, movie fan magazines, Sunday papers, daily papers, can easily eat up hundreds of thousands of dollars, as can ads on television.

The distributor must calculate how to best promote a motion picture so that it provides him with the most money. The producer may be killed by the distributor's decision.

For example, a producer is constantly hounded by the thought that the bank loan is due 24 months after it was made.

If, based on early forecasts, the picture can play in

such a way that the distributor will gross $1,000,000, then the producer will want that $1,000,000 to be grossed within one year so that every creditor can be paid off quickly and interest expense will cease.

In order to gather that $1,000,000 within 12 months, the producer may have to order 200 prints, thus requiring a cash outlay of $100,000.

But the distributor may not have $100,000 available for that purpose. He may order only 40 prints for $20,000, thus saving $80,000.

It will take the distributor three years, instead of one year, to gross that $1,000,000. The additional time will cause the bank loan to be not paid in full, will cause the producer trouble with other creditors and backers. But the distributor does not care. He has saved an immediate $80,000 and has a better chance to steal more of the incoming $1,000,000.

Once a producer gave a $2,000,000 picture to a distributor for distribution. The distributor made just enough prints to service one city at a time (about 40 prints). The distributor did not bother advertising. This allowed the distributor, with almost no investment, to get his distribution fee and his money back for the prints. The distributor made money. The producer and his backers were killed financially.

Thus, producers who are entering into contracts with distributors should seek to have the distributors promise to make at least a minimum number of prints and to spend at least a minimum on advertising. The producer may also want maximums in prints and ads.

The black and white film is a rarity today, although color productions cost 20% more than films made in black and white. A color film can bring in higher revenue because the distributor can charge theatres more for it.

Most black and white films made today are made in Europe by European countries, but they get U.S. distribution because they are cheaply made and usually have made their money back in Europe before they are released here.

FOREIGN PRODUCTION

and

DISTRIBUTION

Is this book going to discuss foreign production and distribution?

No. That's saved for another book.

T H E A T R E S

Some are bigger; some are smaller. Some belong to chains; some don't.

Some play only specialized pictures; some play for general audiences.

Some are comfortable; some are uncomfortable.

Some are open only week-ends; some, every day.

Some are open only evenings; some from noon to midnight; some are open all night.

Some are four-wall; some are drive-ins.

Many theatres are listed geographically by state and city, if the city has more than three theatres, and identified by the circuit of which they are members in *THE INTERNATIONAL MOTION PICTURE ALMANAC*, published by Quigley, price $13.00.

STATES RIGHTS DISTRIBUTORS

In other businesses, the concept of (1) national distributor, (2) local distributor, (3) retail establishment, is fairly common.

The step (2) local distributor may be a branch office owned by (1) the national distributor. Or, the (2) local distributor may be an independent businessman who buys from (1) the national distributor, the exclusive right to commercially exploit the picture in a specified geographic area.

Thus, a states right "local distributor" may "buy" a territory such as (1) California, or (2) New York City, or (3) Georgia - Carolinas, or (4) Eleven Western States, etc. The territory may be "bought" for seven years or one year or any period of time.

The time of payment by the states righter to the distributor may be partly at the time of the contract, partly before the prints are sent to the states righter, partly after showing of the film.

A national distributor who promises use of prints (for example: 40) for a certain period of time (for example: the month of March), must be sure that he can deliver the prints on time.

Prints are frequently mislaid by air freight companies,

and distributors often spend worried hours at freight terminals
trying to find prints needed for immediate showing that day.

The producer who is willing to let producers get 40% of
gross rentals, may find that the states righter takes 40% of
the gross, and remits 60%; then the national distributor takes
40% of that 60% (which equals 24% of the original 100%), thus
giving the producer only 60% of 60% (or only 36% of the original 100%).

Certain national distributors own certain states rights
corporations. Thus, the national and local distributors together get 64% of gross instead of the 40% the producer thinks
he is paying.

Producers dealing with such national distributors
should be aware of the paragraph in the distribution contract
which expressly allows such double distribution fees.

DISTRIBUTION

THE $250 C.O.D. CAPER

I

A young and new distributor long distance telephoned
a theatre owner to discuss booking a film we will call *PORRIDGE*
because that is not its title.

Theatre owner: "I just have a little theatre so I can
just pay you $250 for a one-week run."

The young distributor agreed on the terms: $250; one
week run.

The theatre owner looked at his calendar and said,
"I'll run your movie October 1-7."

The distributor looked at his print availability calendar and promised to have his print air-freighted to the distributor in time.

II

Several days later the young distributor lunched with
a senior citizen distributor. They discussed how the newcomer
was getting along, and the newcomer told about his $250 one-
week October 1-7 booking.

Said the senior citizen, "I know that theatre owner.
He does not pay weak exhibitors. Since you have no other films
that he wants, he won't pay you the $250. Since he is in a
town over 1000 miles away, you can't sue him."

The new distributor asked, "Should I call off the date?"

"No," replied the senior citizen distributor. "I have an idea. The exhibitor needs the print on October 1. His theatre opens at noon. Ship the print to him on September 30, so that it will be available at the airport in the theatre owner's city on the morning of October 1. Ship the print C.O.D. for $250. The theatre owner will need the print so badly that he will pay the $250 to get the print."

III

The young distributor followed the advice. On September 30 he shipped the print for $250 C.O.D. The exhibitor needed the print so badly that he paid the $250 C.O.D. charges.

IV

A month later the senior citizen distributor met the young distributor. He asked, "Whatever happened to the exhibitor who promised to pay you $250 for a one-week run?"

"Well," said the young distributor, "the exhibitor paid the $250 C.O.D. when I shipped him the print. Then he played the print for two weeks instead of one. Then he sent me back the print, C.O.D. for $300.

"I had no choice but to pay the $300. I did not want to leave my print in that exhibitor's hands."

V

The story you have just read is fictitious, incorrect, and untrue. Any coincidences herein which may remind you of an exhibitor you know is purely coincidental.

PERCENTAGE OF BOX OFFICE RECEIPTS

I

The customer may sneak into the theatre; or may have
a pass; or may pay to get into the theatre. The money paid
by the customers is called "box office receipts."

The theatre owner would love all the money to stick,
but he is forced to pay some expenses (labor, advertising, at
least one printer of tickets, rent, utilities). He might even
pay money to a distributor for the use of film.

II

The theatre may pay a flat rental for the run (such as
$250 for a run of one week).

The theatre may buy for flat sums such short items as
cartoons or the "second feature" or even the "A" picture.

The second feature years ago was a "B" low-budget picture. Sometimes an expensive "A" picture with stars but without
box office drawing power would become the "second feature."

An "A" picture which has had its run as an "A" picture
sometimes thereafter is used as a "B" picture. Thus, it can
earn more revenue.

The competition of such "A" pictures hurt the "B"
pictures, which they replaced in theatres.

III

The contract between the distributor and the exhibitor

may call for the distributor to be paid a percentage of box

office receipts.

The simplest percentage arrangement, which is given for

purpose of illustration only, would be that the distributor and

the exhibitor share 50%-50%. The distributor furnishes the fea-

tures and short subjects and pays his expenses of operation;

the theatre owner furnishes the theatre and pays his expenses

of operation.

The percentages are adjustable; instead of 50-50, they

could be 60-40 or 40-60 or any other variation.

IV

In Part II of this chapter we discussed the flat fee

rental paid by the exhibitor to the distributor. In that case,

it was the *film print which was rented.*

Sometimes a distributor has enough confidence in a film

to pay a flat sum to an exhibitor for the *rental of the theatre.*

The theatre owner computes his costs of operating the theatre,

adds profit, and arrives at the amount he wants the distributor

to pay to rent the theatre and to keep 100% of box office re-

ceipts.

Such a contract might require either side to pay person-

nel (management, ushers, nurse, candy counter, box office, etc.).

Such a contract might give candy counter operation con-

trol and receipts to either party.

A theatre owner wishing to cash in on the box office

value of "X" pictures, but not quite willing to chance being arrested, may be happy to go on vacation while renting out the theatre for a flat sum.

V

Now it is time to combine the flat rental method and the percentage method.

The distributor and the exhibitor may provide in their contract that box office receipts be divided as follows:

1. FIRST, the exhibitor receives the first $1000 each week.

2. SECOND, the distributor is reimbursed for his advertising expense, but no more than $500 each week.

3. THIRD, the exhibitor and the distributor split the excess in some fashion. Since the distributor has taken the greater risk, his percentage is greater than it would have been had he taken less risk.

On some powerhouse films, the excess over the exhibitor's first take may be divided 90-10, with 90% going to the distributor.

VI

This chapter concerns box office receipts and how the amount paid to the distributor is allocated.

How the distributor allocates his gross receipts among his "A" film, his second feature, and his short subjects is discussed in another chapter.

VII

Do exhibitors try to cheat distributors? Of course.
How? Various ways.

You may have had the experience of buying a ticket at
a theatre box office, and of giving up the whole ticket to the
doorman, and of having been waved inside the theatre without
getting your ticket back. The doorman then easily can return
the whole ticket to the cashier who re-sells it. The money
for the twice-sold ticket may be shared by the cashier and the
doorman.

If the theatre owner shifts his personnel around from
cashier to doorman to candy counter to usher, and if the manager and assistant perform all jobs in turn, then everybody can
steal a little.

Sometimes a ticket buyer may receive a ticket from the
"second roll." The first roll of numbered tickets is the official roll which is counted (first and last ticket numbers are
entered each day each time the price is changed). The second
roll of tickets is the exhibitor's (or exhibitor's employees')
private roll. The exhibitor accounts to the distributor for
all "first roll" tickets, but does not account for "second roll"
tickets.

Does the distributor know what is going on? Let's get
down to personalities. The distributor's salesman who catches
a cheating exhibitor is going to keep his fool mouth shut; he
is not going to chance losing as customers the cheating exhibitor and all other exhibitors who cheat.

Anyway, the salesman has his own racket going with the
exhibitor. The exhibitor slips the salesman $25 so that the
salesman will give the exhibitor better film-rental terms.

Distributors hired Confidential Reports and other companies to check on theatres. These checking companies hired
persons, often senior citizens (cheap and reliable labor) to
buy tickets at various theatres, to keep track of how many
people were in the theatre each half hour, to count the people
coming into the theatre each quarter hour. One checking would
balance another check. One employee would double-check another
checker.

This system worked well in chains where the absentee
theatre owner feared being short-counted by his employees.
After all, every dollar stolen by an employee hurt both the
theatre owner and the distributor.

But the system often failed where a brazen theatre
owner denied the accuracy of the checker's report. The theatre
owner would argue that it was his duty to share only his receipts, and the receipts left to him after the employees'
thefts. Since the distributor could not prove that the stolen

money landed in the pockets of the distributor (rather than in the pockets of his thieving employees), the distributor had to accept the short count.

Usually a distributor and/or his branch manager and/or his salesman need a theatre more than a theatre needs any particular distributor - this comment is expressly limited to the issue of whether a distributor should risk offending a cheating theatre, merely because the exhibitor cheats.

Let's see - whom have we accused of stealing? All the theatre personnel. Some of the distributor's personnel. This total accusation is totally unjust to somebody. We apologize to somebody, but we don't know to whom.

Please, exhibitors, don't take our attempts at humor too seriously. It is just that we have experience and information.

As one distributor of a tremendous box office hit said, "My contract with the theatre calls for $5,000 weekly and a percentage of box office. I expect $5,000 weekly."

GROSS RENTAL RECEIPTS

I

The amounts paid by the exhibitors to the distributors are gross rental receipts.

II

The receiving distributors may be branches of a national distribution company such as MGM, Warners, Columbia, and the other majors and big minors, or they may be "States rights distributors" who have acquired the exclusive right to lease the film in their geographic territory for a stated number of years (often 7 years).

III

The contract between the theatre and the distributor may call for the distributor to supply two feature films and a short, and for the theatre to pay the distributor.

IV

It is usually up to the distributor to allocate the gross rental receipts between the "A" film, the "B" film, and the short subject.

In fact, it is up to the distributor which feature he will call the "A" film, and which the "B" film.

The distributor may have no reason to cheat; possibly he owns both films outright and nobody is entitled to share in receipts or profit.

On the other hand, the distributor may have a reason to cheat. He may own one film and not the other. One film may have recovered enough money so that the producer may soon have to be paid, while the second film is not anywhere near profit. One film was made by a producer with continuing product while the other was made by a passe' producer. There are lots of reasons for cheating.

IV

Let's assume that we are making up non-existing film titles. I surely hope we are. Let's call one film "Eek" and the second film "Uck." The distributor favors applying the maximum gross rentals to "Eek," and he is willing to hurt "Uck."

A theatre which has used the double feature "Eek" and "Uck" (no short subjects or trailers) pays a distributor the sum of $1000.

How can the distributor allocate the money?

The distributor can arbitrarily divide the proceeds 50-50, 60-40, 70-30, 80-20, 90-10, 100-0. You object to 100-0? Why? How is the producer of "Uck" ever going to find out?

The distributor can arbitrarily decide that "Eek" is the "A" picture entitled to all gross receipts, but having to pay a fee to "Uck." The fee could be $500, $400, $300, $200, $100, $0. You object to $0? How is the producer of "Uck" ever going to find out?

Such distribution is done at the branch. The branch
then sends information to the main office. This information
may be on a summary sheet showing only film and rental, and/or
on detached sheets showing theatre, runs, co-features, key
distribution terms, rentals, etc. If the producer audits the
national distributor, the producer's accountant may be shown
only summary sheets. If the accountant wants more information,
it may be "in our dead files," "in New York," "with our
accountants," etc.

V

So far, we have been talking only about Line 1 of the
distributor's report to the producer.

Other lines of this report are also truly fascinating.

Assume that one of the income headings is supposed to
deal with income from foreign countries. The distributor may
sell the distribution rights in Great Britain for $50,000 plus
costs of prints, freight, insurance. The British pay the
$50,000, but the $50,000 fails to show up in the royalty report
to the producer for six months. During this six months' period,
the distributor has been using the $50,000 for his own purposes
instead of paying the $50,000 to the bank financing the picture.
The value of $50,000 for 6 months when interest is 10% per annum
is $2,500. This means the distributor has cheated the producer
out of $2,500.

According to the producer-distributor contract, the

distributor paid the costs of prints as an interest-bearing advance to the producer. When the distributor gets prints from the lab to send to Great Britain, the distributor shows in its books that the producer owes the distributor the cost of the prints. Soon the distributor will be reimbursed the cost of the prints by the British sub-distributor. At that time, the distributor should show in the producer's account that the distributor has received the money; that therefore the producer's debt to the distributor is reduced. But does the distributor always remember to make that bookkeeping entry? What do you think? How can you be so suspicious?

THE PRINTS

The distributor orders prints from the laboratory.
Each print is assigned a name and code (the name and code number
of the movie) and a number (the prints are numbered 1, 2, 3, etc.

Each print's life is recorded on a card. The card is
with the print when the print is on the premises, and in a file.
(Files are arranged by movie and the print cards are filed nu-
merically. The movie may be filed alphabetically or by code
number given to the movie.)

Each print's card contains a life history of the print.
(2/5 Chicago, Theatre: _____; 2/19 Detroit, Theatre: _____;
3/5 St. Louis, Theatre: _____; 3/14 Returned here. 100' replaced. 3/26 New York, Theatre _____).

The producer who sees a print card can prepare a table
with the following columns:

Column 1	2	3	4	5
Date	City	Theatre	Rental	Extra Income
January				
1				
2				
3				
4				
5				
6				
. . .				

The producer can then learn where the print was on each day.

The producer can prepare a worksheet:

Column 1 City/Theatre			
Date	Print 1	Print 2	Print 3 .... Print 40
January			
1			
2			
3			
4			
5			

The work sheet can become more complicated, in that extra boxes are added for (1) rental received, (2) trailer rental received, (3) other income received, (4) incoming freight paid.

Prints are sometimes shipped from the distributor to the print center and then returned to the distributor. Prints are sent "freight collect." Each recipient pays freight for the prints he receives.

Sometimes a print is sent from one theatre to another in accorance with the wishes of the distributor. The distributor will request that the New York theatre sends its print directly to a designated theatre in Detroit. The Detroit theatre will, after the run, send the print to a specific theatre in Chicago. The print card in the distributor's home office is supposed to keep track of the print.

Sometimes, prints get "lost."

A New York theatre was supposed to return a print to Los Angeles. But the print arrived in L.A. only when it was seven (7) days overdue. The distributor called the New Yorker, who apologized for his shipping clerk's error in losing the print behind some cartons.

The distributor kept a <u>trailer</u> checklist.

Date	Trailer prints by City and Theatre		
December	TP1	TP2	TP3
26	New York	Los Angeles	Albany
27	"	"	"
28	"	"	"
29	"	"	"
30	"	"	"
31	"	"	"

A trailer print is used by a theatre for a week or so just before the theatre uses the print.

The trailer print worksheet showed trailer prints had been sent to New York, Los Angeles, and Albany theatres. But the regular prints followed trailers into only New York and Los Angeles. No print had been sent to Albany. Why had Albany ordered a trailer but no print?

There were two mysteries:

1. Why had Albany not ordered a print?

2. Why had New York been a week late in returning its print?

The distributor had a clipping service which clipped mentions of his movie out of newspaper. The distributor looked through his clippings for December and found the Albany theatre

had advertised his movie as forthcoming soon. In January, the

Albany theatre had advertised his picture as being shown.

The distributor quietly billed the Albany exhibitor

for running the picture for one week. The Albany exhibitor

quickly paid.

The distributor felt very righteous for having caught

the exhibitor. On his books, the distributor should have added

the proceeds to the picture's gross receipts. He did not.

Since there had been no contract with the exhibitor,

the distributor believed that the producer would not catch the

distributor's cheating.

The producer did not catch the distributor.

It would have been worthwhile for the producer to insist

in his distribution contract to inspect the print rooms (receiv-

ing, inspection, repair, storage, shipping, bookkeeping) at all

times. This function could be fulfilled by a producer's print

rep, and may be fulfilled by a certified public accountant's

office.

Is there any such occupation as producer's print repre-

sentative? There should be such a profession. Would their

presence interfere with the operation of the work? Very little.

The print department ships not only prints and trailers,

but also press books, posters, mats, and promotion gimmicks.

The exhibitors pay for all but press books. Sometimes, trailers

are used, not for the billable purpose as trailers to be shown
to the public, but as a non-billable sample of the movie to be
seen by the exhibitor to use to determine whether he should exhibit the picture.

Does the producer share with the distributor the proceeds from the exhibitors for posters, pictures, mats and gimmicks? This depends on the distribution contract. Producers
who are unaware of these receipts don't miss absent clauses in
the distribution contracts.

The various activities of the print department have
their respective forms: summaries of prints received, in-
spected, repaired, stored, shipped.

TELEVISION

Television uses motion pictures. Relatively few pictures are attractive enough to television to draw million-dollar rental fees. Dozens of pictures have drawn rental fees over half a million dollars.

These few and these dozens have sometimes been under-sold by having been sold as part of a block of pictures sold as a unit.

The distributor then allocates to each picture the share of the total amount that the distributor desires. Pro rata sharing is unfair to independent producers who produced the superior pictures which made the package attractive to the TV station buyers.

There were several production attempts in which a TV station organization provided 50% of the financing of $300,000 (or so) pictures in exchange for TV rights. Generally, the TV stations were better off spending $150,000 for TV rights of al-ready produced $1,000,000 pictures.

For a while producers would try to arrange the financing of a picture with a 60% bank loan, 20% miscellaneous sources and deferrals, 20% advance by a TV group for TV rights. But then banks realized that they were lending money against theatre re-ceipts only, and banks felt insecure.

Black and white pictures are at a disadvantage when trying to get TV plays. TV viewers prefer color pictures to black and white pictures; therefore radio stations prefer color pictures to black and white pictures; therefore radio stations prefer color pictures, too.

For a while the question was asked whether TV would show nude scenes in movies. The question has been answered. TV stations have shown nude views in several pictures during prime viewing hours.

Will pay-TV show new multi-million pix? We don't know. Will pay-TV show skin-flix? Why not?

CATALOGS AND PRICE LISTS

(e.g. Optical Effects)

The producer can obtain catalogs and price lists from various companies.

Announcements of new free catalogs appear in *THE HOLLY-WOOD REPORTER*, in other trade publications, and in magazines catering to the industry generally and to specific crafts.

Price lists are frequently dated, and contain the warning that prices are subject to change.

Catalogs may contain (1) list of services available, followed by "Estimates for any of the above on request," and (2) list of services in one column, with price variations in the following columns.

Sometimes two men get together; one is an experienced and broke producer who knows (1) whom to buy; (2) where to buy; (3) how much to pay; the other is a man with extra money who wants to learn how to become a producer. The man with experience needs the man with money to get a picture rolling. The man with money feels he needs to learn, and plans that after two or three pictures he will dump the experience-man because the money-man will have obtained enough experience.

The experience-man knows the thinking of the money-man; the experience-man therefore makes every effort to be able to use the money-man's sources of money after the money-man has left the experience-man.

The catalogs and price lists offer education to the money-man.

Recently one title and art studio produced a catalog in which they listed the following services as being performed by them.

SERVICES AVAILABLE

ART WORK:	Creative Title Design; Set Design; Illustrations; Silk Screening; Product Reproductions; Color Correction of Package and Labels; Airbrushing.
COMPLETE ANIMATION:	Art and Camera.
CONVERSIONS:	Anamorphic; De-Anamorphic; 35mm and 16mm.
LABORATORY:	Complete black and white developing and printing.
MATTES:	Art and Photographic.
OPTICAL EFFECTS:	Standard; Titles, TV Commercials and Custom Work.
ORIGINAL PHOTOGRAPHY:	Stage; Inserts.
REVERSAL DUPES:	Black and White.
TITLES:	Hand Lettered; Printed (Hot Press).

ESTIMATES FOR ANY OF THE ABOVE

ON REQUEST.

The catalog then gave prices for *OPTICAL EFFECTS* (35mm - 16mm).

	STANDARD		CUSTOM	
	Black & White	Color	Black & White	Color
Fades	$ 2.70	$ 5.40	$ 3.45	$ 6.90
Dissolves	5.40	10.80	6.90	13.75
Wipes	9.15	18.35	11.15	22.40
Optical Cuts/Hold Frames	2.70	5.40	3.60	5.70
Flopovers/Repositionings	7.00	7.00	9.15	9.15
Enlargements	13.50	16.20	17.50	17.50
Zooms - Center	20.25	28.35	25.75	35.20
Zooms - Off Center . . .	34.00	48.60	43.20	58.70
Reductions	16.20	18.90	22.50	25.75
Flips	20.80	29.15	25.75	38.80
Oil Effects	21.60	37.80	25.75	38.80
Out of Focus Effects . .	16.20	19.40	17.50	19.40
Telescope/Binocular . . .	9.20	9.20	9.20	9.20
Tilts	27.00	40.50	37.80	51.50
Spins/Vortex	37.80	51.50	37.80	51.50
Split Screens (Mattes Additional)				
2 Way	32.40	43.20	43.20	58.70
3 Way	48.60	59.40	62.95	87.00
4 Way	64.80	75.60	83.60	115.65

An inkling of the variety of processes, procedures and combinations available to the producer can be gleaned from the following price list of *OPTICAL DUPES* (35mm - 16mm).

Some producers who shoot in locations which weigh against carrying around bulky 35mm cameras use 16mm cameras. The film is then blown up to 35mm. The price that follows shows that the black and white cost is 38¢/foot, and the color cost is 76¢/foot.

Here's a list of further services rendered by the art
and title studio:

	Per Foot	
	BLACK & WHITE	COLOR

DUPES - INTERNEGATIVES

	BLACK & WHITE	COLOR
Dupes	$ .18	$ .60
Dupes - Titles and Commercials . . .	.21	.65
Double-exposed dupes without mattes .	.49	1.15
Double-exposed dupes with mattes . .	.59	1.36
Triple-exposed dupes without mattes .	.87	2.13
Triple-exposed dupes with mattes . .	1.16	2.62
Skip Frame/Double Frame	.58	1.32
Reverse Action/Rock Frame	.42	1.06
Blow-Up Dupes - 16mm and 35mm	.38	.76
Paper to Paper - add to the above . .	.025	.05

Minimum $5.00

REVERSAL DUPES

35mm to 35mm	$ .054	
Reversal Overlays	.16	
Prices include paper to paper.		

Minimum $5.00

COLOR MASTERS

Interpositives from EK		$ .54
Separation Masters from EK		.82

SQUEEZING AND UNSQUEEZING

	BLACK & WHITE	COLOR
Dupes - Internegatives		
Individual Scenes	$ .38	$ .84
Reduction 35mm to 16mm		
(Per 35mm foot)		.50
Full Features		
35mm to 35mm		.52
Finegrains - Interpositives	.38	.84

AMERICAN FEDERATION OF MUSICIANS

PERSONAL SERVICE CONTRACT BLANK

By

Rene Hall

The producer is provided with a numbered Personal

Service Contract Blank by American Federation of Musicians,

for use for all motion picture films, television films, in-

dustrial films, documentaries, newsreels, and miscellaneous

films.

The form asks identifying data: Date, Place, Time,

Hours, Title of Picture, Employer. The form has columns con-

cerning the employees: name, address, local, social security

number, hours worked, number of doubles, scale wages, pension

contributions.

The form requests information concerning the orches-

trator, arranger, copyist.

The form enables the producer to calculate the total

pension contributions, and instructs: Make check payable in

this amount to "AFM & EPW Fund."

The copies are distributed eventually as follows:

Copy #1 - To Pension Fund.

#2 - Kept by Producer.

#3 - To Local, returned by Local to Producer.

#4 - To Local, kept by Local.

#5 - To Local, forwarded to American Federation
of Musicians headquarters.

#6 - To Local, forwarded to the session leader.

The Personal Service Contract Blank contains on its
obverse side the following *ADDITIONAL TERMS AND CONDITIONS*:

"The Producer shall at all times have complete control
of the services which the employees will render under the specifications of this contract. The Producer will distribute to the
musicians, including leader, composer or orchestra manager, not
less than the prescribed union scale for their services. He may
do this directly or through the leader, composer or orchestra
manager. All such payments are to be made in accordance with
the provisions of the basic agreement.

1. The Producer hereby authorizes the Leader, Composer
or Orchestra Manager to replace any Employee who by illness, absence, or for any other reason does not perform any or all of
the services provided for under this contract. The agreement
of the Employees to perform is subject to proven detention by
sickness, accidents, or accidents to means of transportation,
riots, strikes, epidemics, acts of God, or any other legitimate
conditions beyond the control of the Employees.

2. To the extent that their inclusion and enforcement
are not prohibited by a valid federal or state statute, the
rules, laws and regulations of the American Federation of
Musicians and the rules, laws and regulations of the Local in

whose jurisdiction the musicians perform, insofar as they are
not in conflict with those of the Federation, are made part of
this contract, and to such extent nothing in this contract shall
ever be construed as to interfere with any obligation which any
employee hereunder may owe to the American Federation of Musicians pursuant thereto.

3.   Any member or members who are parties to or affected
by this contract, whose services thereunder or covered thereby,
are prevented, suspended or stopped by reason of any strike, ban,
unfair list order or requirement of the Federation shall be free
to accept and engage in other employment of the same or similar
character, or otherwise, for other employers or persons without
any restraint, hindrance, penalty, obligation or liability whatever, any other provisions of this contract to the contrary notwithstanding.

4.   This contract shall not become effective unless it
shall be approved by the Federation or an authorized representative.

5.   This contract is ineffective and invalid unless
the Producer is signatory to a basic agreement with the American Federation of Musicians.

6.   All the terms and provisions set forth in the basic
agreement between the Producer and the American Federation of
Musicians shall be deemed part of this agreement with the same
force and effect as though fully set forth herein and nothing

herein contained shall be deemed to amend or supersede any provision of such basic agreement.

  7. In consideration of the common interests of all the
members of the A.F. of M. in the terms and conditions of this
personal service contract and the basic agreement between the
Producer and the A.F. of M., incorporated herein, the Employees
authorize the A.F. of M. exclusively and irrevocably to take
any and all steps and proceedings in its name and behalf and/or
the Employees' behalf and/or in behalf of any of its members
for the enforcement of all rights under this contract and/or
the said basic agreement, all of which rights of the Employees
are hereby assigned to the A.F. of M., and said A.F. of M., in
behalf of any of its members is irrevocably authorized to agree
to any change, modification and/or substitution of any or all
of the provisions of this contract and/or the said basic agreement, except that nothing herein contained shall deprive the
Employees of any money compensation agreed to be paid to such
Employees for services in connection with the making of such
motion picture and sound track."

AMERICAN FEDERATION OF MUSICIANS

and

EMPLOYERS' PENSION WELFARE FUND

(AFM & EPW FUND)

Room 1205, 205 East 42nd Street
New York City, New York 10017

MOTION PICTURE FILMS (Theatrical & Non-Theatrical)

TELEVISION FILMS (MPPA PATTERN)

"Contributions shall be made to the trustees of the
American Federation of Musicians' and Employers' Pension Welfare Fund, created pursuant to the trust indenture dated October 2, 1959, in a sum equal to 3 per cent of all wages earned
under the agreement, computed at scale. Checks shall be made
payable to the order of the "American Federation of Musicians'
and Employers' Pension Welfare Fund" at Room 1205, 205 East
42nd Street, New York, New York 10017."

TELEVISION FILM (Network Pattern)

"Effective July 1, 1961, Employer shall contribute
5 per cent of all earnings of whatever nature covered by this
agreement, computed at scale, to the American Federation of
Musicians' and Employers' Pension Welfare Fund. Employer
shall be bound by the Trust Agreement of the AFM & EPW Fund
dated October 2, 1959.

Such payments shall be made in accordance with the conditions of the applicable Labor Agreement with a copy of the
letter transmitting the payment simultaneously mailed to the
Federation Studio Representative. The trustees may agree with
contributors upon different dates of payment."

BANK-PRODUCER CONTRACTS

The bank and the producer will cover the following:

1. Note payable to bank. Loan agreement.
   Guarantees.

2. Security agreement.

3. Distributor's agreement (to pay bank, to obey
   certain instructions, to surrender distribution rights to bank).

4. Subordination agreements (laboratory, deferrals, early lenders).

5. Laboratory agreements concerning physical
   negatives, prints, etc., and subordination.

6. Completion agreements.

ACADEMY OF MOTION PICTURE ARTS AND SCIENCES

The Academy is an honorary organization of motion
picture industry craftsmen. Its purposes are to advance the
arts and sciences of motion pictures, and to foster coopera-
tion among the creative leadership of all branches of the
industry for cultural, education and technological progress.

The Academy is entirely free of all labor relations
responsibilities, and has no concern with economic or politi-
cal matters.

The Academy publishes the *ACADEMY PLAYERS DIRECTORY*
every four months as a cooperative service to the players and
production studios in Hollywood. It is distributed to the casting department, directors and executives of the participating
studios and to others concerned with the employment of motion
picture, television and radio talent.

The *ACADEMY PLAYERS DIRECTORY* currently is published in
two volumes; Volume One covering bands and specialties, leading women, ingenues, characters and comediennes, children;
Volume Two covers leading men, younger leading men, characters
and comedians.

Anyone desiring to purchase the latest edition can inquire as to price by writing to the Academy of Motion Picture
Arts and Sciences, 9038 Melrose Avenue, Hollywood, California
90069 (CRestview 5-1146).

BALLOTING INFORMATION CHART

Forty-second Annual Awards – 1969 Calendar Year   Academy of Motion Picture Arts and Sciences

AWARD	MAXIMUM NUMBER OF NOMINATIONS	NOMINATIONS BALLOTING — NOMINATING GROUPS	FINAL BALLOTING
ACTOR ACTRESS SUPPORTING ACTOR SUPPORTING ACTRESS	5 5 5 5	Academy Actors Branch Members.	**Final Balloting by Active**
ART DIRECTION	5	Preliminary Balloting by Art Director and Set Decorator members of the Academy Art Directors Branch. Nominations Balloting by all members of the Academy Art Directors Branch except Costume Designers.	
CINEMATOGRAPHY	5	Preliminary and Nominations Balloting by Academy Cinematographers Branch Members.	
COSTUME DESIGN	5	Preliminary and Nominations Balloting by Costume Designer Members of the Academy Art Directors Branch.	
DIRECTING	5	Academy Directors Branch Members.	
DOCUMENTARY AWARDS: Features, more than 3,000 feet Short Subjects, 3,000 feet or less	5 5	Documentary Awards Committee.	
FILM EDITING	5	Preliminary and Nominations Balloting by Academy Film Editors Branch Members.	
FOREIGN LANGUAGE FILM AWARD	5	Foreign Language Film Award Nominating Committee.	

Academy Membership

Category		
MUSIC:		
BEST ORIGINAL SCORE — for a motion picture (not a musical)	5	*Preliminary and Nominations Balloting by Academy Music Branch Members.*
BEST SCORE OF A MUSICAL PICTURE — (original or adaptation)	5	
BEST SONG (original for the picture)	5	
BEST PICTURE	5	*All Active Academy Members.*
SHORT SUBJECTS:		
CARTOONS, 3,000 feet or less	5	*Academy Short Subjects Branch Members.*
LIVE ACTION SUBJECTS, 3,000 feet or less	5	
SOUND	5	*Academy Sound Branch Members.*
SPECIAL VISUAL EFFECTS	2	*Special Visual Effects Award Nominating Committee.*
WRITING:		
SCREENPLAY — Based on material from another medium	5	*Academy Writers Branch Members.*
STORY AND SCREENPLAY — based on material not previously published or produced	5	
OTHER AWARDS:		
SCIENTIFIC OR TECHNICAL AWARDS		*Voted by Board of Governors, Based on Recommendations of the Scientific or Technical Awards Committee.*
JEAN HERSHOLT HUMANITARIAN AWARD		*Voted by Board of Governors.*
THALBERG MEMORIAL AWARD		*Voted by Board of Governors.*
HONORARY AWARDS:		
HONORARY AWARDS		*Voted by Board of Governors.*

Any actor, actress, or aspirant can advertise himself
or herself in the *ACADEMY PLAYERS DIRECTORY*. Almost every personality in the book pays for his ad. Generally, advertisers
supply two pictures (head and shoulders) showing different arrangement of facial muscles and different clothing. The advertisements show the name of the actor in large bold type, and
then in smaller type the name and telephone of the actor's agent
or manager, or both. Some advertisements also include some
credits.

The Academy of Motion Picture Arts and Sciences maintains educational and entertaining programs for Academy members,
programs being historical, biographical, or current. Motion
pictures are shown to members, and sometimes guests may speak.

The Academy maintains a motion picture theatre in which
membership, press, and other previews are shown.

The Academy of Motion Picture Arts and Sciences is most
famous for its presentation of Academy Awards. While the rules
for the conduct of the balloting may vary from time to time,
the rules for the 1970 Academy Awards for achievements during
1969 may be of interest to the reader. After all, there may
be Academy Awards in your future.

PART II

B O O K   R E V I E W S

This part of the book reviews other books, most of
which are available to the reader in libraries, paperback and
regular bookstores, in stores specializing in movie material,
or directly from publishers.

The reader may be surprised at the nature of these
reviews - the *business aspects* of the reviewed books are described, mentioned, and small portions are occasionally quoted.
It is hoped that the reader of this business book will read and
re-read the reviewed books from time to time, as the reader's
realization of various business aspects increases.

FINANCING A THEATRICAL PRODUCTION

(Book Review)

A symposium of the Committee on the Law of the Theatre of the Federal Bar Association of New York, New Jersey and Connecticut was edited by Joseph Taubman, and was published by Federal Legal Publications, Inc., 95 Morton Street, New York, N.Y. 10014, under the title, *FINANCING A THEATRICAL PRODUCTION*.

In the chapter, "Legal and Business Aspects of Financing Broadway Productions," Paul J. Sherman wrote, *"Not too long ago, 'angeldom' on Broadway was a select and privileged rank achieved mainly by those with great personal wealth or close connections with producers . . .*

"A key factor in the appearance of many new investors on the Broadway scene has been the reduction in the size of the investment presently required. . . ."

Other chapters of the book are:

"Production Costs and Offerings"
"Theatrical Limited Partnerships and Joint Ventures"
"Some Thoughts on New Methods of Theatrical Investments"
"The Producer's Share"
"S.E.C. Practice and Procedure"
"S.E.C. Policy"

While *FINANCING A THEATRICAL PRODUCTION* is aimed at lawyers advising Broadway producers, the information in the book will greatly benefit attorneys advising motion picture producers, and the businessman who is the money man of a production team.

PRODUCTION FINANCING

(Book Review)

The Beverly Hills Bar Association and the University of Southern California Law Center annually present programs on Legal Aspects of the Entertainment Industry. The fourteenth such program dealt with PRODUCTION FINANCING.

Section I dealt with FINANCING INDEPENDENT MOTION PICTURE PROJECTS. Appendices included:

1. Bank Loan Agreement.

2. Assignment of Profit Participation and Distributor's Acceptance.

3. Distributor's Acceptance (of Assignment to Bank).

4. Distributor's Acceptance and Acknowledgement (of Assignment to Laboratory).

5. Notice of Irrevocable Authority (Distributor's Acceptance of Appointment as Pledgeholder for Laboratory).

6. Laboratory Pledgeholder Agreement.

7. Guaranty and Completion Agreement.

8. Security Agreement.

8A. Security Agreement - Union Residual Clause.

9. Laboratory Loan Agreement.

10. Mortgage of Copyright.

11A&B. Completion Guarantees (English).

12. Provisions for Distributor's Guarantee of Payment.

12A. Distribution Agreement with Guarantee.

13. Power of Attorney Coupled with an Interest.

14.   Co-Production Agreement.

15.   Production Advance Agreement.

16.   Distributor's Guarantee of Laboratory Loan to Producer.

17.   Distribution Agreement (for Distribution in United
        States, Canada, Their Territories, Possessions and
        Enclaves).

While all of the above is in the first section of PRODUC-
TION FINANCING, the other sections of the book concern: Financing
Independent Phonograph Record Production; Foreign Film Subsidies
and Other State Aid As An Aspect of Financing; Financing Entertainment Vehicles under the Uniform Commercial Code.

Basically, the money-lenders such as banks, credit-providers
such as laboratories, deferral takers, investors, loan guarantors
want some security and want the distributor to make appropriate
payments.

THE LIVELIEST ART

(Book Review)

Arthur Knight's *THE LIVELIEST ART, A Panoramic History of the Movies*, Mentor Books, MQ824, 95¢, provides much business information in its various parts:

Knight recognizes the inventor (flickers, sound, color, etc.), the artist (writer, director, etc.), and the businessman as the three points in the triangle of the film creation.

Many business problems come again and again. For example, movies for general distribution developed from silent to sound, from black and white to color.

The new technology and expense hurt the value of pictures using the old technology. Thus, silent films lost most of their commercial value when sound became established. Similarly, the

market value of a black and white film is less than it would
be if it were in color (generally).

This ends the book review for the moment. The following is comment:

The business lessons must be remembered by investors
and creditors contributing to a motion picture.

"X" rated pictures, rated for "adults" only, for a
long time were silent pictures. Then "voice over" was added;
dialog was avoided because of the expense of synchronization.
As more "X" films became available, technological improvements
were added; distributors and theaters no longer wanted silent
pictures and paid less than before for "voice overs." Recently
a producer of a black and white picture was told by an exhibitor
that the box office value of the feature would have been three
times as high if the black and white picture had been shot in
color.

Now back to the book review of THE LIVELIEST ART by
Arthur Knight.

Knight discusses big studios in "The Stamp of the
Studio."

"But as movies grew longer, more elaborate and expensive
to produce, the problems of administration became increasingly

demanding. The studios were forced to enlarge their operations to stay in business, the producers forced to devote more of their attention to matters of distribution and exhibition and less to production itself. The distance between the studios and the 'front office' began to expand. And early in the twenties, when the movies turned into a vast, multi-million-dollar industry almost overnight, the creative talent was suddenly widely separated from the men who guided the financial destinies of their studios. Soon the studios were being spoken of as 'the factory' or 'the plant,' and pictures became 'the product.' The movies had become big business; and since the very essence of big business is standardization and control, methods of production were introduced that would permit a close calculation of costs and a reasonably exact estimate of profits. Directors quickly learned their position in the complex chain of command that extended from the studio floor up through the new echelons of assistant producers, associate producers, producers, vice presidents in charge of production and on back to the board rooms and executive suites of the company's top brass, generally situated in New York."

MAN AND THE MOVIES

(Book Review)

This is basically a business book for persons interested in commercial aspects of motion pictures. Frequently, business books make difficult reading. In an attempt to try to maintain reader interest, this book has tried to keep its chapters short, and to jump from story to text to book to law and back and forth.

W. R. Robinson, editor of *MAN AND THE MOVIES*, Pelican Book A 1061, $1.95, has a variety of articles on:

1. The Monitor Image (John Huston's *Treasure of the Sierra Madre*, *Maltese Falcon*, *The Red Badge of Courage*).

2. Osborne's *TOM JONES: Adapting a Classic*.

3. Cowboys, Movies, Myths, and Cadillacs: Realism in the Western.

4. Twenty-Six Propositions about Skin Flicks.

5. Poetry and Danger in the Horror Film.

6. Films, Television and Tennis.

7. The Movies, Too, Will Make You Free.

8. The Rhetoric of Hitchcock's Thrillers.

9. Griffith in Retrospect.

10. Antonioni's Films.

11. Fellini: Analyst Without Portfolio.

12. Luchino Visconti, Italian Director.

13. The New Mystique of L'Actuelle.

14. A Poet and the Movies.

15. Don't Make Waves (A Writer's Autobiography).

16. Faulkner in Hollywood.

17. What Shining Phantom: Writers and the Movies.

18. In the Central Blue.

19. Critics and Criticism.

MAN AND THE MOVIES sections emphasize <u>art</u>: "The Art and Its Forms," "The Artist and His Work," "The Personal Encounter."

The businessman would be well advised to peruse this book and similar books, both for the business information they contain and to get some ideas as to why picture making is more complicated than marching actors in front of a camera.

George Garrett, in his generally humorous article, "Don't Make Waves," writes about studio operation: *"In the beginning, <u>somebody</u>, sometimes a Very Distinguished Director, more often a Producer, the corporate chief, has an 'idea.' Usually based upon a 'property.' Novel, play, article, non-fiction book, newspaper story . . . .*

"A very large part of screen writing, then, consists of writing a screen play 'based on' or 'adapted from' something else.

" . . . . most Producers have Readers. The Readers boil

down the book to a synopsis. . . .

"Next comes the 'treatment.' Treatments vary widely
in form and substance. In essence, though, they are detailed
outlines, in ordinary prose, though a dramatic scene sketch or
two may be thrown in, of the sequence and order of the picture.
Structure, characters, motivation, etc. All these are dealt
with. . . .

"Then begins the first draft of the screenplay. Here,
if the treatment is complete enough, the job is basically a mechanical translation of the treatment into numbered 'master
scenes' (somewhere about 300 scenes is about average), which
are a kind of score of the basic shots of the picture. . . .

" . . . an elaborate process of revision begins. . . .

"Actors are cast.

" . . . Director . . .

" . . . Cutter . . .

"Sets are being built and locations found for exterior
shooting. . . .

"Why so many sets for interior scenes? . . . Chances of
lighting, sound and everything else being right on location are
poor. . . .

"Budget and the person of the Production Manager, the
top sergeant of the whole enterprise, begin to be influential.

" . . . a great many pictures make use of continuity
sketches, made by an artist or Art Director. . . .

"Finally the so-called final shooting script. . . ."

The above quotes are extracts from *MAN AND THE MOVIES*.

Of special interest to the movie money people is the time table and extent of money which is often spent before the first day of shooting.

Frequently a producer seeks cash from contributors for the purpose of acquiring an option to the property. After a designated period of time, the option may lapse, the producer will have no rights, the contributor will have lost his contribution.

Persons who are willing to contribute cash, credit, and time toward production of motion pictures should understand the problems of pre-production and production. Various views and angles of these problems are indicated in *MAN AND THE MOVIES*.

FILM WORLD

(Book Review)

The low cost Pelican series on the movies includes *FILM WORLD* by Ivor Montagu, Pelican A 686, $1.75.

Part One, "Film As Science," has chapters on: (1) Definition; (2) Invention; (3) Distortion; (4) Creation; (5) Sound; (6) Colour; (7) Size, Shape, and Substance.

Part Two, "Film As Art," has chapters on: (1) Shot; (2) Inter-shot; (3) Rhythm; (4) Matter; (5) Marriage; (6) Titles.

Part Three, "Film As Commodity," has chapters on: (1) Scale; (2) Cost; (3) System; (6) Monopoly; (7) Protection; (8) Restriction.

Part Four, "Film As Vehicle," has chapters on: (1) Realism; (2) Range.

Of special interest to businessmen are the chapters in Part Three, "Film As Commodity."

For example, Chapter 1 on "Scale" contains information such as: *"The initial costs - as we have called them here, the production costs - the costs of shooting, editing and producing in toto the married negative with sound - may be gigantic, but however large they can be met by multiplication of performance.*

"The negative, celluloid, can be used to manufacture pictures, each as good as another ad lib., at a cost that is chicken-feed compared to production costs. (The only limitation on the

number of positives, the wearing out of the negative by fric-
tion in the printing-machines, is nearly negligible; and in
any case this is circumvented by duplicating, from a specially
fine-grain positive, one or more so-called dupe negatives, with,
nowadays, practically no loss of quality whatever.) Each copy
can be projected many hundreds of times and, while a part may
be damaged by accident and a new (duped) part substituted, will
only gradually, over hundreds of performances, worsen in its
effect by normal mortality, i.e. dirt, friction, and decay.
Each performance may be given to any number up to hundreds or
even thousands of people."

The dream of persons backing a production is that the distributor will collect tremendous amounts of money from theaters, will in turn pay tremendous amounts of money to producers and the persons backing the producers with money, credit, and time.

Another chapter in *FILM WORLD* discusses "Cost." Sample extracts include: *"But the swollen looking staff is all*
necessary and their intermittent apparent idleness unavoidable.
In film, specialist jobs can only be done in succession. Even
with preliminary rehearsals elsewhere, before studio shooting
begins, the final rehearsals for each shot must be completed

on the set; . . . the lighting cameraman . . . the electricians
. . . the stand-ins . . . the soundmen . . . .   Each separate
shot has to go through this rigmarole . . ."

The chapter on "System" commences, *"In film marketing*
three rivals are competing for the cake.   They are: producer
. . . distributor, exhibitor.   These categories correspond
roughly to the classic three in other economic fields: produc-
er, wholesaler, retailer."

FILM WORLD serves as a good source of information for
potential money men as well as talent men in the motion picture industry.

KING COHN

(Book Review)

Bob Thomas's *KING COHN* is available as a Bantam book for 95¢.

The book serves as a story of Harry Cohn, Columbia Pictures, and motion pictures.

It is one of a series of biographies concerning important movie men, their businesses, and motion pictures.

The businessman who wishes to contribute to a motion picture project as investor, money lender, creditor, etc. may wish to read several of these biographies so that said businessman can better understand the ego-nuts with whom he is dealing.

In *KING COHN* appears the following: *"Symptomatic of Cohn's urge to control was a device he repeatedly employed in the signing of actors: he wanted to change their names. By so doing, he could cloud their former identities and create them, in name, if not in other respects, in a new image dictated by Harry Cohn."*

* * * *

"Being a Cohn assistant was an all-consuming job; many found the pace too exhausting and quit."

* * * *

"All the pioneering studio heads were egoists who required the subservience of their underlings."

BASHFUL BILLIONAIRE

(Book Review)

Albert B. Gerber's *BASHFUL BILLIONAIRE*, about Howard Hughes, was published as a paperback by Dell (95¢).

Of business interest is the chapter, "Howard Hughes and His Motion Picture Studio."

The following are extracts:

"In 1927 Joseph P. Kennedy, father of the late President, acquired the controlling interest in the Keith-Albee-Orpheum Corporation. Like many other American corporations, Keith-Albee was unable to withstand the depression and on January 27, 1933, it went into receivership. At this time it became known as RKO Corporation.

"Floyd Odlum, the West Coast financier, first became interested in RKO in 1935 while the company was still in receivership. By the time receivership ended in 1940, Odlum owned the largest single block of stock and became chairman of the board."

* * *

"Odlum decided to sell his RKO stock. In the year 1946 the value of a share of stock had fluctuated between $15.00 and $28.00. The company enjoyed a prestige position in the motion picture industry. It maintained major studios in Hollywood and Culver City, ninety acres of land in Los Angeles, and a film-producing company in Mexico City. Also, RKO had a wholly owned

subsidiary which controlled a chain of one hundred and twenty-
four motion picture theaters throughout the United States.
Fifty-three of these were owned in fee and the balance were
leased. There were twenty-six theaters in New York City alone.
The nation-wide chain ranged from center city theaters in major
cities to two in Sioux City, Iowa, and one in Champaign, Illinois.
The company had a net worth in excess of $100 million with an
earned surplus of $23.5 million. It had paid out dividends to
shareholders averaging $3.5 million annually for several years."

       * * * *

      "In May, 1948, Hughes bought Odlum's stock and took over
control of RKO. He paid $9.50 per share, or a total of $8,825,500."

      "FORTUNE gives as the reason for his purchase that he was
moved by 'two of his abiding interests, prestige and money.' Unquestionably, he was especially interested in the one hundred
and twenty-four theaters of which he gained control in the transaction. He had always experienced a considerable amount of distribution difficulty, but he had confidence in his own productions and believed that if they were exhibited properly they
would make money. The RKO deal gave him a means of distribution.
Also, he had two films rapidly approaching completion - MAD WEDNES-
DAY and VENDETTA. The two pictures had cost him in excess of $5
million and he wanted to be sure of outlets."

The moneymen who read this book may have some money or a lot; all probably wish they had more.

In planning motion picture empires, businessmen should be interested in all three major aspects: production, distribution, and exhibition.

The more powerful distributors can get more and better theaters to show pictures for longer periods of time than the weak distributors. Such power may be at local level, state level, national level, or may lie outside the basic industry.

There are very few natural "hit" movies which are so good that theaters want them at any price. Most pictures are such that theaters "can take them or leave them alone."

The position of Hughes as motion picture producer of two pictures which had cost him in excess of $5,000,000 was probably quite simple: (1) Hughes wanted a distributor he could trust (and the best and perhaps only way a producer can trust a distributor is to be the distributor himself); (2) Hughes wanted distribution power, and the RKO theater chain gave power to his distribution set-up; (3) Considering the degree of entertainment success of the two movies, Hughes would probably have been wiped out by any other distributor. (Producer's share less prints less advertising = $0.00).

BASHFUL BILLIONAIRE has other chapters on the motion picture industry and Howard Hughes. "Howard Hughes and His Bosomy Western" concerns the movie, *THE OUTLAW*, actress Miss Jane

Russell, publicist Russell Birdwell, the Hays Office.

Gerber wrote: *"The supreme promotion coup occurred when,*
as one commentator said, 'The picture's publicity man had achieved
a literal new high in vulgarity. Over Pasadena, a skywriting
plane traced THE OUTLAW, then drew two huge circles side by side
and placed a dot in the center of each.'"

(Comment: Many producers make the mistake of spending
all their money in motion picture production, instead of reserv-
ing a healthy amount for publicity, promotion and advertising.
These last three are functions of the distributor. That's why
the producer should have his own money for publicity, promotion
and advertising of his choice.)

MAN AND WIFE

(Book Review)

MAN AND WIFE, published by the Institute for Adult Education, $5.00, is an important book to the motion picture industry.

The concept of a motion picture theatre as an entertainment center includes:

1. A place where a film is shown.
2. A place to sit, whether or not the shown film is watched.
3. A place to buy and consume refreshments.
4. A place to advertise features in other theatres, forthcoming features, books and records available at other locations.

Generally, motion picture theatres have avoided the retailing business. The only products retailed by theatre candy counters or candy machines have been those meeting simplicity requirements: inexpensive, easy to sell, easy to purchase in appropriate quantity and quality. One essential requirement of the retail product was that it did not require return to the source of any unsold items. Theatres did not want to take the time, trouble, and expense of processing returns. Theatres generally avoided selling books and records associated with the films being shown because of the problem of returns. (Other reasons given were the problems of inventory control, inside theft, and the desire to avoid burglary.)

Eventually, some enterprising motion picture producer

had to get around to providing film viewers a chance to buy a book associated with the film at the theatres which were showing the film.

The book, *MAN AND WIFE*, retails for $5.00. Thus, there is a big $5.00 pie to be cut up by the various parties interested in the book, its distribution, and its retailing.

Many paperback book-industry retailers and many record-industry retailers are serviced by rack jobbers. Rack jobbers service many retailers who have no knowledge of the merchandise - rack jobbers decide what merchandise they wish to place in the "location," deliver the new merchandise, and make counts to determine how much merchandise was sold.

The vending machines will become more important in selling records (e.g., motion picture sound tracks), and books (e.g. written versions of films, or originals on which films are based) in motion picture theatres.

Important reasons why theatres have not sold records and books in the past include: (1) economic reasons; (2) laziness.

The tough-minded men whose "X" films are making more money per dollar invested than most major studio productions, and who are getting more theatres around the country to play their "X" product each month, are making changes in production, distribution, and exhibition.

One of the changes may be the introduction of more retailing in theatres. Such retailing may include distribution of
the Institute for Adult Education's *MAN AND WIFE* and Grove
Press's *I AM CURIOUS (YELLOW)*.

Due to the nature of this business book on the one hand,
and the naturalness of *MAN AND WIFE* on the other, there will
be no illustrative quotes from *MAN AND WIFE* in this book, even
though *MAN AND WIFE* will prove an important book in the development of the motion picture industry.

PEOPLE WHO MAKE MOVIES

(Book Review)

Theodore Taylor's *PEOPLE WHO MAKE MOVIES*, Avon Camelot Books, 75¢, is aimed at readers with high school level intelligence, so it can easily be understood by persons who went to college.

Its chapters are:

    1. The Producer
    2. The Director
    3. The Writer and the Story
    4. The Cameraman
    5. The Unit Production Manager
          and the Assistant Director
    6. Art Direction, Set Decoration, and Costumes
    7. The New Face Department
    8. The Working Core
    9. Those Magicians, the Special Effects Men
   10. Actors and Actresses
   11. The Stuntmen
   12. The Film Editor
   13. Music and the Musical
   14. The Publicist
   15. On the Fringe of Hollywood
   16. Selling the Picture

Theodore Taylor writes this business book in a readable manner, frequently using names and movies to illustrate points. Since he is writing for a high school audience, Taylor correctly assumes that his readers would like to learn about a subject they do not know. Too many movie books are written by critics for an audience which can appreciate fully the critic's writing only if they are as expert in movie history and technique as the critic.

Therefore, of all the paperbacks reviewed herein, this
is probably the best business book that a producer can give to a
potential backer.

HOLLYWOOD UNCENSORED

(Book Review)

     *HOLLYWOOD UNCENSORED, The Stars - Their Secrets and
Their Scandals*, Pyramid Books R-1135, 50¢, has articles about
Tony Curtis, Keenan Wynn, Tuesday Weld, Jerry Lewis, Rory
Calhoun, George Maharis, Jimmy Durante, Steve McQueen, Jayne
Mansfield, Mickey Rooney, Dean Martin, Robert Vaughn, and
John Wayne.

     Some wives of potential money men may be simply
"thrilled" to read about the stars.

DRAT! (About W.C. Fields)

(Book Review)

Richard J. Anobile's *DRAT! (being the encapsulated view
of life by W.C. FIELDS in his own words)*, Signet Books, Q3933,
95¢, has an introduction by Ed McMahon and an article by Richard
F. Shephard.

The book has over 100 photographs with captions of
Field's quotes, such as:

*"I was in love with a beautiful blonde once - she drove
me to drink - 'tis the one thing I'm indebted to her for."*

*"I told Baby LeRoy's nurse to get me a racing form and
I would play nurse until she returned. I quietly removed the
nipple from Baby LeRoy's bottle, dropped in a couple of noggins
of gin, and returned to Baby LeRoy. After sucking on the paci-
fier for a few minutes, he staggered through the scene like a
Barrymore."*

"Any man who hates children can't be all bad."

*"Alcohol, of course, can take care of itself - which is
more than a dog can do."*

If the producer is producing a comedy, then this book
may make a good gift to a potential backer.

THE STUDIO

(Book Review)

Leo Guild's *THE STUDIO*, Holloway House HH-168, 95¢, may make ideal lending by a producer to a money man who has heard that starlets favor a money man who has influence with the producer financially backed by the money man.

The producer must be careful not to increase his production expenses by too much just to satisfy money men's girl friends. However, we have heard of a producer who used more night-working girls than day-working girls in his business operation. He reasoned that getting money through night work was as important as day work.

Naturally the producer must not place himself in any illegal position: Some of the laws the producer should not break are indicated in Leo Guild's *THE STUDIO*.

For the edification of the readers, we present several California laws on procuring, pandering, prostitution.

CALIFORNIA PENAL CODE, Section 266d. - Paid Procuring of Female - Pandering. "Any person who receives any money or other valuable thing for or on account of his placing in custody any female for the purpose of causing her to cohabit with any male to whom she is not married, is guilty of a felony."

Section 266e. - Hiring Panderer. - "Every person who purchases, or pays any money or other valuable thing for, any

female person for the purpose of prostitution, or for the purpose of placing her, for immoral purposes, in any house or place
against her will, is guilty of a felony."

Section 266f. - *Selling Female for Illicit Use.* - "Every
person who sells any female person or receives any money or other
valuable thing for or on account of his placing in custody, for
immoral purposes, any female person, whether with or without her
consent, is gulty of a felony."

Section 266g. - *Prostituting Wife.* - "Every man who, by
force, intimidation, threats, persuasion, promises, or any other
means, places or leaves, or procures any other person or persons
to place or leave, his wife in a house of prostitution, or con-
nives at or consents to, or permits, the placing or leaving of
his wife in a house of prostitution, or allows or permits her
to remain therein, is guilty of a felony and punishable by im-
prisonment in the State prison for not less than three nor more
than ten years; and in all prosecutions under this section a
wife is a competent witness against her husband."

Section 266h. - *Pimping.* - "Any male person who, knowing a female person is a prostitute, lives or derives support or
maintenance in whole or in part from the earnings or proceeds
of her prostitution, or from money loaned or advanced to or

charged against her by any keeper or manager or inmate of a
house or other place where prostitution is practiced or allowed,
or who solicits or receives compensation for soliciting for her,
is guilty of pimping, a felony, and is punishable by imprison-
ment in the state prison for not less than one year nor more
than 10 years.

"Any female person referred to in this section is a
competent witness in any prosecution hereunder to testify for
or against the accused as to any transaction or as to any conversation with the accused or by him with another person or
persons in her presence, notwithstanding her having married
the accused before or after the violation of any of the provisions of this section, whether called as a witness during
the existence of the marriage or after its dissolution."

Unfortunately for some people, there are many other
anti-sex laws.

TELL IT TO LOUELLA

(Book Review)

*"The best selling intimate story of your favorite stars
. . . TELL IT TO LOUELLA by Hollywood's Leading Columnist, Louella Parsons,"* it says on the front cover. Lancer Books, 74-861,
75¢.

The producer who wants to drop names would do well to
read this book.

The producer who wants his name publicized may be able
to learn a lot of publicity-causing items. The producer can
paraphrase the items, substitute the names of himself, his director, writer, stars, backers, etc., and give this material to
his public relations man. Then it is the job of the P.R. (Public
Relations) man to get these stories and items into print.

I.E. AN AUTOBIOGRAPHY

(Book Review)

    Mickey Rooney's *I.E. AN AUTOBIOGRAPHY*, Bantam Books
S3241, 75¢, is an interesting book.

    "One day, when I was about a year and a half, I quit
backstage for a new playpen. Clutching a penny whistle, I followed the orchestra to the pit, crawled into the pit, crawled
onto a drum and began to go through the motions of playing.
Burlesque was informal entertainment. The orchestra leader
went along with me immediately. So did the audience. It must
have looked pretty funny: an infant, dressed like a dandy,
going through all the motions of being a musician. One comic
later complained to my mother, 'Nobody paid any attention to me,
with that damn kid of yours hamming it up on the damn drum.'

    "TODDLER SHOW STOPPER, *Variety* might headline. Pat
White was so pleased he invested $50 for a tuxedo custom-made
to my size. Forty inches of it - all of it. Mother still has
the tuxedo; it would be too small for an adolescent chimpanzee."

    "The McGuire series was a success from the start, just
as later the Andy Hardy series succeeded from its beginning,
which, by the way, was a 1937 quickie called *A Family Affair*.
I think I made fifteen or sixteen Andy Hardy pictures."

    "After Shakespeare, I was offered several strong roles
at MGM. There was *Ah, Wilderness!*, the only comedy Eugene

O'Neill ever wrote."

"In 1936, I made *The Devil Is a Sissy* and *Little Lord Fauntleroy*. Freddie Bartholomew was the little lord himself."

"During the late 1930's, Metro-Goldwyn-Mayer was geared to a schedule of fifty-two pictures a year, one movie a week. There were sets by the acre, directors by the dozen, writers by the score and, the studio advertised, 'more stars than there are in the heavens.'"

"Anyway, the reason there's so much sex in movies today comes down to two words: box office.

"If the day comes when sex ceases to be box office, those daring, audacious, shocking movies we see advertised will disappear. If sex ceases to be box office. . . . Forget the premise. I'm just making a point.

"As Mayer saw it and as almost everyone has seen it since, we are in the movie *business*, the movie industry."

"When the public reaction to Andy, by mail, by phone, by wire and by box office receipts, turned out to be so strong, MGM, like General Motors with a hot new car, was perfectly e-quipped to roll. They had writers ready to pound out scripts, directors ready to plan camera angles, press agents ready to promote. And, happily, they had girls."

"An actor, however good he may be, needs an agent to find him roles and to negotiate contracts. Then he may also need a personal manager. The manager looks for roles, negotiates contracts and watches the agent. Finally, the actor needs a lawyer. The lawyer watches the manager watching the agent.

"An actor acts, but he is also a property, like *Three acres, two-bedroom house, pool, view, $125,000, Pacific Palisades*. The actor concentrates on his acting. The others concentrate on him as a property. Without good people around him, an actor may go out of business. There are thousands of actors around and it is easy for producers to forget. A good agent and a good manager do not let producers forget. In exchange, they won a piece of the property."

The businessman who is asked to back a movie frequently complains about the high salaries of stars. The producer may be able to use Mickey Rooney's autobiography to supply information about (a) the money needs of stars; (b) the needs of producers for stars; (c) the tremendous negotiability of salaries of men temporarily unemployed.

The film budget may allow 10% of budget for the various producers: producer, executive producer, associate producer, co-producer.

10% of a picture budget for $100,000 is $10,000.

10% of a million-dollar picture is $100,000, or ten times the producer's share of a $100,000 picture.

The higher amount of a producer's share in a higher budget picture than in a low budget picture is one reason why producers prefer high budget pictures.

Pictures have places in their budgets for stars. Some stars demand more than others.

(1) The higher the salaries to the stars = (2) the higher the budget of the picture = (3) the higher the amount in the budget for the producers.

Thus, if the producer is spending somebody else's money, and there is sufficient money to make a picture, the producer may not mind stars' requests for high salaries.

Richard Bernstein tells the story of a producer who had studio approval to spend $3,000,000 on a picture. The producer's assistant, a budget-minded production man, told the producer he had calculated how the picture could be brought in for only $2,000,000. The producer fired his assistant.

S I N A T R A

(Book Review)

Arnold Shaw's *SINATRA, Twentieth Century Romantic,*
Pocket Books 671-77111-095, 95¢ contains business information
concerning Frank Sinatra and facets of the entertainment industry.

"The fountainhead of Sinatra's power is his unique and
unsurpassed singing. Although he has worn many other hats -
screen actor, television impresario, film director, musical con-
ductor, record and movie producer - the figure that hypnotizes
even today is the man in the snap-brim at the microphone. His
sex appeal stems from it." . . . .

"IT WAS DURING THE ERA of the Big Bands in the booming
days of the New Deal that Francis Albert Sinatra mastered the
art of which he became the most celebrated and most imitated
exponent of our time." . . . .

"THE DORSEY AFFILIATION was, of course, the realization
of a dream. Only recently Frank told of how, in his Harry James
days, all the young singers wanted to connect either with Dorsey
or Miller." . . . .

"Though Evans never acknowledged that he rounded up
girls to swoon, Jack Keller, a West Coast associate, conceded
that Evans stationed ambulances outside the box office where
bobbysoxers waiting to enter the shrine could see them and

react. On the occasion of Frank's fiftieth birthday, Keller

went further in admitting that they had primed the pump. 'We

outfitted Frank,' he said, 'with breakaway suits and hired

girls to scream when he sexily rolled a note. But we needn't

have. . . . The girls we hired to scream swooned, and hundreds

more we didn't hire swooned with them.'" . . . .

"As his income grew, Frank entered the music publishing

field. Instead of payola, insured through open or covert affili-

ation with an established publisher, Frank wanted ownership."

THE DISNEY VERSION
(Book Review)

Richard Schickel's *THE DISNEY VERSION*, Avon Discus Books W148, $1.25, has a quote of Pauline Kael on its cover: "The story of how Disney built an empire on corrupt popular art has more surprises than might have been anticipated . . . a revealing part of American cultural history. Schickel makes it an important story."

The book may inspire potential producers and their money men. Of special interest is the following quote concerning a producer's deciding that the best distributor is the producer himself.

"The first of these was the formation of Disney's own distribution subsidiary, Buena Vista, named after the street on which the studio's main gate is situated. The company was largely Roy Disney's invention, and he was motivated largely by the reluctance of Disney's long-time distributor, RKO Radio, to get behind THE LIVING DESERT with suitable enthusiasm and by a similar lack of interest among RKO's competitors. In addition, the Disneys had long chafed under the heavy percentage of their grosses that went to their distributors, even though the 30 per cent RKO was getting was close to rock bottom in the industry. By setting up the lean Buena Vista operation, the Disney people cut distribution costs to 15 per cent of the gross and, equally

important, gained direct control over the handling of their
films in the market. They could keep them off double-feature
bills where they might be paired with products deemed unsuitable
to them, and they could begin to package entire programs, consisting, for example, of a feature, a cartoon and a nature film,
which usually ran a bit longer than the usual short subject and
was thus often hard to wedge into other people's programs. Compared to the other events of this decade in Disney's land, the
founding of Buena Vista was not very glamorous or exciting, but
it did represent, for the Disneys, the final step in gaining
complete control of their own destiny, complete freedom from interference by outsiders in the creation and exploitation of their
products. It also, of course, symbolized their rise out of the
ranks of the independents to a status in every way coequal with
the major Hollywood production companies, which had all along
had their own distribution arms. Most important of all, the
studio was able to time the release of its films so that they
could most effectively be coordinated with ancillary activities
(i.e., the big film is released in a period where television-
viewing is at a peak, and more people are likely to see the commercials for it). The studio also gained a very valuable form
of self-protection: no one will ever be able to sell out a

Disney product at a discount or in a hurry merely to improve the distributor's cash flow, a problem that constantly besets the independent producer."

We wonder how this ties in with RKO's decision to go out of the distributing business? What were the differences between Buena Vista and RKO in distribution operations?

THE DISNEY VERSION is a business book. The characters met in other biographies of studio heads are met again in *THE DISNEY VERSION*.

HOLLYWOOD CONFIDENTIAL

(Book Review)

HOLLYWOOD CONFIDENTIAL, edited by Phil Hirsch, has stories about Marlon Brando, Judy Garland, Barbara Payton, Lee Marvin, Alan Ladd, Robert Mitchum, Jack Carter, Jack Palance, David Niven, George C. Scott, Peter O'Toole.

About Alan Ladd, the book indicates that "In the mid-1950's he formed his own company, Jaguar Productions. In addition, Warner's paid Ladd a $150,000 salary for each picture and cut him in for 50 per cent of the profits. This unique step enabled him to earn nearly a million dollars in 1957, his most lucrative year."

* * *

The 50%-of-the-profits for a big star can be more easily promised by a production company which handles its own distribution than by a one-picture-at-a-time producer. The producer-distributor can make its money through distribution. In fact, every $1 the producer-distributor kept in its distribution division, was $1 in profit for the corporation; however, every $1 passed on by the distribution division to the production division meant 50¢ for the star and only 50¢ for the corporation.

Since the distributor-producer has accounting control, it can often decide where dollars should stay - in the distribution division or the production division.

Thus, a distributor-producer can more easily afford to give a star 50% of producer's profits than can a small producer. The small producer may be well advised to pass a deal in which the star is promised 50% of net profit.

Now we'll argue the other side - in favor of a small producer dealing with a star of "50% of profit" caliber.

The budget of such a picture will probably be quite high - and so will the producer's share of the budget. If the producer takes a healthy portion of the fee in cash, and more in deferral, or somehow ahead of "profit," the picture may never be in "profit." 50% of $0 profit is not much. Quite a few stars have learned that.

HOLLYWOOD CONFIDENTIAL contains other business information. Also, add *HOLLYWOOD CONFIDENTIAL* to other books providing biographies of stars, and the reader can play the "Who will we cast" game.

The "Who will we cast" game is played by producers and distributors. Producers submit proposed stars (male, female), featured actors and actresses, directors, cameramen to the distributor. The distributor may state that he likes the submitted persons, and that he is willing to release a picture with such personnel. The producer knows that there will be a time lapse

between this meeting and the first day of shooting; the producer knows that he may be unable to have the submitted personnel at the time of the shooting.

        The producer therefore submits to the distributor
whether the distributor will approve Star B if Star A is unavailable. Will the distributor approve, in lieu of Director D, Directors E or F?

        The producer may have to educate the money men concerning
substitutions of stars, directors, and others.

        The money man whose wife allowed him to invest in a Burt
Lancaster picture, or an Elizabeth Taylor picture, must be edu-
cated into leaving his money in a project in which the stars are
not Burt Lancaster and Elizabeth Taylor, and the director is not
John Huston.

        This book is a pablum way to learn some names and some
business.

THE CARPETBAGGERS

(Book Review)

Harold Robbins' *THE CARPETBAGGERS*, Pocket Books G.C.999, 95¢, Trident Press, $5.95, is a goldmine of information about the motion picture industry.

The following extract is dedicated to producers who leave reading producer-distributor contracts to their lawyers.

(Bernie Norman is a studio head; his sister has forced him to hire her son, David. Nevada Smith is the better-liked of the heroes of *THE CARPETBAGGERS*. Rina Marlowe is the wife of Nevada Smith at the time of the extract):

"IT STARTED OUT AS A QUIET WEDDING BUT IT TURNED into a circus, the biggest publicity stunt ever to come out of Hollywood. And all because David Woolf had finally made it into the bed of the redheaded extra who had a bit-role in *The Renegade*.

"Though he was a junior publicist, just one step above the lowest clerk in the department, and made only thirty-five a week, David was a very big man with the girls. This could be explained in one word. Nepotism. Bernie Norman was his uncle."

"Bernie Norman prided himself on being the first executive in the studio each day. . . . . ."

"He arrived at the door to his own private office that morning about eight o'clock, his inspection having taken a little longer than usual. He sighed heavily and opened his door.

Problems, always problems." . . . .

"David closed the door. 'Next month, before the picture opens, Nevada Smith and Rina Marlowe are getting married,'
he said.

"'You're telling me something?' His uncle glowered.
'Who cares? They didn't even invite me to the wedding. Besides,
Nevada's finished.'

"'Maybe,' David said. 'But the girl isn't. You saw the
picture?'

"'Of course I saw the picture!' Norman snapped. 'We're
sneaking it tonight.'

"'Well, after the sneak, she's going to be the hottest
thing in the business.'

"His uncle looked up at him, a respect dawning in his
eyes. 'So?'

"'From the papers, I see nobody's got her under contract,'
David said. 'You sign her this morning. Then - '

"His uncle was already nodding his head.

"'Then you tell them you want to give them the wedding.
As a present from the studio. We'll make it the biggest thing
ever to hit Hollywood. 'It'll add five million to the gross.'

"'So what good does that do us?' Norman asked. 'We

don't own any of the picture, we don't share in the profits.'

  "'We get a distribution fee, don't we?' David asked,
his confidence growing as he saw the intent look on his uncle's
face. 'Twenty-five per cent of five million is one and a quarter million dollars. Enough to carry half the cost of our
whole distribution setup for a whole year. And the beautiful
thing about it is we can charge all our expenses for the wedding
to publicity and slap the charges right back against the picture.
That way, it doesn't cost us one penny. Cord pays everything
out of his share of the profit.'"

  (Cord is the independent producer of the motion picture
starring Nevada Smith and Rina Marlowe.)

  The nepotism angle is well-known. The deductions that
distributors take out of the producer's share of proceeds are
not as well known.

  You may wish to re-read *THE CARPETBAGGERS* more carefully,
this time for movie business knowledge.

V A L E N T I N O

(Book Review)

Irving Shulman's *VALENTINO*, Pocket Books 77026, 95¢;
Trident Press, $ More.

This book on Valentino, like at least one other, starts
with Valentino's well-publicized funeral.

"At the hospital, the sober announcement of death had
been delivered to the assembled press corps by Joseph Schenck,
chairman of the board of directors of United Artists. Halting-
ly, his voice breaking, and pausing occasionally to pat the arm
of a weeping nurse or aide, Schenck at last managed to announce
that the romantic star had lost his brave battle, then went on
to say that he had lost a friend, the industry had lost a star
and the world had lost a lover. But - take heart - heaven had
gained an immortal." . . . .

"But there was more urgent business: it was imperative
to make new prints of *THE SON OF THE SHEIK* and rush them into
movie theaters if United Artists hoped to profit from the publicity attending Valentino's funeral. Schenck hoped the Valentino estate might prosper from this, since the actor had died
deeply in debt. It seemed inconceivable that a man could squan-
der a million dollars in one year and have nothing to show for
his efforts, but Valentino had accomplished this impossibility.
With some comfort Schenck reflected that United Artists had

shown foresight in insuring the star's life." . . . .

"That night, at the film laboratories, men began to
work around the clock to produce scores of new prints of *THE
SON OF THE SHEIK* and other Valentino films. In constant touch
with the situation, United Artists' executives began to feel
an increasing confidence in the ringmastership of Frank E.
Campbell. With things going so well, the ceremonies might be
prolonged for a week, possibly for two. Was this possible?"
. . . .

"But perhaps the most vexing problem of all was the
projected transcontinental visit by Pola Negri. Adolph Zukor,
in New York, had received a telephone call from the studio in
Hollywood: 'Pola is overwrought and she's heading to New York
for the funeral.' Zukor had advised putting a nurse and publicity man on the train and gave strict orders that Pola was
to guard her statements to the press. Obviously, Paramount intended to make Pola's sad pilgrimage more important than Valentino's demise."

The importance of publicity cannot be over-emphasized.
But, publicity often is not included in the producer's budget.
There should be publicity before the picture: Producer _____
has taken an option to film novelist _____'s forthcoming

book "_____."

    The next week the name of the forthcoming book can be
changed for the next publicity release.

    Next release, _____ will be executive producer of
(producer's) forthcoming film, "_____," based on novelist
_____'s forthcoming book.

    For other releases, see *The Hollywood Reporter,*
Variety and *Daily Variety, Independent Film Journal, Box Office*
and movie columns in newspapers.

    Releases during production, both during the shooting
weeks and the editing months, will be able to have more factual
information.

    Because fan magazines are monthlies, information for
such fan magazines must be furnished with the idea that the
magazines need information which will still be readable 60 to
90 days later.

    Producers may be lazy enough to allow publicity to be
handled by free-lance publicity men. However, good free-lance
publicity men are overworked and do not have enough time to
service each client. The producer should daily bug his publicity man with, *"Show me the clippings* which mention my name or
the name of the movie" and with, "What are you sending out to
what paper today? Be sure to send me a copy of each release you
are sending tonight."

    Did the publicity about Valentino's funeral pay off for
Valentino, the producer, distributor, and theatres? Yes!

INTERNATIONAL FILM GUIDE

(Book Review)

This paperback, edited by Peter Cowie, TANTIVY PRESS,

7 Sedley Place, London W.1., England; A.3. Barnes & Co., Inc.,

New York, U.S.A., $2.95, is an annual handbook for film enthusi-

asts, covering 29 countries, and commercial movies, festivals,

archives, animation, 16mm. and 35mm., film schools, books and

magazines.

Producers may remember how a foreign film with limited

distribution inspired the American production, *THE MAGNIFICENT

SEVEN*, and its sequels, *THE RETURN OF THE SEVEN*, etc. (Query:

Will we live to see *THE SON OF THE SEVEN*?)

Books like *INTERNATIONAL FILM GUIDE* provide information

annually about foreign films, and provide information about

foreign magazines (some in the English language) which can furn-

ish such information faster. Of course, *Weekly Variety* is faster

than magazines and books; possibly producers can be served by

following up *Weekly Variety* reviews by reading the words and

seeing the pictures in the foreign publications.

The "in" look in movie books is almost square: 6-1/4"

by 5-1/4" - the size of *INTERNATIONAL FILM GUIDE*.

Distributors may be interested in the foreign films

potentially available for distribution in the United States.

Exhibitors who play "X" pictures and who want to play

art pictures for policy reasons, may be interested in relatively
unknown foreign pictures offered by weak distributors.

Businessmen who weigh the advantages of Hollywood (technical skill, availability of personnel and facilities) against
disadvantages (higher wages) consider shooting elsewhere. However, uneconomic operations concerning communication, transportation, ignorance of customs, ignorance of available services,
frequently cause outside-of-Hollywood production to cost way
over expected budget.

INTERNATIONAL FILM GUIDE provides some information
about foreign directors, producers, cameramen, unions, trade
boards, suppliers, sources of information, etc. For example,
Laterna Film advertised its studio at Naerum, north of Copen-
hagen, Denmark.

Producers who hunt awards so that their pictures can
be publicized as award winners, can send inquiries to San Sebas-
tian, San Francisco, Sydney, Tours, Trieste, Venice, at the
addresses listed in *INTERNATIONAL FILM GUIDE 1969*.

INTERNATIONAL FILM GUIDE is an easy-to-read reference
book.

For example, what are the commercial possibilities arising out of the article on East Germany?

"Without doubt the best achievement among documentaries
is the mammoth, 4-part *Piloto in Pyjamas*, an account of the visit
paid to North Vietnam by Walter Heynowski and Gerhard Scheumann.
The films consist of 10 interviews in depth with American pilots
shot down over North Vietnam. They are made cleanly and clini-
cally in the style developed by this GDR team in *The Laughing
Man* (reviewed in IFG 1968). By some strange alchemy, these 4
full-length films reveal a good deal more about the American
condition and the climate that could provoke the murder of Martin Luther King and the Kennedys than any other films I have
seen. This group (originally shown as a series on television)
constitutes a remarkable achievement that will stand the test
of time."

P I C T U R E

(Book Review)

Lillian Ross's *PICTURE*, Avon Discus Books W-134, $1.25, is an excellent book.

Library Journal reviewed, "*PICTURE* is of incomparable value to any student of film-making."

It is the story of a specific film, John Huston's *THE RED BADGE OF COURAGE*. It provides insight in the making of any movie. The reader is able to enjoy the conflicts as if this history were a novel.

Lillian Ross introduces the studio (Metro-Goldwyn-Mayer), the picture (*THE RED BADGE OF COURAGE*), the source (the novel by Stephen Crane), columnists (Hedda Hopper), trade papers (*Variety*), the writer-director (John Huston), headquarters of the producer-distributor (as opposed to the studio) in the opening paragraph.

In swiftly moving dialogue and narrative, *PICTURE* discusses Dore Shary, MGM vice president in charge of production; Louis Mayer, MGM vice president in charge of the studio, and, finally, "kills" Nicholas M. Schenck, president of Loew's.

Producer Gottfried Reinhardt, star Audie Murphy, actors Royal Dano, Bill Mauldin, Douglas Dick, and John Dierkes appear and reappear regularly.

Of interest to the businessmen readers of this book may

be the <u>proposed</u> operating budget.

"The operating budget for Production No. 1512 was by now complete. It showed that the total cost was supposed to come to $1,434,789, including:

Direction	$156,010
Story and Continuity	41,992
Cast	82,250
Departmental Overhead	238,000
Rent and Purchase Props	80,800
Extras	145,058
Cameramen	25,500
Sound	35,177
Cutters and Projectionists	15,650
Producer's Unit Charge	102,120
Production Staff	30,915
Stills and Stillmen	6,995
Picture Film and Dev.	17,524
Sound Film and Dev.	8,855
Music	12,620
Wardrobe	43,000
Makeup and Hairdressers	13,915
Auto and Truck Hire	49,125
Meals and Lodging	35,385
Travel and Transportation	6,360
Location Fees and Expenses	18,255
Misc.	23,850

. . . ."

The budget is then broken down further on pages 62 - 64 of *PICTURE*.

The preparation of a workable budget is something the motion picture producer generally likes to leave to somebody else. That way, if a mistake is made, the producer can blame the budget preparer. And the producer always needs someone to blame for everything that goes wrong.

THE NEW AMERICAN CINEMA

(Book Review)

THE NEW AMERICAN CINEMA, a critical anthology edited by Gregory Battcock, Dutton Paperback D200, $1.75, provides information about younger film makers.

As a courtesy to the men who labored to produce this book, the following extracts are published here:

"Most of the films mentioned in this book can be rented for showing. Those interested should write for a catalogue of films to Film-Makers' Cooperative, 175 Lexington Avenue, N.Y., N.Y. 10016."

"The New American Cinema is a term sufficiently elastic to embrace an extraordinary variety of artistically and sometimes technically amateurish ambitious productions that have recently attracted critical attention in New York City and elsewhere. In New York, indeed, what are sometimes referred to as 'underground' movies have almost achieved the status of cult objects among the art public." . . . .

"The films of the New American Cinema are by contrast intensely personal and idiosyncratic statements even when the personality of the filmmaker is deliberately hidden within his work. Each film is the creation of a single artist, usually working on a budget so limited as to preclude any display of smooth proficiency in camera work, editing, directing, and the

like. The actors are nearly always drawn from the artist's circle of friends and are neither professional nor paid. The entire,
and only, purpose of every production is to express the artistic
intention of its maker." . . . .

"The present book aspires to be no more than a general
introduction to today's independent cinema, but it is hoped that
it will convey something of the vitality and dedication of the
many artists who are contributing fresh insights to the value
and meaning of film as an art form today."

The TABLE OF CONTENTS is as follows:

Part I: SURVEY

Part II: THEORY AND CRITICISM

Part III: FILMS AND FILMMAKERS

Toby Mussman: Marcel Duchamp's *Anemic Cinema*
Toby Mussman: The Images of Robert Whitman
P. Adams Sitney: Harry Smith Interview
Stan VanDerBeek: "Culture: Intercom" and
     Expanded Cinema
James Stoller: Shooting Up
Carl Linder: Notes for *The Devil Is Dead*
Gregory Markopoulos: Three Filmmakers
Brian O'Doherty: Bruce Conner and His Films
Dwight Macdonald: Objections to the New American Cinema
Susan Sontag: Jack Smith's *Flaming Creatures*
Stan Brakhage: The Camera Eye - My Eye
John Bragin: The Work of Bruce Baillie
Gregory Battcock: Four Films by Andy Warhol

In the article "Four Films by Andy Warhol," writer Gregory Battcock states, "Potentially the most influential of the New York filmmakers is Andy Warhol, a comparative newcomer to cinema, to which he turned only after having acquired a considerable reputation in the plastic arts . . . .

"*Empire* is now a classic of the avant-garde.

"The burden of appreciating the film, *Screen Test*, rests squarely on the audience. The audience, never catered to, is abused, exposed, and ridiculed. It is, at the same time, very much considered."

Producers may be able to get from *THE NEW AMERICAN CINEMA* the following: (1) Ideas; (2) Gimmicks; (3) Names of people who may be able and eager to join the commercial American cinema. Some of the most commercial work is made by men with the chronological age of 30 who can reach those with the chronological age of 15 - 20.

GUIDE TO FILM-MAKING

and

CREATIVE FILM-MAKING

Edward Pincus' *GUIDE TO FILM-MAKING*, Signet Non-Fiction W3992, $1.50, is a practical production manual for the student, teacher and independent film maker. Kirk Smallman's *CREATIVE FILM-MAKING*, Collier Books 08200, $3.95, is a concise introduction to the fundamentals of film making.

GUIDE TO FILM-MAKING can benefit the potential backer who wants to know where his money is going, the producer who wants to understand what his technical staff is talking about, the moneymen who want to know the business so that less money will be wasted.

Topics covered in *GUIDE TO FILM-MAKING* include:

I. 8mm and 16mm: Persistence of vision; Various film sizes; 16mm film; 16mm film compared with 8mm film; Super 8, single 8 and regular 8.

II. The Camera: General considerations; Lens mounts; Interchangeable lenses and turrets; Camera weight and balance; Viewing systems; Automatic exposure and automatic diaphragm; Camera motors; Camera film capacity; Single frame exposure; Variable shutter; Footage counter; Cleaning the aperture and pressure plate; In-camera effects; Attaching filters; Camera noise; Camera quality; Purchasing equipment; Testing equipment; Renting equipment.

III. The Lens: Focal length; Perspective; Depth of field; Lens aperture or diaphragm; F/stops; Lens quality; Zoom lenses; Focusing a zoom lens; Close-ups with zoom lenses; Additional lenses; Changing the zoom range; Choice of zoom ranges; Care of the lens; Lens shades; The matte box.

IV. Exposure: Underexposure and overexposure; Automatic exposure; Setting for the proper exposure; Reflected-light readings; Taking a reflected-light reading; Spot meters; Incident light readings; Exposure meters.

V. Film Raw Stock: Composition of raw stock; Negative film; Reversal film; Comparative costs; Comparative handling; Comparative quality; ASA ratings; Forced processing; Color versus black and white; General comparisons of films; 16mm films; Care of film.

VI. Filming: Editing and filming; Shooting ratios; Film time and film space; Continuity shooting; Camera supports; Pans and tilts; The moving camera; Zooming; Cutting from a camera movement; Panning to simulate a moving camera; Actual vehicle speed versus its appearance on film; Focusing and framing; Field work; Assistants; Image sharpness.

VII. Lighting: Key light; Fill light; Lighting ratio; Back light; Types of lighting; Viewing glasses; Types of lighting equipment; Problems with daylight filming.

VIII. The Laboratory: Choosing a lab; Information to be sent to the lab; Exposure tests; Timing; Storing the original;

Film cans;   Edge-numbers;   Single- and double-perforated workprints;   8mm and the lab;   Emulsion position and winds;   Other
lab services;   Color workprints;   Scene-to-scene color duplicate
negatives;   The optical house;   Optical effects;   Generations;
Homemade optical printer;   The answer print.

IX.   Problems of Color Filming: Color balance;   Color
filming in daylight;   Color filming with incandescent light;
Color filming with window light;   Color filming with fluorescent
light;   Color filming from a television receiver.

X.   Filters: Filter factors;   Neutral density filters;
Diffusion filters;   Fog filters;   Filters to protect the lens;
Filters for black and white films;   Filters for color film.

XI.   Picture Editing: The 180° rule;   Cutting and pacing;
The cut-away;   Continuity editing;   Jump-cutting;   The mechanics
of editing;   Film rewinds;   The action viewer;   Splicers;   Other
editing equipment;   Leader;   Cutting shots;   Workprinting;   Handling film;   Scratches.

XII.   Preparing the Original for Printing: Marking the
workprint;   Matching edge-numbers;   Leader;   Lining up the optical track.

XIII.   Sound: Synchronization;   Optical track;   Magnetic
track;   Separate sound tracks;   Magnetic stripe;   Making the
optical track;   16mm magnetic track.

XIV.   Sound Recording: Tape recorders;   Microphones;
Tape speed;   Tape;   Recording.

The reader is not babied in this book. New words, concepts and equipment are introduced swiftly. If a reader is over-whelmed by the quantity of knowledge furnished, he may be advised to read Kirk Smallman's *CREATIVE FILM-MAKING* first, and then to read *GUIDE TO FILM-MAKING*. In any event, the producer who does not know the information in *GUIDE TO FILM-MAKING* is in danger of being plucked by suppliers of equipment.

The nepotism and wheeling in studios can cause over-charging to producers. The studio provides services to the distributor at cost plus. The studio buys lumber for sets from

a relative of the studio boss who owns a lumber company on paper.
The Nepotism Paper Lumber Company buys all lumber from a legitimate company, and then doubles the price when selling it to the studio.

What is the net result of this?

Assume the legitimate Lumber Company sells the lumber for $1,000 to the Nepotism Paper Lumber Company.

The Nepotism Paper Lumber Company doubles the price, and sells the lumber to the studio at $2,000.

The studio charges cost plus. The "plus" may be 30%. $2,000 times 30% = $600. The producer is charged $2,600.

If the studio had bought the lumber legitimately for $1,000, then the 30% plus would have been $300, and the charge to the producer would have been $1,300.

Because of Nepotism Paper Lumber Co., the producer is cheated out of the additional $1,300.

The effect of this cheating $1,300 becomes worse as the studio charges interest for "lending" the producer the $1,300. Interest may be charged until the distributor has collected enough money to repay the $1,300.

Assume interest for three years at 10% interest. The $1,300 has grown annually to $1,430 in one year, $1,573 in two years, and $1,730 in three years.

When gross receipts come in, the distributor collects a distribution fee, which may be 40%, while the other 60% is allocated to the producer.

Thus it will take almost $3,000 of the distributor gross income to allocate $1,800 to the producer to pay for the crooked $1,000 profit of the Nepotism Paper Lumber Company.

This tale of the Nepotism Paper Lumber Company may be repeated in every aspect of film-making.

It is easier to cheat a producer out of time, supplies, equipment, money, if the producer cannot accurately budget everything with understanding, than when the producer does understand the technical aspects of film-making.

The headings of chapters in *CREATIVE WRITING* are:

1. The Illusion of Motion
2. Film Stock Formats
3. Camera Features
4. Lighting
5. Film Stock Emulsions
6. Exposure Control
7. Looking at Action
8. Moving Camera
9. Lenses and Perspective
10. Matching the Action in Cuts
11. Expanding and Compressing Time
12. Slow, Fast, and Reverse Motion
13. Animating Real Objects
14. Superimposed Images
15. Special Visual Effects
16. Directing Non-Actors
17. Ways of Recording Sound
18. Editing Sound and Picture
19. Mixing Sounds Together
20. Preparing for Composite Prints
21. Filmic Expression

CREATIVE FILM-MAKING is excellent for beginners in readability, large type, double spacing, numerous photographs, good writing; all facilitate learning. This is probably the best

book for beginners. Producers may benefit themselves by giving
a copy of *CREATIVE FILM-MAKING* to potential backers. Or, it may
be psychologically better to <u>sell</u> the large paperback book to a
potential investor. Sometimes the drawing of first blood ($3.95
for *CREATIVE FILM-MAKING*) makes easier the drawing of additional blood in buckets.

THE MARKETING OF MOTION PICTURES
(Book Review)

Chris Musun's *THE MARKETING OF MOTION PICTURES*, Chris Musun Company, Los Angeles.

Chris Musun has written an excellent business book on *THE MARKETING OF MOTION PICTURES*.

Mr. Musun discusses:

        Part I.   The Consumer
            II.   Channels of Distribution
           III.   Trade Practices
            IV.   Promotion
             V.   Financial
            VI.   Forecasting Motion Picture Gross and
                   Pre-Production Planning

These six parts are discussed in fifteen chapters.

Mr. Musun has enabled the reader of his dissertation to learn about business aspects of motion picture distribution.

Any reader of our tome, who enjoys our tome, should read Chris Musun's *THE MARKETING OF MOTION PICTURES*. It is written intelligently, and without the sarcasm rampart in this book.

Mr. Musun emphasizes the value of market research at all levels of pre-production, production, and distribution in various marketing areas of the United States and foreign areas.

HOLLYWOOD BABYLON

(Book Review)

Kenneth Anger's *HOLLYWOOD BABYLON* is so informative that the distributor claimed that it recalled the entire first edition, and warehoused the recalled first edition. Would you believe it?

HOLLYWOOD BABYLON is one man's history of Hollywood. Readers of books about the moguls' and stars' business and motion picture activities may be interested in alleged off-duty hours activities of moguls and stars.

PART III

TRADE PUBLICATIONS AND MAGAZINES

Part of the expensive delays during production of pictures is due to the producer's not quite knowing who does what. The various publications can help educate producers with brief easy-to-read regular columns, articles, advertisements, etc. Many people who are too impatient to read books are willing to peruse magazines.

TRADE PRESS

THE HOLLYWOOD REPORTER

   THE HOLLYWOOD REPORTER, 6715 Sunset Boulevard, Hollywood, California 90028, is published daily except Saturdays,
Sundays, and holidays. $30 per year subscription.

   This daily trade paper contains articles on unions
(*Nabet Plugs for Dual Unionism*), stock market (*Disney Stock
Again Breaks the Ceiling*), knowledge fighters (*Catholic Film
Office Blasts 1969 Movies*), day dreams (*MGM's Record, Music
Dept. Poised for Bounce to Black*), trade associations (*Hock Re-
Elected Chairman Ad-Pub Committee, MPAA*), personnel changes and
promotions (*Yablans Named New Para Gen'l Sales Manager*), forth-
coming pictures (*Fonda Re-Teams Hopper with "Last Movie"*).

   THE HOLLYWOOD REPORTER covers First Amendment cases
(*Charge Police Disobey Law in Action on "Curious, Yellow"*),
promotions (*Project 7 Films, Inc. Goes Public on Market*),
columns (*Sound Track, Coast to Coast, Rambling Reporter*), regular information items (*Travel Logs, Word from the Sponsor,
Artists and Agents, The Note Book, Wedding Bells, Ill and Injured,
TV-Radio Briefs, Nitery Notes*).

   Producers have found that potential backers are mightily
impressed by the printed word. The printed word in trade publications such as *THE HOLLYWOOD REPORTER* may contain such items
as: (Substitute names yourself).

TRAVEL LOGS: Pete Producer, Park Punset Productions, in Panama for conferences with William Writer.

COLUMN ITEM: Pete Producer wishes he could persuade Greta Garbo and Mary Pickford to join the bridge-players in Producer's forthcoming *TEENAGERS' CHILDREN*.

NEWS ITEM: _____ has been signed by
                          (star)
producer _____ to re-team with _____
                                                      (star)
in _____, which _____
            (new movie)   *(director)*
directs beginning _____, in _____.
                       (date)   *(place)*

ARTISTS & AGENTS: _____
                                          (actor)
with _____ through personal management firm
            (agency)
_____.
            (firm)

Sometimes backers who can find other backers want to see their names in print: "Pete Producer, producer of the forthcoming picture, *I LOVE YOU*, and Bob Backer, executive producer, negotiating with John Huston to direct the picture."

We have casually dropped names in the preceding example. The misuse of names is dangerous. The trade publication may check on the veracity of the story by calling the name, "Hello, John Huston, are you really negotiating with Peter Producer and Bob Backer?"

Whether or not the story is true is important; also important is whether the name has cleared the story in advance. Even if a story is true, the name may not wish to let anyone

else know that he or she is negotiating with Pete Producer.
Somebody else who was thinking of hiring the name may be misled
into believing the name was not available for his project because the name's time had been taken up by Peter Producer.

The lack of veracity of many publicity items causes
concern to trade publications such as *THE HOLLYWOOD REPORTER*.
It is expensive and difficult to verify every story. Therefore,
many stories are accepted from trusted publicity men, which
would not be accepted from untrusted strangers.

Backers and producers may benefit from publicity in the
trade press. On the other hand, if other backers are shown untrue stories, this may (1) shake the confidence of potential
investors; (2) cause potential investors to believe the untrue representations in the trade press, and later sue for
fraud because they were misled by the representations.

Advertisers in the trade press include night clubs,
networks, actors, other talented persons, travel agencies,
auditioners, producers, distributors, publishers, real estate
brokers, etc.

Should a person or company spend money (1) by paying
a publicist whose job it is to get free space in a trade publication, or (2) by paying the trade press directly for an advertisement, or (3) both?

Does a person pay twice for publicity: (1) by buying
an ad to induce the trade press to run the publicity, (2) by

paying a publicist to give publicity to the trade press?

No matter what the answers (1) are, or (2) are believed to be, part of the expense of producing a picture is the publicity expense.

Publicity should be before-the-production, during-the-production, and after-the-production. The producer must constantly do his best to educate all those who are in a position to help the picture: newspaper columnists (who read the trade press for items), potential movie reviewers, personnel of the distributor (who have more work than time to do it in), theatre and circuit film buyers (renters).

In the producer-distributor contracts, distributors are allowed to spend money as advances-to-the-producer by buying advertisements in the trade press. This is very clever of the distributor. He spends money in order to keep relations with the trade press for his distribution company, and he does so at somebody else's expense (the producer's expense).

The distributor may even cheat a little bit. He may use an advertising agency owned by him or a relative. The distributor pays his agency the full cost of the ad (and charges the producer the full cost of the ad). The agency then keeps its commission 15% as agency and 2% for early payment.

Persons thinking of buying ads should first get rate cards so that they may be studied. Sometimes, some other trade publications use their rate card as a top amount to be charged to strangers, and are willing to negotiate rates.

Very often an individual trade press advertisment or publicity item may get no response, sometimes there may be un-expectedly high response.

While many regular readers of trade publications have grains of doubt concerning the veracity of editorial and adver-tising matter, if such readers do not receive contrary informa-tion, the readers may ultimately act because of relying on what they read.

For example, if a trade publication carries a story that _____ film in _____ theatre had a box office record gross of $50,000 in one week, a reader may study that story.

If the theatre has seats: 400 seats and is open noon to midnight: 12 hours and each double feature show requires 4 hours, then there are how many shows per day? 3 shows; if the theatre is open ____ days weekly: 7 days; then each week has _____ shows: 21 shows.

Times Seats = 21 x 400 seats = 8400 maximum show-seats.

Average or Maximum Tickets Cost = $2 each.

8400 seats @ $2 each = $16,800 maximum box office receipts per week in theatre with 400 seats, open 4 hours seven days a week.

Thus if every seat is filled for every show by a person who sees one complete show and pays the average (or maximum) price per ticket, the maximum gross can be calculated.

(Naturally, as a practical matter, seats are not filled every show).

If the trade press story carried a bigger amount as the theatre's gross, the trade press story can be taken with a grain of salt.

But few readers bother with analyzing stories.

Thus the trade press is very useful (1) to plant information and (2) to secure information.

THE HOLLYWOOD REPORTER is generally the most helpful daily trade publication for newcomers and new producers.

TRADE PRESS - VARIETY

VARIETY is published weekly at 154 West 46th Street, New York, N.Y. 10036. Annual subscription, $20.00; two years, $37.50; three years, $50.00.

Weekly *VARIETY* is an excellent trade publication; it is difficult to imagine a better way to spend $50.00 than for a 3-year-subscription to Weekly *VARIETY*.

The stories are sometimes short, often long, detailed, informative. Weekly *VARIETY* carries many pages of box office receipts of specific theatres in numerous cities.

The aware reader can compare alleged box office receipts of usually similar theatres in different towns which are showing the same film.

The theatre may reduce the actual box office receipts if the theatre has to pay a percentage of receipts to a distributor.

The theatre may blow up the actual box office receipts if the theatre is owned by the distributor.

The theatre may always reduce box office receipts to persuade distributors that flat fee rentals of films should be lower. For example, a theatre with smaller box office potential generally pays less than a theatre with bigger box office potential.

Weekly *VARIETY* contains information such as *St. Louis, Dec. 17, 1969, Loew's Mid-City (Loew) (1,100; 90-$1.50) - "All Loving Couples" (UMF) (3rd wk), Good, $6,500. Last week, $8,000.*

Weekly *VARIETY* carries articles and charts summarizing box office receipts.

Producers would be well-advised to clip all mention of their pictures. That way, they can get ready for humorous scenes with their distributors when the distributors tell the producers how badly the pictures are doing.

One of the problems of distributors is that they have to sell horrible (horrible = money-losing) pictures.

In order to pressure a theatre into taking a poor film, the distributor may make a package deal. "I'll give you *BIG HIT* for 4 weeks if you take four horribles for one week each."

The distributor emphasizes that he has the power to withhold forthcoming hits from the exhibitor. The distributor uses various means of communication to reach the exhibitor. One excellent means of such communication is a full-page ad in Weekly *VARIETY*.

Such an ad may contain columns of (1) Expected release date; (2) Picture, stars, running time, rating; (3) Photographs of the star(s); (4) Lists of "name" producer, director, stars.

Circuits show how powerful they are in news stories. This information may be read by national distributors, branch

branch supervisors, and salesmen.

Weekly *VARIETY* carries stories concerning foreign film production, U.S. major producers, independent producers, distributors of various sizes and specialties, exhibitors, trade organizations, stock market, reviews of U.S. and foreign movies, TV shows, etc.

Weekly *VARIETY* carries many long (more than 6 column inches) stories.

Weekly *VARIETY* has many pages concerning Films, Video, TV Films, Radio, Music, Stage.

Aware readers can use charts such as the full-page "50 Top Grossing Films," but must be careful to analyze it by number and type of theatres playing each film.

MAGAZINES - FILMS AND FILMING

FILMS AND FILMING is published monthly by the proprietors, Hansom Books at Artillery Mansions, 75 Victoria Street, London SW1, England. Dollar cheques accepted for subscriptions. $8.25 for 12 months; $15.75 for 2 years; $24.75 for 3 years and a loose-leaf binder.

One of the values of this British magazine, which is a combination trade and fan publication, is the revelation concerning markets.

Frequently in contracts between copyright creators (such as producers) and merchandisers (such as distributors), the merchandiser promises to pay to the creator certain percentages of certain receipts. The contract may be absolutely silent concerning other receipts. You may wish to check your contracts concerning receipts from 16mm distribution.

FILMS AND FILMING contains advertisements of distributors of 16mm films, including 20th Century Fox and United Artists films. The markets for 16mm film include cinema clubs, schools, churches, towns without regular theatres, hospitals, and other organizations.

The 16mm film distributors distribute many big-star features which are not available in 35mm theatres at the time (possibly big theatre distribution occurred years before, or

possibly there never was big theatre distribution). As color
films take over the big screen, the 16mm distribution of black
and white films may become ever more important.

One of the routine ways with which royalty payers
(distributors) cheat royalty receivers (producers) is to totally
omit all receipts from specific sources (theatres).

Producers sometimes use clipping services to clip from
newspapers all items concerning a picture. The producer thus
receives information concerning where his picture played and
for how long. Thus the producer's accountant can prepare a
check list of play dates and places, and can check that against
the information provided by the distributor.

FILMS AND FILMING contains advertisements, publicity
releases and reviews (which indicate releases) as well as play
dates in certain theatres.

It is interesting to watch the so-called pornography
(illegal) field shrinking in scope as the commercial theatres
legally provide more information. The conservative British
FILMS AND FILMING recently had (1) a nude scene on the cover;
(2) a picture story on a movie about cannibalism; (3) nude
scenes of various movies.

Add: (1) The development of mama-papa mini-theatres
(without projectionists) in hotels, shopping centers, and other
locations, and (2) The continuous cheap availability of old

movies with stars appealing to current users of hotels, motels,
shopping centers, etc., and (3) Reviews in *FILMS AND FILMING*
of 20-year-old pictures, and you might have a lot of money from
old pictures.

Pay attention to duration of contract between the producer and the distributor, and regular quarterly auditing of
the books and records of the distributor by the producer, and
the making certain that the distributor must pay the producer
on every dollar received by the distributor and the distributor's licensees.

TRADE PRESS - FILM TV DAILY

FILM TV DAILY, 330 West 58th Street, New York, N.Y.
(Hollywood Office at 6425 Hollywood Boulevard). Subscription
$25.00 for one year.

FILM TV DAILY is a daily, Monday - Friday, trade paper.
The subscription price includes an annual, which alone is worth
the entire cost of subscription.

Frequently businessmen are approached by fakers who
claim production credits to which they are not entitled. A
businessman can search the annuals for credits of the credit
claimer. Each annual contains articles and summaries concerning the business during the covered year. A reader of several
annuals, one after another, can learn facts, hopes and cliches;
such reading can help a businessman take a potential producer's
puffing in stride.

Many of the items appearing in one trade press publication are submitted by a publicist to just that publication
("exclusive"); other items are simultaneously sent to each
trade paper.

One trade paper receiving a long release, which would
require 12 column inches to print in full, might give it the
biggest headline of the day. Another trade paper may only print
the lead paragraph as a news story, or the lead sentence as part

of a column. Therefore, it often pays to send stories to all
the trade papers.

Advertisers have problems concerning in which paper
they should advertise. Often an advertisement pays for itself
if just one account is picked up. For example, Cinerama Releasing Corporation had a full-page advertisement concerning
its "Release Schedule Through Summer '70" in several trade
papers. If this advertisement persuaded just one producer to
release a forthcoming picture through Cinerama Leasing Corp.,
then the ad was worthwhile. If the advertisement persuaded
just one major theatre to pay what it owed to Cinerama, or to
cheat less on a receipt-sharing contract, or to do business
with Cinerama, then the ad in the specific publication read by
the Cinerama customer was worthwhile.

FILM TV DAILY carries film reviews. Distributors often
use trade press reviews in publicity. The greater the number
of trade press reviewers, the greater is the possibility of the
reviews containing phrases or sentences which are quotable in
trade ads.

Several trade publications are based in New York;
others are based in Hollywood. Publicists may wish to keep in
mind that each publication wants a story: (1) First choice -
exclusively; (2) Second choice - simultaneously with other
trade papers. A trade publication does not want a story: (3)
After the competition has carried it.

Actually, it may be better to have a story appear on different days in different papers. Many motion picture industry executives read several trade papers at the start of the business day. If for some reasons the executive skips his reading on one day, he may never bother reading them or at best may skim the papers hurriedly. Therefore, it may pay for the publicist to release stories concerning the same subject to different papers on different days. However, the publicist must rewrite the story for each trade paper.

MAGAZINES - FILM SOCIETY REVIEW

FILM SOCIETY REVIEW is published nine times annually
by the American Federation of Film Societies, 144 Bleeker Street,
New York, N.Y. 10012.   Subscription, $5.00/year.

The full-page advertisements by Columbia Cinematheque,
Universal Education and Visual Arts, Janus Films, United Artists,
Hurlock Cineworld, Walter Reade 16, Swank Motion Pictures, Inc.,
Audio Film Center, NTS Films, Paradigm Films, Roa's Films, Inc.
Warner Brothers-Seven Arts, Brandon Films, Inc. indicate that
this publication is deemed important enough to advertise in by
major distributors.

The distributors distribute 16mm film.

The news, letters, articles, etc. concern students, both
film students and generally.

How big is the 16mm film market?   What do the contracts
between producers and distributors state concerning 16mm distribution receipts?   Does the distributor sell 16mm distribution
rights to a subsidiary for a flat sum?   How is the sum divided?
How long does the producer-distributor contract give distribution rights to the distributor?   The contract usually contains
a clause that any contracts made by distributors with third parties may continue even after termination of the producer-
distributor contract.   This encourages the distributor to make

very long contracts with third parties, such as subsidiaries
distributing 16mm, television, foreign areas, etc.

There are various distributors in the United States.
Some can distribute a film better than others. Some are fat,
and some are lean. Some are big enough to distribute their
own 16mm film; some are not.

What kind of films are distributed to 16mm renters?
Who are the renters?

In the early 1960's when a few book publishers were
specializing in sex books, many of these publishers published
excellent mysteries, romances, adventure stories, etc., with
sex thrown in on pages 10-11, 80-81 and 131-132.

The book publishers aiming at book buyers who liked to
read about lesbians, threw in lesbian affairs on those pages.
The same or another publisher aiming at book buyers enjoying
homosexual books, might use the same or similar main story,
and throw in homosexual episodes on the "special" pages.

In the late 1960's many movies had nude scenes or sex
action scenes which could be deleted for showing in censorship
cities, for TV, or the "institution" portion of the 16mm
market.

The "stag film" audience of the past was mostly a 16mm
audience.

It is interesting to see how 16mm and 35mm markets
change.

Apparently there are many films which never see 35mm distribution, but which are distributed in 16mm.

There are also films which receive 16mm distribution for many years after they receive no attention from the 35mm market.

MAGAZINES - FILMMAKERS NEWSLETTER

FILMMAKERS NEWSLETTER, 80 Wooster Street, New York, N.Y.
10012. Monthly except in the summer. $4.00 for one year; $8.00
for two years and a 208-page paperback book full of basic tips
and techniques on still photography and filmmaking. $2.00 per
year more to get the magazine by first class mail.

FILMMAKERS NEWSLETTER editorial and advertising portions
emphasize equipment and technique. Articles and ads concern
cameras, labs, lenses, how to . . ., music services, titles,
screening and editing facilities, etc.

Both Super-8 and 16mm are discussed.

The CineScene Calendar is a regular monthly feature. It
is a services intended to increase the supporting audience for
independent avant garde/experimental/underground/student films.
It lists many theatres by name, address, and in some cases,
program.

To be quite blunt about it, the ability of a magazine
to draw an audience is sometimes indicated by the non-house ads.

A house ad is one run by the publisher. A non-house
ad is run by a cash-paying advertiser. House ads are often
under a name other than that of the publisher, but use the
publisher's address or box number.

FILMMAKERS NEWSLETTER contains non-house ads.

MAGAZINES - FILM CULTURE

FILM CULTURE, G.P.O. Box 1499, New York, N.Y. 10001.
Quarterly. Subscription $4.00 annually.

Most of the other film buff publications have photographs on most pages, have articles about stars and other
talents who are well-publicized, and generally have materials
to please fans and newcomers among students of the cinema.

FILM CULTURE is for knowledgeable students, teachers
and professionals, and is not easy reading for beginners.
Young film professionals may be interested in comparing notes
of their own educational and thinking progress with that of
the article writers and their subjects.

MAGAZINES - CINEMA

CINEMA is published quarterly at 9667 Wilshire Boulevard, Beverly Hills, California 90212. Subscription rates are $4.00 for four issues; $5.00 six issues; $9.00 twelve issues; $13.00 eighteen issues.

Picture stories concern U.S. and foreign personalities and movies. Regular features are "Books," "Reviews," "Previews."

A recent issue had articles on "Fellini on Fellini on Satyricon," "An Interview with Fellini," "An Interview with Jeanne Moreau," "Sam Peckinpah Going to Mexico," "Four-in-one Cinema," "An Interview with Arthur Penn."

Herbert Luft, who contributed an article on Samuel Goldwyn to *FILMS IN REVIEW*, also contributes articles to other publications, including *CINEMA*.

The politics and currents of the motion picture industry are very interesting.

Every now and then a company such as MGM is in financial trouble, and a "sweep" is made. Naturally the "swept out" persons may harbor resentments. Often the "swept out" personnel have knowledges, uses and powers of which their bosses are unaware or forget. One person may be a relative of a power in a trade press; another may be a friend of a buyer for a circuit;

a third may have publicity and promotion power; a fourth may

be a key witness in an infringement suit.

    CINEMA is enjoyable at various levels - professional,

buff and fun.

MAGAZINES - SCREEN FACTS

SCREEN FACTS, Box 154, Kew Gardens, N.Y. 11415. Subscription Rate: $7.00 for six issues. Contains picture and
text stories concerning motion pictures, and stars of the
present time and of the past. Books about movies and movie
soundtrack recordings are advertised.

The editor is Alan G. Barbour; the co-publishers are
Alan G. Barbour and Larry Edmunds Bookshop; the editorial
assistant is Jean Barbour. Most ads have the post office box
of *SCREEN FACTS* or Larry Edmunds Bookshop.

Larry Edmunds Bookshop, 6658 Hollywood Boulevard,
Hollywood, California 90028 advertises itself as "The world's
largest collection of books and related materials on motion
pictures!

"The most complete list of film publications in existence.
Books, magazines, annuals, directories, pressbooks, posters and
stills. History, biography, criticism, and technique."

The catalogs of Larry Edmunds Bookshops have become
collectors' items.

MAGAZINES - FILMS IN REVIEW

FILMS IN REVIEW is published ten times a year by the National Board of Review of Motion Pictures, Inc., 31 Union Square, New York, N.Y. 10003. Subscription: $7.00 annually.

FILMS IN REVIEW carries long articles on producers, stars, writers, and other talents; contains reviews of new and old motion pictures, has various columns.

The December, 1969 issue was Volume XX, No. 10, which indicates that *FILMS IN REVIEW* has been around a long time.

There are various kinds of previews for various purposes. One type of preview is an unannounced preview so that a producer can check audience reaction. Such a preview may be held near UCLA on the theory that such a preview audience will react typically (whether such audience is typical does not matter as long as its reaction to the film is typical). The movie producer may have preview interviewers and audience reaction cards, and may tape the audience reaction during and after the movie.

Another type of preview is the "favored audience" preview. Such a preview may be held at the Theatre of the Academy of Motion Picture Arts and Sciences.

Such previews allow Academy members to see some of the latest pictures, allow Academy members to meet each other in

friendly circumstances, allow potential users of talent to see
work done by potential employees.

Other previews are "press" previews and "foreign press"
previews.

The "press" previews are presented by producers and/or
distributors to an invited list of representatives of leading
newspapers, magazines, trade and general and fun press.

The "foreign press" members may make their livings in
a variety of ways. It is a touchy situation, sometimes, when
a "foreign press" preview attender is asked which paper he represents. He must never be asked what he does for a living! He
often has two lives. In one life, he has a job for the purpose
of making a living. In his other job he writes movie reviews
and columns which may be read by hundreds or millions of readers.

The reviews of members of the foreign press may be made
directly or indirectly to distributors and exhibitors in their
respective countries. Such persons may be eager to immediately
lease or purchase rights or prints or both. Swift payment to
the world distributor may speed up the time that the producer
may receive his profit.

Thus a man who has trouble landing a job in the production portions of the industry because of a language barrier or
lack of contacts, may be very important in educating key businessmen and numerous consumers regarding the commercial and enjoyment worth of a picture.

Publicists paid by clients can afford to write free articles, reviews, letters for film buff publications. These reach (1) potential commercial users of the films; (2) potential ticket buyers; (3) clients and potential clients of the publicist when the publicist shows his publicity scrapbook to them.

MAGAZINES - SIGHT AND SOUND

SIGHT AND SOUND, British Film Institute, 81 Dean Street,
London W.1. England. American subscriptions and advertising
inquiries should be directed to Eastern News Distributors, 155
West 15th Street, New York, N.Y. 10011.

SIGHT AND SOUND is an independent critical magazine
sponsored and published by the British Film Institute. It is
not an organ for the expression of official British Film Institute policy; signed articles represent the views of their
authors, and not necessarily those of the Editorial Board.

This British publication covers the international movie
scene: '69 festivals in Berlin, Edinburgh, Moscow, Venice;
American movies "The Wild Bunch," "Easy Rider," "Midnight
Cowboy"; the Polish Borowczyk who has made films in France for
ten years, the Indian Satyajit Ray, the Cuban cinema; Film
censorship (Dutch, Scandinavian, French, India, Denmark's pro-
test against John Wayne's "Green Berets"), American directors
Sam Peckinpah and Sidney Lumet.

Most ads are British. U.S. advertisers include Columbia
Cinematheque (16mm), Universal Education and Visual Arts (16mm),
Gotham Book Mart in New York, Larry Edmunds Bookshop in Holly-
wood.

MAGAZINES - MONTHLY FILM BULLETIN

MONTHLY FILM BULLETIN, published quarterly by The

British Film Institute, 81 Dean Street, London W.1., England.

Subscription: 30 shillings per year in Great Britain; $4 in

the United States.

MONTHLY FILM BULLETIN reviews feature films primarily,

and also some non-fiction and short films. The films are re-

viewed in the form under which they have been passed and certi-

fied for public exhibition by the British Board of Film Censors

or by a licensing authority in Great Britain. Authorities and

censorship boards in other countries and parts of the Common-

wealth may pass the same films for public exhibition in a form

different from that in which they were passed in Great Britain.

Reviews give extensive credits to distributors, produc-

tion company, executive producer, producer, associate producer,

production supervisor, production manager, 2nd unit director,

assistant director, script writer, script adaption, dialogue

coach, photography, color process, special effects, special

photographic effects, editor, supervising editor, art director,

set director, special effects, music, music director, costumes,

choreography, sound, sound editor, sound recording, commentary,

animation.

Of special interest are the tables which show how

critics of leading publications reviewed the film.   The rating

of a circle indicates antipathy;   one star to four stars indi-

cates degree of praise.   The tables can indicate to the American

producer whatever tables indicate: how well-publicized the film

was;   in what cities the film was probably played, etc.   The

American who can get British newspapers and magazines will know

in what magazines he can see his reviews.   In Hollywood, numer-

ous British magazines are available in the paperbook store on

Cahuenga near Hollywood Boulevard.

MAGAZINES - SCREEN ACTOR

SCREEN ACTOR is published bi-monthly by the Screen Actors Guild, affiliated with the American Federation of Labor - Congress of Industrial Organizations. The Screen Actors Guild is a branch of the Associated Actors and Artistes of America, 7750 Sunset Boulevard, Los Angeles, California 90048. Subscription $6.00/year.

A recent issue contained an editorial "War on the Exporting of American Jobs," an announcement of a membership meeting, news concerning a Guild election, and "U.S. Court Rebuffs Theatre Owners, O.K.'s Subscription Television," news concerning negotiations in the TV Commercial Field, ("We are waging a vigorous attack on Dealer Commercials"), a question, Are Some Nudes Good Nudes," a picture story, "The Guild Goes to a Convention," an article on the speaking voice by a speech pathologist, "Vocal Suicide in the Theatrical Profession," a story, "Mr. Wong Signs a Contract," (praising the Guild for improving contracts and stating today's producers must sign an approved Guild contract), a picture story, on NAACP awards, a story, "An Acting Lesson," San Francisco Notes, Activity in Florida, Books, Letters, List of Agents Franchised by Guild, Advertisements (Schools, Phone Service, Travel, Business Management, Insurance, Restaurant, Photographer, Old Movie Posters,

Real Estate, Clothing, Cars, Tax Service, Dentist, Make-up, Eye-

lashes, Hotels, Burglar Alarms, Health Foods), In Memoriam,

Producer Unfair List, Residual Checks Await Claimants.

The Producer Unfair List page contains the following

information:

"REMINDER!"

"Guild Rule One provides that no member shall work as an
actor for any producer who is not signed to a Guild contract.
No matter who offers you an acting job in the Guild's field -
producer, talent agent, casting office or friend - it is YOUR
obligation and responsibility to make certain that the producer
wishing to employ you is a Guild signatory. It is not enough
just to check the Guild's Unfair List (see below). New companies entering production and companies who have not previously
used Guild members may not yet have signed Guild agreements.
Always telephone the nearest Guild office. Guild members are
subject to disciplinary action by the Guild if they work for a
non-signatory. They may be fined, suspended or expelled. Keep
the Guild strong! Protect your Guild conditions and pension
and welfare benefits! Don't violate Guild Rule One!

Do Not Work for These Producers on Unfair List

The following companies have been placed on the Unfair
List by the Board of Directors because of their refusal to sign
Guild Basic Agreements or for violations which caused cancella-
tion of their contracts.

Members are instructed not to work for these companies
until further notice: . . . ."

MAGAZINES

ACTION, DIRECTORS GUILD OF AMERICA

ACTION, DIRECTORS GUILD OF AMERICA, 7950 Sunset Boulevard, Hollywood, California 90046. Subscription: $4.00/year.

ACTION is published by the Directors Guild of America
as a means of communicating with members and as a medium for
the exchange of ideas and information of professional interest.

Articles concern such directors as Mitchell Leisen,
John Sturges, new director Ossie Davis. Short quotes of sayings
by directors are used under the heading, "What Directors Are
Saying." The "Bulletin Board" page contains news of the Guild.
Books are mentioned and reviewed, such books being about movies,
about specific directors or stars, about technical improvements,
about any other aspects of the industry.

A producer may want to subscribe to *ACTION* in order to
collect information about numerous directors.

When a producer talks with potential backers, bankers,
distributors, stars, etc., the producer is asked about the di-
rector(s) the producer may employ.

The producer can use photocopies of articles in *ACTION*
and in movie buff magazines concerning directors to persuade
all concerned (backers, bankers, distributor, laboratory giving
credit, stars) that the director chosen by the producer will
create a money-making picture.

INDEPENDENT FILM JOURNAL

THE INDEPENDENT FILM JOURNAL is a trade publication.

THE INDEPENDENT FILM JOURNAL reaches exhibitors and
film buyers all over the country. So do *BOX OFFICE*, *MOTION
PICTURE HERALD*, *THE EXHIBITOR*, and Weekly *VARIETY*.

THE INDEPENDENT FILM JOURNAL contains rough editorials
from the viewpoint of the independent exhibitor. The distributor is the heavy.

Since the exhibitors buy the ads, and keep buying ads
in *THE INDEPENDENT FILM JOURNAL*, a reader's first reaction might
be to admire *THE INDEPENDENT JOURNAL* for its daring. A second
reaction is one of admiration: *THE INDEPENDENT FILM JOURNAL*
gets readership through its editorials and other contents; the
high and selective readership allow *THE INDEPENDENT JOURNAL* to
get the ads.

Every once in a while exhibitors act as if they believe
that producers-distributors make a lot of money, and exhibitors
announce plans of producing a lot of pictures.

The exhibitors work on the theory that they will make
back a lot of their money by exhibiting the films in their own
theatres and in the theatres owned by friends.

The exhibitor-turned-producer soon learns about production through his mistakes. He learns about distribution when
his exhibitor "friends" refuse to play the picture unless terms

are more favorable to the exhibitor than the usual distributor-
exhibitor contract.

The exhibitor-turned-producer soon drops his plans to
produce pictures because of the cost, and soon drops his plans
to distribute because he does not have enough time to properly
run his theatres and to distribute films.

THE INDEPENDENT FILM JOURNAL carries stories from
various production centers and distribution centers, as well
as from exhibitors.

FAN MAGAZINES

Producers should constantly publicize themselves, their pictures, their stars, their feature players, their hopes, plans, romances, etc. in fan magazines.

Fan magazines are read by the millions (*PHOTOPLAY*) and the hundreds of thousands (*TEEN SCREEN*). Each fan magazine should be studied to ascertain how it can be reached: (1) by complete stories and photographs; (2) by gossip items; (3) by letters to the editor; (4) by individual photographs and captions; (5) by listing fan clubs, etc. Some magazines are completely written by one staff writer in one week, who will be writing under various pseudonyms. The pseudonyms may be house names (owned by the magazine) or may be names of stars who like the publicity that the column gives them. Other magazines accept copy from publicists, professional writers and photographers.

Fan magazines prepare copy 30-60 days before they are on the stands. Writers should beware of this time element. For example, if a publicist writing in February knows a picture will open at Radio City Music Hall on March 15, the writer should <u>not</u> write about the opening "next month."

Different magazines write about different persons. Some magazines have Kennedy stories; some have Elizabeth Taylor-Richard Burton stories; some write about only movie stars;

others concentrate on TV stars;   others concentrate on recording stars.

Magazines want (1) stories and photographs which will
induce browsers to buy and readers to subscribe;   (2) to get
stories and photographs for as little as possible.   However,
routine stories about unknown artists, while they may even be
free for the magazine, are often rejected because they hurt the
sale of magazines.   Sometimes magazine publishers or editors
accept fees from newcomers who are willing to pay to get
mentions.

BEST ACTRESS, 1946

OLIVIA DE HAVILLAND
in "To Each His Own"

Olivia de Havilland doesn't have the look of a fighter. Best known for her work as a gentlewoman on the screen, she proved her spirit in 1943 by taking on a fight with her home studio, Warner Brothers, at a time when movie studios wielded more power than General Electric. It was a legal battle over suspension time added to her studio contract and, by standing up for her cause, Miss de Havilland flirted with career suicide.

Since her entry into pictures in 1935, Olivia de Havilland had been dedicated to the pursuit of good screen work, but only twice in nine years did she have really worthwhile roles: on a loan-out to Selznick for *Gone With the Wind*; on a loan-out to Paramount for *Hold Back the Dawn*. At her home studio, she spent most of her time wearing hoopskirts in Errol Flynn pictures or playing inconsequential ingenues. When her seven-year contract with Warner Brothers ended in 1943, the studio informed her she still owed them six months work, time that had accumulated while she was on suspension. Since an old California law limited to seven years the period that any employer could enforce a contract against an employee, she disputed the studio's right to the added time and fought the case through three courts at a personal cost of $13,000 and two years of her time, during which no other studio could employ her. She won the case, and the respect of the industry. The District Court of Appeals upheld her contention that a studio could not add suspension time to a player's contract.

Fortunately for Miss de Havilland, the lengthy inactivity and suit against an all-powerful studio didn't end her career, and she had no trouble finding good roles.

During her court battle, Charles Brackett asked her to do *To Each His Own* and then waited a year until she was legally free to do it. Nunnally Johnson gave her a showy part as identical twin sisters in *The Dark Mirror* and between the two of them she was back in business and a forerunner for 1946's acting awards.

To Each His Own was a Tiffany tear-jerker in the old tradition of *Madame X* and *Sin of Madelon Claudet*. Directed by Mitchell Leisen, the picture spanned two wars and told of twenty-seven unhappy years in the life of an unwed mother who loses custody of her son, becomes his 'Aunt Jody' when he is adopted by another family, and meets him years later in wartime London. Miss de Havilland was required to age from a bubbling young girl to a brusk middle-aged business woman and her effective work

turned the picture into a believable drama. The sentimental song, *To Each His Own*, which helped attract a sizable audience to see the film, wasn't used in the picture. It was written by Ray Evans and Jay Livingstone after the picture was completed, for exploitation.

The picture brought Olivia de Havilland her first Academy Award and offers to play rich, dramatic roles that had never come within her neighborhood at Warner Brothers. For the next three years she did the most consistent high level of work of any actress on the screen, and won her second Academy Award three years later for *The Heiress*.

OTHER ACTRESS NOMINEES, 1946

CELIA JOHNSON in Brief Encounter (British)
JENNIFER JONES in Duel in the Sun
ROSALIND RUSSEL in Sister Kenny
JANE WYMAN in The Yearling

Olivia de Havilland as young Jody

Another time, another war: Olivia de Havilland and a younger generation

BEST SUPPORTING ACTOR, 1946
HAROLD RUSSELL
in "The Best Years of Our Lives"

OTHER SUPPORTING NOMINEES, 1946

CHARLES COBURN in The Green Years
WILLIAM DEMAREST in The Jolson Story
CLAUDE RAINS in Notorious
CLIFTON WEBB in The Razor's Edge

DIRECTOR
Clarence Brown, THE YEARLING
Frank Capra, IT'S A WONDERFUL
  LIFE
David Lean, BRIEF ENCOUNTER
Robert Siodmak, THE KILLERS
*William Wyler, THE BEST YEARS OF
  OUR LIVES

WRITING
(Original Story)
THE DARK MIRROR, Vladimir Pozner
THE STRANGE LOVE OF MARTHA
  IVERS, Jack Patrick
THE STRANGER, Victor Trivas
TO EACH HIS OWN, Charles Brackett
*VACATION FROM MARRIAGE
  (British), Clemence Dane
    (Original Screenplay)
THE BLUE DAHLIA, Raymond
  Chandler
CHILDREN OF PARADISE (French),
  Jacques Prevert
NOTORIOUS, Ben Hecht
THE ROAD TO UTOPIA, Norman
  Panama, Melvin Frank
*THE SEVENTH VEIL (British),
  Muriel Box, Sydney Box
    Screenplay
ANNA AND THE KING OF SIAM,
  Sally Benson, Talbot Jennings
*THE BEST YEARS OF OUR LIVES,
  Robert E. Sherwood
BRIEF ENCOUNTER (British),
  Anthony Havelock-Allan, David
  Lean, Ronald Neame
THE KILLERS, Anthony Veiller
OPEN CITY (Italian), Sergio Amidei,
  F. Fellini

CINEMATOGRAPHY
Black-and-White
*ANNA AND THE KING OF SIAM,
  Arthur Miller
THE GREEN YEARS, George Folsey
    Color
THE JOLSON STORY, Joseph Walker
*THE YEARLING, Charles Rosher,
  Leonard Smith, Arthur Arling

INTERIOR DECORATION
Black-and-White
*ANNA AND THE KING OF SIAM,
  Lyle Wheeler, William Darling;
  Thomas Little, Frank E. Hughes
KITTY, Hans Dreier, Walter Tyler;
  Sam Comer, Ray Moyer
THE RAZOR'S EDGE, Richard Day,
  Nathan Juran; Thomas Little,
  Paul S. Fox
    Color
CAESAR AND CLEOPATRA (British),
  John Bryan
HENRY V, Paul Sheriff, Carmen Dillon
*THE YEARLING, Cedric Gibbons,
  Paul Groesse; Edwin B. Willis
SOUND RECORDING
THE BEST YEARS OF OUR LIVES,
  Gordon Sawyer
IT'S A WONDERFUL LIFE, John
  Aalberg
*THE JOLSON STORY, John Livadary

SHORT SUBJECTS
Cartoons
*THE CAT CONCERTO, M-G-M
CHOPIN'S MUSICAL MOMENTS,
  Universal
JOHN HENRY AND THE INKY POO,
  Geo. Pal-Paramount
SQUATTER'S RIGHTS, Disney-RKO
WALKY TALKY HAWKY, Warner Bros.
    One-Reel
DIVE-HI CHAMPS, Paramount
*FACING YOUR DANGER, Warner
  Bros.
GOLDEN HORSES, 20th Century-Fox
SMART AS A FOX, Warner Bros.
SURE CURES, M-G-M
    Two-Reel
*A BOY AND HIS DOG, Warner Bros.
COLLEGE QUEEN, Paramount
HISS AND YELL, Columbia
THE LUCKIEST GUY IN THE WORLD,
  M-G-M

DOCUMENTARY
Short Subjects
ATOMIC POWER, 20th Century-Fox
LIFE AT THE ZOO, Artkino
PARAMOUNT NEWS ISSUE #37,
  Paramount

MUSIC
Best Song

ALL THROUGH THE DAY (Centennial
Summer), Jerome Kern, Oscar
Hammerstein II
I CAN'T BEGIN TO TELL YOU (The
Dolly Sisters), James Monaco,
Mack Gordon
OLE BUTTERMILK SKY (Canyon
Passage), Hoagy Carmichael, Jack
Brooks
*ON THE ATCHISON, TOPEKA AND
SANTA FE (The Harvey Girls),
Harry Warren, Johnny Mercer
YOU KEEP COMING BACK LIKE A
SONG (Blue Skies), Irving Berlin

Best Score
**(Scoring of a Dramatic or
Comedy Picture)**

ANNA AND THE KING OF SIAM,
Bernard Herrmann
*THE BEST YEARS OF OUR LIVES,
Hugo Friedhofer
HENRY V (British), William Walton
HUMORESQUE, Franz Waxman
THE KILLERS, Miklos Rozsa
(Scoring of a Musical Picture)
BLUE SKIES, Robert Emmett Dolan
CENTENNIAL SUMMER, Alfred
Newman
THE HARVEY GIRLS, Lennie Hayton
*THE JOLSON STORY, Morris Stoloff
NIGHT AND DAY, Ray Heindorf, Max
Steiner

FILM EDITING
*THE BEST YEARS OF OUR LIVES,
Daniel Mandell
IT'S A WONDERFUL LIFE, William
Hornbeck
THE JOLSON STORY, William Lyon
THE KILLERS, Arthur Hilton
THE YEARLING, Harold Kress

SPECIAL EFFECTS
*BLITHE SPIRIT (British), Thomas
Howard
A STOLEN LIFE, William McGann,
Nathan Levinson

SPECIAL AWARDS
To Laurence Olivier for his outstanding achievement as actor, producer
and director in bringing HENRY V
to the screen. (statuette)
To Harold Russell for bringing hope
and courage to his fellow veterans
through his appearance in THE
BEST YEARS OF OUR LIVES.
(statuette)
To Ernst Lubitsch for his distinguished contributions to the art
of the motion picture. (scroll)
To Claude Jarman, Jr., outstanding
child actor of 1946. (miniature
statuette)

1946 IRVING J. THALBERG
MEMORIAL AWARD
SAMUEL GOLDWYN

SCIENTIFIC OR TECHNICAL
Class I
None
Class II
None
Class III
To HARLAN L. BAUMBACH and the
PARAMOUNT WEST COAST LABOR-
ATORY
To HERBERT E. BRITT
To BURTON F. MILLER and the WAR-
NER BROS. STUDIO SOUND AND
ELECTRICAL DEPTS.
To CARL FAULKNER
To MOLE-RICHARDSON COMPANY
To ARTHUR F. BLINN, ROBERT O.
COOK, C. O. SLYFIELD and the
WALT DISNEY STUDIO SOUND
DEPT.
To BURTON F. MILLER and the WAR-
NER BROS. STUDIO SOUND DEPT.
To MARTY MARTIN and HAL ADKINS
of the RKO Radio Studio
To HAROLD NYE and the WARNER
BROS. STUDIO ELECTRICAL DEPT.
*Denotes winner

BEST SUPPORTING ACTRESS, 1946
ANNE BAXTER
in "The Razor's Edge"

OTHER SUPPORTING NOMINEES, 1946

ETHEL BARRYMORE in The Spiral Staircase
LILLIAN GISH in Duel in the Sun
FLORA ROBSON in Saratoga Trunk
GALE SONDERGAARD in Anna and the King of Siam

Fredric March shows winner Loretta Young he didn't make a mistake

Expected winner Rosalind Russell arrives at the ceremony

Zanuck, Loretta Young, Gwenn, Celeste Holm, Colman

THE TWENTIETH YEAR

1947

The Big Upset . . .

They put a surprise ending on the 1947 Academy Award show. *Daily Variety*, a trade publication, took a straw-poll of Academy voters prior to the presentation of awards and published the results. Predicted winners were *Gentlemen's Agreement* (film), Ronald Colman in a narrow margin over Gregory Peck as best actor, Edmund Gwenn and Celeste Holm as supporting players. But the biggest runaway, according to all soothsayers, was Rosalind Russell as best actress. If there was to be any contest, according to the poll, the runners-up were (in order): Dorothy McGuire (#2), Joan Crawford (#3), Susan Hayward (#4) and, trailing, Loretta Young. The odds on a Russell victory were four-to-one against the field, and it was no secret that a post-award celebration party was being planned in her honor.

As the Academy Award show — March 20, 1948 at the Shrine Auditorium — progressed along its merry way, things were going as expected, with Dick Powell and Agnes Moorehead in charge of the proceedings. *Gentlemen's Agreement* and *Miracle On 34th Street* each won three awards, and, for the first time, a special award was given to a foreign-language film, *Shoe-Shine*, from Italy. Visitor Jean Simmons made her way to the stage four times to accept awards for J. Arthur Rank's British productions of *Great Expectations* and *Black Narcissus*. In the big races, *Gentlemen's Agreement*, Ronald Colman, Celeste Holm and Edmund Gwenn won, as predicted. It was all over but the shouting — almost.

Some attendees in the rear of the auditorium began to file toward the exits as Fredric March ripped open the envelope containing the name of the year's best actress. Candidate Russell was halfway out of her seat. The name — totally unexpected — was Loretta Young. The gasp that arose from the audience stopped everyone dead in their tracks. Even winner Young was stunned. It was something like a 100-1 shot running away with the Kentucky Derby and she had difficulty getting to the stage in a huge emerald-green taffeta dress that clearly hadn't been designed for climbing stairs. All she could gasp was "At long last!" and clutch her Oscar.

Backstage, posing for photographers and newsreels, winner Young — who happened to be Rosalind Russell's closest chum — found more words. "What about Roz?" she asked her husband. "What'll I say to Roz?"

At the Mocambo nightclub party, following the ceremony, all eyes were on the two ladies when Miss Russell appeared in the doorway, an hour later. Instead of pulling hair, the two pros greeted each other with a frantic bearhug that put a fitting capper on the biggest upset in Academy history.

A thoughtless drunk creates a scene: Gregory Peck, Celeste Holm, John Garfield

John Garfield

Celeste Holm

Dean Stockwell

Gregory Peck, Dorothy McGuire

BEST PICTURE, 1947
"Gentlemen's Agreement"

GENTLEMEN'S AGREEMENT (20TH CENTURY-FOX)
Producer: Darryl F. Zanuck
Director: Elia Kazan
Screenplay: Moss Hart
From the novel by Laura Z. Hobson

Phil Green	GREGORY PECK
Kathy Lacey	DOROTHY McGUIRE
Dave Goldman	JOHN GARFIELD
Anne Dettrey	Celeste Holm
Mrs. Green	Anne Revere
Elaine Wales	June Havoc
Mr. Minify	Albert Dekker
Jane	Jane Wyatt
Tommy Green	Dean Stockwell
and Sam Jaffe, Frank Wilcox, Gene Nelson	

While Bing Crosby, Betty Grable, and Ingrid Bergman were still holding court at the 1947 box-office, Hollywood began to use the screen to have a three-year look at minority groups. In 1947, two excellent studies of anti-Semitism appeared: *Crossfire* and *Gentlemen's Agreement*, and in 1949, four major works about the Negro problem (*Home of the Brave*, *Lost Boundaries*, *Intruder in the Dust*, *Pinky*) were produced. The cycle ended almost as quickly as it began, but while it was with us it proved the post-war screen could attract audiences with strong, mature themes, and without Abbott and Costello.

Gentlemen's Agreement, a pet project of Darryl F. Zanuck at 20th Century-Fox, was about a writer who poses as a Jew for six months in order to do a series of articles on anti-semitism. He finds that most of the people he knows are touched by the problem; his secretary has changed her name to avoid intolerance in their office, his fiance is irritated that she can't tell friends he "isn't really Jewish," and he finds himself discriminated against by his landlord and people of the community.

Directed by Elia Kazan, it was a strong preachment of the unwritten 'gentlemen's agreements' that exist on the subtle side of religious prejudices. The cast — headed by Gregory Peck, Dorothy McGuire, and John Garfield — all worked as an inspired team on top of an important project. The picture, based on a best seller by Laura Z. Hobson, didn't disappoint its large public and won three Academy Awards: picture, supporting actress, director, and gained a new respect for movie story-telling from even the severest critics.

For Celeste Holm, a recent Broadway success as Ado Annie in *Oklahoma!*, the picture made an auspicious debut. Peck, Dorothy McGuire and Anne Revere all received Academy nominations for their performances and John Garfield — already well established as a leading actor — accepted his small part as a labor of love for the project. For winner Kazan, who had also directed 1947's semi-documentary *Boomerang*, it was the first of two trips to the Academy winners circle and the first of five nominations as best director.

OTHER PICTURE NOMINEES, 1947

THE BISHOP'S WIFE, Goldwyn-RKO Radio
CROSSFIRE, RKO Radio
GREAT EXPECTATIONS, Universal-International (British)
MIRACLE ON 34TH STREET, 20th Century-Fox

M A G A Z I N E S

Producers should study each magazine; and hound his publicist about each magazine. What kind of material will each magazine print?

A movie shot in Peru may be publicized in *NATIONAL GEOGRAPHIC* as the still photographer contrasts the three civilizations: yesterday, today, and the movie. A comparison of five directors' work may publicize five pictures all distributed by one distributor, in a photography magazine.

The making of a movie may provide a dramatic photo story for *LIFE* or *LOOK*. The bit role played by royalty or nobility may get the movie a plug in a "People" column in a news magazine.

The stuntman portion of a picture may be publicized in an action magazine.

The stars' wardrobe and hair style may be publicized in fashion and beauty magazines.

Recently American publishers like Grove Press and Ballantine have published movie scripts; probably general magazines will soon carry scripts or portions.

All kinds of prizes may be sought as the magazine's movie of the month, star of the month, newcomer of the month, director of the month, friend of the publisher of the month.

PART IV

P A R T N E R S H I P S

The judge listened attentively as the cross-examining attorney asked the producer to identify his signature on the last page of a long contract involving $7,500.

Producer: "That's my signature."

Cross-examiner: "Did you read the contract?"

Producer: "No."

Cross-examiner: "Why not?"

Producer: "Why should I? I produce. My lawyer told me to sign. I signed."

Cross-examiner: "Do you realize that you, and not your lawyer, are liable for the $7,500?"

Producer: "Now I do. I think that from now on I'll read contracts before I sign them."

The contracts in this book are not standard contracts, are not endorsed by anybody, *some are probably as unfair as any other bunch of contracts*, some are as fair as any other bunch of contracts. They do provide basis for comparison.

This part on partnerships provides pleasant, easy, boring, necessary, informative, dull, essential reading material for all potential partners - and that means *you*. If you wish to skim, you can read the italicized portions only.

SIX MEN WITH CASH

Once upon a time there were six men with cash to spare. They wanted to combine their extra money in a joint venture which would back show-business projects.

These six men are totally fictitious, and they had the unlikely names of:

1. AAA AAA
2. BBB BBB
3. CCC CCC
4. DDD DDD
5. EEE EEE
6. AND BRIAN.

The first five men did not have any time to spend on the project, so they asked BRIAN to take care of things.

Brian had prepared for him a *CERTIFICATE OF LIMITED PARTNERSHIP*.

Brian had a mind which was curious about everything. He decided to learn about limited partnerships. Since Brian lived in California, Brian looked in California's Corporation Code.

Because many states have adopted the Uniform Limited Partnership Act, many states have laws similar to or identical to the statutes set forth in the next chapter.

LIMITED PARTNERSHIP ACT

It is time for a warning to readers. You are about to
be able to read laws passed by the State of California, in effect
January 1, 1970.

Please notice (1) the State, and (2) the time, (3) the
incompleteness.

(1) The laws of California may or may not be (a) identical to, (b) similar to, (c) different from the laws in your own
State.

(2) The laws in effect at the time of this writing, on
January 1, 1970, may be changed at any time, and may not be effective when you read this.

(3) These laws are not _all_ the laws concerning limited
partnerships.

You may be too lazy to read all the law at this time.
Please read at least sections 15502 (certificate), 15505 (sorry,
ego), 15507 (liability of limited partner), and 15519 (assignment
of interest).

Are you allowed to back movies without learning about
limited partnerships?

Of course you are!

The following extracts are from *WEST'S ANNOTATED CALIFORNIA CODES.*

"*Section 15501. Limited partnership defined; liability of limited partners.* A limited partnership is a partnership formed by two or more persons under the provisions of Section 15502, having as members one or more general partners and one or more limited partners. The limited partners as such shall not be bound by the obligations of the partnership. (Added Stats. 1949, c. 383, p. 688, Section 1.)"

"*Section 15502. Formation.* (1) Two or more persons desiring to form a limited partnership shall: (a) Sign and acknowledge a certificate, which shall state:

I.   The name of the partnership,
II.   The character of the business,
III.   The location of the principal place of business,
IV.   The name and place of residence of each member; general and limited partners being respectively designated,
V.   The term for which the partnership is to exist,
VI.   The amount of cash and a description of and the agreed value of the other property contributed by each limited partner,
VII.   The additional contributions, if any, agreed to be made by each limited partner and the times at which or events on the happening of which they shall be made,
VIII. The time, if agreed upon, when the contribution of each limited partner is to be returned,
IX.   The share of the profits or the other compensation by way of income which each limited partner shall receive by reason of his contribution,
X.   The right, if given, of a limited partner to substitute an assignee as contributor in his place, and the terms and conditions of the substitution,
XI.   The right, if given, of the partners to admit additional limited partners,
XII.   The right, if given, of one or more of the limited

partners to priority over other limited partners,
as to contributions or as to compensation by way
of income, and the nature of such priority,

XIII.   The right, if given, of the remaining general partner or partners to continue the business on the
death, retirement, or insanity of a general partner,

XIV.   The right, if given, of a limited partner to demand
and receive property other than cash in return for
his contribution,

XV.   The right, if given, of a limited partner to vote
upon any of the matters described in subdivision (b)
of Section 15507, and the vote required for election
or removal of general partners, or to cause other
action to be effective as to the limited partnership.

    (b) Record said certificate in the office of
the recorder of the county in which the principal
place of business of the partnership is situated.

    (2) A limited partnership is formed if there has
been substantial compliance in good faith with the requirements of paragraph one.

    (3) If the partnership has places of business
situated in, or holds title to real property in, different counties, it shall cause either such recorded
certificate, or a copy of such recorded certificate,
certified by the recorder in whose office it is recorded, to be recorded in the office of the recorder
of each such different county.

    (4) Recording of the certificate in accordance
with (1) (b) above or recording of the recorded certificate, or a copy thereof in accordance with (3) above
shall create the same conclusive presumptions as provided in Section 15010.5 of this code; any other person
claiming to be a partner who has been omitted from any
such statement shall have the right to record a cor-
rective statement as provided in said Section 15010.5.
(As amended Stats. 1955, c. 614, p. 1103, Section 1;
Stats. 1959, c. 998, p. 3019, Section 1; Stats. 1963,
c. 870, p. 2110, Section 1.)"

"*Section 15503. Permissible business; banking; insurance.* A limited partnership may carry on any business which
a partnership without limited partners may carry on, except

banking and insurance.   (Added Stats. 1949, c. 383, p. 690,

Section 1.)"

"Section 15504.   *Contribution of limited partner.*   The
contribution of a limited partner may be cash or other property,
but not services. (Added Stats. 1949, c. 383, p. 690, Sec. 1.)"

"Section 15505.   *Partnership name.*

(1)   *Use of limited partner's name.*   The surname of a
limited partner shall not appear in the partnership name, unless

(a)   It is also the surname of a general partner, or
(b)   Prior to the time when the limited partner became such the business had been carried on under a name in which
his surname appeared.

(2)   *Liability of limited partner whose name appears in
partnership name.*   A limited partner whose name appears in a
partnership name contrary to the provisions of paragraph one is
liable as a general partner to partnership creditors who extend
credit to the partnership without actual knowledge that he is
not a general partner. (Added Stats. 1949, c. 383, p. 690,
Section 1.)"

"Section 15506.   *False statement in certificate;   liability of signer.*   If the certificate contains a false statement, one who suffers loss by reliance on such statement may
hold liable any party to the certificate who knew the statement
to be false,

(a)   At the time he signed the certificate, or
(b)   Subsequently, but within a sufficient time before the statement was relied upon to enable him to cancel or
amend the certificate, or to file a petition for its cancellation or amendment as provided in subdivision three of Section
15525. (Added Stats. 1949, c. 383, p. 690, Section 1.)"

"Section 15507.   *Liability of limited partner.*

(a)   A limited partner shall not become liable as a
general partner unless, in addition to the exercise of his
rights and powers as a limited partner, he takes part in the
control of business.

(b)   A limited partner shall not be deemed to take

part in the control of the business by virtue of his possessing or exercising a power, specified in the certificate, to vote upon matters affecting the basic structure of the partnership, including the following matters or others of a similar nature:

    I.   Election or removal of general partners.
    II. Termination of the partnership.
  III. Amendment of the partnership agreement.
    IV. Sale of all or substantially all of the assets of the partnership.

     (c) The statement of powers set forth in subdivision (b) shall not be construed as exclusive or as indicating that any other powers possessed or exercised by a limited partner shall be sufficient to cause such limited partner to be deemed to take part in the control of the business within the meaning of subdivision (a). (As amended Stats. 1963, c. 870, p. 2111, Section 2.)"

"Section 15508. Admission of new limited partners; amendment to original certificate. After the formation of a limited partnership, additional limited partners may be admitted upon filing an amendment to the original certificate in accordance with the requirements of Section 15525 or Section 15525.5. (As amended Stats. 1967, c. 896, p. 2346, Sec. 1.)"

"Section 15509. Rights, powers, and liabilities of general partners.

    (1) A general partner shall have all the rights and powers and be subject to all the restrictions and liabilities of a partner in a partnership without limited partners, except that without the written consent or ratification of the specific act by all the limited partners, a general partner or all of the general partners have no authority to

    (a) Do any act in contravention of the certificate,
    (b) Do any act which would make it impossible to carry on the ordinary business of the partnership,
    (c) Confess a judgment against the partnership,
    (d) Possess partnership property, or assign their rights in specific partnership property, for

other than a partnership purpose,
   (e) Admit a person as a general partner,
   (f) Admit a person as a limited partner, unless
the right so to do is given in the certificate,
   (g) Continue the business with partnership property
on the death, retirement or insanity of a general partner, unless the right so to do is given in the certificate.

   (2) In the event of the removal or failure of re-election of a general partner, pursuant to the vote of the limited
partners in accordance with the certificate, such general partner shall cease to be liable as such upon the filing of an
amended certificate of limited partnership as provided in Sections 15524 and 15525 hereof, and compliance by the partnership or the partner with all of the requirements of notice and
publication of a former partner in a partnership without limited
partners. (As amended Stats. 1963, c. 870, p. 2111, Section 3.)"

   "Section 15510. *Rights of limited partners.* (1) A

limited partner shall have the same rights as a general partner

to
   (a) Have the partnership books kept at the principal place of business of the partnership, and at all times to
inspect and copy any of them,
   (b) Have on demand true and full information of
all things affecting the partnership, and a formal account of
partnership affairs whenever circumstances render it just and
reasonable, and
   (c) Have dissolution and winding up by decree of
court.

   (2) A limited partner shall have the right to receive

a share of the profits or other compensation by way of income,

and to the return of his contribution as provided in Sections

15515 and 15516. (Added Stats. 1949, c. 383, p. 691, Sec. 1.)"

   "Section 15511. *Status of person erroneously believing*

himself to be a limited partner. A person who has contributed

to the capital of a business conducted by a person or partner-

ship erroneously believing that he has become a limited partner

in a limited partnership, is not, by reason of his exercise of the rights of a limited partner, a general partner with the person or in the partnership carrying on the business, or bound by the obligations of such person or partnership; provided, that on ascertaining the mistake he promptly renounces his interest in the profits of the business, or other compensation by way of income. (Added Stats. 1949, c. 383, p. 691, Section 1.)"

"*Section 15512. One person as both general and limited partner; rights, powers, and liabilities.* (1) A person may be a general partner and a limited partner in the same partnership at the same time.

(2) A person who is a general, and also at the same time a limited partner, shall have all the rights and powers and be subject to all the restrictions of a general partner; except that, in respect to his contribution, he shall have the rights against the other members, which he would have had if he were not also a general partner. (Added Stats. 1949, c. 383, p. 691, Section 1.)"

"*Section 15513. Loans and other transactions between partnership and limited partner; fraudulent conveyances.*

(1) A limited partner also may loan money to and transact other business with the partnership, and, unless he is also a general partner, receive on account of resulting claims against the partnership, with general creditors, a pro rata share of the assets. No limited partner shall in respect to any such claim

(a) Receive or hold as collateral security any partnership property, or
(b) Receive from a general partner of the partnership any payment, conveyance, or release from liability, if at the time the assets of the partnership are not sufficient

to discharge partnership liabilities to persons not claiming as general or limited partners.

(2)   The receiving of collateral security, or a payment, conveyance, or release in violation of the provisions of paragraph one is a fraud on the creditors of the partnership. (Added Stats. 1949, c. 383, p. 691, Section 1.)"

"*Section 15514. Priorities among limited partners.* Where there are several limited partners the members may agree that one or more of the limited partners shall have a priority over other limited partners as to the return of their contributions, as to their compensation by way of income, or as to any other matter. If such an agreement is made it shall be stated in the certificate, and in the absence of such a statement all the limited partners shall stand upon equal footing. (Added Stats. 1949, c. 383, p. 691, Section 1.)"

"*Section 15515. Income payment to limited partner.* A limited partner may receive from the partnership the share of the profits or the compensation by way of income stipulated for in the certificate; provided, that after such payment is made, whether from the property of the partnership or that of a general partner, the partnership assets are in excess of all liabilities of the partnership except liabiliteis to limited partners on account of their contributions and to general partners. (Added Stats. 1949, c. 383, p. 692, Section 1.)"

"*Section 15516. Withdrawal of limited partner's contribution.*

(1)   *Limitations on withdrawal.* A limited partner shall not receive from a general partner or out of partnership property any part of his contribution until

(a)   All liabilities of the partnership, except liabilities to general partners and to limited partners on account of their contributions, have been paid or there remains property of the partnership sufficient to pay them,

(b)   The consent of all members is had, unless the return of the contribution may be rightfully demanded under the provisions of paragraph two, and

(c)   The certificate is canceled or so amended as to set forth the withdrawal or reduction.

(2)   *Right to return of contribution.* Subject to the provisions of paragraph one a limited partner may rightfully

demand the return of his contribution

       (a)   On the dissolution of a partnership, or

       (b)   When the date specified in the certificate for its return has arrived, or

       (c)   After he has given six months' notice in writing to all other members, if no time is specified in the certificate either for the return of the contribution or for the dissolution of the partnership.

       (3) *Return of contribution in cash.* In the absence of any statement in the certificate to the contrary or the consent of all members, a limited partner, irrespective of the nature of his contribution, has only the right to demand and receive cash in return for his contribution.

       (4) *Limited partner's right to dissolve partnership.* A limited partner may have the partnership dissolved and its affairs wound up when

       (a)   He rightfully but unsuccessfully demands the return of his contribution, or

       (b)   The other liabilities of the partnership have not been paid, or the partnership property is insufficient for their payment as required by paragraph 1(a) and the limited partner would otherwise be entitled to the return of his contribution. (Added Stats. 1949, c. 383, p. 692, Section 1.)"

"Section 15517. *Liability of limited partnership.*

       (1) *Unpaid contributions.* A limited partner is liable to the partnership

       (a)   For the difference between his contribution as actually made and that stated in the certificate as having been made, and

       (b)   For any unpaid contribution which he agreed in the certificate to make in the future at the time and on the conditions stated in the certificate.

       (2) *Trustee of money or property.* A limited partner holds as trustee for the partnership

       (a)   Specific property stated in the certificate as contributed or which has been wrongfully returned, and

(3) *Waiver or compromise of liability*. The liabilities of a limited partner as set forth in this section can be waived or compromised only by the consent of all members; but a waiver or compromise shall not affect the right of a creditor of a partnership who extended credit or whose claim arose after the filing and before a cancellation or amendment of the certificate, to enforce such liabilities.

(4) *Liability after rightful return of contribution*. When a contributor has rightfully received the return in whole or in part of the capital of his contribution, he is nevertheless liable to the partnership for any sum, not in excess of such return with interest, necessary to discharge its liabilities to all creditors who extended credit or whose claims arose before such return. (Added Stats. 1949, c. 383, p. 692, Sec. 1.)"

"*Section 15518. Limited partner's interest in partnership*. A limited partner's interest in the partnership is personal property. (Added Stats. 1949, c. 383, p. 693, Sec. 1.)"

"*Section 15519. Assignment of interest; substituted limited partner*.

(1) *Assignability of interest*. A limited partner's interest is assignable.

(2) *Substituted limited partner*. A substituted limited partner is a person admitted to all the rights of a limited partner who has died or has assigned his interest in a partnership.

(3) *Rights of assignee not a substituted limited partner*. An assignee, who does not become a substituted limited partner, has no right to require any information or account of the partnership transaction, to inspect the partnership books, or to vote on any of the matters as to which a limited partner would be entitled to vote pursuant to the provisions of Section 15507 and the certificate of limited partnership; he is only entitled to receive the share of the profits or other compensation by way of income, or the return of his contributions, to which his assignor would otherwise be entitled.

(4) *Assignee's right to become substituted partner*. An assignee shall have the right to become a substituted limited partner if all the members (except the assignor) consent thereto or if the assignor, being thereunto empowered by the certificate, gives the assignee that right.

(5) *When substitution occurs; amendment to certificate*.

An assignee becomes a substituted limited partner when the certificate is appropriately amended in accordance with Section
15525.

(6) *Rights, powers, and liabilities of substituted
limited partner.* The substituted limited partner has all the
rights and powers, and is subject to all the restrictions and
liabilities of his assignor, except those liabilities of which
he was ignorant at the time he became a limited partner and
which could not be ascertained from the certificate.

(7) *Effect of substitution on liability of assignor.*
The substitution of the assignee as a limited partner does not
release the assignor from liability to the partnership under
Sections 15506 and 15517. (As amended Stats. 1963, c. 870,
p. 2112, Section 4.)"

"*Section 15520. Retirement, death, insanity, removal
or failure of re-election of general partner.*

The retirement, death, insanity, removal or failure of
re-election of a general partner dissolves the partnership, unless the business is continued by the remaining general partners and/or the general partner or general partners elected in
place thereof

(a) Under a right so to do stated in the certificate, or
(b) With the consent of all members. (As amended
Stats. 1963, c. 870, p. 2112, Section 5.)"

"*Section 15521. Death of limited partner.*

(1) *Rights of personal representative.* On the death
of a limited partner his executor or administrator shall have
all the rights of a limited partner for the purpose of settling
his estate, and such power as the deceased had to constitute
his assignee a substituted limited partner.

(2) *Liability of estate.* The estate of a deceased
limited partner shall be liable for all his liabilities as a
limited partner. (Added Stats. 1949, c. 383, p. 693, Sec. 1.)"

"*Section 15522. Creditors' remedy to reach limited
partner's interest in partnership.*

(1) *Charge on interest; appointment of receiver.* On
due application to a court of competent jurisdiction by any
creditor of a limited partner, the court may charge the interest

of the indebted limited partner with payment of the unsatisfied amount of such claim; and may appoint a receiver, and make all other orders, directions, and inquiries which the circumstances of the case may require.

(2) *Redemption*. The interest may be redeemed with the separate property of any general partner, but may not be redeemed with the partnership property.

(3) *Non-exclusive remedy*. The remedies conferred by paragraph one shall not be deemed exclusive of others which may exist.

(4) *Statutory exemption*. Nothing in this act shall be held to deprive a limited partner of his statutory exemption. (Added Stats. 1949, c. 383, p. 694, Section 1.)"

"Section 15523. *Distribution of partnership assets.*

(1) *Priorities in payment of liabilities*. In settling accounts after dissolution the liabilities of the partnership shall be entitled to payment in the following order:

(a) Those to creditors, in the order of priority as provided by law, except those to limited partners on account of their contributions, and to general partners,

(b) Those to limited partners in respect to their share of the profits and other compensation by way of income on their contributions,

(c) Those to limited partners in respect to the capital of their contributions,

(d) Those to general partners other than for capital and profits,

(e) Those to general partners in respect to profits,

(f) Those to general partners in respect to capital.

(2) *Proportionate claims of limited partners*. Subject to any statement in the certificate or to subsequent agreement, limited partners share in the partnership assets in respect to their claims for capital, and in respect to their claims for profits or for compensation by way of income on their contributions respectively, in proportion to the respective amounts of such claims. (Added Stats. 1949, c. 383, p. 694, Sec. 1.)"

"*Section 15524.   Cancellation and amendment of certificate; when required.*

(1)   The certificate shall be canceled when the partnership is dissolved or all limited partners cease to be such.

(2)   A certificate shall be amended when

(a)   There is a change in the name of the partnership or in the amount or character of the contribution of any limited partner,
(b)   A person is substituted as a limited partner,
(c)   An additional limited partner is admitted,
(d)   A person is admitted as a general partner,
(e)   A general partner retires, dies, or becomes insane, and the business is continued under Section 15520,
(f)   There is a change in the character of the business of the partnership,
(g)   There is a false or erroneous statement in the certificate,
(h)   There is a change in the time as stated in the certificate for the dissolution of the partnership or for the return of contribution,
(i)   A time is fixed for the dissolution of the partnership, or the return of a contribution, no time having been specified in the certificate,
(j)   The members desire to make a change in any other statement in the certificate in order that it shall accurately represent the agreement between them, or
(k)   There is a change in the right to vote upon any of the matters described in subdivision (b) of Section 15507.   (As amended Stats. 1963, c. 870, p. 2113, Section 6.)"

"*Section 15525.   Formalities for amendment or cancellation of certificate.*

(1)   *Contents and execution of amendment.*   The writing to amend a certificate shall

(a)   Conform to the requirements of subdivision 1a of Section 15502 as far as necessary to set forth clearly the change in the certificate which it is desired to make, and
(b)   Be signed and acknowledged by all members, and an amendment substituting a limited partner or adding a limited or general partner shall be signed also by the member to be substituted or added, and when a limited partner is to be substituted, the amendment shall also be signed by the assigning limited partner.

(2) *Execution of cancellation.* The writing to cancel a certificate shall be signed by all members.

(3) *Refusal to execute cancellation or amendment; petition to court.* A person desiring the cancellation or amendment of a certificate, if any person designated in paragraphs one and two as a person who must execute the writing refuses to do so, may petition the superior court in the county where the principal place of the partnership is situated to direct a cancellation or amendment thereof.

(4) *Court order for cancellation or amendment.* If the court finds that the petitioner has a right to have the writing executed by a person who refuses to do so, it shall order the county recorder of the county in which the original certificate is recorded to record the cancellation or amendment of the certificate; and where the certificate is to be amended, the court shall also cause to be filed for record in said office a certified copy of its decree setting forth the amendment.

(5) *Recording.* A certificate is amended or canceled when there is recorded in the office referred to in paragraph (1) (b) of Section 15502 of this code:

(a) A writing in accordance with the provisions of paragraph one or two, or
(b) A certified copy of the order of court in accordance with the provisions of paragraph four. Provided, however, that such amendment or cancellation shall be void as against a purchaser or encumbrancer in good faith and for value of real property in a 'different county' referred to in paragraph (3) of Section 15502 of this code, whose conveyance is duly recorded before such recorded writing, or a copy thereof certified by the recorder in whose office it is recorded, or a certified copy of such court order, has been recorded in the office of the recorder in such different county.

(6) *Status of amended certificate.* After the certificate is duly amended in accordance with this section, the amended certificate shall thereafter be for all purposes the certificate provided for by this act except as to a purchaser or encumbrancer in good faith and for value under the circumstances set forth in the proviso to paragraph (5). (As amended Stats. 1959, c. 489, p. 2424, Section 1.)"

"*Section 15525.5.   Partnership having 25 or more limited partners; signing writing to amend certificate in certain cases.*

Notwithstanding the provisions of paragraph (b) of subdivision (1) of Section 15525, if the partnership certificate permits and the partnership has 25 or more limited partners immediately prior to the event requiring amendment of the certificate under this chapter, the writing to amend the certificate may be signed by a general partner and by the member to be substituted or added in the case of an amendment substituting a limited partner or adding a limited or general partner and shall be signed also by the assigning limited partner when a limited partner is to be substituted, and if the amendment reflects the retirement, death or insanity of a general partner, and the business is continued under Section 15520, the amendment may be signed by any general partner. (Added Stats. 1967, c. 896, p. 2347, Section 2.)"

"*Section 15526.   Proper parties to actions;   limited partner.* A contributor, unless he is a general partner, is not a proper party to proceedings by or against a partnership, except where the object is to enforce a limited partner's right against or liability to the partnership. (Added Stats. 1949, c. 383, p. 695, Section 1.)"

"*Section 15527. Title of chapter.* This chapter may be cited as The Uniform Limited Partnership Act. (Added Stats. 1949, c. 383, p. 695, Section 1.)"

"*Section 15528.   Interpretation and construction.*

(1) The rule that statutes in derogation of the common law are to be strictly construed shall have no application to this act.

(2) This act shall be so interpreted and construed as to effect its general purpose to make uniform the law of those states which enact it.

(3) This act shall not be so construed as to impair the obligations of any contract existing when the act goes into effect, nor to affect any action or proceedings begun or right accrued before this act takes effect. (Added Stats. 1949, c. 383, p. 696, Section 1.)"

"*Section 15529. Application of rules of law and equity.* In any case not provided for in this act the rules of law and equity, including the law merchant, shall govern. (Added Stats. 1949, c. 383, p. 696, Section 1.)"

"*Section 15530.   Prior limited partnerships.*

(1) *Election to come under chapter.* A limited partnership formed under any statute of this State prior to the adoption of this act, may become a limited partnership under this act by complying with the provisions of Section 15502, provided the certificate set forth

(a) The amount of the original contribution of each limited partner, and the time when the contribution was made, and

(b) That the property of the partnership exceeds the amount sufficient to discharge its liabilities to persons not claiming as general or limited partners by an amount greater than the sum of the contributions of its limited partners.

(2) *Continuation under old law.* A limited partnership formed under any statute of this State prior to the adoption of this act, until or unless it becomes a limited partnership under this act, shall continue to be governed by the provisions of Chapter 3 of Title 10 of Part 4 of Division 3 of the Civil Code as they existed prior to the repeal thereof, except that such partnership shall not be renewed unless so provided in the original agreement. (Added Stats. 1949, c. 383, p. 696, Section 1.)"

"*Section 15531.   Fraud; offense.* Every member of a special or limited partnership who commits any fraud in the affairs of the partnership is guilty of a misdemeanor. (Added Stats. 1949, c. 383, p. 696, Section 1.)"

(NOTE: The same or similar laws are in effect in the following states: Alaska, Arizona, Arkansas, California, Colorado, Florida, Georgia, Hawaii, Idaho, Illinois, Indiana, Iowa, Maryland, Massachusetts, Michigan, Minnesota, Missouri, Montana, Nebraska, Nevada, New Hampshire, New Jersey, New Mexico, New York, North Carolina, Oklahoma, Pennsylvania, Rhode Island, South Dakota, Tennessee, Utah, Vermont, Virginia, Washington, West Virginia, Wisconsin.)

LIMITED PARTNERSHIP AGREEMENT

Warning to reader: The sample *LIMITED PARTNERSHIP AGREE-MENT* is only a sample. It may or may not be useful, but is educational. You can learn some of the items a limited partnership can contain. Frequently such agreements are much shorter, since autographs of money men are usually easier to get on one-page agreements than on longer agreements.

There may be several limited partnerships for different purposes.

For example, the *ANGEL LIMITED PARTNERSHIP* may be formed for the purpose of backing various projects as these projects come along. One project may be backed solely with one or more loans. Another project may be backed solely with money supplied by a limited partner.

Thus, *PRODUCTION COMPANY LIMITED PARTNERSHIP* may be a joint venture with the producer as the producer as general partner and *ANGEL LIMITED PARTNERSHIP* as one of the limited partnerships.

The benefits to the original money men supplying money to *ANGEL LIMITED PARTNERSHIP* are various. They are not backing any particular picture with "all eggs in one basket."

MOTION PICTURE BACKING
LIMITED PARTNERSHIP AGREEMENT

The parties hereto, effective as of this day, enter into and form a limited partnership as follows:

I. LAW

A copy of the *CALIFORNIA CORPORATION CODE* chapter on the *Uniform Limited Partnership Act* will be furnished by the Partnership to each partner on request.

This limited partnership is organized pursuant to the provisions of the *Uniform Limited Partnership Act of the State of California (CORPORATIONS CODE Sections 15501 et seq.)*, and the rights and liabilities of the general and limited partners shall be as provided in that act, except as herein otherwise expressly stated.

II. The **NAME** of the partnership shall be MOTION PICTURE BACKING LIMITED PARTNERSHIP NO. 7.

III. PURPOSE

The purpose of this partnership is to engage in the business of backing motion pictures.

The backing may consist of lending money to a producer or distributor, lending credit for a laboratory fee, purchasing stock in a corporation producing a picture, contributing money as a limited partner to a partnership producing a picture, or in such other manner as may be deemed advisable by the general partner(s)

The limited partners understand that the general partner has various activities such as investor, producer, distributor. The limited partners consent to the general partner's wearing two hats, but require that the general partner clearly indicate to all concerned the limited purposes of this limited partnership. For example, a producer seeking money may deal with the general partner representing this limited partnership; the producer may also deal with the man who is a general partner hereof while he is wearing his hat as distributor. The general partner should always make clear to the producer in communications and in contracts when such general partner is wearing the hat of general partner and when he is wearing the hat of distributor.

The limited partners hereby consent to and approve the limited partnership's backing producers and projects with which the general partner also has producer-distributor relations.

This limited partnership may not be the general partner of a motion picture production partnership.

This limited partnership authorizes the general partner hereof to become the general partner of a motion picture production partnership which is backed by the limited partnership.

IV.   PRINCIPAL PLACE OF BUSINESS

A.   *Principal Place of Business.*   The principal place of business of the partnership will be at _____ _____ , City of Los Angeles, State of California.

B.   *Additional Places of Business.*   The partnership shall have such other places of business as from time to time shall be determined.

V.   DESIGNATION OF GENERAL PARTNERS AND THEIR
      RESPECTIVE CAPITAL CONTRIBUTIONS

A.   *General Partner(s).*   The following person(s) shall be general partner(s):

Name	Residence	$ Contribution
1.		
2.		
3.		

B.   LOANS

A general partner may lend money as a creditor to the limited partnership.

VI.   DESIGNATION OF LIMITED PARTNERS AND THEIR
       RESPECTIVE CAPITAL CONTRIBUTIONS

Name	Residence
1.	
2.	
3.	

VI.   LIMITED PARTNERS (Continued)

Name   Residence

4. _____

5. _____

6. _____

A.   *Limited Partners.*   The above members of the partnership shall be the limited partners.

B.   *Capital Contributions of Limited Partners.*   The capital contributions of each limited partner are as follows:

Name   Cash   Other Property

1. _____

2. _____

3. _____

4. _____

5. _____

6. _____

C.   *Receipt of Contributions.*   Receipt of the capital contributions of each of the limited partners as above specified is acknowledged by the partnership and its members to the extent indicated in receipts issued by the general partner for the partnership.

D.   *Additional Contributions.*   No limited partner has agreed to contribute as capital any additional cash or property.   A limited partner may lend money as a creditor to the limited partnership.

VII.   DUTIES AND RIGHTS OF PARTNERS

A.   *General Partners; Duties.*   Each of the general partners shall diligently and exclusively apply himself in and about the business of the partnership to the utmost of his skill and power, full time or part time, as the need may be.

B.   *General Partners; Right to Engage in Similar Business.*   Each general partner may, at any time during the term hereof, engage directly or indirectly in any business similar to the business of the said copartnership without obtaining the written approval of any of the other parties hereto.

C.   *Limited Partners; Rights and Duties.*   No limited partner shall have any right to be active in the conduct of the partnership's business, nor have power to bind the partnership in any contract, agreement, promise or undertaking.

VIII.   FEES OF GENERAL PARTNER

A.   *Amount of Fee.*   For the services rendered by them to the partnership, the general partners shall be entitled to fees which are initially fixed as hereinbelow indicated:

Name	Amount
1. _____	*
2. _____	*
3. _____	*

* All general partners will share a total of 10% of the net profit of the limited partnership, computed and payable as of the last day of each March, June, September, and December.

B. *Expense of Operation*. Such fees shall be treated as an expense of operation of the partnership business and shall be payable irrespective of whether or not the partnership shall operate at a profit.

C. *Other Expenses*. The limited partnership shall be charged with no overhead expenses (such as salaries, rent, telephone). Such expenses shall be borne by the general partner(s). The limited partnership shall pay fees for its legal, accounting, secretarial services, long distance telephone expenses, any taxes, license fees, etc. Because of the nature of this business - backing motion pictures - the limited partners expect the possibility of profits, losses, loans being overdue, guaranteed obligations not being paid on time, and realize that these items may cause expenses.

IX. DISTRIBUTION OF PROFITS

A. *Determination*. The general partners or a surviving partner shall have the right, except as hereinafter provided, to determine whether partnership profits from time to time shall be distributed in cash or shall be left in the business, in which latter event the capital account of all partners shall be increased.

B. However, in the event more than one-fourth of the assets of this limited partnership are utilized to back a motion picture project by loans and/or equity, then as this limited partnership receives funds, then to the extent they are not needed to meet expenses, such funds shall be distributed to the partners.

    X.   PROFIT AND LOSS SHARING BY LIMITED PARTNERS

    A. *Net Profits.* The limited partners shall receive the following shares of the net profits of the partnership:

	Name	Amount
1.	_____	_____ %
2.	_____	_____ %
3.	_____	_____ %
4.	_____	_____ %
5.	_____	_____ %
6.	_____	_____ %

    B. *Losses.* After giving effect to the share of losses chargeable against the capital contributions of limited partners, the remaining partnership losses shall be borne by the general partners in the same proportions in which, as between themselves, they share profits.

    XII. BOOKS OF ACCOUNT

    A. *Books of Account to Be Kept.* It is agreed among the parties that there shall at all times be kept during the continuance of this partnership good, just and true books of account of all transactions, assets and liabilities of the partnership. Said book shall be balanced and closed at the end of each year, and at any other time on reasonable request of any general partner.

B. *Fiscal Year Basis.* The profits and losses of the partnership and its books of account shall be maintained on a fiscal year basis determined by all the general partners.

C. *Place Where Book Is to Be Kept; Inspection.* Said books of account are to be kept at the principal place of business of the partnership, and are to be open for inspection by any partner at all reasonable times.

XIII. SUBSTITUTIONS, ASSIGNMENTS, AND ADMISSION OF ADDITIONAL PARTNERS

A. *Substitution for General Partner; Sale or Assignment of Interest.* No general partner may, without consent in writing of the other general partner(s), substitute a partner in his stead, or sell or assign all or any part of his interest in the partnership business.

B. *Additional General or Limited Partners.* Additional general or limited partners may be admitted to this partnership on such terms as may be agreed on in writing between the general partners and such new partners. The terms so agreed on shall constitute an amendment of this partnership agreement.

C. *Substitution of Assignee for Limited Partner.* A limited partner may assign his interest. An assignee is entitled to receive the share of the profits or other compensation by way of income, or the return of his contributions, to which his assignor would otherwise be entitled. No limited partner may substitute an assignee as a limited partner in his or her stead, but the person or persons entitled by will or by the intestate laws, as the case may be, shall succeed to all the rights of the limited partner, as a substituted limited partner.

XIV. TERMINATION OF INTEREST OF LIMITED PARTNER;

RETURN OF CAPITAL CONTRIBUTION

A. *Termination of Interest.* The interest of any limited partner may be terminated as follows:

1. By dissolution of the partnership for any reason provided herein;

2. By the agreement of all partners; and

3. By the consent of the personal representative of a deceased limited partner and the partnership.

B. *Return of Capital Contributions.* On the termination of the interest of a limited partner, there shall be payable to such limited partner, or his or her estate, as the case may be, a sum to be determined by all the partners, which sum shall be no less than the capital account of the limited partner as shown on the books at the time of the termination, including profits or losses from the last closing of the books of the partnership to the date of the termination, when the interest in profits and losses terminated. The amount payable shall be an obligation payable only out of partnership assets and in the option of the partnership may be paid within one year after the termination of the interest, provided however, that interest at the rate of eight per cent (8%) shall be paid on the unpaid balance.

XV.   BORROWING BY A PARTNER

In case of necessity as determined by a majority
vote of all the partners, a partner may borrow up to one thous-
and dollars ($1,000) from the partnership which shall be repay-
able together with interest thereon at the rate of ten per cent
(10%) per annum.

XVI.   TERM OF PARTNERSHIP DISSOLUTION

The partnership term commences as of the date above
the signatures, and continues thereafter for an unstipulated
time ending

A.   On the dissolution of the partnership by law;
or

B.   On dissolution at any time agreed on by the
general partners;   or

C.   On dissolution following ninety (90) days written notice by a general partner to the other general partner or
partners;   or

D.   On dissolution at the close of the month following the qualification and appointment of the personal representative of a deceased general partner, and following the exercise
by the surviving general partner or partners of an option hereby
granted to cause the partnership to be dissolved as of the close
of such month.

XVIII.   AMENDMENTS

This agreement, except with respect to vested rights of partners, may be amended at any time by a majority vote as measured by the interest in the sharing of profits and losses.

XIX.   BINDING EFFECT OF AGREEMENT

This agreement shall be binding on the parties hereto and their respective heirs, executors, administrators, successors and assigns.

IN WITNESS WHEREOF, the parties have executed this agreement on the following date: _____

GENERAL PARTNERS:

1. _____

2. _____

3. _____

LIMITED PARTNERS:

1. _____

2. _____

3. _____

4. _____

5. _____

6. _____

LIMITED PARTNERSHIP AGREEMENT
OF THE
JOE YORE STORY COMPANY

LIMITED PARTNERSHIP AGREEMENT between ABLE BARKER (herein called "the General Partner") and the parties who shall execute this agreement as hereinafter provided (each of whom is herein called a "Limited Partner").

1. The parties hereby form a limited partnership (herein called "the Partnership") pursuant to the provisions of Article 8 of the Partnership Law of the State of New York for the purpose of producing, distributing and exhibiting a motion picture tentatively entitled *JOE YORE STORY* (herein called "the Motion Picture"), and for the purpose of exploiting and turning to account the rights at any time held by the Partnership in connection therewith, and for no other purpose. The Partnership shall be conducted under the firm name of The Joe Yore Story Company. The principal office of the partnership shall be care of Able Baker, _____, New York, N.Y.

2. The Partnership shall commence on the day upon which, pursuant to the New York Partnership Law, the Certificate of Limited Partnership is duly filed in the Office of the Clerk of New York County, and shall continue until terminated as in this agreement provided. A notice containing the substance of the Certificate of Limited Partnership shall be published as required by the New York Partnership Law.

3.   The capital of the Partnership shall be $100,000.
Each Limited Partner shall contribute to the capital of the
Partnership the sum set forth as his contribution opposite his
signature hereto. The contribution of each Limited Partner
shall be payable at the time of execution of this agreement
but shall be held in escrow until the full amount of $100,000
shall have been so paid in, except as may be otherwise agreed
to by the Limited Partner making such contribution. Of such
amount, (a) $90,000 shall be used for the payment of all ex-
penses incurred in connection with the production, distribution
and exhibition of the Motion Picture, and the exploitation and
turning to account of all rights therein, and (b) $10,000 shall
be paid as underwriting commissions and expenses in connection
with the raising of the capital of the Partnership. If the expenses referred to in (a) above shall exceed $90,000, the Gene-
ral Partner agrees, either by making cash contributions himself as a Limited Partner or by obtaining contributions from
the other Limited Partners, or by making loans to the Partnership, to make available to the Partnership such sums as shall
equal the excess, but such additional contributions or loans
shall not have the effect of reducing the share of net profits
payable to the original Limited Partners. The General Partner,
however, shall not be obligated to obtain additional contributions or loans if the cost of the production shall be increased
as a result of extraordinary events, such as enemy invasions,

strikes, Acts of God, etc. In the event that loans are made to the Partnership, they shall be entitled to be repaid in full, without interest, prior to the return of any contributions to the Limited Partners.

4. VILLA YORE PRODUCTIONS, INC. ("Villa") has made the following contractual arrangements with respect to the Motion Picture:

A. VILLA has acquired from Book Publisher, Inc. ("BOOK"), the owner of all motion picture rights in and to the novel entitled *JOE YORE STORY* by Woodrow Olivetti, and the owner of all rights in and to the screenplay written by Woodrow Olivetti (and certain other persons) adapted from such novel, the rights to produce, distribute and exhibit one motion picture based upon said novel and said screenplay and to exploit and turn to account all rights therein. These rights are exclusive for seven years, after which BOOK shall have the right to produce, distribute and exhibit remakes of and sequels to the Motion Picture, and to require VILLA to withdraw the Motion Picture from distribution and exhibition for five years after the commencement of principal photography of a remake or sequel. All such rights of VILLA shall terminate unless (a) at least $100,000 of the capital of the Partnership is contributed by April 30, 1972; (b) principal photography of the Motion Picture is commenced not later than June 30, 1972; and (c) the Motion Picture is completed not later than March 31, 1973.

B.   VILLA has made arrangements with _____ ("DIREC-
TOR") whereby DIRECTOR is to direct the Motion Picture.

C.   All of the rights and obligations of VILLA pursuant to the agreements described in subparagraphs A and B above
shall be assigned to the Partnership upon its formation.

D.   The financial arrangements among VILLA (and, accordingly, the Partnership when the rights and obligations of
VILLA are assigned to the Partnership upon its formation), BOOK
and DIRECTOR, as set forth in the agreements referred to in sub-
paragraphs A and B above, are as follows: The entire gross receipts derived from the exhibition, distribution or other exploitation of the Motion Picture are to be allocated and distributed among the Partnership, BOOK and DIRECTOR as follows:

(1) First, to the payment of, or provision for
the payment of all distribution costs, fees and expenses;

(2) Second, the next $400,000 available there-
after shall be paid to BOOK and the Partnership in the propor-
tions of 10% thereof to BOOK and 90% thereof to the Partnership;
that is, until a total of $40,000 is paid to BOOK and a total
of $360,000 is paid to the Partnership; provided, however, that
the Partnership shall receive the first $5,000 payable to BOOK
as recoupment of an advance payment made to BOOK upon the execution of the agreement between VILLA and BOOK.

(3) Third, out of the next monies available
thereafter there shall be paid to the Partnership any amounts

expended by the Partnership in connection with Motion Picture
in excess of $100,000 until such excess, if any, shall have been
fully recouped by the Partnership.

(4) Fourth, the remaining gross receipts shall
be distributed (a) 15% thereof to BOOK: (b) 15% thereof to
DIRECTOR; (c) 70% thereof to the Partnership.

5. The contributions of the Limited Partners shall be
returned to them at the following times:

At such time after the commencement of exhibition
of the Motion Picture as the Partnership has a cash reserve of
not less than $10,000 after the payment or reasonable provision
for payment of all debts, liabilities, taxes, and contingent
liabilities in connection with the production, distribution and
exhibition of the Motion Picture, all cash (in excess of such
reserve) which (a) has not to that date been expended by the
Partnership, and (b) is received from time to time by the Partnership as its share of the gross receipts derived from the
exhibition of the Motion Picture pursuant to the agreements
with BOOK and DIRECTOR referred to in Paragraph 4 above and
agreements with distributors, shall be paid monthly to the Limited Partners until such time as the Limited Partners shall
have received $100,000 from such sources. Each Limited Partner
shall receive that proportion of such monthly excess of cash as
the total of his contribution bears to the aggregate amount of
all contributions made by all Limited Partners.

6. When the total contributions of the Limited Partners shall have been returned to them pursuant to the provisions of Paragraph 5 above, the remaining amounts to which the Partnership is entitled as its share of gross receipts derived from the exhibition of the Motion Picture pursuant to the agreements between BOOK and DIRECTOR referred to in Paragraph 4 above and agreements with distributors in excess of the cash reserve of $10,000 referred to in Paragraph 5 above, and after payment of reasonable provision for payment of all debts, liabilities, taxes, and contingent liabilities in connection with the production, distribution and exhibition of the Motion Picture shall be deemed to be "net profits" and shall be distributed and divided among the General Partner and the Limited Partners in the following proportions:

The Limited Partners shall each receive that proportion of 60% of the net profits which his contribution bears to the aggregate limited contribution (excluding, however, from such limited partners all persons who, pursuant to Paragraph 3 hereof, may be entitled to compensation only from the share of the General Partner in such net profits, and excluding from such aggregate limited contributions the contributions as limited partners so made by such persons). The General Partner shall receive the remaining 40% of net profits.

7. The Partnership shall continue until the completion of all distribution of the Motion Picture or until the termina-

tion of the Partnership's rights in the Motion Picture. In this
connection, the General Partner shall have the right, whenever
in his discretion he shall deem it necessary, to abandon the
production of the Motion Picture at any time. The General Partner shall also have the right to sell, or otherwise dispose of,
any or all rights in the Motion Picture, and if all such rights
shall be sold, or otherwise disposed of, then the Partnership
shall terminate. The Partnership shall also terminate upon
the death or insanity or retirement of the General Partner. If
a Limited Partner shall die, his executors, administrators, or,
if he shall become insane, his committee or other representatives, shall have the same rights that the Limited Partner would
have had if he had not died or become insane, and the share of
such Limited Partner in the assets of the Partnership shall, until the termination of the Partnership, be subject to all terms,
provisions and conditions of this agreement as if such Limited
Partner had not died or become insane.

8. The General Partner has heretofore incurred or paid
and, prior to the inception of the Partnership will incur or pay
certain production expenses (including without limitation an
advance payment of $5,000 made to BOOK) and the amount thereof,
and no more, shall be included in the production expenses, and
the General Partner shall be reimbursed therefor immediately
after the full amount of $100,000 is paid in.

9. No Limited Partner shall be personally liable for

any debts, obligations or loss of the Partnership beyond the
amount of his contribution to the capital of the Partnership.
If any sum by way of repayment of contribution or distribution
of profits shall have been paid prior or subsequent to the termination date of the Partnership and at any time subsequent to
such repayment there shall be any unpaid debts, taxes, liabilities or obligations of the Partnership, and the Partnership
shall not have sufficient assets to meet them, then each Limited Partner and the General Partner shall be obligated to repay
to the Partnership up to the amount of capital so returned to
him, and profits so distributed to him, as the General Partner
may need for such purpose and demand.

10. Solely for the purpose of determining whether or
not any contributions are to be repaid or net profits are to be
distributed, the monthly financial reports prepared by the accountants for the Partnership shall be conclusive.

11. Upon the termination of the Partnership, the assets
of the Partnership shall be liquidated as promptly as possible
and the cash proceeds shall be applied as follows in the following order of priority:

A. To the payment of debts, taxes, obligations
and liabilities of the Partnership and the necessary expenses
of liquidation. Where there is a contingent debt, obligation
or liability, a reserve shall be set up to meet it, and if and
when said contingency shall cease to exist, the monies, if any,

in said reserve shall be distributed as herein provided for in this Paragraph.

B.   To the repayment of capital contributed by the Limited Partners (if any shall then remain unpaid), said Limited Partners sharing each such repayment proportionately to their respective contributions.

C.   The surplus, if any, of the said assets then remaining shall be divided among all the partners in the proportion that they share in net profits.

12.   The General Partner agrees:

A.   Upon commencement of the Partnership, to open and maintain in New York City a special bank account in which shall be deposited the Partnership funds.

B.   To keep full and faithful books of account in which shall be entered fully and accurately each transaction of the Partnership.

C.   To furnish each Limited Partner with a statement of expenses within ninety (90) days after the commencement of exhibition of the Motion Picture, and a statement of income and expenses not less frequently than semi-annually following the commencement of exhibition of the Motion Picture; to furnish each Limited Partner with all so-called "information returns" (prior to the filing thereof with the Federal and State governments), showing the income of the Partnership and of each Partner received therefrom; to have all of such statements prepared by a firm of accountants experienced in the motion picture business.

D. To render in connection with the Motion Picture services customarily and usually rendered by motion picture producers, and to devote as much time thereto as may be necessary, its being understood and agreed, however, that the General Partner may engage in other businesses, including other motion picture productions, and the Limited Partners shall have no right to share in the proceeds therefrom.

13. The General Partner shall have complete control of the production, distribution and exhibition of the Motion Picture, and the exploitation and turning to account of all rights therein. Without limitation, the General Partner shall have the complete control over all business decisions with respect to the Motion Picture, including the sale or other disposition thereof, distribution and exhibition arrangements, and any other marketing arrangements.

14. No assignee of a Limited Partner shall have the right to become a substitute Limited Partner in the place of his assignor.

15. The Limited Partners shall have no right to demand and receive property other than cash in return for their contributions. In the repayment of capital contributions, the division of profits or otherwise, no Limited Partners shall have any priority over any other Limited Partner.

16. This agreement may be executed in counterparts, all of which taken together shall be deemed one original.

17. Any dispute arising under, out of, in connection with, or in relation to this agreement, or the making or validity thereof, or its interpretation, or any breach thereof, shall be determined and settled by arbitration in New York City, pursuant to the rules then obtaining of the American Arbitration Association. Any award rendered shall be final and conclusive upon the parties, and a judgment thereon may be entered in the highest court of the forum, State or Federal, having jurisdiction.

18. Each of the Limited Partners does hereby make, constitute and appoint the General Partner his true and lawful attorney, and in his name, place and stead to make, execute, sign, acknowledge and file:

A. The Certificate of Limited Partnership of the Partnership, and to include therein all information required by the laws of the State of New York;

B. Such amended Certificate of Limited Partnership as may be required pursuant to Paragraph 3 hereof; and

C. All papers which may be required to effectuate the dissolution of the Partnership after its termination.

IN WITNESS WHEREOF, the parties hereto have set their hands and seals as of the _____ day of _____, 1971.

General Partner   Limited Partner(s)
Residence Address   Residences, Contributions, %'s

PART V

DISTRIBUTION PRACTICES

You are about to read about film distribution practices. A little spice is added because many of these practices are illegal. The guest author is the great Justice Douglas of the United States Supreme Court; in fact, what we did was copy decisions of The Supreme Court of The United States.

The cases present a variety of defendants: major and minor distributors, circuits and combinations.

The producer-distributor-theatre combinations have been broken up. Please remember theatres and distributors had basic reasons for each rightful and wrongful act. Theoretically, most reasons still exist.

We hope you enjoy and can get useful information from these well-written stories.

Please remember that these cases took place many years ago.

UNITED STATES v. . . . . (Introduction)

I

"The history of the motion picture industry is one of
almost continuous innovations and successions of combinations
to control markets. *Innovations* occurred in cameras and pro-
jectors, in film and screens, in distribution organization, in
theatre structure, and in techniques of operation throughout
the industry. *Combinations* were based on control of patents,
actors, distribution facilities, and theatres. The *innovations*
worked to promote entry of new firms into the industry, and the
combinations were designed to deter entry."

Conant, *Antitrust in the Motion Picture Industry.*

II

Case: U.S. v. Crescent

"Mr. Justice Douglas delivered the opinion of the Court.

"The United States brought this civil suit against nine
affiliated companies (whom we will call the exhibitors) operating motion picture theatres in some 70 small towns in Alabama,
Arkansas, Kentucky, Mississippi and Tennessee; against certain
officers of these companies; and against eight major distributors of motion picture films, charging them with a conspiracy
unreasonably to restrain interstate trade and commerce in motion-
picture films and to monopolize the exhibition of films in this
area in violation of Section 1 and Section 2 of the Sherman

Act . . . ."

Case of *U.S. v. CRESCENT AMUSEMENT CO*, Supreme

Court of the U.S. (1944), 323 US 173, 65 S Ct 254, 89 L ed 168.

III

Case: U.S. v. Griffith

"Mr. Justice Douglas delivered the opinion of the Court.

"This is a suit brought by the United States in the District Court to prevent and restrain appellees from violating Sections 1 and 2 of the Sherman Act . . . .

"The appellees are four affiliated corporations and two individuals who are associated with them as stockholders and officers. The corporations operate (or own stock in corporations which operate) moving picture theatres in Oklahoma, Texas, and New Mexico. . . . . the corporate appellees had interests in theatres in 85 towns . . . Five years earlier the corporate appellees had theatres in approximately 37 towns."

Case of the *U.S. v. Griffith*, Supreme Court of the U.S. (1948), 334 U.S. 100, 68 S Ct 941, 92 L ed 1236.

IV

Case: Schine Chain Theatres, Inc. v. U.S.

"Mr. Justice Douglas delivered the opinion.

" . . . . The appellants, who were defendants below, are a parent company, three of its officers and directors, and five of its wholly owned subsidiaries - to whom we refer collectively as Schine. As of May 19, 1942, Schine owned or had a

financial interest in a chain of approximately 148 motion picture theatres (these figures do not include 18 which were closed
and had been or were being converted to other uses), located in
76 towns in 6 states (New York - 78; Ohio - 36; Kentucky - 18;
Maryland - 12; Delaware - 2; Virginia - 2), the greater portion being 78 theatres in 41 towns in New York and 36 theatres
in 17 towns in Ohio."

Case of *Schine Chain Theatres v. U.S.*, Supreme Court
of the U.S. (1948) 334 U.S. 110, 68 S Ct 947, 92 L ed 1245.

V

Case: U.S. v. Paramount Pictures, Inc.

This is the big case. The Court's opinion runs 51
pages.

"Mr. Justice Douglas delivered the opinion of the Court.
. . . .

The suit was instituted by the United States under Section 4 of the Sherman Act to prevent and restrain violations of
it. The defendants fall into three groups: (1) Paramount Pictures, Inc., Loew's Incorporated, Radio-Keith-Orpheum Corporation, Warner Brothers Pictures, Inc., Twentieth Century-Fox
Film Corporation, which produce motion pictures and their respective subsidiaries or affiliates which distribute and exhibit
films. These are known as the five major defendants or exhibitor-defendants. (2) Columbia Pictures Corporation and Universal Corporation, which produce motion pictures, and their

subsidiaries which distribute films. (3) United Artists Corporation, which is engaged only in the distribution of motion
pictures. The five majors, through their subsidiaries or affiliates, own or control theatres; the other defendants do
not."

Case of *The U.S. v. Paramount Pictures, Inc.*, Supreme
Court of the U.S., (1948), 334 U.S. 131, 68 S Ct 915, 92 L
ed 1260.

VI

These cases are helpful for various reasons to various
readers. The cases have historical value. The cases provide
a background for the constant headaches written about in *The
Independent Film Journal*, *Weekly Variety*, *Daily Variety*, *Box
Office*, *The Hollywood Reporter*, and other trade publications.
The cases provide education in trade practices, including fair
trade practices, which men who have dreams and schemes may use
tomorrow. Men in production, distribution and exhibition today
are still accusing each other of unfair trade practices. Men
in all fields are today threatening opponents with treble-
damage (plus attorneys' fees) anti-trust actions. How will
you make money with this knowledge?

U.S. v. CRESCENT AMUSEMENT CO.

The following case is copied from an official publication of the U.S. Superintendent of Documents, Government Printing Office, Washington, D.C.

This anti-trust action was filed against eight major distributors of films and nine affiliated companies (exhibitors) operating motion picture theatres in some 70 small towns in Alabama, Arkansas, Kentucky, Mississippi, and Tennessee.

Justice Douglas wrote the opinion for the U.S. Supreme Court.

U. S. *v.* CRESCENT AMUSEMENT CO.   173

166   Syllabus.

whether the courts may afford relief where the board refuses or fails to perform a function delegated to it by Congress, since the board is not a party. Neither the pleadings nor the prayers disclose a situation in which the question of the availability of such remedies antecedent to, or subsequent to, the election or certification need be discussed or decided.

The writ is accordingly dismissed.

MR. JUSTICE RUTLEDGE concurs in the result.

UNITED STATES *v.* CRESCENT AMUSEMENT CO.
ET AL.

NOS. 17 AND 18.   APPEALS FROM THE DISTRICT COURT OF THE UNITED STATES FOR THE MIDDLE DISTRICT OF TENNESSEE.*

Argued November 6, 7, 1944.—Decided December 11, 1944.

1. The motions in the District Court to amend the findings in this case raised questions of substance, and an appeal applied for and allowed while such motions were pending was premature and must be dismissed. P. 177.
2. That the District Court has allowed a premature appeal does not deprive it of jurisdiction to allow a subsequent and timely appeal. P. 177.
3. The Sherman Antitrust Act may apply to the business of exhibiting motion pictures, when a regular interchange of films in interstate commerce is involved. P. 180.
4. On appeal this Court considers only the alleged errors which have been included in the assignments of error. P. 180.
5. The evidence sustains the District Court's findings of a conspiracy of the defendant exhibitors of motion pictures, and certain officers thereof, unreasonably to restrain interstate trade and commerce in motion picture films and to monopolize the exhibition of films in the areas in question, in violation of § 1 and § 2 of the Sherman Act. P. 181.

---

*Together with No. 19, *Crescent Amusement Co. et al.* v. *United States*, also on appeal from the District Court of the United States for the Middle District of Tennessee.

(a) There was ample evidence that the combination used its buying power for the purpose either of restricting the ability of its competitors to license films or of eliminating competition by acquiring the competitor's property or otherwise. P. 181.

(b) Whether the distributors were technically co-conspirators is immaterial, since action by a combination of exhibitors to obtain an agreement with a distributor whereby commerce with a competing exhibitor is suppressed or restrained is itself a conspiracy in restraint of trade and a conspiracy to monopolize a part of the trade or commerce among the States, each of which is prohibited by the Sherman Act. P. 183.

(c) Even if error be assumed in the introduction of certain evidence—consisting of letters or reports written by employees of certain of the major distributors to other employees or officers in the same company stating reasons why the distributor was discriminating against an independent and in favor of the defendants— there is sufficient other evidence to establish the restraints of trade and monopolistic practices, and the burden of showing prejudice has not been sustained. P. 184.

(d) Though the findings leave much to be desired in the light of the function of the trial court, they are supported by the evidence and must therefore be sustained. P. 184.

6. Upon consideration of objections to provisions of the decree in this case, *held:*

(1) Lest the public interest be not adequately protected, the decree should be revised so as to prohibit future acquisitions of a financial interest in additional theatres outside of Nashville "except after an affirmative showing that such acquisition will not unreasonably restrain competition." P. 185.

(2) Provisions of the decree enjoining the defendant exhibitors from making franchises with certain distributors "with the purpose and effect of maintaining their theatre monopolies and preventing independent theatres from competing with them" and from entering into "any similar combinations and conspiracies having similar purposes and objects"; from combining, in licensing films, their closed towns with their competitive situations "for the purpose and with the effect of compelling the major distributors to license films on a non-competitive basis in competitive situations and to discriminate" against the independents; and enjoining each defendant exhibitor "from conditioning the licensing of films in any competitive situation (outside Nashville) upon the licensing of films in any other theatre situation"—are sustained. P. 187.

U. S. *v.* CRESCENT AMUSEMENT CO.   175

(a) The franchise agreements and the licensing system were the chief instruments of the unlawful practices, and it was the duty of the court to enjoin their continuance and resumption. P. 188.

(b) These provisions of the decree are not unenforceable as too vague and general. P. 188.

(3) The divestiture provisions of the decree—requiring each corporate exhibitor to divest itself of the ownership of any stock or other interest in any other corporate defendant or affiliated corporation, and enjoining it from acquiring any interest in those companies; requiring one of the individual defendants to resign as an officer of any corporation (except Crescent) which is affiliated with any defendant exhibitor and enjoining him from acquiring control over any such affiliate by acting as officer or otherwise; requiring another of the individual defendants to resign as an officer of the affiliates (except one corporation of his choice) and enjoining him from acquiring any control over the others by acting as an officer or otherwise; and allowing a year from the date of the decree for completion of the divestiture—are sustained. P. 189.

(a) In this type of Sherman Act case, the Government should not be confined to an injunction against further violations; dissolution of the combination may be ordered where the creation of the combination is itself the violation. P. 189.

(b) Those who violate the Act may not reap the benefits of their violations and avoid an undoing of their unlawful project on the plea of hardship or inconvenience. P. 189.

(c) The fact that minority stockholders of the affiliated companies are not parties to the suit does not bar a separation of the companies. P. 190.

(d) The requirement that two of the defendant corporate exhibitors sell their respective half-interests in two companies which were not made parties to the proceedings is sustained, since it does not appear on this record that any legal right of any other stockholder would be affected. P. 190.

No. 17 dismissed.

No. 18 reversed.

No. 19 affirmed.

DIRECT APPEALS under the Expediting Act from a decree against defendants in a civil suit under the Sherman Antitrust Act. Two of the appeals were taken by the Government, the other by certain of the defendants.

Assistant Attorney General Berge and *Mr. Robert L. Wright,* with whom *Solicitor General Fahy* and *Messrs. Charles H. Weston* and *Chester T. Lane* were on the brief, for the United States.

Mr. William Waller, with whom *Mr. Geo. H. Armistead, Jr.* was on the brief, for appellees in Nos. 17 and 18 and appellants in No. 19.

MR. JUSTICE DOUGLAS delivered the opinion of the Court.

The United States brought this civil suit against nine affiliated companies (whom we will call the exhibitors) operating motion picture theatres in some 70 small towns in Alabama, Arkansas, Kentucky, Mississippi, and Tennessee; against certain officers of these companies; and against eight major distributors of motion picture films, charging them with a conspiracy unreasonably to restrain interstate trade and commerce in motion-picture films and to monopolize the exhibition of films in this area in violation of § 1 and § 2 of the Sherman Act. 26 Stat. 209, 15 U. S. C. §§ 1, 2. The suit was dismissed against five of the distributors on motion of the United States.[1] Of the other three the Court found that only one had violated the Sherman Act. The court also found that seven of the exhibitors and three of the individual defendants had violated the Sherman Act substantially as charged. It entered a decree against them. From the judgment en-

---

[1] This was done after a consent decree had been entered against five of the major distributors in *United States* v. *Paramount Pictures, Inc.* This dismissal did not eliminate the charge that these distributors had conspired with the defendant exhibitors to restrain and monopolize trade. And some of the distributors, though dismissed from the case, were found to be co-conspirators with the exhibitors in making franchise agreements and in licensing films for the purpose of maintaining the exhibitors' theatre monopolies and of preventing the independents from competing.

U. S. *v.* CRESCENT AMUSEMENT CO.   177

tered the United States, six of the exhibitors, and three individual defendants appeal directly to this Court under § 2 of the Act of February 11, 1903, 32 Stat. 823, 15 U. S. C. § 29 and § 238 of the Judicial Code, as amended by the Act of February 13, 1925, 43 Stat. 936, 938, 28 U. S. C. § 345.

I. Before we come to the merits there is a preliminary question as to whether the appeal of the United States in No. 17 is premature. The District Court entered a final judgment in this case on May 17, 1943. On the sixtieth day after judgment there were motions pending to amend the findings. On that day the appeal was applied for and allowed. On August 30, 1943, the court ruled on the motions to amend its findings. Within sixty days thereafter the United States applied for the appeal in No. 18 and it was allowed. The appeal in No. 17 was filed here at the same time as that in No. 18. The appellees move to dismiss No. 17 on the ground that it was premature and to dismiss No. 18 on the ground that the District Court by allowing the first appeal lost jurisdiction of the cause and was without power to allow a further appeal. We think the motion to dismiss the appeal in No. 17 must be granted and the motion to dismiss the appeal in No. 18 denied.

The motion to amend the findings tolled the time to appeal if it was not addressed to "mere matters of form but raised questions of substance," e. g., if it sought a "reconsideration of certain basic findings of fact and the alteration of the conclusions of the court." *Leishman* v. *Associated Electric Co.,* 318 U. S. 203, 205. An examination of the motion makes plain that matters of substance were raised. The appeal in No. 17 was accordingly premature. *Zimmern* v. *United States,* 298 U. S. 167. But it does not follow that the District Court had no jurisdiction to allow the appeal in No. 18. An appeal can hardly be premature (and therefore a nullity) here and yet not premature (and therefore binding) below. Under these circumstances an appellant may rely upon the later appeal (*Ohio Public Service Co.* v. *Fritz,* 274 U. S. 12) and not run the risk of losing an appellate review on the appeal first allowed. Cf. *Wilentz* v. *Sovereign Camp,* 306 U. S. 573.

II. We turn to the merits. Crescent, the principal exhibitor,[2] owns 50% of the stock of Cumberland and Lyric. The majority of Crescent's stock is owned by defendant Sudekum, by certain of his relatives, and by defendants Stengel and Baulch. Prior to 1937 Crescent owned almost two-thirds of the stock of Muscle Shoals; since that time Muscle Shoals was run as a partnership in which Sudekum's wife had a half-interest. Defendant Stengel, Sudekum's son-in-law, is the record holder of all of Rockwood's stock. Rockwood owns 50% of the stock of Cherokee and Kentucky and of five other theatre corporations. Rockwood was operated as a "virtual branch" of the Crescent business under the immediate supervision of Stengel. Sudekum is president of Crescent, Cumberland, and Lyric; Stengel is an officer and director of Kentucky and Cherokee. Sudekum was paid $200 a week by Cherokee "for his advice and assistance in running the business." Each of these companies was an exhibitor operating motion picture theatres.

In the five-year period ended in August 1939 when this bill was filed the exhibitors experienced a rather rapid growth—in the number of towns where their theatres were operated; in the number of towns where they operated without competition; in their earnings and surplus. The United States claims that that growth was the prod-

---

[2] Crescent is used for Crescent Amusement Co.; Cumberland for Cumberland Amusement Co.; Lyric for Lyric Amusement Co., Inc.; Cherokee for Cherokee Amusements, Inc.; Kentucky for Kentucky Amusement Co., Inc.; Muscle Shoals for Muscle Shoals Theatres; and Rockwood for Rockwood Amusement Co.

U. S. *v.* CRESCENT AMUSEMENT CO.   179

uct of restraints of trade in violation of § 1 of the Sherman Act and of monopolistic practices in violation of § 2.

The District Court found that each of the seven exhibitors had violated the Sherman Act by

"A. Creating and maintaining an unreasonable monopoly of the business of operating theatres in the towns of Tennessee, Northern Alabama, and Central and Western Kentucky, in which each has theatres.

"B. Combining its closed towns with its competitive situations in licensing films for the purpose and with the effect of compelling the major distributors to license films on a non-competitive basis in competitive situations and to discriminate against its independent competitors in licensing films.

"C. Coercing or attempting to coerce independent operators into selling out to it, or to abandon plans to compete with it by predatory practices."

The court found that these violations were effected (a) by combining with each other and with certain major distributors in making franchises, i. e. term contracts for the licensing of films, with the purpose and effect of maintaining their theatre monopolies and preventing independents from competing with them; (b) by combining with each other for the purpose of dividing the territory in which theatres might be operated by any of them; (c) by combining with each other for the purpose and with the effect of eliminating, suppressing, and preventing independents from competing in the territory in which each operated; and (d) by combining with each other and with certain major distributors in licensing films for the purpose and with the effect of maintaining their theatre monopolies and preventing independents from competing with them. Three of the individual defendants were found to have participated actively in these violations.

U. S. *v.* CRESCENT AMUSEMENT CO.   181

The crux of the government's case was the use of the buying power of the combination for the purpose of eliminating competition with the exhibitors and acquiring a monopoly in the areas in question.   There was ample evidence that the combination used its buying power for the purpose either of restricting the ability of its competitors to license films or of eliminating competition by acquiring the competitor's property or otherwise.   For example, the defendants would insist that a distributor give them monopoly rights in towns where they had competition or else defendants would not give the distributor any business in the closed towns where they had no competition.   The competitor not being able to renew his contract for films would frequently go out of business or come to terms and sell out to the combination with an agreement not to compete for a term of years.   The mere threat would at times be sufficient and cause the competitor to sell out to the combination "because his mule was scared."   In that way some of the affiliates were born.   In summarizing various deals of this character the District Court said, "Each of these agreements not to compete with Crescent or its affiliates in other towns extended far beyond the protection of the business being sold, and demonstrated a clear intention to monopolize theatre operation wherever they or their affiliates secured a foothold." [4]

---

[4] The expansion of the combination during this period was summarized by the District Court as follows:

"On August 11, 1934, the defendant exhibitors and their affiliates operated in thirty-two towns in Tennessee (excluding Nashville), Kentucky, and Alabama, in six of which they had competition. On August 11, 1939, the defendant exhibitors and their affiliates, with the exception of Strand, heretofore dismissed as a defendant, operated in seventy-eight towns in Tennessee (excluding Nashville), Kentucky, Alabama, and North Carolina, in five of which they had competition, and the only towns in which they have competition today outside of Nashville, are Gadsden, Alabama, Harriman, Gallatin and McMinn-

182   OCTOBER TERM, 1944.

Opinion of the Court.   323 U.S.

The same type of warfare was waged with franchise contracts with certain major distributors covering a term of years. These gave the defendants important exclusive film-licensing agreements. Their details varied. But generally they gave the defendant exhibitors the right to first-run exhibition of all feature pictures which they chose to select in their designated towns. Clearances over the same or nearby towns were provided, i. e. a time lag was established between the showing by the defendant exhibitors and a subsequent showing by others. The opportunity of competitors to obtain feature pictures for subsequent runs was further curtailed by repeat provisions

---

ville, Tennessee, and Franklin, Kentucky. In two of these towns—Gadsden, Alabama, and Harriman, Tennessee—the independent theatres have opened since the filing of this suit and two more—Franklin, Kentucky, and Gallatin, Tennessee—are towns which Crescent entered less than two years before the filing of this suit.

"Of the forty-five towns in Tennessee listed in the 1940 census as having populations between 2,500 and 10,000, Crescent and its affiliates now operate theatres in all but nine. The independents operating in three of those nine towns have already been approached by Sudekum emissaries with the suggestion that they sell to one of the defendant exhibitors."

Their financial growth was found to be "out of all proportion" to their physical expansion:

"During the five-year period immediately preceding the suit, the Crescent and Rockwood companies each experienced a phenomenal growth in earnings and surplus which was out of all proportion to the increase in gross receipts and gross assets resulting from physical expansion of the business and improving general economic conditions. During the five-year fiscal period from June 30, 1934 to June 30, 1939, Crescent's total assets were less than doubled, but its surplus was increased thirty times. During the last fiscal year of said period its gross receipts were less than twice the amount of its gross receipts for the first fiscal year of said period, but its net profits (exclusive of dividends received) were more than five times those of the first year. During the five-year period, its net earnings (exclusive of dividends received) averaged about 35 per cent per annum, on its capitalization."

U. S. *v.* CRESCENT AMUSEMENT CO. **183**

which gave the defendant exhibitors the option of show-ing the pictures in their theatres a second time. In re-viewing one of these franchise agreements the District Court concluded, "The repeat-run clause in the franchise was completely effective in preventing the sale of a second-run of any Paramount features to any opposition theatre."

We are now told, however, that the independents were eliminated by the normal processes of competition; that their theatres were less attractive; that their service was inferior; that they were not as efficient businessmen as the defendants. We may assume that if a single exhibitor launched such a plan of economic warfare he would not run afoul of the Sherman Act.[5] But the vice of this under-taking was the combination of several exhibitors in a plan of concerted action. They had unity of purpose and unity of action. They pooled their buying power for a common end. It will not do to analogize this to a case where purchasing power is pooled so that the buyers may obtain more favorable terms. The plan here was to crush competition and to build a circuit for the exhibitors. The District Court found that some of the distributors were co-conspirators on certain phases of the program. But we can put that circumstance to one side and not stop to inquire whether the findings are adequate on that phase of the case. For it is immaterial whether the distributors technically were or were not members of the conspiracy. The showing of motion pictures is of course a local affair. But action by a combination of exhibitors to obtain an agreement with a distributor whereby commerce with a competing exhibitor is suppressed or restrained is a con-spiracy in restraint of trade and a conspiracy to monopo-

---

[5] A union of the exhibitor with a distributor in such a program would of course constitute a conspiracy under the Sherman Act as held in *Interstate Circuit* v. *United States*, 306 U. S. 208.

184 OCTOBER TERM, 1944.

Opinion of the Court. 323 U. S.

lize a part of the trade or commerce among the States, each of which is prohibited by the Sherman Act. And as we have said, the course of business which involves a regular exchange of films in interstate commerce is adequate to bring the exhibitors within the reach of the Sherman Act. *Interstate Circuit* v. *United States, supra.*

The exhibitors, however, claim that the findings against them on the facts must fall because of improper evidence. The evidence to which this objection is directed consists of letters or reports written by employees of certain of the major distributors to other employees or officers in the same company stating reasons why the distributor was discriminating against an independent in favor of the defendants. The United States asserts that these letters or reports were declarations of one conspirator in furtherance of the common objective and therefore admissible as evidence against all under the rule of *Hitchman Coal & Coke Co.* v. *Mitchell,* 245 U. S. 229, 249. And it is argued that it makes no difference that these distributors were dismissed out of the case (*Delaney* v. *United States,* 263 U. S. 586, 590) since they were charged with being co-conspirators and since the findings are with certain exceptions adequate to support the charge. We do not come to that question. The other evidence established the position of the distributors and their relations to the theatres involved, what the distributors in fact did, the combination of the defendants, the character and extent of their buying power, and how it was in fact used. This other evidence was sufficient to establish the restraints of trade and monopolistic practices; the purpose, character, and extent of the combination are inferable from it alone. Thus even if error be assumed in the introduction of the letters and reports, the burden of showing prejudice has not been sustained.

The defendants finally object to the findings on the ground that they were mainly taken verbatim from the

U. S. *v.* CRESCENT AMUSEMENT CO.   185

government's brief. The findings leave much to be desired in light of the function of the trial court. See *United States* v. *Forness,* 125 F. 2d 928, 942–943. But they are nonetheless the findings of the District Court. And they must stand or fall depending on whether they are supported by evidence. We think they are.

IV. The major controversy here has turned on the provisions of the decree.

A. *Objections of the United States.* The United States objects to the provision of the decree that no defendant exhibitor shall acquire a financial interest in any additional theatre outside Nashville in any town where there already is a theatre "unless the owner of such theatre should voluntarily offer to sell same to either of the exhibitor defendants, and when none of said defendants, their officers, agents or servants are guilty of any of the acts or practices prohibited by paragraph nine (9) hereof." Paragraph 9 referred to enjoins the defendants "from coercing or attempting to coerce independent operators into selling out to it, or to abandon plans to compete with it by predatory practices." It asks that there be substituted for that provision one which the District Court had earlier approved restraining such acquisitions "except after an affirmative showing that such acquisition will not unreasonably restrain competition."

The Court at times has rather freely modified decrees in Sherman Act cases where it approved the conclusions of the District Court as to the nature and character of the violations. *Standard Oil Co.* v. *United States,* 221 U. S. 1, 78–82. *United States* v. *American Tobacco Co.,* 221 U. S. 106, 184–188. We recognize however that there is a wide range of discretion in the District Court to mould the decree to the exigencies of the particular case; and where the findings of violations are sustained, we will not direct a recasting of the decree except on a showing of abuse of discretion. See *Ethyl Gasoline Corp.* v. *United*

States, 309 U. S. 436, 461; *United States* v. *Bausch & Lomb Co.,* 321 U. S. 707, 725, 728. We think this is a case where we should act lest the public interest not be adequately protected by the decree as cast.

The generality of this provision of the decree bids fair to call for a retrial of a Sherman Act case any time a citation for contempt is issued. The crucial facts in each case would be subtle ones as is usually true where purpose and motive are at issue. This type of provision is often the only practical remedy against continuation of illegal trade practices. But we are dealing here with a situation which permits of a more select treatment. The growth of this combine has been the result of predatory practices condemned by the Sherman Act. The object of the conspiracy was the destruction or absorption of competitors. It was successful in that endeavor. The pattern of past conduct is not easily forsaken. Where the proclivity for unlawful activity has been as manifest as here, the decree should operate as an effective deterrent to a repetition of the unlawful conduct and yet not stand as a barrier to healthy growth on a competitive basis. The acquisition of a competing theatre terminates at once its competition. Punishment for contempt does not restore the competition which has been eliminated. And where businesses have been merged or purchased and closed out it is commonly impossible to turn back the clock. Moreover if the District Court were to supervise future acquisitions in this case, it would not be undertaking an onerous and absorbing administrative burden. The burden would not seem more onerous than under the alternative provision where in substance the issue would be violation of the Sherman Act *vel non.*

These considerations impel us to conclude that the decree should be revised so as to prohibit future acquisitions of a financial interest in additional theatres outside of

U. S. *v.* CRESCENT AMUSEMENT CO.   187

Nashville "except after an affirmative showing that such acquisition will not unreasonably restrain competition."

B. *Objections of the Defendants.*   (1) The decree enjoins the defendant exhibitors from making franchises with certain distributors "with the purpose and effect of maintaining their theatre monopolies and preventing independent theatres from competing with them" and from entering into "any similar combinations and conspiracies having similar purposes and objects." The decree also enjoins them from combining, in licensing films, their closed towns with their competitive situations "for the purpose and with the effect of compelling the major distributors to license films on a non-competitive basis in competitive situations and to discriminate" against the independents. The decree also enjoins each defendant exhibitor "from conditioning the licensing of films in any competitive situation (outside Nashville) upon the licensing of films in any other theatre situation."

It is argued that these provisions will aggrandize the distributors at the expense of the exhibitors, that if such measures are taken they should be taken against the distributors, that they deprive the exhibitors of group purchasing power, that the franchise agreements are normal and necessary both for distributors and exhibitors, and that these provisions of the decree are so vague and general as to greatly burden the conduct of these businesses.

It is not for us, however, to pick and choose between competing business and economic theories in applying this law. Congress has made that choice. It has declared that the rule of trade and commerce should be competition, not combination. *United States* v. *Trenton Potteries Co.,* 273 U. S. 392, 397; *Fashion Originators' Guild* v. *Federal Trade Commission,* 312 U. S. 457, 465. Since Congress has made that choice, we cannot refuse to sustain a decree because by some other measure of the public good the result may not seem desirable. *United States* v. *Socony-Vacuum Oil Co.*, 310 U. S. 150, 221–222. The duty of the Court in these cases is "to frame its decree so as to suppress the unlawful practices and to take such reasonable measures as would preclude their revival." *Ethyl Gasoline Corp.* v. *United States, supra,* p. 461. The chief weapons used by this combination in its unlawful warfare were the franchise agreements and the licensing system. The fact that those instruments could be lawfully used does not mean that the defendants may leave the court unfettered. Civil suits under the Sherman Act would indeed be idle gestures if the injunction did not run against the continuance or resumption of the unlawful practice. And it is hard to see how the decree could be made less general and more specific. If it is a burden which cannot be lightened by application to the court for exercise of the power which it has reserved over the decree, it is a burden which those who have violated the Act must carry. And the fact that there may be somewhere in the background a greater conspiracy from which flow consequences more serious than we have here is no warrant for a refusal to deal with the lesser one which is before us.

(2) Serious complaint is made of the divestiture provisions of the decree. It requires each corporate exhibitor to divest itself of the ownership of any stock or other interest in any other corporate defendant or affiliated corporation,[6] and enjoins it from acquiring any interest in those companies. Sudekum is required to resign as an officer of any corporation (except Crescent) which is affiliated with any defendant exhibitor and he is enjoined from acquiring control over any such affiliate (except Crescent) by acting as officer or otherwise. Stengel is required to resign as

---

[6] Defined in the decree to exclude certain companies.

U. S. *v.* CRESCENT AMUSEMENT CO. 189

178 Opinion of the Court.

officer of the affiliates (except one corporation of his choice) and is enjoined from acquiring any control over the others by acting as an officer or otherwise. A year from the date of entry of the decree is allowed for completing this divestiture.

It is said that these provisions are inequitable and harsh income tax wise, that they exceed any reasonable requirement for the prevention of future violations, and that they are therefore punitive.

The Court has quite consistently recognized in this type of Sherman Act case that the government should not be confined to an injunction against further violations. Dissolution of the combination will be ordered where the creation of the combination is itself the violation. See *Northern Securities Co.* v. *United States,* 193 U. S. 197, 354–360; *Standard Oil Co.* v. *United States, supra; United States* v. *American Tobacco Co., supra,* pp. 186–188; *United States* v. *Union Pacific R. Co.,* 226 U. S. 61, 97; *United States* v. *Reading Co.,* 253 U. S. 26, 63; *United States* v. *Lehigh Valley R. Co.,* 254 U. S. 255; *United States* v. *Southern Pacific Co.,* 259 U. S. 214; *United States* v. *Corn Products Refining Co.,* 234 F. 964, 1018. Those who violate the Act may not reap the benefits of their violations and avoid an undoing of their unlawful project on the plea of hardship or inconvenience. That principle is adequate here to justify divestiture of all interest in some of the affiliates since their acquisition was part of the fruits of the conspiracy. But the relief need not, and under these facts should not, be so restricted. The fact that the companies were affiliated induced joint action and agreement. Common control was one of the instruments in bringing about unity of purpose and unity of action and in making the conspiracy effective. If that affiliation continues, there will be tempting opportunity for these exhibitors to continue to act in combination against the independents.   The proclivity in the past to use that affiliation for an unlawful end warrants effective assurance that no such opportunity will be available in the future.   Hence we do not think the District Court abused its discretion in failing to limit the relief to an injunction against future violations.   There is no reason why the protection of the public interest should depend solely on that somewhat cumbersome procedure when another effective one is available.

The fact that minority stockholders of the affiliated companies are not parties to the suit is no legal barrier to a separation of the companies.   *United States* v. *American Tobacco Co., supra.*   No legal right of one stockholder is normally affected if another stockholder is required to sell his stock.   And no exception to that rule has been shown to exist here.   Only business inconvenience and hardship are asserted.   It is said, however, that the decree requires Rockwood and Cherokee (two defendant exhibitors) to sell their respective half-interests in two companies which were not made parties to the proceedings. The argument is that the latter companies are indispensable parties if such divestiture is required.   Reliance is placed on *Minnesota* v. *Northern Securities Co.*, 184 U. S. 199.   In that case Minnesota brought an original action in this Court alleging that the acquisition by Northern Securities Co. of the majority stock of two railroad companies effected a consolidation of the railroads in violation of Minnesota law.   Minnesota asked, among other things, for an injunction against Northern Securities Co. voting the stock of those companies.   The Court held that the two railroad companies were indispensable parties; and since the jurisdiction of the Court would have been defeated if they were joined, leave to file the bill was denied. Denial of the right of a majority stockholder to vote his stock would deprive the corporation of a board of direc-

U. S. *v.* CRESCENT AMUSEMENT CO.   191

173   Opinion of the Court.

tors elected in accordance with state law. If such a step were taken, the corporation should be a party so that all corporate interests might be represented. *Minnesota* v. *Northern Securities Co.* goes no farther than that. Here there is no showing of any complication of that order. If such a complication appeared, the District Court could bring in the two affiliates as parties in order to effectuate the decree. *United States* v. *Southern Pacific Co., supra,* p. 241. But on this record it does not appear that if Rockwood and Cherokee are required to sell their half-interests in those companies any legal right of any other stockholder would be affected. Cf. *Morgan* v. *Struthers,* 131 U. S. 246.

We have considered the other contentions and find them without merit.

The appeal in No. 17 is dismissed.

The judgment in No. 18 is reversed.

The judgment in No. 19 is affirmed.

It is so ordered.

MR. JUSTICE FRANKFURTER, MR. JUSTICE MURPHY, and MR. JUSTICE JACKSON took no part in the consideration or decision of these cases.

MR. JUSTICE ROBERTS dissents.

U.S. v. GRIFFITH *

    The following case is copied from an official publica-

tion of the U.S. Superintendent of Documents, Government Print-

ing Office, Washington, D.C.

    This anti-trust action was filed against four affiliated

corporations and two individuals who were associated with them

as stockholders and officers (exhibitors in Oklahoma, Texas and

New Mexico). They had theatres in approximately 37 towns one

year, and in approximately 85 towns five years later.

*Supreme Court of the U.S. (1948), 334 U.S. 100, 68 S Ct 941,

    92 L Ed 1236.

100   OCTOBER TERM, 1947.

Syllabus.   334 U. S.

UNITED STATES v. GRIFFITH ET AL.

APPEAL FROM THE DISTRICT COURT OF THE UNITED STATES FOR THE WESTERN DISTRICT OF OKLAHOMA.

No. 64. Argued December 15, 1947.—Decided May 3, 1948.

1. Even in the absence of a specific intent to restrain or monopolize trade, it is violative of §§ 1 and 2 of the Sherman Act for four affiliated corporations operating motion picture theatres in numerous towns in three states and having no competitors in some of these towns to use the buying power of the entire circuit to obtain exclusive privileges from film distributors which prevent competitors from obtaining enough first- or second-run films to operate successfully. Pp. 101–110.

   (a) It is not always necessary to find a specific intent to restrain trade or to build a monopoly in order to find that §§ 1 and 2 of the Sherman Act have been violated. It is sufficient that a restraint of trade or monopoly results as the consequence of the defendants' conduct or business arrangements. P. 105.

   (b) Specific intent in the sense in which the common law used the term is necessary only where the acts fall short of the results prohibited by the Sherman Act. P. 105.

   (c) The use of monopoly power, however lawfully acquired, to foreclose competition, to gain a competitive advantage, or to destroy a competitor, is unlawful. Pp. 106–107.

   (d) It is unlawful for the operator of a circuit of motion picture theatres to use his monopoly in towns in which he has no competitors to obtain exclusive rights to films for towns in which he has competitors. Pp. 107–109.

   (e) The exhibitors in this case having combined with each other and with the distributors to obtain monopoly rights, had formed a conspiracy in violation of §§ 1 and 2 of the Sherman Act. P. 109.

2. The District Court having erroneously dismissed the complaint in this case without making adequate findings as to the effect of the practices found by this Court to be unlawful, the case is remanded to the District Court for further findings and the fashioning of a decree which will undo as near as may be the wrongs that were done and prevent their recurrence in the future. Pp. 109–110.

68 F. Supp. 180, reversed.

UNITED STATES *v.* GRIFFITH. 101

100 Opinion of the Court.

In a suit by the United States to restrain violations of §§ 1 and 2 of the Sherman Act, the District Court found that there was no violation of the Act and dismissed the complaint on the merits. 68 F. Supp. 180. On appeal to this Court, *reversed and remanded*, p. 110.

Robert L. Wright argued the cause for the United States. With him on the brief were *Solicitor General Perlman, Assistant Attorney General Sonnett, Milton A. Kallis* and *Robert W. Ginnane.*

Charles B. Cochran argued the cause for appellees. With him on the brief was *John B. Dudley.*

MR. JUSTICE DOUGLAS delivered the opinion of the Court.

This is a suit brought by the United States in the District Court to prevent and restrain appellees from violating §§ 1 and 2 of the Sherman Act. 26 Stat. 209, as amended, 50 Stat. 693, 15 U. S. C. §§ 1, 2. The District Court, finding there was no violation of the Act in any of the respects charged in the complaint, dismissed the complaint on the merits. 68 F. Supp. 180. The case is here by appeal under § 2 of the Expediting Act of February 11, 1903, 32 Stat. 823, as amended, 15 U. S. C. § 29, and § 238 of the Judicial Code, as amended by the Act of February 13, 1925, 43 Stat. 936, 938, 28 U. S. C. § 345.

The appellees are four affiliated corporations and two individuals who are associated with them as stockholders and officers.[1] The corporations operate (or own stock in

___

[1] Griffith Amusement Co., Consolidated Theatres, Inc., R. E. Griffith Theatres, Inc., Westex Theatres, Inc., H. J. Griffith, and L. C. Griffith. R. E. Griffith, a brother of H. J. and L. C. Griffith, was a defendant, but died while the suit was pending in the District Court and the action was not revived against his estate or personal representative.

Opinion of the Court.   334 U. S.

corporations which operate) moving picture theatres in Oklahoma, Texas, and New Mexico. With minor exceptions, the theatres which each corporation owns do not compete with those of its affiliates but are in separate towns. In April, 1939, when the complaint was filed, the corporate appellees had interests in theatres in 85 towns. In 32 of those towns there were competing theatres. Fifty-three of the towns (62 per cent) were closed towns, *i. e.* towns in which there were no competing theatres. Five years earlier the corporate appellees had theatres in approximately 37 towns, 18 of which were competitive and 19 of which (51 per cent) were closed. It was during that five-year period that the acts and practices occurred which, according to the allegations of the complaint, constitute violations of §§ 1 and 2 of the Sherman Act.

Prior to the 1938–1939 season these exhibitors used a common agent to negotiate with the distributors for films for the entire circuit.[2] Beginning with the 1938–1939 season one agent negotiated for the circuit represented by two of the corporate appellees, and another agent negotiated for the circuit represented by the other two corporate appellees. A master agreement was usually executed with each distributor covering films to be released by the distributor during an entire season.[3] There were variations among the master agreements. But in the main they provided as follows: (a) They lumped together towns in which the appellees had no competition and towns in which there were competing

---

[2] The circuit includes the four corporate appellees and their affiliated exhibitors. When less than the full ownership of a theatre was acquired, the contract would provide that the buying and booking of films was exclusively in the hands of the Griffith interests.

[3] The agreement negotiated by the common agent would be executed between a distributor and each of the corporate appellees or between a distributor and an individual exhibitor.

UNITED STATES *v.* GRIFFITH. 103

100 Opinion of the Court.

theatres. (b) They generally licensed the first-run exhibition in practically all of the theatres in which appellees had a substantial interest of substantially all of the films to be released by the distributor during the period of a year.[4] (c) They specified the towns for which second runs were licensed for exhibition by appellees, the second-run rental sometimes being included in the first-run rental. (d) The rental specified often was the total minimum required to be paid (in equal weekly or quarterly installments) by the circuit as a whole for use of the films throughout the circuit, the appellees subsequently allocating the rental among the theatres where the films were exhibited. (e) Films could be played out of the order of their release, so that a specified film need not be played in a particular theatre at any specified time.[5]

The complaint charged that certain exclusive privileges which these agreements granted the appellee exhibitors over their competitors unreasonably restrained competition by preventing their competitors from obtaining enough first- or second-run films from the distributors[6] to operate successfully. The exclusive privileges charged as violations were preemption in the selection of films and the receipt of clearances over competing theatres. It

---

[4] There were a few franchise agreements covering films to be released by a distributor during a term of years, usually for three years and in one instance for five years.

The theatres of appellees in Oklahoma City were second, not first, run theatres.

[5] The privilege was frequently conditioned on the playing of, or paying for, a designated quantity of the film obligation during stated portions of the season.

[6] Those are the eight major film distributors who originally were defendants. The charge that these distributors conspired with each other was eliminated from the complaint and they were dismissed as defendants by stipulation or on motion of appellant. But the charge that each of the distributors had conspired with the appellee exhibitors was retained.

104   OCTOBER TERM, 1947.

also charged that the use of the buying power of the entire circuit in acquiring those exclusive privileges violated the Act.

The District Court found no conspiracy between the appellee exhibitors or between them and the distributors, which violated the Act. It found that the agreements under which films were distributed were not in restraint of trade; that the appellees did not monopolize or attempt to monopolize the licensing or supply of film for first run or for any subsequent run; that the appellees did not conspire to compel the distributors to grant them the exclusive privilege of selecting films before the films were made available to any competing exhibitor; that there was no agreement between defendants and distributors granting defendants unreasonable clearances; that the appellees did not compel or attempt to compel distributors to grant them privileges not granted their competitors or which gave them any substantial advantage over their competitors; and that appellees did not condition the licensing of films in any competitive situation on the licensing of such films in a non-competitive situation, or *vice versa*.

The appellant introduced evidence designed to show the effect of the master agreements in some twenty-odd competitive situations. The District Court made detailed findings on this phase of the case to the effect that difficulties which competitors had in getting desirable films after appellee exhibitors entered their towns, the inroads appellees made on the business of competitors, and the purchases by appellees of their competitors were not the result of threats or coercion nor the result of an unlawful conspiracy, but solely the consequence of lawful competitive practices.

In *United States* v. *Crescent Amusement Co.*, 323 U. S. 173, a group of affiliated exhibitors, such as we have in the present case, were found to have violated §§ 1 and 2 of the Sherman Act by the pooling of their buying power

UNITED STATES *v.* GRIFFITH. 105

and the negotiation of master agreements similar to those we have here. A difference between that case and the present one, which the District Court deemed to be vital, was that in the former the buying power was used for the avowed purpose of eliminating competition and of acquiring a monopoly of theatres in the several towns, while no such purpose was found to exist here. To be more specific, the defendants in the former case through the pooling of their buying power increased their leverage over their competitive situations by insisting that they be given monopoly rights in towns where they had competition, else they would give a distributor no business in their closed towns.

It is, however, not always necessary to find a specific intent to restrain trade or to build a monopoly in order to find that the anti-trust laws have been violated. It is sufficient that a restraint of trade or monopoly results as the consequence of a defendant's conduct or business arrangements. *United States* v. *Patten*, 226 U. S. 525, 543; *United States* v. *Masonite Corp.*, 316 U. S. 265, 275. To require a greater showing would cripple the Act. As stated in *United States* v. *Aluminum Co. of America*, 148 F. 2d 416, 432, "no monopolist monopolizes unconscious of what he is doing." Specific intent in the sense in which the common law used the term is necessary only where the acts fall short of the results condemned by the Act. The classical statement is that of Mr. Justice Holmes speaking for the Court in *Swift & Co.* v. *United States*, 196 U. S. 375, 396:

"Where acts are not sufficient in themselves to produce a result which the law seeks to prevent—for instance, the monopoly—but require further acts in addition to the mere forces of nature to bring that result to pass, an intent to bring it to pass is necessary in order to produce a dangerous probability that it will happen. *Commonwealth* v. *Peaslee*, 177 Massachusetts, 267, 272.   But when that intent and the consequent dangerous probability exist, this statute, like many others and like the common law in some cases, directs itself against that dangerous probability as well as against the completed result."

And see *United States* v. *Aluminum Co. of America, supra,* pp. 431–432.   And so, even if we accept the District Court's findings that appellees had no intent or purpose unreasonably to restrain trade or to monopolize, we are left with the question whether a necessary and direct result of the master agreements was the restraining or monopolizing of trade within the meaning of the Sherman Act.

Anyone who owns and operates the single theatre in a town, or who acquires the exclusive right to exhibit a film, has a monopoly in the popular sense.   But he usually does not violate § 2 of the Sherman Act unless he has acquired or maintained his strategic position, or sought to expand his monopoly, or expanded it by means of those restraints of trade which are cognizable under § 1.   For those things which are condemned by § 2 are in large measure merely the end products of conduct which violates § 1.   *Standard Oil Co.* v. *United States,* 221 U. S. 1, 61.   But that is not always true.   Section 1 covers contracts, combinations, or conspiracies in restraint of trade.[7]   Section 2 is not restricted to conspiracies or combinations to monopolize[8] but also makes it a crime for any person to monopolize or to attempt to monopolize any part of

---

[7] Section 1 provides: "Every contract, combination in the form of trust or otherwise, or conspiracy, in restraint of trade or commerce among the several States, or with foreign nations, is hereby declared to be illegal. . . ."

[8] Section 2 provides: "Every person who shall monopolize, or attempt to monopolize, or combine or conspire with any other person or persons, to monopolize any part of the trade or commerce among the several States, or with foreign nations, shall be deemed guilty of a misdemeanor . . . ."

UNITED STATES *v.* GRIFFITH.   107

interstate or foreign trade or commerce. So it is that monopoly power, whether lawfully or unlawfully acquired, may itself constitute an evil and stand condemned under § 2 even though it remains unexercised.[9] For § 2 of the Act is aimed, *inter alia*, at the acquisition or retention of effective market control. See *United States* v. *Aluminum Co. of America*, 148 F. 2d 416, 428, 429. Hence the existence of power "to exclude competition when it is desired to do so" is itself a violation of § 2, provided it is coupled with the purpose or intent to exercise that power. *American Tobacco Co.* v. *United States*, 328 U. S. 781, 809, 811, 814. It is indeed "unreasonable, *per se*, to foreclose competitors from any substantial market." *International Salt Co.* v. *United States*, 332 U. S. 392, 396. The anti-trust laws are as much violated by the prevention of competition as by its destruction. *United States* v. *Aluminum Co. of America, supra.* It follows *a fortiori* that the use of monopoly power, however lawfully acquired, to foreclose competition, to gain a competitive advantage, or to destroy a competitor, is unlawful.

A man with a monopoly of theatres in any one town commands the entrance for all films into that area. If he uses that strategic position to acquire exclusive privileges in a city where he has competitors, he is employing his monopoly power as a trade weapon against his competitors. It may be a feeble, ineffective weapon where he has only one closed or monopoly town. But as those towns increase in number throughout a region, his monopoly power in them may be used with crushing effect on competitors in other places.[10] He need

---

[9] So also a conspiracy to monopolize violates § 2 even though monopoly power was never acquired. *American Tobacco Co.* v. *United States*, 328 U. S. 781, 789.

[10] It was said in *United States* v. *United States Steel Corp.*, 251 U. S. 417, 451, that mere size is not outlawed by § 2. But size is of course an earmark of monopoly power. Moreover, as stated by

108   OCTOBER TERM, 1947.

Opinion of the Court.   334 U. S.

not be as crass as the exhibitors in *United States* v. *Crescent Amusement Co.*, *supra*, in order to make his monopoly power effective in his competitive situations. Though he makes no threat to withhold the business of his closed or monopoly towns unless the distributors give him the exclusive film rights in the towns where he has competitors, the effect is likely to be the same where the two are joined. When the buying power of the entire circuit is used to negotiate films for his competitive as well as his closed towns, he is using monopoly power to expand his empire. And even if we assume that a specific intent to accomplish that result is absent, he is chargeable in legal contemplation with that purpose since the end result is the necessary and direct consequence of what he did. *United States* v. *Patten*, *supra*, p. 543.

The consequence of such a use of monopoly power is that films are licensed on a non-competitive basis in what would otherwise be competitive situations. That is the effect whether one exhibitor makes the bargain with the distributor or whether two or more exhibitors lump together their buying power, as appellees did here. It is in either case a misuse of monopoly power under the Sherman Act. If monopoly power can be used *to beget* monopoly, the Act becomes a feeble instrument indeed. Large-scale buying is not, of course, unlawful *per se*. It may yield price or other lawful advantages to the buyer. It may not, however, be used to monopolize or to attempt to monopolize interstate trade or commerce. Nor, as we hold in *United States* v. *Paramount Pictures, Inc.*, *post*, p. 131, may it be used to stifle competition by denying competitors less favorably situated access to the market.

Justice Cardozo, speaking for the Court in *United States* v *Swift & Co.*, 286 U. S. 106, 116, "size carries with it an opportunity for abuse that is not to be ignored when the opportunity is proved to have been utilized in the past."

UNITED STATES *v.* GRIFFITH.   109

100   Opinion of the Court.

Appellees were concededly using their circuit buying power to obtain films. Their closed towns were linked with their competitive towns. No effort of concealment was made as evidenced by the fact that the rental specified was at times the total minimum amount required to be paid by the circuit as a whole. Monopoly rights in the form of certain exclusive privileges were bargained for and obtained. These exclusive privileges, being acquired by the use of monopoly power, were unlawfully acquired. The appellees, having combined with each other and with the distributors to obtain those monopoly rights, formed a conspiracy in violation of §§ 1 and 2 of the Act. It is plain from the course of business that the commerce affected was interstate. *United States* v. *Crescent Amusement Co., supra,* pp. 180, 183–184.

What effect these practices actually had on the competitors of appellee exhibitors or on the growth of the Griffith circuit we do not know. The District Court, having started with the assumption that the use of circuit buying power was wholly lawful, naturally attributed no evil to it and thus treated the master agreements as legitimate weapons of competition. Since it found that no competitors were driven out of business, or acquired by appellees, or impeded in their business by threats or coercion, it concluded that appellees had not violated the Sherman Act in any of the ways charged in the complaint. These findings are plainly inadequate if we start, as we must, from the premise that the circuit buying power was unlawfully employed. On the record as we read it, it cannot be doubted that the monopoly power of appellees had some effect on their competitors and on the growth of the Griffith circuit. Its extent must be determined on a remand of the cause. We remit to the District Court not only that problem but also the fashioning of a decree which will undo as near as may be the wrongs that were done and prevent their recurrence in the future. See *United*

110 OCTOBER TERM, 1947.

States v. *Crescent Amusement Co., supra,* pp. 189–190;
Schine Chain Theatres v. *United States, post,* p. 110;
United States v. *Paramount Pictures, Inc., post,* p. 131.

Reversed.

MR. JUSTICE FRANKFURTER dissents, substantially for the reasons set forth in the opinion of the District Court, 68 F. Supp. 180.

MR. JUSTICE MURPHY and MR. JUSTICE JACKSON took no part in the consideration or decision of this case.

SCHINE CHAIN THEATRES, INC. ET AL. v. UNITED STATES.

APPEAL FROM THE DISTRICT COURT OF THE UNITED STATES FOR THE WESTERN DISTRICT OF NEW YORK.

No. 10. Argued December 15, 1947.—Decided May 3, 1948.

The United States sued to restrain violations of §§ 1 and 2 of the Sherman Act by a parent corporation, three of its officers and directors and five of its subsidiaries, which owned or had a financial interest in a large chain of motion picture theatres located in six states. The District Court found that they had used the combined buying power of the entire circuit to negotiate master agreements with the major film distributors, which had the effect of depriving competitors of first- and second-run films; obtained from the distributors unreasonable "clearances," long-term agreements for rentals of films and other concessions which gave them unreasonable advantages over competitors; threatened to build theatres or to open closed theatres in order to stop or prevent competition; cut admission prices; obtained from competitors whom they bought out agreements not to compete for long terms of years, which sometimes extended to towns other than those in which the purchased theatres operated; and thus conspired with each other and with the eight major film distributors to violate §§ 1 and 2 of the Sherman Act. The District Court enjoined these practices and ordered defendants to divest themselves of certain theatres. Defendants appealed. *Held:*

SCHINE CHAIN THEATRES, INC. v. U.S.

Supreme Court of the U.S. (1948) 334 U.S. 110, 68 S Ct 947, 92 L Ed
1245.

The following extracts of the Supreme Court of the
United States opinion in this case are copied from an official
publication of the U.S. Superintendent of Documents, Government
Printing Office, Washington, D.C.

" . . . .

SCHINE CHAIN THEATRES, INC. ET AL.

V.

UNITED STATES.

APPEAL FROM THE DISTRICT COURT OF THE UNITED STATES

FOR THE WESTERN DISTRICT OF NEW YORK.

No. 10.   Argued December 15, 1947. - Decided May 3, 1948.

The United States sued to restrain violations of Sections 1 and 2 of the Sherman Act by a parent corporation, three
of its officers and directors and five of its subsidiaries, which
owned interest in a large chain of motion picture theatres located
in six states. The District Court found that they had used the
combined buying power of the entire circuit to negotiate master
agreements with the major film distributors, which had the effect of depriving competitors of first-and second-run films; obtained from the distributors unreasonable 'clearances,' long-term
agreements for rentals of films and other concessions which gave

them unreasonable advantages over competitors; threatened to

build theatres or to open closed theatres in order to stop or

prevent competition; cut admission prices; obtained from com-

petitors whom they bought out agreements not to compete for long

terms of years, which sometimes extended to towns other than

those in which the purchased theatres operated; and thus con-

spired with each other and with the eight major film distributors

to violate Sections 1 and 2 of the Sherman Act. The District

Court enjoined these practices and ordered defendants to divest

themselves of certain theatres. Defendants appealed. *Held:*

The judgment of the District Court is affirmed in part and re-

versed in part and the cause is remanded to it for proceedings

in conformity with this opinion. . . ."

"This is a companion case to No. 64, United States v.

Griffith (334 US 101, ante, 1240, 68 S Ct 941), and is here by

way of appeal from the District Court. The appellants, who were

defendants below, are a parent company, three of its officers

and directors, and five of its wholly owned subsidiaries - to

whom we refer collectively as Schine. As of May 19, 1942, Schine

owned or had a financial interest in a chain of approximately

148 motion picture theatres located in 76 towns in 6 states,

the greater portion being 78 theatres in 41 towns in New York

and 36 theatres in 17 towns in Ohio. Of the 76 towns, 60 were

closed towns, i.e., places where Schine had the only theatre or

all the theatres in town. This chain was acquired beginning in

in 1920 and is the largest independent theatre circuit in the
country. Since 1931 Schine acquired 118 theatres. Since 1928
the closed towns increased by 56. In 1941 there were only three
towns in which Schine's competitors were playing major film
products." . . . .

" . . . . the combining of the open and closed towns
for the negotiation of films for the circuit was a restraint of
trade and the use of monopoly power in violation of Section 1
and Section 2 of the Act. The concerted action of the parent
company, its subsidiaries, and the named officers and directors
in that endeavor was a conspiracy which was not immunized by
reason of the fact that the members were closely affiliated
rather than independent." . . . . "The negotiations which Schine
had with the distributors resulted in the execution of master
agreements between the distributors and exhibitors. This
brought the distributors into unlawful combinations with the
Schine defendants." . . . .

"As we read the evidence underlying this finding, it
was the use of Schine's monopoly power - represented by combining the buying power of the open and closed towns - which enabled
it to obtain that which its competitors could not obtain. Depri-
vation of competitors of first- and second-run pictures in that
way was indeed arbitrary in the sense that it was the product of
monopoly power, not of competitive forces." . . . .

"For the franchise agreements as employed by Schine are

unreasonable restraints of trade for the reasons stated; and

they must be permanently enjoined, even though we assume their

collateral aspects are not accurately described by the District

Court and so may not be condemned." . . . .

   "We reach the same result as respects the agreements

not to compete which Schine exacted from competitors whom it

bought out. It is not enough that the agreements may be valid

under local law. Even an otherwise lawful device may be used

as a weapon in restraint of trade or in an effort to monopolize

a part of trade or commerce. Agreements not to compete have at

times been used for that unlawful purpose." . . . .

   "There is evidence to support the findings that minimum

prices were fixed. It is well settled that the fixing of minimum

prices like other types of price fixing, is unlawful per se." . . .

   "For the self-interest of exhibitors which would call

for long clearances would militate against the best interests

of distributors." . . . .

   "We accordingly set aside the divestiture provisions

of the decree so that the District Court can make the findings

necessary for an appropriate decree. We approve the dissolution

of the pooling agreements, the prohibition against buying or

booking films for theatres in which Schine has no financial in-

terest, and the restriction on future acquisitions of theatres.

See United States v. Crescent Amusement Co. supra (323 US pp

185-187, 89 L ed 169-171, 65 S Ct 254). We do not reach the

the question of the appointment of a trustee to sell theatres
as that merely implements the divestiture provisions which must
be reconsidered by the District Court.

The judgment of the District Court is affirmed in part
and reversed in part and the cause is remanded to it for proceedings in conformity with this opinion.

So ordered.

Mr. Justice *Frankfurter* concurs in the result.

Mr. Justice *Murphy* and Mr. Justice *Jackson* took no
part in the consideration or decision of the case.

U.S. v. PARAMOUNT PICTURES, INC. *

The following case is copied from an official publication of the U.S. Superintendent of Documents, Government
Printing Office, Washington, D.C.

Of interest are the sub-headings.

First - Restraint of Trade:

      (1) Price Fixing
      (2) Clearances and Runs
      (3) Pooling Agreements; Joint Ownership
      (4) Formula Deals, Master Agreements and
            Franchises
      (5) Block Booking
      (6) Discrimination

Second - Competitive Bidding.

Third - Monopoly, Expansion of Theatre Holdings,
       Divestiture.

Fourth - (Arbitration)

Fifth - Intervention.

Several tables are interesting, such as "Theatres
jointly owned with independents," "Theatres jointly owned by
two defendants," "The number of feature films released during
the 1943-1944 season by the eleven largest distributors."

Mr. Justice Douglas delivered the opinion of the Supreme
Court. Mr. Justice Jackson took no part in the consideration or
decision of these cases. Mr. Justice Frankfurter dissented in
part.

*Supreme Court of the U.S., (1948), 334 U.S. 131, 68 S Ct 915,
  92 L Ed 1260.*

UNITED STATES *v.* PARAMOUNT PICTURES. 131

Syllabus.

UNITED STATES *v.* PARAMOUNT PICTURES, INC. ET AL.

NO. 79. APPEAL FROM THE DISTRICT COURT OF THE UNITED STATES FOR THE SOUTHERN DISTRICT OF NEW YORK.*

Argued February 9–11, 1948.—Decided May 3, 1948.

The United States sued to restrain violations of §§ 1 and 2 of the Sherman Act by (1) five corporations which produce motion pictures and their respective subsidiaries or affiliates which distribute and exhibit films and own or control theatres, (2) two corporations which produce motion pictures and their subsidiaries which distribute films, and (3) one corporation engaged only in the distribution of motion pictures. The complaint charged that the first group of defendants conspired to and did restrain and monopolize interstate trade in the exhibition of motion pictures in most of the larger cities of the country and that their combination of producing, distributing and exhibiting motion pictures violated §§ 1 and 2 of the Act. It also charged that all of the defendants, as distributors, conspired to and did restrain and monopolize interstate trade in the distribution and exhibition of films. After a trial, the District Court granted an injunction and other relief. *Held:*

   1. The District Court's finding that price-fixing conspiracies existed between all defendants and between each distributor-defendant and its licensees, which resulted in exhibitors being required to charge substantially uniform minimum admission prices, is sustained. Pp. 141–142.

   2. Its injunction against defendants or their affiliates granting any license (except to their own theatres) in which minimum prices for admission to a theatre are fixed, is sustained. Pp. 142–144.

---

*Together with No. 80, *Loew's, Incorporated et al.* v. *United States;* No. 81, *Paramount Pictures, Inc. et al.* v. *United States;* No. 82, *Columbia Pictures Corp. et al.* v. *United States;* No. 83, *United Artists Corp.* v. *United States;* No. 84, *Universal Corp. et al.* v. *United States;* No. 85, *American Theatres Assn., Inc. et al.* v. *United States et al.;* and No. 86, *Allred et al.* v. *United States et al.,* also on appeal from the same court.

(a) The fact that defendants owned copyrights to their films and merely licensed their use by exhibitors did not entitle them to conspire with each other to fix uniform prices of admission to be charged by exhibitors. P. 143.

(b) Nor did it justify the conspiracy between each distributor-defendant and its licensees to fix and maintain uniform minimum admission prices which had the effect of suppressing price competition between exhibitors. Pp. 143–144.

(c) A copyright may no more be used than a patent to deter competition between rivals in the exploitation of their licenses. P. 144.

3. The District Court's finding that there was a conspiracy to restrain trade by imposing unreasonable "clearances" is sustained. Pp. 144–147.

4. Its injunction against defendants and their affiliates agreeing with each other or with any exhibitors or distributors to maintain a system of "clearances," or granting any "clearance" between theatres not in substantial competition, or granting or enforcing any "clearance" against theatres in substantial competition with the theatre receiving the license for exhibition in excess of what is reasonably necessary to protect the licensee, is sustained. Pp. 147–148.

(a) A request that it be construed or modified so as to allow licensors in granting "clearances" to take into consideration what is reasonably necessary for a fair return to the licensor is rejected. Pp. 147–148.

(b) In the setting of this case, the only measure of reasonableness of a clearance by Sherman Act standards is the special needs of the licensee for the competitive advantages it affords. P. 148.

5. A provision of the decree that, "Whenever any clearance provision is attacked as not legal . . . the burden shall be upon the distributor to sustain the legality thereof," is sustained. P. 148.

6. The District Court's finding that the exhibitor-defendants had "pooling agreements" whereby normally competitive theatres were operated as a unit, or managed by a joint committee or by one of the exhibitors, the profits being shared according to prearranged percentages, and that these agreements resulted in the elimination of competition *pro tanto* both in exhibition and in distribution of feature pictures, is sustained. P. 149.

UNITED STATES *v.* PARAMOUNT PICTURES. 133

131   Syllabus.

7. Its requirement that existing "pooling agreements" be dissolved and its injunction against any future arrangement of that character are sustained. P. 149.

8. Its findings as to the restraint of trade by means of arrangements under which many theatres are owned jointly by two or more exhibitor-defendants, its requirement that the exhibitor-defendants terminate such joint ownership of theatres, and its injunction against future acquisitions of such interests, are sustained. Pp. 149–151.

9. Its order that certain other relationships involving joint ownership of theatres by an exhibitor-defendant and an independent be dissolved and its injunction against future acquisitions of such joint interests must be revised after further inquiries and findings upon remand of the cases. Pp. 151–153.

(a) It erred in failing to inquire into the circumstances under which each particular interest had been acquired and in treating all relationships alike in this portion of the decree. P. 152.

(b) To the extent that these acquisitions were the fruits of monopolistic practices or restraints of trade, they should be divested and no permission to buy out the other owner should be given a defendant. P. 152.

(c) Even if lawfully acquired, divestiture of such interests would be justified if they have been utilized as part of the conspiracy to eliminate or suppress competition. P. 152.

(d) If the joint ownership is an alliance with one who is or would be an operator but for the joint ownership, divorce should be decreed, even though the affiliation was innocently acquired. P. 153.

(e) In those instances where joint ownership involves no more than innocent investments by those who are not actual or potential operators and it was not used in furtherance of the conspiracy and did not result in a monopoly, its retention by defendants would be justified and they might be given permission to acquire the interests of the independents on a showing by them and a finding by the Court that neither monopoly nor unreasonable restraint of trade in the exhibition of films would result.   P. 153.

10. The District Court's findings that certain "formula deals" covering the exhibition of feature pictures in entire circuits of theatres and certain "master agreements" covering their exhibition in two or more theatres in a particular circuit unlawfully restrain

134   OCTOBER TERM, 1947.

trade, and its injunction against the making or further performance of such arrangements, are sustained. Pp. 153–155.

(a) Such arrangements are devices for stifling competition
and diverting the cream of the business to the large operators.
P. 154.

(b) The pooling of the purchasing power of an entire circuit
in bidding for films is a misuse of monopoly power insofar as it
combines theatres having no competitors with those having competitors. *United States* v. *Griffith, ante,* p. 100; *Schine Chain
Theatres* v. *United States, ante,* p. 110.   Pp. 154–155.

(c) Distributors who join in such arrangements by exhibitors
are active participants in effectuating a restraint of trade and a
monopolistic practice. P. 155.

11. The findings of the District Court with reference to "franchises" whereby exhibitors obtain all feature pictures released by
a distributor over a period of more than a motion picture season
are set aside, so that the court may examine the problem in the
light of the elimination from the decree of the provision for competitive bidding. Pp. 155–156.

12. On the record in this case, it cannot be said that "franchises"
are illegal *per se* when extended to any theatre or circuit no matter
how small. P. 156.

13. The findings of the District Court as to "block-booking"
and its injunction against defendants performing or entering into
any license in which the right to exhibit one feature is conditioned
upon the licensee's taking one or more other features, are sustained.
Pp. 156–159.

(a) The result of this practice is to add to the monopoly of
the copyright in violation of the principle of the patent cases involving tying clauses. P. 158.

(b) *Transparent-Wrap Machine Corp.* v. *Stokes & Smith Co.,*
329 U. S. 637, distinguished. P. 159.

(c) The selling of films in blocks or groups, when there is
no requirement, express or implied, for the purchase of more than
one film is not illegal; but it is illegal to refuse to license one or
more copyrights unless another copyright is accepted. P. 159.

14. The provision of the decree regulating the practice of "blind-
selling," whereby a distributor licenses a feature picture before
the exhibitor is afforded an opportunity to view it, is sustained.
P. 157, n. 11.

15. The District Court's findings that defendants had unreasonably discriminated against small independent exhibitors and in

UNITED STATES *v.* PARAMOUNT PICTURES. 135

favor of large affiliated and unaffiliated circuits through various kinds of contract provisions and that these discriminations resulted in restraints of trade in violation of the Sherman Act, are sustained. Pp. 159–160.

16. On remand of these cases, the District Court should provide effective relief against continuance of these discriminatory practices, in the light of the elimination from the decree of the provision for competitive bidding. P. 161.

17. That large exhibitors with whom defendants dealt fathered the illegal practices and forced them onto defendants is no excuse, if true; since acquiescence in an illegal scheme is as much a violation of the Sherman Act as the creation and promotion of one. P. 161.

18. The requirement of the decree that films be licensed on a competitive bidding basis should be eliminated, because it would involve the judiciary too deeply in the daily operation of this nation-wide business and would uproot business arrangements and established relationships without opening up to competition the markets which defendants' unlawful restraints have dominated. Pp. 161–166.

19. On remand of these cases, the freedom of the District Court to reconsider the adequacy of the decree in the light of the elimination of the provision for competitive bidding is not limited to those parts specifically indicated. P. 166.

20. Motion pictures, like newspapers and radio, are included in the press whose freedom is guaranteed by the First Amendment; but the problem involved in these cases bears only remotely, if at all, on any question of freedom of the press, save only as timeliness of release may be a factor of importance in specific situations. Pp. 166–167.

21. The findings of the District Court on the subjects of monopoly in exhibition and the need for divestiture are set aside as being deficient in the light of the principles stated in this opinion, in *United States* v. *Griffith, ante,* p. 100, and in *Schine Chain Theatres* v. *United States, ante,* p. 110, and because of the elimination from the decree of the provisions for competitive bidding. The injunction against the five major defendants expanding their theatre holdings in any manner is also set aside, in order that the District Court may make an entirely fresh start on these phases of the problems. Pp. 167–175.

(a) In determining the need for divestiture, it is not enough to conclude, as the District Court did, that none of the defendants was organized or has been maintained for the purpose of achieving a "national monopoly," nor that the five major defendants through their present theatre holdings "alone" do not and cannot collectively or individually have a monopoly of exhibition. P. 171.

(b) When the starting point is a conspiracy to effect a monopoly through restraints of trade, it is relevant to determine what the results of the conspiracy were, even if they fell short of monopoly. P. 171.

(c) While a monopoly resulting from the ownership of the only theatre in a town usually does not constitute a violation of the Sherman Act, even such an ownership is vulnerable in a suit under the Sherman Act if the property was acquired, or its strategic position maintained, as a result of practices which constitute unreasonable restraints of trade. *United States* v. *Griffith, ante,* p. 100. P. 171.

(d) The problem of the District Court did not end with enjoining continuance of the unlawful restraints nor with dissolving the combination which launched their conspiracy; its function includes also undoing what the conspiracy achieved. P. 171.

(e) The problem under the Sherman Act is not solved merely by measuring monopoly in terms of size or extent of holdings or by concluding that single ownerships were not obtained "for the purpose of achieving a national monopoly." P. 172.

(f) It is the relationship of the unreasonable restraints of trade to the position of the defendants in the exhibition field (and more particularly in the first-run phase of that business) that is of first importance on the divestiture phase of these cases. P. 172.

(g) The fruits of the conspiracy must be denied to the five major defendants, as they were to the independents in *Schine Chain Theatres* v. *United States, ante,* p. 110. P. 172.

(h) Section 1 of the Sherman Act outlaws unreasonable restraints irrespective of the amount of trade or commerce involved and § 2 condemns monopoly of any appreciable part of trade or commerce. P. 173.

(i) Specific intent is not a necessary element of a purpose or intent to create a monopoly; the requisite purpose or intent is present if monopoly results as a necessary consequence of what was done. P. 173.

(j) Monopoly power, whether lawfully or unlawfully acquired, may violate § 2 of the Sherman Act though it remains unexercised; the existence of the power to exclude competition when it is

UNITED STATES *v.* PARAMOUNT PICTURES.   137

desired to do so is itself a violation of § 2, if it is coupled with the purpose or intent to exercise that power.   P. 173.

(k) The setting aside of the provision of the decree enjoining the five major defendants from further expanding their theatre holdings is not to be taken as intimating in any way that the District Court erred in including this prohibition.   P. 175.

22. Vertical integration of producing, distributing and exhibiting motion pictures is not illegal *per se;* its legality depends upon (1) the purpose or intent with which it was conceived or (2) the power it creates and the attendant purpose or intent.   Pp. 173–174.

(a) It violates the Sherman Act if it was a calculated scheme to gain control over an appreciable segment of the market and to restrain or suppress competition, rather than an expansion to meet legitimate business needs.   P. 174.

(b) A vertically integrated enterprise will constitute a monopoly which, though unexercised, violates the Sherman Act, if a power to exclude competition is coupled with a purpose or intent to do so.   P. 174.

(c) The fact that the power created by size was utilized in the past to crush or prevent competition is potent evidence that the requisite purpose or intent attends the presence of monopoly power.   P. 174.

(d) Likewise bearing on the question whether monopoly power is created by a vertical integration, is the nature of the market to be served and the leverage on the market which the particular vertical integration creates or makes possible.   P. 174.

23. Whether an injunction against the licensing of films among the five major defendants would, in the absence of competitive bidding, serve as a short-range remedy in certain situations to dissipate the effects of the conspiracy is a question for the District Court.   P. 175.

24. The District Court has no power to force or require parties to submit to arbitration in lieu of the remedies afforded by Congress for enforcing the antitrust laws; but it may authorize the maintenance of a voluntary system of arbitration by those parties who consent, and it may provide the rules and procedure under which such a system is to operate.   P. 176.

(a) The Government did not consent to a permanent system of arbitration under the consent decree.   P. 176.

(b) Whether a voluntary system of arbitration should be inaugurated is for the discretion of the District Court.   P. 176.

138   OCTOBER TERM, 1947.

25. In view of the elimination from the decree of the provision for competitive bidding, the District Court's denial of motions of certain associations of exhibitors and a number of independent exhibitors for leave to intervene in opposition to the system of competitive bidding is affirmed and their motions for leave to intervene in this Court are denied.   Pp. 176–178.

66 F. Supp. 323; 70 F. Supp. 53, affirmed in part and reversed in part.

In a suit by the United States to restrain violations of §§ 1 and 2 of the Sherman Act by major motion picture producers, distributors and exhibitors, the District Court granted an injunction and other relief. 66 F. Supp. 323; 70 F. Supp. 53. On appeal to this Court, *affirmed in part, reversed in part and remanded,* p. 178.

Attorney General Clark and *Assistant Attorney General Sonnett* argued the cause for the United States in No. 79, and *Robert L. Wright* for the United States in Nos. 80–86. *Solicitor General Perlman, Mr. Sonnett, Mr. Wright, Kenneth L. Kimble, Stanley M. Silverberg* and *Philip Marcus* were on the briefs.

John W. Davis argued the cause for Loew's Incorporated, appellant in No. 80.   With him on the brief were *J. Robert Rubin, S. Hazard Gillespie, Jr.* and *Benjamin Melniker.*

William J. Donovan argued the cause for the Radio-Keith-Orpheum Corp. et al., appellants in No. 80.   With him on the brief were *George S. Leisure, Ralstone R. Irvine, Gordon E. Youngman* and *Roy W. McDonald.*

Joseph M. Proskauer argued the cause for Warner Bros. Pictures, Inc. et al., appellants in No. 80.   With him on the brief were *Robert W. Perkins* and *Harold Berkowitz.*

James F. Byrnes argued the cause for the Twentieth Century-Fox Film Corp. et al., appellants in No. 80.

UNITED STATES *v.* PARAMOUNT PICTURES. 139

131   Counsel for Parties.

With him on the brief were *Otto E. Koegel, John F. Caskey* and *Frederick W. R. Pride.*

Whitney North Seymour argued the cause for Paramount Pictures, Inc. et al., appellants in No. 81. With him on the brief were *Louis Phillips* and *Albert C. Bickford.*

Louis D. Frohlich argued the cause for Columbia Pictures Corp. et al., appellants in No. 82. With him on the brief was *Arthur H. Schwartz.*

George A. Raftery argued the cause for the United Artists Corp., appellant in No. 83. With him on the brief were *Edward C. Raftery* and *Arthur F. Driscoll. T. Newman Lawler* was also of counsel.

Thomas Turner Cooke argued the cause for Universal Pictures Co., Inc. et al., appellants in No. 84. With him on the brief were *Adolph Schimel* and *Frank W. Ford.*

Thurman Arnold argued the cause for the American Theatres Association, Inc. et al., appellants in No. 85. With him on the brief were *Paul Williams* and *Milton W. Freeman.*

John G. Jackson and *Robert T. Barton, Jr.* argued the cause for Allred et al., appellants in No. 86. With them on the brief was *George B. Brooks.*

Briefs of *amici curiae* supporting the United States in No. 79 were filed by *Abram F. Myers* for the Conference of Independent Exhibitors' Associations; *Morris L. Ernst, Loyd Wright* and *James M. Barnes* for the Society of Independent Motion Picture Producers; *Herman M. Levy* for independent members of the Motion Picture Theatre Owners of America; and *Harold J. Sherman, Wendell Berge, James Lawrence Fly* and *C. Dickerman Williams* for the American Civil Liberties Union.

140 OCTOBER TERM, 1947.

Opinion of the Court. 334 U. S.

MR. JUSTICE DOUGLAS delivered the opinion of the Court.

These cases are here on appeal [1] from a judgment of a three-judge District Court [2] holding that the defendants had violated § 1 and § 2 of the Sherman Act, 26 Stat. 209, as amended, 50 Stat. 693, 15 U. S. C. §§ 1, 2, and granting an injunction and other relief. 66 F. Supp. 323; 70 F. Supp. 53.

The suit was instituted by the United States under § 4 of the Sherman Act to prevent and restrain violations of it. The defendants fall into three groups: (1) Paramount Pictures, Inc., Loew's, Incorporated, Radio-Keith-Orpheum Corporation, Warner Bros. Pictures, Inc., Twentieth Century-Fox Film Corporation, which produce motion pictures, and their respective subsidiaries or affiliates which distribute and exhibit films. These are known as the five major defendants or exhibitor-defendants. (2) Columbia Pictures Corporation and Universal Corporation, which produce motion pictures, and their subsidiaries which distribute films. (3) United Artists Corporation, which is engaged only in the distribution of motion pictures. The five majors, through their subsidiaries or affiliates, own or control theatres; the other defendants do not.

The complaint charged that the producer defendants had attempted to monopolize and had monopolized the production of motion pictures. The District Court found to the contrary and that finding is not challenged here. The complaint charged that all the defendants, as distributors, had conspired to restrain and monopolize and

[1] Sec. 2 of the Expediting Act of February 11, 1903, 32 Stat. 823, as amended, 15 U. S. C. § 29, and § 238 of the Judicial Code, as amended by the Act of February 13, 1925, 43 Stat. 936, 938, 28 U. S. C. § 345.

[2] The court was convened pursuant to the provisions of the Act of April 6, 1942, 56 Stat. 198, 199, 15 U. S. C. § 28.

UNITED STATES *v.* PARAMOUNT PICTURES. 141

131   Opinion of the Court.

had restrained and monopolized interstate trade in the distribution and exhibition of films by specific practices which we will shortly relate.   It also charged that the five major defendants had engaged in a conspiracy to restrain and monopolize, and had restrained and monopolized, interstate trade in the exhibition of motion pictures in most of the larger cities of the country.   It charged that the vertical combination of producing, distributing, and exhibiting motion pictures by each of the five major defendants violated § 1 and § 2 of the Act.   It charged that each distributor-defendant had entered into various contracts with exhibitors which unreasonably restrained trade.   Issue was joined; and a trial was had.[3]

First. Restraint of Trade—(1) *Price Fixing.*

No film is sold to an exhibitor in the distribution of motion pictures. The right to exhibit under copyright is licensed. The District Court found that the defendants in the licenses they issued fixed minimum admission prices which the exhibitors agreed to charge, whether the rental of the film was a flat amount or a percentage of the receipts. It found that substantially uniform minimum prices had been established in the licenses of all defendants. Minimum prices were established in master agreements or franchises which were made between various defendants as distributors and various defendants as exhibitors and in joint operating agreements made by the five majors with each other

---

[3] Before trial, negotiations for a settlement were undertaken. As a result, a consent decree against the five major defendants was entered November 20, 1940. The consent decree contained no admission of violation of law and adjudicated no issue of fact or law, except that the complaint stated a cause of action. The decree reserved to the United States the right at the end of a three-year trial period to seek the relief prayed for in the amended complaint. After the end of the three-year period the United States moved for trial against all the defendants.

and with independent theatre owners covering the operation of certain theatres.[4] By these later contracts minimum admission prices were often fixed for dozens of theatres owned by a particular defendant in a given area of the United States. Minimum prices were fixed in licenses of each of the five major defendants. The other three defendants made the same requirement in licenses granted to the exhibitor-defendants. We do not stop to elaborate on these findings. They are adequately detailed by the District Court in its opinion. See 66 F. Supp. 334–339.

The District Court found that two price-fixing conspiracies existed—a horizontal one between all the defendants; a vertical one between each distributor-defendant and its licensees. The latter was based on express agreements and was plainly established. The former was inferred from the pattern of price-fixing disclosed in the record. We think there was adequate foundation for it too. It is not necessary to find an express agreement in order to find a conspiracy. It is enough that a concert of action is contemplated and that the defendants conformed to the arrangement. *Interstate Circuit v. United States*, 306 U. S. 208. 226–227; *United States v. Masonite Corp.*, 316 U. S. 265, 275. That was shown here.

On this phase of the case the main attack is on the decree which enjoins the defendants and their affili-

---

[4] A master agreement is a licensing agreement or "blanket deal" covering the exhibition of features in a number of theatres, usually comprising a circuit.

A franchise is a licensing agreement, or series of licensing agreements, entered into as part of the same transaction, in effect for more than one motion picture season and covering the exhibition of features released by one distributor during the entire period of the agreement.

An independent as used in these cases means a producer, distributor, or exhibitor, as the context requires, which is not a defendant in the action, or a subsidiary or affiliate of a defendant.

UNITED STATES *v.* PARAMOUNT PICTURES. 143

ates from granting any license, except to their own theatres, in which minimum prices for admission to a theatre are fixed in any manner or by any means. The argument runs as follows: *United States* v. *General Electric Co.,* 272 U. S. 476, held that an owner of a patent could, without violating the Sherman Act, grant a license to manufacture and vend, and could fix the price at which the licensee could sell the patented article. It is pointed out that defendants do not sell the films to exhibitors, but only license them and that the Copyright Act (35 Stat. 1075, 1088, 17 U. S. C. § 1), like the patent statutes. grants the owner exclusive rights.[5] And it is argued that if the patentee can fix the price at which his licensee may sell the patented article, the owner of the copyright should be allowed the same privilege. It is maintained that such a privilege is essential to protect the value of the copyrighted films.

We start, of course, from the premise that so far as the Sherman Act is concerned, a price-fixing combination is illegal *per se*. *United States* v. *Socony-Vacuum Oil Co.,* 310 U. S. 150; *United States* v. *Masonite Corporation, supra*. We recently held in *United States* v. *Gypsum Co.,* 333 U. S. 364, 400, that even patentees could not regiment an entire industry by licenses containing price-fixing agreements. What was said there is adequate to bar defendants, through their horizontal conspiracy, from fixing prices for the exhibition of films in the movie industry. Certainly the rights of the copyright owner are no greater than those of the patentee.

Nor can the result be different when we come to the vertical conspiracy between each distributor-defendant and his licensees. The District Court stated in its findings:

"In agreeing to maintain a stipulated minimum admission price, each exhibitor thereby consents to

_____
[5] See note 12, *infra*.

the minimum price level at which it will compete against other licensees of the same distributor whether they exhibit on the same run or not. The total effect is that through the separate contracts between the distributor and its licensees a price structure is erected which regulates the licensees' ability to compete against one another in admission prices."

That consequence seems to us to be incontestable. We stated in *United States* v. *Gypsum Co., supra*, p. 401, that "The rewards which flow to the patentee and his licensees from the suppression of competition through the regulation of an industry are not reasonably and normally adapted to secure pecuniary reward for the patentee's monopoly." The same is true of the rewards of the copyright owners and their licensees in the present case. For here too the licenses are but a part of the general plan to suppress competition. The case where a distributor fixes admission prices to be charged by a single independent exhibitor, no other licensees or exhibitors being in contemplation, seems to be wholly academic, as the District Court pointed out. It is, therefore, plain that *United States* v. *General Electric Co., supra*, as applied in the patent cases, affords no haven to the defendants in this case. For a copyright may no more be used than a patent to deter competition between rivals in the exploitation of their licenses. See *Interstate Circuit* v. *United States, supra*, p. 230.

(2) *Clearances and Runs.*

Clearances are designed to protect a particular run of a film against a subsequent run.[6] The District Court

---

[6] A clearance is the period of time, usually stipulated in license contracts, which must elapse between runs of the same feature within a particular area or in specified theatres.

Runs are successive exhibitions of a feature in a given area, first-run being the first exhibition in that area, second-run being the next

UNITED STATES *v.* PARAMOUNT PICTURES. 145

found that all of the distributor-defendants used clearance provisions and that they were stated in several different ways or in combinations: in terms of a given period between designated runs; in terms of admission prices charged by competing theatres; in terms of a given period of clearance over specifically named theatres; in terms of so many days' clearance over specified areas or towns; or in terms of clearances as fixed by other distributors.

The Department of Justice maintained below that clearances are unlawful *per se* under the Sherman Act. But that is a question we need not consider, for the District Court ruled otherwise and that conclusion is not challenged here.   In its view their justification was found in the assurance they give the exhibitor that the distributor will not license a competitor to show the film either at the same time or so soon thereafter that the exhibitor's expected income from the run will be greatly diminished.   A clearance when used to protect that interest of the exhibitor was reasonable, in the view of the court, when not unduly extended as to area or duration.   Thus the court concluded that although clearances might indirectly affect admission prices, they do not fix them and that they may be reasonable restraints of trade under the Sherman Act.

The District Court held that in determining whether a clearance is unreasonable, the following factors are relevant:

(1) The admission prices of the theatres involved, as set by the exhibitors;

(2) The character and location of the theatres involved, including size, type of entertainment, appointments, transit facilities, etc.;

---

subsequent, and so on, and include successive exhibitions in different theatres, even though such theatres may be under a common ownership or management.

146   OCTOBER TERM, 1947.

Opinion of the Court.   334 U. S.

(3) The policy of operation of the theatres involved, such as the showing of double features, gift nights, give-aways, premiums, cut-rate tickets, lotteries, etc.;

(4) The rental terms and license fees paid by the theatres involved and the revenues derived by the distributor-defendant from such theatres;

(5) The extent to which the theatres involved compete with each other for patronage;

(6) The fact that a theatre involved is affiliated with a defendant-distributor or with an independent circuit of theatres should be disregarded; and

(7) There should be no clearance between theatres not in substantial competition.

It reviewed the evidence in light of these standards and concluded that many of the clearances granted by the defendants were unreasonable. We do not stop to retrace those steps. The evidence is ample to show, as the District Court plainly demonstrated, see 66 F. Supp. pp. 343–346, that many clearances had no relation to the competitive factors which alone could justify them.[7] The clearances which were in vogue had, indeed, acquired a fixed and uniform character and were made applicable to situations without regard to the special circumstances which are necessary to sustain them as reasonable restraints of trade. The evidence is ample to support the

---

[7] Thus the District Court found:

"Some licenses granted clearance to sell to all theatres which the exhibitor party to the contract might thereafter own, lease, control, manage, or operate against all theatres in the immediate vicinity of the exhibitor's theatre thereafter erected or opened. The purpose of this type of clearance agreements was to fix the run and clearance status of any theatre thereafter opened not on the basis of its appointments, size, location, and other competitive features normally entering into such determination, but rather upon the sole basis of whether it were operated by the exhibitor party to the agreement."

UNITED STATES *v.* PARAMOUNT PICTURES. 147

131   Opinion of the Court.

finding of the District Court that the defendants either
participated in evolving this uniform system of clearances
or acquiesced in it and so furthered its existence. That
evidence, like the evidence on the price-fixing phase of
the case, is therefore adequate to support the finding of
a conspiracy to restrain trade by imposing unreasonable
clearances.

The District Court enjoined defendants and their affiliates from agreeing with each other or with any exhibitors
or distributors to maintain a system of clearances, or from
granting any clearance between theatres not in substantial
competition, or from granting or enforcing any clearance
against theatres in substantial competition with the theatre receiving the license for exhibition in excess of what
is reasonably necessary to protect the licensee in the run
granted. In view of the findings this relief was plainly
warranted.

Some of the defendants ask that this provision be
construed (or, if necessary, modified) to allow licensors
in granting clearances to take into consideration what
is reasonably necessary for a fair return to the licensor.
We reject that suggestion. If that were allowed, then
the exhibitor-defendants would have an easy method of
keeping alive at least some of the consequences of the
effective conspiracy which they launched. For they
could then justify clearances granted by other distributors
in favor of their theatres in terms of the competitive
requirements of those theatres, and at the same time
justify the restrictions they impose upon independents in
terms of the necessity of protecting their film rental as
licensor. That is too potent a weapon to leave in the
hands of those whose proclivity to unlawful conduct has
been so marked. It plainly should not be allowed so long
as the exhibitor-defendants own theatres. For in its bald-
est terms it is in the hands of the defendants no less than
a power to restrict the competition of others in the way

deemed most desirable by them. In the setting of this case the only measure of reasonableness of a clearance by Sherman Act standards is the special needs of the licensee for the competitive advantages it affords.

Whether the same restrictions would be applicable to a producer who had not been a party to such a conspiracy is a question we do not reach.

Objection is made to a further provision of this part of the decree stating that "Whenever any clearance provision is attacked as not legal under the provisions of this decree, the burden shall be upon the distributor to sustain the legality thereof." We think that provision was justified. Clearances have been used along with price fixing to suppress competition with the theatres of the exhibitor-defendants and with other favored exhibitors. The District Court could therefore have eliminated clearances completely for a substantial period of time, even though, as it thought, they were not illegal *per se*. For equity has the power to uproot all parts of an illegal scheme—the valid as well as the invalid—in order to rid the trade or commerce of all taint of the conspiracy. *United States v. Bausch & Lomb Co.*, 321 U. S. 707, 724. The court certainly then could take the lesser step of making them *prima facie* invalid. But we do not rest on that alone. As we have said, the only justification for clearances in the setting of this case is in terms of the special needs of the licensee for the competitive advantages they afford. To place on the distributor the burden of showing their reasonableness is to place it on the one party in the best position to evaluate their competitive effects. Those who have shown such a marked proclivity for unlawful conduct are in no position to complain that they carry the burden of showing that their future clearances come within the law. Cf. *United States v. Crescent Amusement Co.*, 323 U. S. 173, 188.

UNITED STATES *v.* PARAMOUNT PICTURES. **149**

Opinion of the Court.

(3) *Pooling Agreements; Joint Ownership.*

The District Court found the exhibitor-defendants had agreements with each other and their affiliates by which theatres of two or more of them, normally competitive, were operated as a unit, or managed by a joint committee or by one of the exhibitors, the profits being shared according to prearranged percentages. Some of these agreements provided that the parties might not acquire other competitive theatres without first offering them for inclusion in the pool. The court concluded that the result of these agreements was to eliminate competition *pro tanto* both in exhibition and in distribution of features,[8] since the parties would naturally direct the films to the theatres in whose earnings they were interested.

The District Court also found that the exhibitor-defendants had like agreements with certain independent exhibitors. Those alliances had, in its view, the effect of nullifying competition between the allied theatres and of making more effective the competition of the group against theatres not members of the pool. The court found that in some cases the operating agreements were achieved through leases of theatres, the rentals being measured by a percentage of profits earned by the theatres in the pool. The District Court required the dissolution of existing pooling agreements and enjoined any future arrangement of that character.

These provisions of the decree will stand. The practices were bald efforts to substitute monopoly for competition and to strengthen the hold of the exhibitor-defendants on the industry by alignment of competitors on their side. Clearer restraints of trade are difficult to imagine.

There was another type of business arrangement that the District Court found to have the same effect as the

---

[8] A feature is any motion picture, regardless of topic, the length of film of which is in excess of 4,000 feet.

150 OCTOBER TERM, 1947.

Opinion of the Court. 334 U. S.

pooling agreements just mentioned. Many theatres are owned jointly by two or more exhibitor-defendants or by an exhibitor-defendant and an independent.* The result is, according to the District Court, that the theatres are operated "collectively, rather than competitively." And where the joint owners are an exhibitor-defendant and an independent the effect is, according to the District Court, the elimination by the exhibitor-defendant of "putative competition between itself and the other joint owner, who otherwise would be in a position to operate theatres independently." The District Court found these joint ownerships of theatres to be unreasonable restraints of trade within the meaning of the Sherman Act.

The District Court ordered the exhibitor-defendants to disaffiliate by terminating their joint ownership of the-

---

Theatres jointly owned with independents:

Paramount	993
Warner	20
Fox	66
RKO	187
Loew's	21
Total	1287

Theatres jointly owned by two defendants:

Paramount-Fox	6
Paramount-Loew's	14
Paramount-Warner	25
Paramount-RKO	150
Loew's-RKO	3
Loew's-Warner	5
Fox-RKO	1
Warner-RKO	10
Total	214

Of the 1287 jointly owned with independents, 209 would not be affected by the decree since one of the ownership interests is less than 5 per cent, an amount which the District Court treated as *de minimis*

UNITED STATES *v.* PARAMOUNT PICTURES. 151

131   Opinion of the Court.

atres; and it enjoined future acquisitions of such interests. One is authorized to buy out the other if it shows to the satisfaction of the District Court and that court first finds that such acquisition "will not unduly restrain competition in the exhibition of feature motion pictures." This dissolution and prohibition of joint ownership as between exhibitor-defendants was plainly warranted. To the extent that they have joint interests in the outlets for their films each in practical effect grants the other a priority for the exhibition of its films. For in this situation, as in the case where theatres are jointly managed, the natural gravitation of films is to the theatres in whose earnings the distributors have an interest. Joint ownership between exhibitor-defendants then becomes a device for strengthening their competitive position as exhibitors by forming an alliance as distributors. An express agreement to grant each other the preference would be a most effective weapon to stifle competition. A working arrangement or business device that has that necessary consequence gathers no immunity because of its subtlety. Each is a restraint of trade condemned by the Sherman Act.

The District Court also ordered disaffiliation in those instances where theatres were jointly owned by an exhibitor-defendant and an independent, and where the interest of the exhibitor-defendant was "greater than five per cent unless such interest shall be ninety-five per cent or more," an independent being defined for this part of the decree as "any former, present or putative motion picture theatre operator which is not owned or controlled by the defendant holding the interest in question." The exhibitor-defendants are authorized to acquire existing interests of the independents in these theatres if they establish, and if the District Court first finds, that the acquisition "will not unduly restrain competition in the

exhibition of feature motion pictures." All other acquisitions of such joint interests were enjoined.

This phase of the decree is strenuously attacked. We
are asked to eliminate it for lack of findings to support it.
The argument is that the findings show no more than
the existence of joint ownership of theatres by exhibitor-
defendants and independents. The statement by the
District Court that the joint ownership eliminates "putative competition" is said to be a mere conclusion without
evidentiary support. For it is said that the facts of the
record show that many of the instances of joint ownership
with an independent interest are cases wholly devoid of
any history of or relationship to restraints of trade or monopolistic practices. Some are said to be rather fortui-
tous results of bankruptcies; others are said to be the
results of investments by outside interests who have no
desire or capacity to operate theatres, and so on.

It is conceded that the District Court made no inquiry
into the circumstances under which a particular interest
had been acquired. It treated all relationships alike, insofar as the disaffiliation provision of the decree is concerned. In this we think it erred.

We have gone into the record far enough to be con-
fident that at least some of these acquisitions by the exhibitor-defendants were the products of the unlawful
practices which the defendants have inflicted on the industry. To the extent that these acquisitions were the
fruits of monopolistic practices or restraints of trade, they
should be divested. And no permission to buy out the
other owner should be given a defendant. *United States
v. Crescent Amusement Co., supra*, p. 189; *Schine Chain
Theatres, Inc.* v. *United States, ante*, p. 110. Moreover,
even if lawfully acquired, they may have been utilized as
part of the conspiracy to eliminate or suppress competition in furtherance of the ends of the conspiracy. In that
event divestiture would likewise be justified. *United*

UNITED STATES *v.* PARAMOUNT PICTURES. 153

131   Opinion of the Court.

States v. *Crescent Amusement Co., supra,* pp. 189–190. In that situation permission to acquire the interest of the independent would have the unlawful effect of permitting the defendants to complete their plan to eliminate him.

Furthermore, if the joint ownership is an alliance with one who is or would be an operator but for the joint ownership, divorce should be decreed even though the affiliation was innocently acquired. For that joint ownership would afford opportunity to perpetuate the effects of the restraints of trade which the exhibitor-defendants have inflicted on the industry.

It seems, however, that some of the cases of joint ownership do not fall into any of the categories we have listed. Some apparently involve no more than innocent investments by those who are not actual or potential operators. If in such cases the acquisition was not improperly used in furtherance of the conspiracy, its retention by defendants would be justified absent a finding that no monopoly resulted. And in those instances permission might be given the defendants to acquire the interests of the independents on a showing by them and a finding by the court that neither monopoly nor unreasonable restraint of trade in the exhibition of films would result. In short, we see no reason to place a ban on this type of ownership, at least so long as theatre ownership by the five majors is not prohibited. The results of inquiry along the lines we have indicated must await further findings of the District Court on remand of the cause.

(4) *Formula Deals, Master Agreements, and Franchises.*

A formula deal is a licensing agreement with a circuit of theatres in which the license fee of a given feature is measured, for the theatres covered by the agreement, by a specified percentage of the feature's national gross. The District Court found that Paramount and RKO

154   OCTOBER TERM, 1947.

Opinion of the Court.   334 U. S.

had made formula deals with independent and affiliated circuits.   The circuit was allowed to allocate playing
time and film rentals among the various theatres as it
saw fit.   The inclusion of theatres of a circuit into a
single agreement gives no opportunity for other theatre
owners to bid for the feature in their respective areas
and, in the view of the District Court, is therefore an unreasonable restraint of trade.   The District Court found
some master agreements [10] open to the same objection.
Those are the master agreements that cover exhibition
in two or more theatres in a particular circuit and allow
the exhibitor to allocate the film rental paid among the
theatres as it sees fit and to exhibit the features upon
such playing time as it deems best, and leaves other terms
to the discretion of the circuit.   The District Court enjoined the making or further performance of any formula
deal of the type described above.   It also enjoined the
making or further performance of any master agreement
covering the exhibition of features in a number of
theatres.

The findings of the District Court in these respects
are supported by facts, its conclusion that the formula
deals and master agreements constitute restraint of trade
is valid, and the relief is proper.   The formula deals
and master agreements are unlawful restraints of trade
in two respects.   In the first place, they eliminate the
possibility of bidding for films theatre by theatre.   In
that way they eliminate the opportunity for the small
competitor to obtain the choice first runs, and put a
premium on the size of the circuit.   They are, therefore,
devices for stifling competition and diverting the cream
of the business to the large operators.   In the second
place, the pooling of the purchasing power of an entire
circuit in bidding for films is a misuse of monopoly power

---

[10] See note 4, *supra.*

UNITED STATES *v.* PARAMOUNT PICTURES. 155

insofar as it combines the theatres in closed towns with competitive situations. The reasons have been stated in *United States* v. *Griffith, ante,* p. 100, and *Schine Chain Theatres, Inc.* v. *United States, ante,* p. 110, and need not be repeated here. It is hardly necessary to add that distributors who join in such arrangements by exhibitors are active participants in effectuating a restraint of trade and a monopolistic practice. See *United States* v. *Crescent Amusement Co., supra,* p. 183.

The District Court also enjoined the making or further performance of any franchise. A franchise is a contract with an exhibitor which extends over a period of more than a motion picture season and covers the exhibition of features released by the distributor during the period of the agreement. The District Court held that a franchise constituted a restraint of trade because a period of more than one season was too long and the inclusion of all features was disadvantageous to competitors. At least that is the way we read its findings.

Universal and United Artists object to the outlawry of franchise agreements. Universal points out that the charge of illegality of franchises in these cases was restricted to franchises with theatres owned by the major defendants and to franchises with circuits or theatres in a circuit, a circuit being defined in the complaint as a group of more than five theatres controlled by the same person or a group of more than five theatres which combine through a common agent in licensing films. It seems, therefore, that the legality of franchises to other exhibitors (except as to block-booking, a practice to which we will later advert) was not in issue in the litigation. Moreover, the findings on franchises are clouded by the statement of the District Court in the opinion that franchises "necessarily contravene the plan of licensing each picture, theatre by theatre, to the highest bidder." As will be seen hereafter, we eliminate from the decree

156   OCTOBER TERM, 1947.

the provision for competitive bidding.   But for its inclusion of competitive bidding the District Court might well have treated the problem of franchises differently.

We can see how if franchises were allowed to be used between the exhibitor-defendants each might be able to strengthen its strategic position in the exhibition field and continue the ill effects of the conspiracy which the decree is designed to dissipate.   Franchise agreements may have been employed as devices to discriminate against some independents in favor of others.   We know from the record that franchise agreements often contained discriminatory clauses operating in favor not only of theatres owned by the defendants but also of the large circuits.   But we cannot say on this record that franchises are illegal *per se* when extended to any theatre or circuit no matter how small.   The findings do not deal with the issue doubtlessly due to the fact that any system of franchises would necessarily conflict with the system of competitive bidding adopted by the District Court.   Hence we set aside the findings on franchises so that the court may examine the problem in the light of the elimination from the decree of competitive bidding.

We do not take that course in the case of formula deals and master agreements, for the findings in these instances seem to stand on their own bottom and apparently have no necessary dependency on the provision for competitive bidding.

(5) *Block-Booking*.

Block-booking is the practice of licensing, or offering for license, one feature or group of features on condition that the exhibitor will also license another feature or group of features released by the distributors during a given period.   The films are licensed in blocks before they are actually produced.   All the defendants, except United Artists, have engaged in the practice.   Block-booking prevents competitors from bidding for single features on their

UNITED STATES *v.* PARAMOUNT PICTURES. 157

individual merits. The District Court held it illegal for
that reason and for the reason that it "adds to the monopoly of a single copyrighted picture that of another copyrighted picture which must be taken and exhibited in
order to secure the first." That enlargement of the
monopoly of the copyright was condemned below in reliance on the principle which forbids the owner of a patent
to condition its use on the purchase or use of patented or
unpatented materials. See *Ethyl Gasoline Corporation*
v. *United States,* 309 U. S. 436, 459; *Morton Salt Co.* v.
Suppiger Co., 314 U. S. 488, 491; *Mercoid Corp.* v. *Mid-
Continent Investment Co.,* 320 U. S. 661, 665. The court
enjoined defendants from performing or entering into any
license in which the right to exhibit one feature is
conditioned upon the licensee's taking one or more other
features.[11]

---

[11] Blind-selling is a practice whereby a distributor licenses a feature
before the exhibitor is afforded an opportunity to view it. To remedy
the problems created by that practice the District Court included the
following provision in its decree:

"To the extent that any of the features have not been trade shown
prior to the granting of the license for more than a single feature, the
licensee shall be given by the licensor the right to reject twenty per
cent of such features not trade shown prior to the granting of the
license, such right of rejection to be exercised in the order of release
within ten days after there has been an opportunity afforded to the
licensee to inspect the feature."

The court advanced the following as its reason for inclusion of this
provision:

"Blind-selling does not appear to be as inherently restrictive of
competition as block-booking, although it is capable of some abuse.
By this practice a distributor could promise a picture of good quality
or of a certain type which when produced might prove to be of poor
quality or of another type—a competing distributor meanwhile being
unable to market its product and in the end losing its outlets for
future pictures. The evidence indicates that trade-shows, which are
designed to prevent such blind-selling, are poorly attended by
exhibitors. Accordingly, exhibitors who choose to obtain their films
for exhibition in quantities, need to be protected against burdensome

We approve that restriction. The copyright law, like the patent statutes, makes reward to the owner a secondary consideration. In *Fox Film Corp.* v. *Doyal,* 286 U. S. 123, 127, Chief Justice Hughes spoke as follows respecting the copyright monopoly granted by Congress, "The sole interest of the United States and the primary object in conferring the monopoly lie in the general benefits derived by the public from the labors of authors." It is said that reward to the author or artist serves to induce release to the public of the products of his creative genius. But the reward does not serve its public purpose if it is not related to the quality of the copyright. Where a high quality film greatly desired is licensed only if an inferior one is taken, the latter borrows quality from the former and strengthens its monopoly by drawing on the other. The practice tends to equalize rather than differentiate the reward for the individual copyrights. Even where all the films included in the package are of equal quality, the requirement that all be taken if one is desired increases the market for some. Each stands not on its own footing but in whole or in part on the appeal which another film may have. As the District Court said, the result is to add to the monopoly of the copyright in violation of the principle of the patent cases involving tying clauses.[12]

---

agreements by being given an option to reject a certain percentage of their blind-licensed pictures within a reasonable time after they shall have become available for inspection."

We approve this provision of the decree.

[12] The exclusive right granted by the Copyright Act, 35 Stat. 1075, 17 U. S. C. § 1, includes no such privilege. It provides, so far as material here, as follows:

"That any person entitled thereto, upon complying with the provisions of this Act, shall have the exclusive right:

"(d). To perform or represent the copyrighted work publicly if it be a drama or, if it be a dramatic work and not reproduced in copies for sale, to vend any manuscript or any record whatsoever thereof;

UNITED STATES *v.* PARAMOUNT PICTURES. 159

131   Opinion of the Court.

It is argued that *Transparent-Wrap Machine Corp.* v. *Stokes & Smith Co.*, 329 U. S. 637, points to a contrary result.   That case held that the inclusion in a patent license of a condition requiring the licensee to assign improvement patents was not *per se* illegal.   But that decision, confined to improvement patents, was greatly influenced by the federal statute governing assignments of patents. It therefore has no controlling significance here.

Columbia Pictures makes an earnest argument that enforcement of the restriction as to block-booking will be very disadvantageous to it and will greatly impair its ability to operate profitably.   But the policy of the anti-trust laws is not qualified or conditioned by the convenience of those whose conduct is regulated.   Nor can a vested interest in a practice which contravenes the policy of the anti-trust laws receive judicial sanction.

We do not suggest that films may not be sold in blocks or groups, when there is no requirement, express or implied, for the purchase of more than one film.   All we hold to be illegal is a refusal to license one or more copyrights unless another copyright is accepted.

(6) *Discrimination.*

The District Court found that defendants had discriminated against small independent exhibitors and in favor of large affiliated and unaffiliated circuits through various kinds of contract provisions.   These included suspension of the terms of a contract if a circuit theatre remained closed for more than eight weeks with reinstatement without liability on reopening; allowing large privileges in the selection and elimination of films;

---

to make or to procure the making of any transcription or record thereof by or from which, in whole or in part, it may in any manner or by any method be exhibited, performed, represented, produced, or reproduced; and to exhibit, perform, represent, produce, or reproduce it in any manner or by any method whatsoever;"

allowing deductions in film rentals if double bills are played; granting moveovers [13] and extended runs; granting road show privileges; [14] allowing overage and underage; [15] granting unlimited playing time; excluding foreign pictures and those of independent producers; and granting rights to question the classification of features for rental purposes. The District Court found that the competitive advantages of these provisions were so great that their inclusion in contracts with the larger circuits and their exclusion from contracts with the small independents constituted an unreasonable discrimination against the latter. Each discriminatory contract constituted a conspiracy between licensor and licensee. Hence the District Court deemed it unnecessary to decide whether the defendants had conspired among themselves to make these discriminations. No provision of the decree specifically enjoins these discriminatory practices because they were thought to be impossible under the system of competitive bidding adopted by the District Court.

These findings are amply supported by the evidence. We concur in the conclusion that these discriminatory practices are included among the restraints of trade which the Sherman Act condemns. See *Interstate Circuit* v. *United States, supra,* p. 231; *United States* v. *Crescent Amusement Co., supra,* pp. 182–183. It will be for the

---

[13] A moveover is the privilege given a licensee to move a picture from one theatre to another as a continuation of the run at the licensee's first theatre.

[14] A road show is a public exhibition of a feature in a limited number of theatres, in advance of its general release, at admission prices higher than those customarily charged in first-run theatres in those areas.

[15] Underage and overage refer to the practice of using excess film rental earned in one circuit theatre to fulfill a rental commitment defaulted by another.

UNITED STATES *v.* PARAMOUNT PICTURES. 161

131   Opinion of the Court.

District Court on remand of these cases to provide effective relief against their continuance, as our elimination of the provision for competitive bidding leaves this phase of the cases unguarded.

There is some suggestion on this as well as on other phases of the cases that large exhibitors with whom defendants dealt fathered the illegal practices and forced them onto the defendants. But as the District Court observed, that circumstance if true does not help the defendants. For acquiescence in an illegal scheme is as much a violation of the Sherman Act as the creation and promotion of one.

Second—Competitive Bidding.

The District Court concluded that the only way competition could be introduced into the existing system of fixed prices, clearances and runs was to require that films be licensed on a competitive bidding basis. Films are to be offered to all exhibitors in each competitive area.[16] The license for the desired run is to be granted to the highest responsible bidder, unless the distributor rejects all offers. The licenses are to be offered and taken theatre by theatre and picture by picture. Licenses to show films in theatres in which the licensor owns directly or indirectly an interest of ninety-five per cent or more are excluded from the requirement for competitive bidding.

Paramount is the only one of the five majors who opposes the competitive bidding system. Columbia Pictures, Universal, and United Artists oppose it. The intervenors representing certain independents oppose it. And

---

[16] Competitive bidding is required only in a "competitive area" where it is "desired by the exhibitors." As the District Court said, "the decree provides an opportunity to bid for any exhibitor in a competitive area who may desire to do so."

The details of the competitive bidding system will be found in 70 F. Supp. pp. 73–74.

the Department of Justice, which apparently proposed the system originally, speaks strongly against it here.

At first blush there is much to commend the system of competitive bidding. The trade victims of this conspiracy have in large measure been the small independent operators. They are the ones that have felt most keenly the discriminatory practices and predatory activities in which defendants have freely indulged. They have been the victims of the massed purchasing power of the larger units in the industry. It is largely out of the ruins of the small operators that the large empires of exhibitors have been built. Thus it would appear to be a great boon to them to substitute open bidding for the private deals and favors on which the large operators have thrived. But after reflection we have concluded that competitive bidding involves the judiciary so deeply in the daily operation of this nation-wide business and promises such dubious benefits that it should not be undertaken.

Each film is to be licensed on a particular run to "the highest responsible bidder, having a theatre of a size, location and equipment adequate to yield a reasonable return to the licensor." The bid "shall state what run such exhibitor desires and what he is willing to pay for such feature, which statement may specify a flat rental, or a percentage of gross receipts, or both, or any other form of rental, and shall also specify what clearance such exhibitor is willing to accept, the time and days when such exhibitor desires to exhibit it, and any other offers which such exhibitor may care to make." We do not doubt that if a competitive bidding system is adopted all these provisions are necessary. For the licensing of films at auction is quite obviously a more complicated matter than the like sales for cash of tobacco, wheat, or other produce. Columbia puts these pertinent queries: "No two exhibitors are likely to make the same bid as to

UNITED STATES *v.* PARAMOUNT PICTURES. 163

131   Opinion of the Court.

dates, clearance, method of fixing rental, etc. May bids containing such diverse factors be readily compared? May a flat rental bid be compared with a percentage bid? May the value of any percentage bid be determined unless the admission price is fixed by the license?"

The question as to who is the highest bidder involves the use of standards incapable of precise definition because the bids being compared contain different ingredients. Determining who is the most responsible bidder likewise cannot be reduced to a formula. The distributor's judgment of the character and integrity of a particular exhibitor might result in acceptance of a lower bid than others offered. Yet to prove that favoritism was shown would be well-nigh impossible, unless perhaps all the exhibitors in the country were given classifications of responsibility. If, indeed, the choice between bidders is not to be entrusted to the uncontrolled discretion of the distributors, some effort to standardize the factors involved in determining "a reasonable return to the licensor" would seem necessary.

We mention these matters merely to indicate the character of the job of supervising such a competitive bidding system. It would involve the judiciary in the administration of intricate and detailed rules governing priority, period of clearance, length of run, competitive areas, reasonable return, and the like.   The system would be apt to require as close a supervision as a continuous receivership, unless the defendants were to be entrusted with vast discretion.   The judiciary is unsuited to affairs of business management; and control through the power of contempt is crude and clumsy and lacking in the flexibility necessary to make continuous and detailed supervision effective. Yet delegation of the management of the system to the discretion of those who had the genius to conceive the present conspiracy and to execute it with the subtlety which this record reveals, could be done only with the

164   OCTOBER TERM, 1947.

Opinion of the Court.   334 U. S.

greatest reluctance. At least such choices should not be faced unless the need for the system is great and its benefits plain.

The system uproots business arrangements and established relationships with no apparent overall benefit to the small independent exhibitor. If each feature must go to the highest responsible bidder, those with the greatest purchasing power would seem to be in a favored position. Those with the longest purse—the exhibitor-defendants and the large circuits—would seem to stand in a preferred position. If in fact they were enabled through the competitive bidding system to take the cream of the business, eliminate the smaller independents, and thus increase their own strategic hold on the industry, they would have the cloak of the court's decree around them for protection. Hence the natural advantage which the larger and financially stronger exhibitors would seem to have in the bidding gives us pause. If a premium is placed on purchasing power, the court-created system may be a powerful factor towards increasing the concentration of economic power in the industry rather than cleansing the competitive system of unwholesome practices. For where the system in operation promises the advantage to the exhibitor who is in the strongest financial position, the injunction against discrimination [17] is apt to hold an empty promise. In this connection it should be noted that, even though the independents in a given competitive area do not want competitive bidding, the exhibitor-defendants can invoke the system.

Our doubts concerning the competitive bidding system are increased by the fact that defendants who own theatres are allowed to pre-empt their own features. They thus start with an inventory which all other exhib-

---

[17] The competitive bidding part of the decree provides: "Each license shall be granted solely upon the merits and without discrimination in favor of affiliates, old customers or others."

UNITED STATES *v.* PARAMOUNT PICTURES. 165

131   Opinion of the Court.

itors lack.   The latter have no prospect of assured runs except what they get by competitive bidding.   The proposed system does not offset in any way the advantages which the exhibitor-defendants have by way of theatre ownership.   It would seem in fact to increase them.   For the independents are deprived of the stability which flows from established business relationships.   Under the proposed system they can get features only if they are the highest responsible bidders.   They can no longer depend on their private sources of supply which their ingenuity has created.   Those sources, built perhaps on private relationships and representing important items of good will, are banned, even though they are free of any taint of illegality.

The system was designed, as some of the defendants put it, to remedy the difficulty of any theatre to break into or change the existing system of runs and clearances. But we do not see how, in practical operation, the proposed system of competitive bidding is likely to open up to competition the markets which defendants' unlawful restraints have dominated.   Rather real danger seems to us to lie in the opportunities the system affords the exhibitor-defendants and the other large operators to strengthen their hold in the industry.   We are reluctant to alter decrees in these cases where there is agreement with the District Court on the nature of the violations. *United States* v. *Crescent Amusement Co., supra,* p. 185; *International Salt Co. v. United States,* 332 U. S. 392, 400.   But the provisions for competitive bidding in these cases promise little in the way of relief against the real evils of the conspiracy.   They implicate the judiciary heavily in the details of business management if supervision is to be effective.   They vest powerful control in the exhibitor-defendants over their competitors if close supervision by the court is not undertaken.   In light of these considerations we conclude that the competitive

166   OCTOBER TERM, 1947.

Opinion of the Court.   334 U. S.

bidding provisions of the decree should be eliminated so that a more effective decree may be fashioned.

We have already indicated in preceding parts of this opinion that this alteration in the decree leaves a hiatus or two which will have to be filled on remand of the cases. We will indicate hereafter another phase of the problem which the District Court should also reconsider in view of this alteration in the decree. But out of an abundance of caution we add this additional word. The competitive bidding system was perhaps the central arch of the decree designed by the District Court. Its elimination may affect the cases in ways other than those which we expressly mention. Hence on remand of the cases the freedom of the District Court to reconsider the adequacy of decree is not limited to those parts we have specifically indicated.

Third. Monopoly, Expansion of Theatre Holdings, Divestiture.

There is a suggestion that the hold the defendants have on the industry is so great that a problem under the First Amendment is raised. Cf. *Associated Press* v. *United States*, 326 U. S. 1. We have no doubt that moving pictures, like newspapers and radio, are included in the press whose freedom is guaranteed by the First Amendment. That issue would be focused here if we had any question concerning monopoly in the production of moving pictures. But monopoly in production was eliminated as an issue in these cases, as we have noted. The chief argument at the bar is phrased in terms of monopoly of exhibition, restraints on exhibition, and the like. Actually, the issue is even narrower than that. The main contest is over the cream of the exhibition business—that of the first-run theatres. By defining the issue so narrowly we do not intend to belittle its importance. It shows, however, that the question here is not

UNITED STATES *v.* PARAMOUNT PICTURES. 167

what the public will see or *if* the public will be permitted to see certain features.   It is clear that under the existing system the public will be denied access to none.   If the public cannot see the features on the first-run, it may do so on the second, third, fourth, or later run.   The central problem presented by these cases is which exhibitors get the highly profitable first-run business.   That problem has important aspects under the Sherman Act.   But it bears only remotely, if at all, on any question of freedom of the press, save only as timeliness of release may be a factor of importance in specific situations.

The controversy over monopoly relates to monopoly in exhibition and more particularly monopoly in the first-run phase of the exhibition business.

The five majors in 1945 had interests in somewhat over 17 per cent of the theatres in the United States—3,137 out of 18,076.[18]   Those theatres paid 45 per cent of the total domestic film rental received by all eight defendants.

In the 92 cities of the country with populations over 100,000 at least 70 per cent of all the first-run theatres are affiliated with one or more of the five majors.   In 4 of those cities the five majors have no theatres.   In 38 of those cities there are no independent first-run theatres.   In none of the remaining 50 cities did less

---

[18] The theatres which each of the five majors owned independently of the others were: Paramount 1,395 or 7.72 per cent; Warner 501 or 2.77 per cent; Loew's 135 or .74 per cent; Fox 636 or 3.52 per cent; RKO 109 or .60 per cent.   There were in addition 361 theatres or about 2 per cent in which two or more of the five majors had joint interests.   These figures exclude connections through film-buying or management contracts or through corporations in which a defendant owns an indirect minority stock interest.

These theatres are located in 922 towns in 48 States and the District of Columbia.   For further description of the distribution of theatres see Bertrand, Evans, and Blanchard, The Motion Picture Industry—A Pattern of Control 15–16 (TNEC Monograph 43, 1941).

than three of the distributor-defendants license their product on first run to theatres of the five majors. In 19 of the 50 cities less than three of the distributor-defendants licensed their product on first run to independent theatres. In a majority of the 50 cities the greater share of all of the features of defendants were licensed for first-run exhibition in the theatres of the five majors.

In about 60 per cent of the 92 cities having populations of over 100,000, independent theatres compete with those of the five majors in first-run exhibition. In about 91 per cent of the 92 cities there is competition between independent theatres and the theatres of the five majors or between theatres of the five majors themselves for first-run exhibition. In all of the 92 cities there is always competition in some run even where there is no competition in first runs.

In cities between 25,000 and 100,000 populations the five majors have interests in 577 of a total of 978 first-run theatres or about 60 per cent. In about 300 additional towns, mostly under 25,000, an operator affiliated with one of the five majors has all of the theatres in the town.

The District Court held that the five majors could not be treated collectively so as to establish claims of general monopolization in exhibition. It found that none of them was organized or had been maintained "for the purpose of achieving a national monopoly" in exhibition. It found that the five majors by their present theatre holdings "alone" (which aggregate a little more than one-sixth of all the theatres in the United States), "do not and cannot collectively or individually, have a monopoly of exhibition." The District Court also found that where a single defendant owns all of the first-run theatres in a town, there is no sufficient proof that the acquisition was for the purpose of creating a monopoly. It found rather that such consequence resulted from the inertness

UNITED STATES *v.* PARAMOUNT PICTURES. 169

of competitors, their lack of financial ability to build theatres comparable to those of the five majors, or the preference of the public for the best-equipped theatres. And the percentage of features on the market which any of the five majors could play in its own theatres was found to be relatively small and in nowise to approximate a monopoly of film exhibition.[19]

Even in respect of the theatres jointly owned or jointly operated by the defendants with each other or with independents, the District Court found no monopoly or attempt to monopolize. Those joint agreements or ownership were found only to be unreasonable restraints of trade. The District Court, indeed, found no monopoly on any phase of the cases, although it did find an attempt to monopolize in the fixing of prices, the granting of un-

---

[19] The number of feature films released during the 1943–44 season by the eleven largest distributors is as follows:

	No. of Films	Percentages of Total With "Westerns" included	With "Westerns" excluded
Fox	33	8.31	9.85
Loew's	33	8.31	9.85
Paramount	31	7.81	9.25
RKO	38	9.57	11.34
Warner	19	4.79	5.67
Columbia	41	10.32	12.24
United Artists	16	4.04	4.78
Universal	49	12.34	14.63
Republic	–29 features	14.86	8.66
	–30 "Westerns"		
Monogram	–26 features	10.58	7.76
	–16 "Westerns"		
PRC	–20 features	9.07	5.97
	–16 "Westerns"		
Totals	397	100.00	100.00
	335 without "Westerns"		

170   OCTOBER TERM, 1947.

Opinion of the Court.   334 U.S.

reasonable clearances, block-booking and the other unlawful restraints of trade we have already discussed. The
"root of the difficulties," according to the District Court,
lay not in theatre ownership but in those unlawful
practices.

The District Court did, however, enjoin the five majors
from expanding their present theatre holdings in any
manner.[20]   It refused to grant the request of the Department of Justice for total divestiture by the five majors
of their theatre holdings. It found that total divestiture
would be injurious to the five majors and damaging to
the public. Its thought on the latter score was that
the new set of theatre owners who would take the place
of the five majors would be unlikely for some years to
give the public as good service as those they supplanted
"in view of the latter's demonstrated experience and skill
in operating what must be regarded as in general the
largest and best equipped theatres." Divestiture was, it
thought, too harsh a remedy where there was available
the alternative of competitive bidding. It accordingly
concluded that divestiture was unnecessary "at least until
the efficiency of that system has been tried and found
wanting."

It is clear, so far as the five majors are concerned, that
the aim of the conspiracy was exclusionary, i. e. it was
designed to strengthen their hold on the exhibition field.
In other words, the conspiracy had monopoly in exhibition
for one of its goals, as the District Court held. Price,
clearance, and run are interdependent. The clearance
and run provisions of the licenses fixed the relative playing
positions of all theatres in a certain area; the minimum
price provisions were based on playing position—the first-
run theatres being required to charge the highest prices,

---

[20] Excepted from this prohibition was the acquisition of interests
in theatres jointly owned, a matter we have discussed in a preceding
portion of this opinion.

UNITED STATES *v.* PARAMOUNT PICTURES. 171

the second-run theatres the next highest, and so on.   As the District Court found, "In effect, the distributor, by the fixing of minimum admission prices, attempts to give the prior-run exhibitors as near a monopoly of the patronage as possible."

It is, therefore, not enough in determining the need for divestiture to conclude with the District Court that none of the defendants was organized or has been maintained for the purpose of achieving a "national monopoly," nor that the five majors through their present theatre holdings "alone" do not and cannot collectively or individually have a monopoly of exhibition.   For when the starting point is a conspiracy to effect a monopoly through restraints of trade, it is relevant to determine what the results of the conspiracy were even if they fell short of monopoly.

An example will illustrate the problem.   In the popular sense there is a monopoly if one person owns the only theatre in town.   That usually does not, however, constitute a violation of the Sherman Act.   But as we noted in *United States* v. *Griffith, ante,* p. 100, and see *Schine Chain Theatres, Inc.* v. *United States, ante,* p. 110, even such an ownership is vulnerable in a suit by the United States under the Sherman Act if the property was acquired, or its strategic position maintained, as a result of practices which constitute unreasonable restraints of trade.   Otherwise, there would be reward from the conspiracy through retention of its fruits.   Hence the problem of the District Court does not end with enjoining continuance of the unlawful restraints nor with dissolving the combination which launched the conspiracy.   Its function includes undoing what the conspiracy achieved.   As we have discussed in *Schine Chain Theatres, Inc.* v. *United States, ante,* p. 110, the requirement that the defendants restore what they unlawfully obtained is no more punishment than the familiar remedy

172   OCTOBER TERM, 1947.

Opinion of the Court.   334 U. S.

of restitution.   What findings would be warranted after such an inquiry in the present cases, we do not know. For the findings of the District Court do not cover this point beyond stating that monopoly was an objective of the several restraints of trade that stand condemned.

Moreover, the problem under the Sherman Act is not solved merely by measuring monopoly in terms of size or extent of holdings or by concluding that single ownerships were not obtained "for the purpose of achieving a national monopoly."   It is the relationship of the unreasonable restraints of trade to the position of the defendants in the exhibition field (and more particularly in the first-run phase of that business) that is of first importance on the divestiture phase of these cases.   That is the position we have taken in *Schine Chain Theatres, Inc.* v. *United States, ante,* p. 110, in dealing with a projection of the same conspiracy through certain large circuits.   Parity of treatment of the unaffiliated and the affiliated circuits requires the same approach here.   For the fruits of the conspiracy which are denied the independents must also be denied the five majors.   In this connection there is a suggestion that one result of the conspiracy was a geographical division of territory among the five majors.   We mention it not to intimate that it is true but only to indicate the appropriate extent of the inquiry concerning the effect of the conspiracy in theatre ownership by the five majors.

The findings of the District Court are deficient on that score and obscure on another.   The District Court in its findings speaks of the absence of a "purpose" on the part of any of the five majors to achieve a "national monopoly" in the exhibition of motion pictures.   First, there is no finding as to the presence or absence of monopoly on the part of the five majors in the *first-run* field for the entire country, in the *first-run* field in the 92 largest cities of the country, or in the *first-run* field in separate localities. Yet the *first-run* field, which constitutes the cream of the

UNITED STATES *v.* PARAMOUNT PICTURES.   173

exhibition business, is the core of the present cases.   Section 1 of the Sherman Act outlaws unreasonable restraints irrespective of the amount of trade or commerce involved (*United States* v. *Socony-Vacuum Oil Co.*, 310 U. S. 150, 224, 225, n. 59), and § 2 condemns monopoly of "any part" of trade or commerce.   "Any part" is construed to mean an appreciable part of interstate or foreign trade or commerce.   *United States* v. *Yellow Cab Co.*, 332 U. S. 218, 225.   Second, we pointed out in *United States* v. *Griffith, ante,* p. 100, that "specific intent" is not necessary to establish a "purpose or intent" to create a monopoly but that the requisite "purpose or intent" is present if monopoly results as a necessary consequence of what was done.   The findings of the District Court on this phase of the cases are not clear, though we take them to mean by the absence of "purpose" the absence of a specific intent.   So construed they are inconclusive.   In any event they are ambiguous and must be recast on remand of the cases.   Third, monopoly power, whether lawfully or unlawfully acquired, may violate § 2 of the Sherman Act though it remains unexercised (*United States* v. *Griffith, ante,* p. 100), for as we stated in *American Tobacco Co.* v. *United States,* 328 U. S. 781, 809, 811, the existence of power "to exclude competition when it is desired to do so" is itself a violation of § 2, provided it is coupled with the purpose or intent to exercise that power.   The District Court, being primarily concerned with the number and extent of the theatre holdings of defendants, did not address itself to this phase of the monopoly problem. Here also, parity of treatment as between independents and the five majors as theatre owners, who were tied into the same general conspiracy, necessitates consideration of this question.

Exploration of these phases of the cases would not be necessary if, as the Department of Justice argues, vertical integration of producing, distributing and exhibit-

ing motion pictures is illegal *per se*.   But the majority
of the Court does not take that view.   In the opinion of
the majority the legality of vertical integration under the
Sherman Act turns on (1) the purpose or intent with
which it was conceived, or (2) the power it creates and the
attendant purpose or intent.   First, it runs afoul of the
Sherman Act if it was a calculated scheme to gain control
over an appreciable segment of the market and to restrain
or suppress competition, rather than an expansion to meet
legitimate business needs.   *United States* v. *Reading Co.*,
253 U. S. 26, 57; *United States* v. *Lehigh Valley R. Co.*,
254 U. S. 255, 269–270.   Second, a vertically integrated
enterprise, like other aggregations of business units
(*United States* v. *Aluminum Co. of America*, 148 F. 2d
416), will constitute monopoly which, though unexercised,
violates the Sherman Act provided a power to exclude
competition is coupled with a purpose or intent to do so.
As we pointed out in *United States* v. *Griffith, ante*, p. 100,
107, n. 10, size is itself an earmark of monopoly power.
For size carries with it an opportunity for abuse.   And the
fact that the power created by size was utilized in the past
to crush or prevent competition is potent evidence that
the requisite purpose or intent attends the presence of
monopoly power.   See *United States* v. *Swift & Co.*, 286
U. S. 106, 116; *United States* v. *Aluminum Co. of America*,
supra, p. 430.   Likewise bearing on the question whether
monopoly power is created by the vertical integration, is
the nature of the market to be served (*United States* v.
Aluminum Co. of America, supra, p. 430), and the leverage on the market which the particular vertical integration creates or makes possible.

These matters were not considered by the District
Court.   For that reason, as well as the others we have
mentioned, the findings on monopoly and divestiture
which we have discussed in this part of the opinion will
be set aside.   There is an independent reason for doing

UNITED STATES *v.* PARAMOUNT PICTURES. 175

131   Opinion of the Court.

that. As we have seen, the District Court considered competitive bidding as an alternative to divestiture in the sense that it concluded that further consideration of divestiture should not be had until competitive bidding had been tried and found wanting. Since we eliminate from the decree the provisions for competitive bidding, it is necessary to set aside the findings on divestiture so that a new start on this phase of the cases may be made on their remand.

It follows that the provision of the decree barring the five majors from further theatre expansion should likewise be eliminated. For it too is related to the monopoly question; and the District Court should be allowed to make an entirely fresh start on the whole of the problem. We in no way intimate, however, that the District Court erred in prohibiting further theatre expansion by the five majors.

The Department of Justice maintains that if total divestiture is denied, licensing of films among the five majors should be barred. As a permanent requirement it would seem to be only an indirect way of forcing divestiture. For the findings reveal that the five majors could not operate their theatres full time on their own films.[21] Whether that step would, in absence of competitive bidding, serve as a short-range remedy in certain situations to dissipate the effects of the conspiracy (*United States* v. *Univis Lens Co.*, 316 U. S. 241, 254; *United States* v. *Bausch & Lomb Co.*, *supra*, p. 724; *United States* v. *Crescent Amusement Co.*, *supra*, p. 188) is a question for the District Court.

---

[21] The District Court found, "Except for a very limited number of theatres in the very largest cities, the 18,000 and more theatres in the United States exhibit the product of more than one distributor. Such theatres could not be operated on the product of only one distributor."

Fourth.

The consent decree created an arbitration system which had, in the view of the District Court, proved useful in its operation. The court indeed thought that the arbitration system had dealt with the problems of clearances and runs "with rare efficiency." But it did not think it had the power to continue an arbitration system which would be binding on the parties, since the consent decree did not bind the defendants who had not consented to it and since the government, acting pursuant to the powers reserved under the consent decree, moved for trial of the issues charged in the complaint. The District Court recommended, however, that some such system be continued. But it included no such provision in its decree.

We agree that the government did not consent to a permanent system of arbitration under the consent decree and that the District Court has no power to force or require parties to submit to arbitration in lieu of the remedies afforded by Congress for enforcing the anti-trust laws. But the District Court has the power to authorize the maintenance of such a system by those parties who consent and to provide the rules and procedure under which it is to operate. The use of the system would not, of course, be mandatory. It would be merely an auxiliary enforcement procedure, barring no one from the use of other remedies the law affords for violations either of the Sherman Act or of the decree of the court. Whether such a system of arbitration should be inaugurated is for the discretion of the District Court.

Fifth—Intervention.

Certain associations of exhibitors and a number of independent exhibitors, appellant-intervenors in Nos. 85 and 86, were denied leave to intervene in the District

UNITED STATES *v.* PARAMOUNT PICTURES. 177

Court. They appeal from those orders. They also filed original motions for leave to intervene in this Court. We postponed consideration of the original motions and of our jurisdiction to hear the appeals until a hearing on the merits of the cases.

Rule 24 (a) of the Rules of Civil Procedure, which provides for intervention as of right, reads in part as follows: "Upon timely application anyone shall be permitted to intervene in an action: . . . (2) when the representation of the applicant's interest by existing parties is or may be inadequate and the applicant is or may be bound by a judgment in the action."

The complaint of the intervenors was directed towards the system of competitive bidding. The Department of Justice is the representative of the public in these anti-trust suits. So far as the protection of the public interest in free competition is concerned, the interests of those intervenors was adequately represented. The intervenors, however, claim that the system of competitive bidding would have operated prejudicially to their rights. Cf. *United States* v. *St. Louis Terminal*, 236 U. S. 194, 199. Their argument is that the plan of competitive bidding under the control of the defendants would be a concert of action that would be illegal but for the decree. If pursuant to the decree defendants acted under that plan, they would gain immunity from any liability under the anti-trust laws which otherwise they might have to the intervenors. Thus, it is argued, the decree would affect their legal rights and be binding on them. The representation of their interests by the Department of Justice on that score was said to be inadequate since that agency proposed the idea of competitive bidding in the District Court.

We need not consider the merits of that argument. Even if we assume that the intervenors are correct in their

178   OCTOBER TERM, 1947.

position, intervention should be denied here and the orders of the District Court denying leave to intervene must be affirmed. Now that the provisions for competitive bidding have been eliminated from the decree, there is no basis for saying that the decree affects their legal rights. Whatever may have been the situation below, no other reason appears why at this stage their intervention is warranted. Any justification for making them parties has disappeared.

The judgment in these cases is affirmed in part and reversed in part, and the cases are remanded to the District Court for proceedings in conformity with this opinion.

So ordered.

MR. JUSTICE JACKSON took no part in the consideration or decision of these cases.

MR. JUSTICE FRANKFURTER, dissenting in part.

"The framing of decrees should take place in the District rather than in Appellate Courts. They are invested with large discretion to model their judgments to fit the exigencies of the particular case." On this guiding consideration, the Court earlier this Term sustained a Sherman Law decree, which was not the outcome of a long trial involving complicated and contested facts and their significance, but the formulation of a summary judgment on the bare bones of pleadings. *International Salt Co.* v. *United States,* 332 U. S. 392, 400–401. The record in this case bespeaks more compelling respect for the decree fashioned by the District Court of three judges to put an end to violations of the Sherman Law and to prevent the recurrence, than that which led this Court not to find abuse of discretion in the decree by a single district judge in the *International Salt* case.

UNITED STATES *v.* PARAMOUNT PICTURES.   179

131   FRANKFURTER, J., dissenting in part.

This Court has both the authority and duty to consider whether a decree is well calculated to undo, as far as is possible, the result of transactions forbidden by the Sherman Law and to guard against their repetition.   But it is not the function of this Court, and it would ill discharge it, to displace the district courts and write decrees *de novo*.   We are, after all, an appellate tribunal even in Sherman Law cases.   It could not be fairly claimed that this Court possesses greater experience, understanding and prophetic insight in relation to the movie industry, and is therefore better equipped to formulate a decree for the movie industry than was the District Court in this case, presided over as it was by one of the wisest of judges.

The terms of the decree in this litigation amount, in effect, to the formulation of a regime for the future conduct of the movie industry.   The terms of such a regime, within the scope of judicial oversight, are not to be derived from precedents in the law reports, nor, for that matter, from any other available repository of knowledge. Inescapably the terms must be derived from an assessment of conflicting interests, not quantitatively measurable, and a prophecy regarding the workings of untried remedies for dealing with disclosed evils so as to advance most the comprehensive public interest.

The crucial legal question before us is not whether we would have drawn the decree as the District Court drew it, but whether, on the basis of what came before the District Court, we can say that in fashioning remedies it did not fairly respond to disclosed violations and therefore abused a discretion, the fair exercise of which we should respect and not treat as an abuse.   Discretion means a choice of available remedies.   As bearing upon this question, it is most relevant to consider whether the District Court showed a sympathetic or mere niggling awareness of the proper scope of the Sherman Law and the range of

its condemnation.   Adequate remedies are not likely to
be fashioned by those who are not hostile to evils to be
remedied.   The District Court's opinion manifests a stout
purpose on the part of that court to enforce its thorough-
going understanding of the requirements of the Sherman
Law as elucidated by this Court.   And so we have before
us the decree of a district court thoroughly aware of the
demands of the Sherman Law and manifestly determined
to enforce it in all its rigors.

How did the District Court go about working out the
terms of the decree some of which this Court now dis-
places?   The case was before that court from October 8,
1945, to January 22, 1947.   A vast body of the evidence
which had to be considered below, and must be considered
here in overturning the lower court's decree, consisted of
documents.   A mere enumeration of these documents, not
printed in the record before us, required a pamphlet of 42
pages.   It took 460 pages for a selection of exhibits
deemed appropriate for printing by the Government.
The printed record in this Court consists of 3,841 pages.
It is on the basis of this vast mass of evidence that the
District Court, on June 11, 1946, filed its careful opinion,
approved here, as to the substantive issues.   Thereafter,
it heard argument for three days as to the terms of the
judgment.   The parties then submitted their proposals
for findings of fact and conclusions of law by the District
Court.   After a long trial, an elaborate opinion on the
merits, full discussion as to the terms of the decree, more
than two months for the gestation of the decree, the terms
were finally promulgated.

I cannot bring myself to conclude that the product
of such a painstaking process of adjudication as to a
decree appropriate for such a complicated situation as
this record discloses was an abuse of discretion, arrived
at as it was after due absorption of all the light that

UNITED STATES *v.* PARAMOUNT PICTURES. 181

131   FRANKFURTER, J., dissenting in part.

could be shed upon remedies appropriate for the future. After all, as to such remedies there is no test, ultimately, except the wisdom of men judged by events.

Accordingly, I would affirm the decree except as to one particular, that regarding an arbitration system for controversies that may arise under the decree. This raises a pure question of law and not a judgment based upon facts and their significance, as are those features of the decree which the Court sets aside. The District Court indicated that "in view of its demonstrated usefulness" such an arbitration system was desirable to aid in the enforcement of the decree. The District Court, however, deemed itself powerless to continue an arbitration system without the consent of the parties. I do not find such want of power in the District Court to select this means of enforcing the decree most effectively, with the least friction and by the most fruitful methods. A decree as detailed and as complicated as is necessary to fit a situation like the one before us is bound, even under the best of circumstances, to raise controversies involving conflicting claims as to facts and their meaning. A court could certainly appoint a master to deal with questions arising under the decree. I do not appreciate why a proved system of arbitration, appropriate as experience has found it to be appropriate for adjudicating numberless questions that arise under such a decree, is not to be treated in effect as a standing master for purposes of this decree. See *Ex parte Peterson*, 253 U. S. 300. I would therefore leave it to the discretion of the District Court to determine whether such a system is not available as an instrument of auxiliary enforcement. With this exception I would affirm the decree of the District Court.

PART VI

CENSORSHIP - COMSTOCK

Anthony Comstock waged his war against "obscenity" from the year 1872 until his death in 1915. Comstock operated on the theory that every human being has an inborn tendency toward wrongdoing which is restrained mainly by fear of the final judgment. Comstock wanted to remove the traps that Satan created. Comstock lobbied for the Federal Anti-Obscenity Act of 1873 and for the New York Act which soon followed.

Comstock arranged for cutting in his New York Society for the Suppression of Vice for one-half of the fines levied on people successfully prosecuted by the Society or its agents.

Source: Supreme Court case of *GINSBERG v. NEW YORK* (1968), 390 US 629, 88 S Ct 1274, 20 L ed 2 195.

The following is an extract from Comstock's "TRAPS FOR THE YOUNG" (1883).

". . . .

APPENDIX I TO OPINION OF
MR. JUSTICE DOUGLAS,
DISSENTING.

A. COMSTOCK, TRAPS FOR THE YOUNG 20-22 (1883)

And it came to pass that as Satan went to and fro upon the earth, watching his traps and rejoicing over his numerous victims, he found room for improvement in some of his schemes. The daily press did not meet all his requirements. The *weekly* illustrated papers of crime would do for young men and sports, for brothels, ginmills, and thieves' resorts, but were found to be so gross, so libidinous, so monstrous, that every decent

person spurned them. They were excluded from the home on sight.
They were too high-priced for children, and too cumbersome to
be conveniently hid from the parent's eye or carried in the boy's
pocket. So he resolved to make another trap for boys and girls
especially." . . . .

        "Satan stirred up certain of his willing tools on earth
by the promise of a few paltry dollars to improve greatly on
the death-dealing quality of the weekly death-traps, and forthwith came a series of new snares of fascinating construction,
small and tempting in price, and baited with high-sounding names."
. . . .

        "This class includes the silly, insipid tale, the coarse,
slangy story in the dialect of the barroom, the blood-and-thunder
romance of border life, and the exaggerated details of crimes,
real and imaginary." . . . . "The unreal far outstrips the real.
Crimes are gilded, and lawlessness is painted to resemble valor,
making a bid for bandits, brigands, murderers, thieves, and criminals in general. Who would go to the State prison, the gambling
saloon, or the brothel to find a suitable companion for the child?
Yet a more insidious foe is selected when these stories are allowed to become associates for the child's mind and to shape and
direct the thoughts." . . . .

        "The leading character in many, if not in the vast
majority of these stories, is some boy or girl who possesses
usually extraordinary beauty of countenance, the most superb
clothing, abundant wealth, the strength of a giant, the agility
of a squirrel, the cunning of a fox, the brazen effrontery of
the most daring villain, and who is utterly destitute of any regard for the laws of God or man. Such a one is foremost among
desperadoes, the companion and beau-ideal of maidens, and the
high favorite of some rich person, who by his patronage and in-
dorsement lifts the young villain into lofty positions in society, and provides liberally of his wealth to secure him immunity for his crimes. These stories link the pure maiden with
the most foul and loathsome criminals. Many of them favor violation of marriage laws and cheapen female virtue."

CENSORSHIP

UNITED ARTISTS CORPORATION v. CITY OF DALLAS

Supreme Court of the United States (1968), 390 US 676, 88 S Ct 1298, 20 L ed 225.

"Mr. Justice Marshall delivered the opinion of the Court.

(1)   Appellants are an exhibitor and the distributor of a motion picture named 'Viva Maria,' which, pursuant to a city ordinance, the Motion Picture Classification Board of the appellee City of Dallas classified as 'not suitable for young persons.' A county court upheld the Board's determination and enjoined exhibition of the film without acceptance by appellants of the requirements imposed by the restricted classification. The Texas Court of Civil Appeals affirmed, and we noted probable jurisdiction, 387 US 903, 18 L Ed 2d 620, 87 S Ct 1685, to consider the First and Fourteenth Amendment issues raised by appellants with respect to appellee's classification ordinance.

That ordinance, adopted in 1965, may be summarized as follows. It establishes a Motion Picture Classification Board, composed of nine appointed members, all of whom serve without pay. The Board classifies films as 'suitable for young persons' or as 'not suitable for young persons,' young persons being defined as children who have not reached their 16th birthday. An exhibitor must be specially licensed to show 'not suitable' films.

The ordinance requires the exhibitor, before any initial showing of a film, to file with the Board a proposed classification of the film together with a summary of its plot and similar information. The proposed classification is approved if the Board affirmatively agrees with it, or takes no action upon it within five days of its filing.

If a majority of the Board is dissatisfied with the proposed classification, the exhibitor is required to project the film before at least five members of the Board at the earliest practicable time. At the showing, the exhibitor may also present testimony or other support for his proposed classification. Within two days the Board must issue its classification order. Should the exhibitor disagree, he must file within two days a notice of nonacceptance. The Board is then required to go to court within three days to seek a temporary injunction, and a hearing is required to be set on that application within five

days thereafter; if the exhibitor agrees to waive notice and
requests a hearing on the merits of a permanent injunction, the
Board is required to waive its application for a temporary injunction and join in the exhibitor's request. If an injunction
does not issue within 10 days of the exhibitor's notice of nonacceptance, the Board's classification order is suspended. The
ordinance does not define the scope of judicial review of the
Board's determination, but the Court of Civil Appeals held that
de novo review in the trial court was required. If an injunction issues and the exhibitor seeks appellate review, or if an
injunction is refused and the Board appeals, the Board must
waive all statutory notices and times, and join a request of the
exhibitor, to advance the case on the appellate court's docket,
i.e., do everything it can to assure a speedy determination."

．．．．

"'Not suitable for young persons' means:

(1) Describing or portraying brutality, criminal vio-
lence or depravity in such a manner as to be, in the judgment
of the Board, likely to incite or encourage crime or delinquency
on the part of young persons; or

(2) Describing or portraying nudity beyond the customary limits of candor in the community, or sexual promiscuity or
extra-marital or abnormal sexual relations in such a manner as
to be, in the judgment of the Board, likely to incite or encourage delinquency or sexual promiscuity on the part of young
persons or to appeal to their prurient interest.

"A film shall be considered likely to incite or encourage' crime delinquency or sexual promiscuity on the part of
young persons, if, in the judgment of the Board, there is a substantial probability that it will create the impression on young
persons that such conduct is profitable, desirable, acceptable,
respectable, praiseworthy or commonly accepted.

"A film shall be considered as appealing to 'prurient
interest' of young persons, if, in the judgment of the Board,
its calculated or dominant effect on young persons is substantially to arouse sexual desire. In determining whether a film
is 'not suitable for young persons,' the Board shall consider
the film as a whole, rather than isolated portions, and shall
determine whether its harmful effects outweigh artistic or
educational values such film may have for young persons."

"(2-4) Appellants attack those standards as unconstitu-
tionally vague. We agree. Motion pictures are, of course, protected by the First Amendment."

. . . .

"(10-11)   Vagueness and the attendant evils we have
described, see supra, at 230, are not rendered less objection-
able because the regulation of expression is one of classification rather than direct suppression. . . . .

"Nor is it an answer to an argument that a particular
regulation of expression is vague to say that it was adopted
for the salutary purpose of protecting children. The permissible extent of vagueness is not directly proportional to, or
a function of, the extent of the power to regulate or control
expression with respect to children. As Chief Judge Fuld has
said:

"'It is . . . essential that legislation aimed at protecting children from allegedly harmful expression - no less
than legislation enacted with respect to adults - be clearly
drawn and that the standards adopted be reasonably precise so
that those who are governed by the law and those that adminis-
ter it will understand its meaning and application.' People
v. Kahan, 15 NY 2d 311, 313, 206 NE 2d 333, 335 (1965) (con-
curring opinion)."

CENSORSHIP - FAME AND FORTUNE

I

Censorship is great for the men who seek publicity in *READER'S DIGEST*, other magazines, newspapers, and especially local community and church papers read by the publicity seeker's customers, clients, potential customers and clients. The publicity seeker gets publicity and money for espousing his cause. As many other cause espousers admit, what else is a good cause for but to provide material for its espousers to use to get publicity and money for themselves?

The censorship boys dismiss the Constitutional provision protecting free speech with a religious sounding, "Free speech does not include obscenity." (Why not? Because I told you so.)

The closest parallel to such reasoning is that of religious leaders espousing holy wars; "The Commandment against killing does not include killing those who don't belong to our religion."

The censorship boys make lots of money selling memberships, pamphlets, books, movies. They get government and private industry jobs. They can exercise their hate with glee.

Why should they not pursue their game?

II

Censorship is great for the X producers. Prices for tickets for XXX productions are higher than are tickets for roadshows. XXX tickets in many theatres along Santa Monica

Boulevard in Hollywood cost $5.00 each, while roadshow tickets

for *Marooned*, *Hello, Dolly* and *Goodbye, Mr. Chips* cost less.

More and more exhibitors in small towns are showing

XXX pictures, while making more money than ever, even after

contributing to (campaign) funds of local government men.

Local prosecutors must weigh the advantages of prosecution

(personal publicity) against the disadvantages (high cost of

prosecution, congestion of the criminal courts, anger of busi-

nessmen benfiting from customers drawn to the neighborhood

by the theatre and then remaining in the neighborhood to do

eating and shopping).

III

The censorship promoters operate at various governmental

and economic levels. The motion picture industry has various

censorship and classification procedures. One such classifica-

tion is that of the G-M-R-X classification.

G - Suggested for General audiences.

M - Suggested for Mature audiences.

R - Restricted - Persons under 16 not admitted unless

accompanied by parent or guardian.

X - Persons under 18 not admitted.

((XXX - An advertising gimmick, is not one of the four

self-censorship ratings.))

The first four ratings, G-M-R-X, apply to films released

after November 1, 1968 in ads submitted and approved under the
Motion Picture Code of Self-Regulation. This rating system was
declared experimental.

IV

There really should be a "B" rating. "B" for Babies.
These would be films fit only for 1-year-old babies sitting in
front of television sets and enjoying the variety of sights and
sounds.

PART VII

LABORATORY CREDIT AGREEMENT

There is no standard laboratory credit agreement. The
Laboratory Credit Agreement in this book is furnished for information only, just as every other agreement in this book is not
"standard" or "approved."

The Laboratory Credit Agreement is usually prepared by
the lab. The lab extends the credit, attaches a price list to
provide certainty, obtains security agreement rights and other
rights, everything possible, obtains a completion and subordination agreement from somebody with credit.

The laboratory thus becomes a money-lender, lending
money to the producer, production company, guarantor; actually,
cash is not loaned but credit is given for services at billing
rates.

Eventually the lab may be paid by the distributor, pursuant to a direction by the producer. Or the lab may be paid
by a guarantor.

The bank will insist that the laboratory subordinate
its rights to those of the bank. The lab will, because the
bank will insist.

LABORATORY CREDIT AGREEMENT

            AGREEMENT executed _____, 19_____,
between _____, herein called "Company," and
_____, herein called "Producer."

            WHEREAS, Producer has commenced or is about to commence
production of a motion picture now entitled "_____
_____" and

            WHEREAS, Producer desires to engage Company to do the
laboratory work in connection with the production of said motion
picture, as hereinafter provided; and

            WHEREAS, Producer has requested that Company extend
credit for its charges in connection with said laboratory work;

            NOW, THEREFORE, IT IS AGREED AS FOLLOWS:

            1. Producer's Lab Work.

            Producer hereby engages Laboratory to do and
perform all negative developing, daily printing, Title and Optical work, and all other items of laboratory work required by
Producer, including the furnishing of negative-cutting facilities, in connection with the production of said motion picture,
and Company hereby agrees to perform and furnish all such work
and facilities which may be required by Producer in connection
with the production of said motion picture, at Company's standard prices current at the time such work and facilities are
done and furnished. Attached hereto and marked Exhibit "A" is
a schedule of Company's current standard prices. It is understood that such prices are exclusive of any sales taxes now or
hereafter imposed by any governmental authority or any additional charges for which Company may become liable by reason of
any legislation, whether municipal, county, state or federal,
or by reason of any executive, administrative or judicial regulation, order or decree. In the event of any increase in Company's manufacturing costs occasioned by an upward revision of
wage scales, including retroactive increases, under any collective bargaining agreement, the prices set forth in Exhibit "A"
may be increased and a new price schedule established for the
work and facilities to be done and furnished hereunder. In the
event of an increase or decrease in the cost to Company of raw
stock film, the prices to be charged by Company and paid by

Producer for raw stock film supplied at a time when such changed
prices are applicable shall be increased or decreased accordingly.

   2.   Prints.

        Producer hereby further agrees to engage Company
to supply all release prints of the foregoing motion picture and
Company agrees to supply such prints upon order of Producer at
the same price for which Distributor is able to secure prints
of the same kind and quality at the time such prints are furnished.

   3.   Billing.

        Company shall bill Producer at monthly intervals
for charges entered against the Producer hereunder. All charges
will become final thirty (30) days following the rendition of
the statement in which such charges are reflected, unless prior
to the expiration of such thirty-day period Producer makes a
claim in writing for the adjustment of any such charge. Such
written claim shall specify the charge which is questioned and
the grounds therefor. Each monthly statement will be accompanied
by a promissory note, payable on demand, in the principal amount
of the charges incurred by Producer hereunder during the accounting period reflected in the statement. Each note shall bear interest at the rate of ten per cent (10%) per annum on the unpaid
balance. Producer agrees to execute each such note promptly and
deliver the same forthwith to Company. Company agrees that it
will not make demand for payment of the indebtedness under any
promissory note except upon the occurrence of the following:

        a.   The default by Producer in any of its
obligations hereunder;
        b.   The sale of the motion picture, or consum-
mation of a distribution agreement with respect thereto, accompanied by Producer's request that the negative of the motion
picture be delivered to Producer or its designee, or that prints
be made from the negative for delivery to Producer or its
designee;
        c.   The expiration of a period of six (6) months
from the date of commencement of photography of the motion picture;   or
        d.   The expiration of a period of three (3)
months following completion of the first trial composite prints
of said motion picture.

4. I A T S E

Without limiting the effect of the provisions of Paragraph 3 hereof, Producer agrees that it will proceed diligently with the production and completion of said motion picture, and agrees that in any event, production of said motion picture will be completed in all respects and the same will be ready for distribution not later than six (6) months following commencement of principal photography, and further agrees that said motion picture will be sold, or a distribution agreement entered into with respect thereto, not later than three (3) months after completion of the first trial composite prints of said motion picture.

Producer agrees to employ only technicians of IATSE or NABET Local Unions and Crafts in the production of said motion picture.

5. Clear Title.

Producer represents and warrants that it is and will be the sole owner of the motion picture and of all properties relating thereto (whether tangible or intangible and including, but without being limited to, all properties referred to in Paragraph 6 hereof), free and clear of any claims, rights, liens or charges thereon, together with the sole, exclusive and unencumbered worldwide silent, sound, synchronized and talking motion picture rights and licenses of every kind in and to the literary, musical, dramatic and other material therein contained or upon which said motion picture is based, in whole or in part, and that no interest in or claim against the motion picture or any of the properties thereof has been transferred to or is now held by anyone whomsoever. The foregoing warranties shall not be deemed violated by the transfer of any interest in the motion picture or the properties thereof, if such transfer is expressly made subject to the rights of Company hereunder.

6. General Lien.

Company shall have a general lien on Producer's "property," hereinafter more particularly described, for unpaid charges against Producer's account. The term "property" as used herein shall include said motion picture, and all of Producer's films, photoplays, photographs, pictures or other physical property from time to time in the possession of Company. If the lien on the property, or any part thereof, should be dependent upon possession of Company, and if Company should relinquish possession of such property and the same should later come again into the possession of Company, said lien shall reattach to such

property; its being understood, however, that the foregoing is
not intended to limit the rights of Company to the extent that
the same are not dependent upon possession by Company of the
property or any part thereof. Said lien shall also extend to
and include all of Producer's interest in all of the following:
The copyright (including common law, statutory, domestic and
foreign) on the property; the copyright on all literary, musical or other material used in, or in connection with, the property; and, in general, all rights in all matters and things
relating to or designed to enable or expedite the exploitation,
exhibition, marketing and distribution of the property, whether
or not specifically mentioned in this agreement.

7.   Additional Documents.

Producer agrees to execute such documents as
may be reasonably required by Company to effectuate the lien
or liens of Company hereunder and to effectuate the other purposes of this agreement.   Without limiting the generality of
the foregoing, Producer agrees to execute a mortgage of chattels - assignment and pledge on the motion picture or any other
items included in the property, a copyright mortgage on the
copyright of those items which are copyrighted or copyrightable,
and a notice of assignment of accounts receivable, in the forms
of the respective documents attached hereto and made a part
hereof, marked Exhibits "B," "C" and "D," or in such other form
as Company may require. In the event of the failure of Producer
to execute any promissory note or notes under Paragraph 3 hereof,
or any of the documents referred to in the next preceding sentence, or any other documents which may be required by Company
pursuant to the provisions of this agreement, Producer hereby
appoints, irrevocably, Company as attorney-in-fact of Producer
with full and complete authority to execute any or all of such
documents and to file and record the same wherever Company may
desire. In addition to any other rights which Company may have
hereunder, Producer agrees that Company's lien may be enforced
in the same manner as provided for enforcement of pledges under

the law of the State of California. Producer expressly waives
demand for payment or performance and notice of sale of any
pledged property, and any such sale may be either public or private, at Company's option, and at any such sale Company may bid
for and purchase the property offered for sale or any part
thereof. The property need not be present at any such sale or
in view of the purchaser or purchasers, and title shall pass upon such sale wherever the property or any part thereof is located with like effect as though all the property were present
and in the possession of the person conducting the sale and
were physically delivered to the purchaser or purchasers.

8. Third Party Actions.

In the event of any claim of right or ownership
adverse to the claim of Producer, with respect to said motion
picture or any other items included in the property, Company
shall have the right to interplead the property concerned or
bring other suitable action to have the adverse claims determined, or to defend against or resist any claim or proceeding
with respect to the property in any manner Company deems advisable. The cost of all such proceedings, including Company's
attorneys' fees, will be paid by Producer. It is expressly understood that the instituting, maintaining or defense of or
resistance to any such proceeding by Company shall not prejudice Company's security or lien rights herein provided for,
nor the right to assert its claim for any unpaid balances.

9. Company's Laboratory Agreement.

Annexed hereto and made a part hereof, marked
Exhibit "E," is Company's Laboratory Agreement. In the event
of any inconsistency between the Laboratory Agreement and this
agreement, the provisions of this agreement shall prevail.

10. Notwithstanding anything to the contrary contained in this agreement, the lien, mortgage, security, and
rights of Company set forth in this agreement shall be subject
to and subordinate to the lien, mortgage, security, and rights
in connection with each of the following:

a. A loan to Producer by _____ (Bank) of
_____ (City) in the amount of $_____,
plus interest; and,

b. A loan, or loans, to Producer by a third
party, or parties, to be designated by Producer, the aggregate
amount of which shall not exceed $_____, plus interest.

The Producer has informed the Company that it intends to re-finance the Motion Picture by substitutions in the place of the persons or firms specified in sub-paragraphs a and b above, different persons or firms having substantially the same rights of the substituted persons or firms. In that event, the Company agrees that its lien, mortgage, security, and rights, as set forth in this agreement, shall be junior to and subordinate to the liens, mortgages, security, and rights of the substituted persons or firms; provided that the aggregate indebtedness payable by Producer in connection with this Motion Picture to such substituted persons or firms shall not exceed, in the aggregate, $150,000.00, plus interest.

COMPANY: _____

By: _____

PRODUCER: _____

By: _____

EXHIBIT "A"

PRICE LIST

(EDITOR'S NOTE: Because of price variations, we are omitting the price list from this book.)

EXHIBIT "B"

SECURITY AGREEMENT

MORTGAGE OF CHATTELS

ASSIGNMENT AND PLEDGE

(Motion Picture)

By this Mortgage, made the _____ day of _____,
19____, by _____ , a _____
corporation, debtor and mortgagor, to the undersigned LABORATORY,
mortgagee and secured party, the debtor and mortgagor, herein
called "Producer," mortgages and assigns to and pledges with
mortgagee and secured party the property herein described as
security for the obligations hereinafter set forth.

1. Description of property. The property hereby mortgaged, pledged, and assigned, is described as follows:

a. The feature-length motion picture photoplay
(herein referred to as the "Picture") now entitled "_____
_____," which title is subject to change, based upon
an original story by _____,
and a shooting script by _____,
starring or featuring _____,
directed by _____,
under _____ as Producer;

b. All of the right, title and interest of Producer
in the literary, musical, dramatic, and other material upon or
from which, in whole or in part, the picture is based or adapted

or which is used or included in the Picture, and in the copyrights, renewals and extensions of copyright, and rights of
copyright, in such material:

      c. The physical properties of the picture, includ-
ing but not limited to all scripts, treatments and other manu-
scripts, negatives, prints, sound tracks, recordings, cut-outs,
and trims, in whatever state of completion, and all duplicates
and copies thereof;

      d. All assignable rights, present and future, in
and to all agreements for personal services, agreements for the
use of studio space and facilities, laboratory contracts, and
all other contracts relating to the production of the Picture;

      e. All copyrights, rights of copyright, and re-
newals and extensions of copyrights, domestic and foreign, heretofore or hereafter obtained on the Picture or any part thereof
and the right to make publication thereof for copyright purposes,
to register claim to copyright, and to renew and extend such
copyrights;

      f. All insurance and insurance policies heretofore
or hereafter placed by Producer on the Picture, the insurable
properties thereof, or any person or person engaged in the making of the Picture, and the proceeds of any such insurance;

      g. The right to market or otherwise exploit the
property in any manner whatever throughout the world; and

      h. All rent, revenue, income, compensation, and
profits of Producer from the release, exhibition, distribution,
or other exploitation of the Picture or of any rights therein
or derived therefrom.

    All of the foregoing property and rights are referred
to collectively in this instrument as the "Property," and this
Mortgage of Chattels, Assignment and Pledge is referred to as
the "Mortgage," or "Security Agreement."

    2. First lien. There are no rights in the property
prior to the rights of Mortgagee under this mortgage, its
being understood that this mortgage constitutes a first lien
on the property.

    3. Obligations secured. This mortgage is executed to
secure:

      a. Those loans and credits, whether or not

evidenced by a promissory note or notes, heretofore or hereafter made or extended by Mortgagee to Producer under an agreement between them dated _____, 19____, or under any renewal or extension thereof (such agreement, renewals, and extensions being herein called the "credit agreement");

b. The performance of each agreement of Producer contained herein or in the credit agreement. The maximum amount the repayment of which is to be secured by this mortgage at any one time shall not exceed $_____ then outstanding and unpaid, not including in such amount any items which theretofore may have been repaid or discharged.

4. Insurance to be provided by Producer. For such time as is customary in the motion picture industry Producer shall keep insured at their full insurable value against loss by fire, theft, or other insurable risks, the negatives, prints, sound tracks, recordings, and all other insurable accessories and properties of the picture, and shall secure such case insurance as is available covering such persons engaged in connection with the Picture as Mortgagee designates from time to time. The policy or policies of insurance shall be delivered to Mortgagee. Each policy shall be so written that the proceeds thereof will be payable to Mortgagee, Producer, and others, as their respective interests appear. Producer shall be entitled to receive all payments made under such policies or any of them prior to the completion of the picture and shall be obligated to use such proceeds for and only for the completion of the picture and as hereafter provided in this paragraph. All of such insurance proceeds remaining and all insurance proceeds received after completion of the picture shall be applied upon the obligations secured hereby in the same manner as the revenue and income received or to be received from the distribution and exploitation of the Picture.

5. Supplementary instruments. From time to time Producer shall execute, acknowledge, and deliver to Mortgagee, such further supplementary mortgages, agreements of pledge, and assignments, of the property or any part thereof as Mortgagee requires to enable it to exercise and to protect its rights hereunder and to maintain and evidence the security provided for herein, and shall deliver to Mortgagee satisfactory evidence that the Picture has been duly copyrighted in the United States of America and in other places where motion picture copyrights are customarily secured by so-called "major producers" of motion pictures, in the name of Producer or of distributor, free and clear of adverse claims and liens.

6. Warranties by Producer. Producer warrants and agrees
that it owns and at all times will own, the full, complete, and
unencumbered title in and to the property, free and clear of any
claims, rights, liens, or charges thereon, together with the
sole, exclusive, and unencumbered world-wide silent, sound, synchronized and talking motion picture rights and licenses of
every kind in and to the literary, musical, dramatic, and other
material therein contained or upon which the Picture is based,
in whole or in part, and that no interest in or claim against
the property has been transferred heretofore to or is now held
by anyone whomsoever.

7. Producer to protect title. Producer agrees to defend, at its own cost, (a) its title to the property as warranted
above; (b) this mortgage as a lien and charge upon the property
and as an assignment and pledge thereof; (c) the Picture and
the rights of Mortgagee as Mortgagee, pledgee, and assignee thereof against all claims of infringement and against all claims whatsoever based on or resulting from the use in the picture of any
story, adaptation, idea, character, impersonation, photography,
music, or other material. The assertion by any one of any such
claim shall not constitute a default hereunder if such claim is
diligently, adequately, and successfully contested by Producer
or is settled or discharged by it with reasonable diligence.

8. Covenant against other encumbrances. Producer
agrees that without Mortgagee's prior written consent Producer
will not suffer or permit any lien, charge, encumbrance, or
adverse claim whatsoever to accrue or be acquired upon or
against the property or any right therein which might be or
become prior or superior to the rights and liens of Mortgagee
under this mortgage.

9. Taxes to be paid by Producer. Producer agrees to
pay promptly and before delinquency all franchise taxes and
license fees required by law and all taxes, whether general or
special, assessments, and other governmental charges, lawfully
levied or assessed against Producer or the property or any part
thereof, and to furnish promptly to Mortgagee the official receipts or other evidence satisfactory to Mortgagee showing
such payments.

10. Mortgagee's right to perform certain acts. If Producer fails to make any payment or to do any act as herein provided, Mortgagee, in its sole discretion and with or without
notice to or demand upon Producer and without releasing Producer from any obligation hereunder may (a) make such payment
or do such act in such manner and to such extent as it deems
necessary to protect the security hereof; (b) commence or

appear in and defend any action or proceeding affecting the security hereof or the rights or powers of Mortgagee; (c) pay,
purchase, contest, or compromise any encumbrance, charge or lien,
which in its judgment is or might be prior or superior hereto;
(d) sell the property or any part thereof or cause it to be sold
at pledgee's sale; (e) foreclose this mortgage; and (f) in exercising any such powers, pay necessary expenses, employ counsel
and pay reasonable counsel fees. Producer shall reimburse mortgages immediately and without demand for all sums so expended
or expenses incurred by Mortgagee, with interest from the date
of expenditure at the rate of seven per cent (7%) per annum.

11.   Declaration of trust. Until the delivery of the
property to distributor, Producer agrees that it holds and will
hold the property as trustee for Mortgagee with the same effect
as though Mortgagee, as pledgee in possession thereof, had delivered possession to Producer to hold as trustee for Mortgagee.

12.   Distributor and others as pledge-holders. Following
delivery of the property or any part thereof to distributor,
and while the possession of distributor continues, distributor
shall hold the property in possession as pledgeholder for Mortgagee with like effect as though the property were in the possession of Mortgagee as pledgee. Every laboratory and other
person, firm or corporation which acquires possession of the
property or any part thereof is also appointed pledge-holder
thereof for Mortgagee in like manner as distributor. Producer
will obtain from distributor and from each such person, firm or
corporation instruments by which such pledge-holder assents to
and agrees to be bound by the provisions of this paragraph and
of Paragraph 16 of this mortgage.

13.   Waiver of statute of limitations. Producer waives
and agrees not to plead, invoke, or set up in any way any statute of limitations as a defense to any action or proceeding for
the payment of any indebtedness hereby secured or for the enforcement of any provision hereof or for any deficiency which
remains after any sale, pursuant to judicial decree or otherwise, of all or any part of the property.

14.   Producer to pay costs of collection. Producer
agrees to pay all costs and expenses, including attorneys'
fees in a reasonable amount, incurred by Mortgagee at any time
in the collection of any obligation hereby secured or in the
protection or enforcement of any of its rights hereunder or
under the credit agreement, or in the care, management, or
protection of the property, whether or not suit is filed, or
in any action to foreclose this mortgage.

15. Events of default. Each of the following shall be an event of default:

    a. If Producer defaults in the due and punctual payment of any indebtedness secured hereby or of any interest thereon;

    b. If Producer defaults in the due performance or observance of any other obligation of Producer under this mortgage or under the credit agreement and fails to cure such default within five days after written notice thereof has been given by Mortgagee to Producer;

    c. If any representation or warranty made by Producer herein or in the credit agreement or in any other statement heretofore or hereafter furnished by Producer to Mortgagee proves to be false or misleading in any material respect;

    d. If Producer abandons production of the picture or fails in any respect to cause it to be completed and delivered to distributor for release and distribution within the time provided in the credit agreement;

    e. If for any reason, whether valid or invalid, distributor fails or refuses to release and distribute the picture or discontinues the distribution thereof or in any material respect breaches the distribution agreement and unless within thirty (30) days after written notice thereof from Mortgagee to Producer such failure, refusal or breach is discontinued or cured or in lieu thereof Producer has substituted another distributor satisfactory to Mortgagee;

    f. If Mortgagee is prevented by any act or neglect of Producer from receiving the assigned revenue and income from the picture for application upon the indebtedness hereby secured;

    g. If Producer becomes insolvent or unable to pay its debts as they mature, or files a voluntary petition in bankruptcy under any chapter of the Bankruptcy Act or files an answer admitting the jurisdiction of the court and the material allegations of any involuntary petition filed pursuant to any chapter of the Bankruptcy Act, or is adjudicated a bankrupt, or makes an assignment for the benefit of creditors, or applies for or consents to the appointment of a receiver or trustee or if a receiver or trustee is appointed for all or a substantial part of the property or of the business of Producer;

    h. If any attachment, execution or other writ is levied upon the property or any substantial part thereof and remains in effect for more than thirty (30) days;

i. If the directors of Producer elect to wind up and dissolve Producer and to distribute its assets or if they elect to enter into any merger or consolidation without first obtaining Mortgagee's written approval.

16. Pledgee's sale. Upon the happening of an event of default, as defined herein, any pledge-holder of the property designated in this mortgage, upon request of Mortgagee shall sell the property or that part thereof then in the possession or under the control of such pledge-holder. Unless within ten days after written request to do so any such pledge-holder conducts such sale or causes it to be conducted such pledge-holder, upon demand therefor by Mortgagee, shall deliver the pledged property then in its possession to Mortgagee and Mortgagee then may sell the pledged property or cause it to be sold. Producer expressly waives demand for payment or performance and notice of sale. Any such sale may be either public or private, at the option of the Mortgagee, only, and at any such sale Mortgagee may bid for and purchase the property offered for sale or any part thereof and by such purchase shall become the owner thereof. The property need not be present at any such sale or in view of the purchaser or purchasers and title shall pass upon such sale wherever the property or any part thereof is located with like effect as though all of the property were present and in the possession of the person conducting the sale and were physically delivered to the purchaser or purchasers. From the gross proceeds of the sale there shall first be deducted the expenses incurred by the pledge-holder or Mortgagee in connection therewith, including attorneys' fees and brokers' commissions. The net proceeds then remaining shall be applied on account of the indebtedness secured by this mortgage, and any further amounts then remaining shall be paid to, or for the account of, Producer.

17. Mortgagee's right to accelerate maturity. At any time after the happening of any event of default, unless such default has been remedied by Producer or waived in writing by Mortgagee, Mortgagee, at its option, may declare immediately due and payable the indebtedness secured hereby and then unpaid, including unpaid interest thereon, and may immediately enforce any or all of its rights hereunder. In no event shall Mortgagee be required to make any other or additional loan or to extend any other or additional credit to Producer under the credit agreement at any time when Producer is in default hereunder or to any receiver, trustee or assignee of Producer.

18. Defeasance. Upon payment in full to Mortgagee of the indebtedness hereby secured and the performance by Producer

of all other of its obligations hereunder Mortgagee will deliver to Producer such instruments of release, reconveyance, and re-assignment, as will be sufficient to discharge Producer of its obligations hereunder and to terminate and release the lien and charge of this mortgage upon the property.

19. <u>Effect of titles</u>. The titles or headings of the various paragraphs of this mortgage are intended solely for con-venience of reference and are not intended and shall not be deemed for any purpose whatever to modify, explain or aid in the construction of any of the provisions of this mortgage.

20. <u>Parties bound</u>. This mortgage shall bind and inure to the benfit of, as the case may require, the parties hereto and their respective successors and assigns.

Executed at _____, _____
on the date first above written.

PRODUCER (Debtor, Mortgagor):   _____

                          By: _____

LABORATORY (Secured Party, Mortgagee):   _____

                          By: _____

EXHIBIT "C"

SECURITY AGREEMENT

MORTGAGE AND ASSIGNMENT OF COPYRIGHTS

_____, a _____

corporation, hereinafter called "Mortgagor," or "Producer,"

hereby mortgages and assigns to the undersigned LABORATORY, here-

inafter called "Mortgagee," the following property:

The copyrights, including all renewals and extensions

thereof, which may be secured under the laws now or hereafter

in effect in the United States of America, or any other coun-

tires, in and to that certain motion picture entitled, "_____

_____."

Said copyright was registered in the United States Copy-

right Office in the name of Mortgagor under entry number _____

_____.

This Mortgage and Assignment is executed pursuant to

the provisions of a Mortgage of Chattels - Pledge and Assign-

ment of said motion picture, hereinafter called the "Picture

Mortgage," dated _____, 19____, and executed by Mort-

gagor in favor of Mortgagee, and is executed as security for:

a. The repayment of all loans and extensions of
credit made and to be made by Mortgagee to Mortgagor in the
principal amount of $_____, and any renewals or ex-
tensions thereof and interest thereon, provided that the maximum amount to be secured hereby and remaining unpaid at any one
time shall not exceed the total sum of $_____.

      b. The payment of all costs, expenses and attorneys' fees in a reasonable amount incurred by Mortgagee in the event of the foreclosure of this Mortgage and Assignment or of the Picture Mortgage or in any action upon the indebtedness of Mortgagor to Mortgagee or in any other action to protect or enforce the rights of Mortgagee hereunder or under said Picture Mortgage or affecting or purporting to affect the security therefor;

      c. The full and faithful performance by Mortgagor of all the provisions contained in or contemplated by this Mortgage and Assignment and the Picture Mortgage.

      In the event of any default of Mortgagor under this Mortgage and Assignment or the Picture Mortgage, the aforesaid copyrights, or any of them, may be sold together with the properties described in the Picture Mortgage in the manner therein provided, and the purchaser at such sale shall thereafter hold said copyrights, or any of them, free of any claims of Mortgagor or of any rights of redemption. The recitals in any Certificate or Certificates of Sale hereunder executed by the Mortgagee, and the recitals in any judicial decree of foreclosure or Certificate or Certificates of Sale made thereunder, shall be conclusive proof of the truthfulness of any matters or facts stated therein, whether set forth in specific or general terms or as conclusions of law or fact. The Mortgagee is hereby irrevocably appointed and empowered as attorney-in-fact for Mortgagor to assign and transfer said copyrights, or any of them, to the purchaser or purchasers thereof at any sale or sales hereunder.

      All rights and remedies of Mortgagee hereunder shall be cumulative, and the exercise of any right or remedy hereunder shall not preclude the exercise of any other right or remedy given Mortgagee by any instrument executed by Mortgagor or by any provision of law or equity.

      Executed at &rule;, &rule;, on &rule;, 19&rule;.

PRODUCER: &rule;

    By: &rule;

LABORATORY: &rule;

    By: &rule;

EXHIBIT "D"

COMPLETION AND SUBORDINATION AGREEMENT

Agreement executed _____, 19_____,

between _____, hereinafter

called "Guarantor," and _____, hereinafter

called "Laboratory."

WHEREAS, _____, a

_____, hereinafter called "Producer," de-

sires to borrow and/or obtain credit from Laboratory up to a

total outstanding at any one time of $ __12,000.00_____

to be used for the production and completion of a motion picture

now entitled "_____,"

hereinafter called the "film" and

WHEREAS, Laboratory requires as a condition precedent to
the lending of any money or extension of credit to Producer for
the production and completion of the film and in consideration
thereof that Guarantor shall unconditionally guarantee the completion of the film as a finished product, for exhibition and
exploitation throughout the world; and

WHEREAS, Guarantor will derive a substantial benefit
from the completion of the film and is willing to guarantee the
completion thereof;

NOW, THEREFORE, in consideration of the premises and in
further consideration of the substantial benefit which will result to Guarantor from the completion of the film, the parties
hereto do hereby mutually agree as follows:

1. All of the recitals hereinabove set forth shall
be deemed to be included herein as though set forth at length
herein.

2.   Guarantor agrees that if, for any reason or under any contingency, Producer shall abandon production of the film, or shall fail to complete the film as a finished product on or prior to _____, 19____, and pay all of the production costs thereof, or if the film is not sold or a distribution agreement entered into with respect thereto within three (3) months after completion of the first trial composite prints thereof, or if the Laboratory takes possession of the film prior to the completion thereof by reason of any default of Producer under the Pledge and Assignment, executed by Producer to Laboratory, and the production of such film shall have been abandoned by Producer or such film is not being completed as aforesaid, or if, for any reason or under any condition the right of Producer to receive any other or further loans or extensions of credit in connection therewith shall be terminated and the production of said film shall have been abandoned or is not being completed, then and in any such event, Guarantor will assume all responsibility for the completion of the film, and, at his own cost and expense, will fully complete or cause the film to be fully completed and made into a finished product for delivery to the distributor on or prior to said date, and will pay all bills, costs and charges in connection with the production and completion of the film, and will cause the film to be sold or cause a distribution agreement to be entered into with respect thereto within said period of three (3) months. In such event, should Laboratory at the time have possession of the film it will make the same available for completion by Guarantor or his monimee.

3.   Guarantor, at his option, may elect not to fully complete the film in the manner hereinabove provided or not to sell the film or enter into a distribution agreement with respect thereto, and in the event he elects not to complete the film or fails to do so on or prior to said date or fails to do so on or prior to said date or fails to sell or enter into a distribution agreement within said period of three months, Guarantor will pay in full all loans and indebtednesses then owing by Producer to Laboratory with respect to the film, not exceeding the sum of $12,000, together with interest thereon; and Guarantor waives any right to require Laboratory to proceed against Producer or exhaust the security of Producer.

4.   Any indebtedness of Producer to Guarantor, with the interest thereon, which shall result from completion of the film by Guarantor at his own cost and expense, if he is required to perform under the provisions of this agreement, shall be and it hereby is, subordinated to the indebtedness of Producer to Laboratory.

5.   Guarantor agrees with Laboratory that the guaranties hereinabove contained are unconditional and create separate and distinct liabilities of Guarantor which Laboratory may enforce by separate action and with or without enforcement of the pledge or the sale or foreclosure of the film or any other security which Laboratory may hold.

6.   Guarantor authorizes Laboratory, without notice or demand and without affecting its guaranties hereunder, from time to time, to:

a.   Assign the guaranties, or any of them, in whole or in part without notice;

b.   Renew, compromise, extend, accelerate or otherwise change the time for payment of, or otherwise change the terms of the loans or credits or any part thereof, including increase or decrease of the rate of interest thereon.

7.   Guarantor waives any right to require Laboratory to:

a.   Proceed against Producer;

b.   Proceed to foreclose the Pledge and Assignment or sell by pledgee's sale the films thereunder or proceed against or exhaust any other security held from Producer or others;

8.   Guarantor waives any defense arising by reason of any disability or other defense of Producer or by reason of the cessation from any cause whatsoever of the liability of Producer.

9.   Guarantor waives all demands for performance and all notices of non-performance and of sale, and all other notices of every kind and character whatsoever.

10.   Guarantor agrees, upon demand by Laboratory, to pay to and reimburse Laboratory for all costs and expenses, including reasonable attorneys' fees, which Laboratory may expend or incur in the enforcement of this agreement.

11.   Guarantor hereby subordinates to and in favor of Laboratory and to the lien and charge of the Mortgage of Chattels-Pledge and Assignment all rights, titles and interest now possessed by Guarantor or which he may hereafter acquire in, on or to the film and the properties thereof, to the end and intent that the lien and charge of Laboratory on the film and

on the revenue and income therefrom which are assigned and
hypothecated to Laboratory under the Mortgage of Chattels -
Pledge and Assignment shall be and remain prior and preferred
to any lien or charge thereon of Guarantor until the loans made
by Laboratory to Producer, with interest thereon, shall have
been fully paid and discharged.

12.   In the event of any assignment by Producer for
the benefit of creditors, or in case of any bankruptcy proceedings instituted by or against Producer, or in case of the appointment of a receiver for Producer's business or assets, or
in case of the appointment of a receiver for Producer's business
or assets, or in case of any liquidation, dissolution or winding
up of the affairs of Producer, Producer and any assignee, trustee in bankruptcy, receiver, or other person or persons in
charge, are hereby authorized and directed to pay to Laboratory
the full amount of Laboratory's claim against Producer before
making any payment of principal or interest to Guarantor, and,
insofar as may be necessary for that purpose, Guarantor hereby
assigns and transfers to Laboratory all rights to any payments,
dividends or distributions out of the assets of Producer.

13.   It shall not be necessary for Laboratory to
inquire into the powers of Producer or any of its officers,
employees, agents or representatives acting or purporting to
act on its behalf.

14.   This agreement shall be construed according to
the laws of the State of California.

IN WITNESS WHEREOF, the parties hereto have
caused this agreement to be executed at Los Angeles, California,
as of the date first hereinabove written.

GUARANTOR: _____

By: _____

LABORATORY: _____

By: _____

PART VIII

PRODUCER-DISTRIBUTOR AGREEMENT

You are now able to read one of the great masterpieces of American literature.

Consider the value of a novel to the average novelist - almost $0 or less.

Consider the value of this contract to the distributor - over $100,000; possibly over $1,000,000.

The Producer hocks his life to make the picture, and this contract gives away his chance of redeeming his life through this picture.

DISTRIBUTOR-PRODUCER ROYALTY REPORT

TITLE		
PRODUCER		
RELEASE NUMBER	REPORT NUMBER	
WEEK OF RELEASE	DATE	

INCOME & EXPENSE	CURRENT	CUMULATIVE
REVENUE		
DOMESTIC THEATRICAL		
ENGLISH THEATRICAL		
CANADIAN THEATRICAL		
FOREIGN THEATRICAL		
DOMESTIC TELEVISION		
CANADIAN TELEVISION		
FOREIGN TELEVISION		
DOMESTIC TRL & ACC		
TOTAL REVENUE		
OFF-TOP EXPENSE		
DOMESTIC THEA PRINTS		
DOMESTIC CO-OP/ADVTG		
DOMESTIC THEA CENSOR		
DOMESTIC EXPRESS		
FGN DIST COST THEA		
FOREIGN DIST COST TV		
CANADA CONV COST		
TOTAL OFF-TOP EXP		
DISTRIBUTION FEES		
DOMESTIC EXCH FEES		
DOM H/O FEES THEA		
ENG H/O FEES THEA		
CANADA H/O FEES THEA		
FOREIGN DIST FEE THT		
DOMESTIC DIST FEE TV		
CANADA H/O FEES TV		
FOREIGN DIST FEE TV		
DOM TRAIL DIST FEE		
TOTAL DISTRIB FEES		
PRODUCERS EXPENSES		
PROD POOL PRINTS		
LESS RENTAL		
LESS SALES		
PROD ADVERTISING		
PROD EXPRESS		
PROD TV COSTS		
PRODUCER MISCELLANY		
NET PRODUCERS CHGS		
NET CR TO PRODUCER		

PRODUCER-DISTRIBUTOR AGREEMENT

PRODUCER-DISTRIBUTOR AGREEMENT

THIS AGREEMENT, made this date: _____

by and between _____ ,

a California corporation, (hereinafter referred to as "Producer"),

and _____ ,

a California corporation, (hereinafter referred to as "Distribu-

tor"),

WITNESSETH:

WHEREAS, Producer contemplates the production of __one__

motion picture photoplay, said photoplay tentatively entitled

_____ ,

being hereinafter referred to individually as "Picture," or "the

subject picture," and

WHEREAS, Distributor is engaged in the business of dis-

tributing motion pictures in the United States through the medium

of franchise holders, and in the rest of the world through any

or all available mediums; and

WHEREAS, Producer and Distributor desire that the Dis-

tributor shall release and distribute the picture to be produced

by Producer upon the terms and conditions hereinafter set forth;

NOW, THEREFORE, in consideration of the mutual promises
and agreements herein contained, and for other good and valuable
consideration, the parties hereto do hereby agree as follows:

    1. <u>PICTURE</u>.

    a. Producer agrees to produce and deliver to Dis-
tributor, for release and distribution by Distributor, <u>one</u>
English language feature-length, sound-and-talking motion picture photoplay photographed in panovision, tentatively entitled
"_____,"
on or before February 28, 1970.

    b. Producer agrees that the picture to be produced
by Producer in accordance with this agreement, shall be of
feature-length (not less than 90 minutes in length), and of competent and merchantable quality.

    c. Distributor shall have the right to approve
screenplay, male and female leads, and the directors of the said
picture. Producer has stated that _____
will direct the picture, and Distributor hereby approves said-
named _____ as Director. If Producer does not
obtain written approval of each of same, Distributor shall be
under no obligation to comply with any of the provisions set
forth in Paragraph 2. Distributor shall have five (5) days
after submission by Producer within which to refuse to accept
the screenplay and/or the names submitted for male and female
leads and/or the director (other than the named director, who

is herein approved as director), and if Distributor shall disapprove any of the said items, all dates for starting and finish-
ing and delivery of the motion picture as herein provided shall
be automatically extended for a period equal to the period of delay in principal photography occasioned by said disapproval.

    2.   DISTRIBUTOR'S GUARANTEE.

    Producer agrees to submit a proposed budget of the pic-
ture to Distributor, for Distributor's approval, no later than
fifteen (15) days prior to the commencement of principal photography of the picture. Upon written approval by Distributor, the
said budget shall be known as the "approved budget" of the
picture.

    Conditioned upon and only in the event that Distributor
shall approve Producer's budget of the picture as provided above,
Distributor unconditionally guarantees and agrees to pay to Producer the total sum of not less than $200,000.00 with respect
to picture, within the period of twenty-four (24) months and
seven (7) days from the date of first general release of picture
in the United States (said period of twenty-four months and
seven days being hereinafter referred to as "the guarantee
period").

    Distributor shall be entitled to credit on said guarantee
of $200,000.00 for such amount of the aforesaid total guarantee
as may actually be paid by Franchise Holders and/or others to
Distributor, for Producer's account, and then paid by Distributor

to Producer as required as aforesaid.

In the event Producer has received less than the total
sum of $200,000.00 within the guarantee period with respect to
the picture from the normal proceeds of distribution and the
aforesaid contracted total guarantee, Distributor agrees to
pay upon the expiration of the guarantee period, the shortage,
if any, between what Producer has received of the aforesaid
gross receipts from the picture and total guarantee and the
total sum of $200,000.00. After Distributor has paid such
shortage, if any, Distributor may recoup said shortage from
Producer's share of the gross receipts from the picture derived from all territories and for all distribution media.

3. DELIVERY.

Full delivery of each picture by Producer shall consist
of making physical delivery, at the sole cost and expense of
Producer, to Distributor, at Distributor's place of business,
or to such person or corporation, at such address as Distributor may designate, of the following:

a. One answer print of the picture, fully cut,
main and end titled, edited and assembled, with the sound track
printed thereon in perfect synchronization with the photographic
action and fit and ready for exhibition and distribution.

b. One wholly original picture negative of the
picture, fully cut, main and end titled, edited and assembled
and conformed in all respects to said sample, composite positive

print, and one wholly original sound track negative, made concurrently with and synchronously with the original picture
negative of the picture, including therein any sound, sound effects or music dubbed into said original sound track negative.

c.   One first-class clear, composite, fine-grain
protection positive print of the picture, fully cut, main and
end titled, edited and assembled with the sound track printed
thereon in perfect synchronization with the photographic action and conformed in all respects to said sample composite
positive print.

d.   Fifty (50) typewritten or mimeographed copies
of a detailed dialogue continuity of the completed picture,
conformed in all respects to the dialogue contained in the completed picture.

e.   Ten (10) copies of music cue sheets of the
picture setting forth the titles of the compositions, the names
of the composers, the place and extent of the uses made of the
compositions in the picture, the name of the owner or owners of
the copyright thereon, if the same has been copyrighted, and the
name and address of the publisher of the compositions, if
published.

f.   The original negative and one positive print of
not less than seventy-five (75) still photographs, 8 x 10 inches
in size, which photographs shall depict different scenes and/or
poses taken from the picture, the majority of which shall depict

the principal members of the cast, suitable for use by Distributor in the preparation of advertising, exhibition and publicity material for the picture. Each said still photograph shall be accompanied by a title descriptive of the scene depicted.

g. Such material as Distributor may reasonably require for the making of trailers to be used in connection with the distribution of the picture.

h. Such other publicity and exploitation material as distributor may reasonably require to be used in connection with the picture.

i. Copies of sound royalty agreements, if any, and a certificate by a corporate officer of Producer to the effect that all costs, expenses or charges incurred in connection with the production of the picture, except deferments or trade credits arranged in accordance with the provisions of this agreement and expressly authorized or approved in writing by Distributor and fully subordinated to the rights of Distributor hereunder, have been paid in full.

j. Duplicate originals, or photostatic copies, if duplicate originals are unavailable, of all licenses, contracts, assignments and/or other written permissions from the proper parties in interest permitting Producer to use any musical, literary, dramatic and other material of whatever nature used by it in the production of the picture (including but not limited to all employment contracts with actors, actresses, directors, producers and writers).

k.   Producer will receive a rating of "G" or the equivalent, accompanied by the original or duplicate original letter of transmittal. Producer will also shoot additional scenes which, if included in the film, would get it an "X" rating.

l.   Six (6) copies of a brief synopsis in the English language of the story of the picture which shall be delivered as soon as possible.

m.   Two (2) copies of the shooting script used in the production of the picture.

Distributor shall have the right to inspect and examine the material and documents tendered as delivery hereunder and shall advise Producer within ten (10) days after the tendered delivery if and wherein the same is not complete, whereupon Producer shall promptly deliver to Distributor such items by which it shall have failed to make delivery in the first instance. Distributor may (but shall not be obligated to) accept delivery of the picture if such delivery shall not be complete, in which event, Distributor may supply or require Producer thereafter to supply at the sole cost and expense of Producer, such items which Producer shall have failed to deliver in the first instance. Such acceptance of incomplete delivery shall not be deemed to be a waiver of Distributor's right to demand and require a full delivery as herein defined.

Producer agrees to deliver the Picture to Distributor

free and clear of all recording, synchronization, dubbing, re-
dubbing and/or distribution royalties, music copyright royalties
and all other patent and/or copyright royalties and any other
payments which may be required to be met with respect thereto,
or any part thereof, as well as with respect to the distribution or exhibition thereof, or prints thereof, for the United
States, and for each and every part of the world, its being the
intention hereof that all such payments shall be made by Producer as and when required, and in the event of failure on Producer's part to make any of said payments Distributor shall have
the right at Distributor's option, but shall not be obligated,
to make the same at Producer's sole cost and expense and deduct
and recoup the amount thereof from Producer's share of the gross
receipts of the Picture.

4. GRANTS OF RIGHTS.

Producer does hereby give, grant, assign and set over
unto Distributor the sole, exclusive and irrevocable right,
license and privilege under copyright to rent, lease, license,
exhibit, distribute, re-issue, deal in and with respect to the
picture and prints, or any part thereof, and trailers thereof,
and to license others to do so, in standard and substandard
gauges throughout the entire world by any and all mediums or
means, (the entire world being hereinafter referred to as the
"licensed territory") for a period of twenty (20) years from
the date of first general release of the Picture in the United

States. The rights granted herein shall include but are not
limited to rentals, leases or licenses to United States Army,
Navy and other military or armed services installations, the
American Red Cross, Veterans' Hospitals or similar facilities
wherever situated throughout the world, whether in 35mm or in
substandard gauges.

The rights herein granted, without limiting the generality of the foregoing, shall include all so-called 'theatrical'
as well as 'non-theatrical' rights in the picture (as those
terms are commonly understood in the motion picture (industry)
and shall include the right to use film of any and all gauges,
and the right to project, exhibit, reproduce, transmit and perform and authorize and license others to project, exhibit, reproduce, transmit and perform and authorize and license others
to project, exhibit, reproduce, transmit and perform the picture
and prints and trailers thereof theatrically and by television,
(whether free, pay-as-you-see or otherwise) and/or by any and
all other scientific, mechanical and/or electrical means, methods
or devices now known or herafter conceived or created.

Distributor agrees that it will not distribute the picture on so-called free television for a period of twenty-four
(24) months after the first general release of the picture in
35mm gauge in the United States.

The Producer reserves the right to require the Distributor to negotiate the sale or license of television rights to the

picture at the end of five (5) years after date of general release of purchase in the United States, if the Distributor has
not already negotiated said Television rights or license at said
time. The rights granted herein shall include but are not
limited to rentals, leases or licenses to the United States Army,
Navy and other Military or armed services installations, the
American Red Cross, Veterans' Hospitals, or similar facilities
wherever situated througout the world, whether in 35mm or in
substandard gauges.

   5.   DISTRIBUTOR'S OBLIGATIONS.

   Distributor agrees to use its best efforts consistent
with good business in distributing and selling and/or causing
the distribution and sale of the Picture as herein provided;
provided, however, that Producer acknowledges and agrees that
Distributor makes no representativons, warranties, guarantees
or agreements as to the gross receipts or net profits to be derived from the Picture, except as is set forth specifically in
this agreement. Distributor shall have the sole, exclusive and
complete control (without let or hindrance by Producer or any
third person) over the leasing, licensing, exploiting, marketing
and/or other distribution of the Picture and/or the rights
therein.

   Distributor shall be under no obligation to lease, license or otherwise turn to account the Picture in any country
or territory of the world outside of the United States where

Distributor in its sole judgment deems it impossible, unprofit-
abile or otherwise not feasible to do so.

The Picture may be distributed, marketed or disposed of
by Distributor or by any other person, firm or corporation whom
Distributor designates, including (but not limited to) Distributor's corporate subsidiaries or affiliates. Without limiting
the generality of the preceding sentence, it is agreed that
Distributor may transfer or assign this agreement, or all or
any part of Distributor's rights hereunder, to any person, firm
or corporation and this agreement shall inure to Distributor's
benefit and the benefit of Distributor's successors and assigns.

It is acknowledged and agreed that Distributor, as well
as such other persons, firms or corporations as may distribute,
market or turn to account the Picture or the rights therein,
shall have sole and complete authority with respect to the distribution, marketing or other turning to account of the Picture
and the rights therein, and the Producer agrees that such distribution, marketing and turning to account may be accomplished
under any plan or plans which Distributor or Distributor's successors and assigns may deem proper and expedient, and upon such
terms and conditions as Distributor or Distributor's successors
and assigns may deem desirable.

Without in any manner limiting the generality of the
foregoing, it is agreed that the Picture may be distributed
singly or in a group including other pictures, and, if

distributed or otherwise disposed of as part of a group including other pictures, the gross receipts allocated to the Picture shall be fixed and determined by Distributor, and any such allocation shall be conclusive and binding upon Producer in all respects.

Distributor and any other person, firm or corporation, distributing, marketing or otherwise turning to account the Picture shall have the right to make and cancel contracts with respect to the distribution or exhibition of the Picture, and the right to adjust and settle all disputes with exhibitors, licensees and other persons, including (but not limited to) the right to make allowances and give credit to such exhibitors, licensees and other persons, and all such acts, including allowances to such exhibitors, licensees and other persons for advertising, publicity and exploitation, shall be conclusive and binding upon Producer.

Nothing herein contained shall be construed to require the constant or continuous distribution of the Picture, after the normal period of distribution shall have expired, or to cause Distributor to re-issue the Picture, and Producer agrees that these are matters with respect to which Distributor's sole judgment and discretion shall be conclusive, and nothing herein contained shall constitute an obligation on Distributor's part with respect to the sale, distribution, marketing or other turning to account of any rights in the Picture (including but not limited to television rights, non-theatrical rights and substandard gauge rights) other than 35mm theatrical rights, its being our agreement and the intention hereof that Distributor shall have the right in Distributor's judgment and discretion to determine whether, when, how and for what price such other rights in the Picture are disposed of.

It is understood and agreed that it is the present intention of Distributor to combine the Picture with another motion picture presently entitled *THE JOE YORE STORY*. Said two (2) pictures shall be merchandised as a twin picture combination in most situations, and it is agreed that all revenue derived from both motion pictures shall be combined, and that the revenue therefrom shall be divided 65% to the Picture and 35% to *THE JOE YORE STORY*. Distributor, however, makes no warranty that the said two (2) pictures will always be contracted for, booked or played together. However, in all cases when the pictures are combined, the total revenue from both pictures shall be divided 65% to the Picture, and 35% to *THE JOE YORE STORY*. Other than as specifically amended and modified by this paragraph, the provisions of the foregoing parts of Paragraph 5 shall prevail.

6. THEATRICAL DISTRIBUTION.

The right to distribute the pictures in motion picture theatres and in theatres generally where motion pictures are exhibited and in other places generally where motion pictures are exhibited to persons who pay admission charge therefor and

and in the theatrical field (as said term is understood and used
in the motion picture industry), whether by the use of standard
or substandard size prints, is hereinafter referred to as the
right to "theatrically distribute" the pictures.

   7.   ALTERING CONTRACTS.

   Distributor shall have the right and power to alter,
amend, modify, change, waive, release or cancel any of its contracts with its Franchise Holders, subdistributors or licensees,
or any of the terms and conditions thereof, and to make any compromise, adjustment, or settlement of disputes thereunder, and
to make any allowances, rebates, refunds or credits thereto.

   In addition to the foregoing, Distributor shall have the
right to alter and cancel contracts with exhibitors, including
the right to adjust and settle all disputes with exhibitors and
the right to make allowances, rebates, refunds, or credits
therewith. All such alterations and cancellations of contracts,
adjustments, settlements, allowances and credits made by distributor in good faith shall be final.

   8.   TIME OF RELEASE.

   Provided that Producer makes full delivery of the Picture
as defined herein to Distributor on or before March 15, 1970,
Distributor agrees to release the Picture in the United States
on or before June 1, 1970, and, for purposes of this agreement,
June 1, 1970 shall be considered the date of first general release in the United States.

9.   FOREIGN LANGUAGE VERSIONS.

Distributor shall have the right to make and to license others to make foreign language versions of the picture, including, but not limited to, cut in, superimposed, dubbed and synchronized versions and exhibition prints thereof.

10.   MUSIC PERFORMANCE RIGHTS.

In addition to, but not by way of limitation of, all rights herein elsewhere granted, Producer hereby grants, sells, assigns, transfers and sets over unto Distributor and its successors, representatives and assigns, for the term of this agreement and any renewals or extensions thereof, any and all rights under copyright to the original music and musical compositions recorded or contained upon the sound track of the Picture, specifically including but not limited to the sole and exclusive public performance rights, which shall be understood to include the rights to publicly perform and to license or cause or permit so-called Performing Rights Societies or others to license the public performance rights (whether for profit or not for profit and whether or not in conjunction with the exhibition or sale of the Picture) of and to any and all of the original music and musical compositions recorded or contained upon the sound track of the Picture (including but not limited to the songs, instrumental and background music). The foregoing grant shall include also the sole and exclusive right to collect and receive, either directly or through any subsidiaries, agent, representatives,

so-called Performing Rights Societies or others, and any and all
royalties, fees and all other forms of remuneration for or in
connection with such rights or the license or the exercise
thereof.

For the purpose of exploiting such rights and collecting the fees, royalties and other remuneration, which may be derived therefrom, Distributor shall be entitled in its own discretion to employ the services of one or more agents or agencies and to permit such agents and agencies to charge and deduct therefrom, their commissions, fees, expenses and other
charges, the remainder of that part of all such fees, royalties
and other remuneration, as have been actually received by Distributor in the United States in U.S. dollars will be added to
and be treated as part of the theatrical gross receipts derived
from the distribution of the picture, and disposed of in accordance with the provisions hereafter set forth.

11. <u>CUTTING, EDITING AND ALTERING FOR CENSORSHIP, ETC.</u>

Distributor shall have the right to make such changes,
additions, alterations, cuts, interpolations and eliminations
as may be required by any duly authorized censorship authority
and as may be required for the distribution of the picture in
television (whether free, pay-as-you-see, or otherwise) and to
deduct the cost thereof from Producer's share of the gross
receipts.

12.   ACCESS TO NEGATIVE, ETC.

Distributor shall have exclusive access to the negative
and the exclusive right to obtain prints hereunder, except however, that Distributor may not order more than 250 prints for
domestic theatrical distribution without obtaining the prior
written approval of Producer. In addition thereto, Distributor
shall have the exclusive right to order such additional prints
for foreign distribution as Distributor deems necessary in Distributor's sole and exclusive discretion. On request or demand
of Distributor, Producer shall advise in writing said laboratory
or any other laboratory or laboratories performing laboratory
work in connection with the picture that Distributor has such
exclusive authority.

Distributor shall also have the right to order dupe
negatives of the picture or other duplicating prints made for
protection purposes, and Distributor may likewise cause to be
made 16mm, 8mm, and other sub-standard size negatives, dupe
negatives or duplicating prints if reasonably necessary in connection with its distribution of the picture.

Distributor in its sole and exclusive discretion is
hereby authorized by the Producer to purchase and advance the
cost of 35mm "pool" prints and to recoup said cost fully from
the Producer's share of the adjusted gross receipts from the
distribution of the picture as hereafter provided; provided,
however, that at the termination of the term of this

distribution agreement, Distributor agrees that Producer shall
not be charged with more than fifty (50) such "pool" prints.
Distributor shall collect from the theatrical exhibitors of the
picture and shall transmit the payment thereof to Producer, the
sum of ten dollars ($10.00) per week per pool print for each
pool print utilized by said exhibitors for all saturation bookings. After said saturation bookings have been completed, Distributor is hereby authorized to sell, lease or otherwise deal
in said pool prints at Distributor's discretion, and without
any further payment therefor to Producer.

Producer agrees to execute any instruments which Distributor may deem necessary for the purpose of causing any
laboratory which may hold the negative of the Picture to comply
with Distributor's instructions with respect to the making and
delivering of positive prints, fine grain prints, dupe negatives
or other laboratory work or services required, or to ship to
Distributor's designee the original negative, upon Distributor's
written request therefor. Such fine-grain prints, dupe negatives
and original negatives shall be kept in a laboratory designated
by Distributor in Distributor's name, for the purpose of enabling
Distributor to acquire such positive prints of the Picture, and
any and all laboratory work and services in connection therewith,
as Distributor may require.

Upon the expiration or sooner termination of Distributor's
rights hereunder, with respect to the Picture, Distributor agrees

to deliver possession to Producer of any such negatives, prints or other physical properties of the picture as may then be in existence. In the event that any such properties become stolen, destroyed or lost, Distributor agrees to notify Producer promptly of the fact of such properties being so stolen, destroyed or lost and to furnish Producer with an affidavit setting forth in reasonable detail the facts surrounding such occurrence. Distributor agrees to exercise every reasonable effort, at its own expense, to recover lost or stolen properties.

If the negatives, prints and other physical properties of the picture become worn, damaged or otherwise no longer in usable condition, Distributor agrees to furnish Producer with an affidavit to this effect, and at Producer's request to deliver the same to Producer. Distributor agrees upon request of Producer to furnish Producer, from time to time, with a list showing the exact location and whereabouts of all negatives, prints and other physical properties of the picture.

However, in the event that Producer enters into a financing agreement with or concerning a laboratory, and in the further event that said agreement provides that said laboratory shall possess a Lender's Lien, or other rights in connection with the picture, Distributor agrees that the negative of the picture shall remain at said laboratory and that domestic prints only for the picture shall be manufactured at said laboratory, provided that Distributor agrees in writing to the use of said laboratory and provided further that the laboratory recognizes, in writing, all the aforesaid Distributor's rights of access, etc.

13. DEFINITION OF GROSS RECEIPTS, ETC.

The term "gross receipts" as used herein shall be deemed to mean all monies received by Distributor and its Franchise Holders, sub-distributors and licensees from the lease, license, rental, dealing in and distribution of the theatrical and television (whether free, pay-as-you-see or otherwise) rights in the picture, including monies received from theatrical and/or television re-issues of the picture (and including any monies actually received as judgments from law suits or otherwise by reason of the infringement or interference by third persons granted to Distributor (after deducting all costs and expenses incurred in litigation in collecting the same, including attorneys' fees).

The term "total gross receipts" shall mean the aggregate of the following, to wit: "domestic theatrical gross receipts," "domestic television receipts" and "foreign gross receipts" as hereinafter defined:

a. The term "domestic theatrical gross receipts" shall mean all net monies (after deducting all costs and expenses incurred in litigation in collecting the same, including attorneys' fees) actually received as film rentals on a percentage basis or from outright disposition of the picture for a flat

sum from the parties exhibiting the picture in the United States
of America, Alaska and Hawaii in the theatrical field after giving effect to any adjustments with exhibitors for rebates, credits, allowances or refunds, less sales tax, if any. Receipts
from rentals, leases or licenses to United States Army, Navy
and other Military or Armed Services installations, the American Red Cross, Veterans' Hospitals or facilities for shut-ins
wherever situated throughout the world shall be deemed a part
of and included in the domestic theatrical gross receipts,
whether in 35mm or in sub-standard gauges.

        b. The term "domestic television gross receipts"
shall mean all net monies (after deducting all costs and expenses incurred in litigation in collecting the same, including
attorneys' fees) actually received by Distributor as film rentals on a percentage basis or from outright dispositions of the
picture for a flat sum from sub-distributors or licensees for
the right to license or make other dispositions of the right to
exhibit the picture in the United States of America, Alaska and
Hawaii in the television field (including pay-as-you-see television rights and any other medium not yet known) after giving
effect to any adjustments for rebates, credits, allowances or
refunds.

        c. The term "foreign gross receipts" shall mean
all net monies (after deducting all costs and expenses incurred
in litigation in collecting the same, including attorneys' fees)

actually received by Distributor from sub-Distributors or licensees for the right to distribute the picture theatrically or by
means of television processes (including pay-as-you-see television rights and any other medium not yet known) in any territories other than the United States, Alaska and Hawaii where
Distributor makes an outright disposition of the picture for
a flat sum to such sub-Distributor or licensee and/or where
Distributor distributes the picture through sub-Distributors
or licensees on a percentage basis.

    14.   ADJUSTED GROSS RECEIPTS.

    From gross receipts shall be deducted and recouped the
following expenses and the balance remaining after making such
deductions is hereby defined as "Adjusted Gross Receipts."

        a. All sums paid or payable by Distributor or any
of its Franchise Holders, sub-Distributors or licensees as
taxes based upon the value of the pictures, or as imposts, taxes,
license fees and like charges, however denominated, imposed,
assessed or levied by any government, or any duly constituted
taxing authority, based upon or relating to the gross receipts
derived on account of or from the distribution or exhibition of
the pictures in any country, subdivision thereof, or territory,
or upon the portion thereof payable to Distributor or its sub-
Distributors or licensees, whether such taxes are denominated
as turnover taxes, sales taxes, film hire taxes, gross business
taxes, or by any other denomination.

Nothing herein contained, however, shall be deemed to mean that Producer shall be obligated to pay or participate in any net income, franchise, excess profits or corporation taxes.

b. Costs and expenses incurred or paid in connection with securing local censorship approvals.

c. Cost and expenses incurred or paid in connection with re-cutting and re-editing the pictures for the purpose of meeting local censorship requirements.

d. Cost of release prints, replacements, dupe negatives and all sums actually expended or incurred by Distributor in processing said material throughout the licensed territory (except for the cost of "pool prints" which are provided for in Paragraph 12 hereof). All laboratory work shall be done at prevailing rates at the laboratory designated by Producer and approved by Distributor. Producer agrees that Distributor shall have the right to order as many prints of the picture for use in the licensed territory as Distributor deems commercially advisable, but no more than 250 prints (including "pool prints") for United States distribution without Producer's consent.

e. All payments made or credits allowed or sums expended by Distributor in connection with advertising and/or exploitation wherein Distributor shares with the exhibitor the cost of such advertising and/or exploitation, i.e. "co-operative advertising" as that term is understood in the motion picture industry and any and all credits allowed or sums expended by by Distributor in connection with advertising and/or exploitation in or in connection with specific campaigns at the theatre level whether or not the exhibitor contributes thereto with the exception of these items enumerated in Paragraph 16 hereof.

Nothing herein contained shall be construed or interpreted to prevent Distributor from making an outright disposition or sale, whether for a fixed sum or otherwise of any of the domestic television or substandard rights or licenses or foreign theatrical and/or television and/or any other foreign rights or licenses in or to the picture to any licensee, sub-Distributor and/or other purchaser; and in said event or events, the total net receipts received by Distributor for any said sale or disposition is herein defined as the "adjusted gross receipts" for the purpose of computing the fees to Distributor.

15. <u>DISTRIBUTION FEES.</u>

From adjusted gross receipts shall be deducted the following distribution fees:

a. From the theatrical receipts as referred to and defined in Paragraph 13a of this agreement an amount of 40% of net money received by Distributor. The above terms and distribution fees shall prevail, except as is otherwise specifically set forth herein-below and for the times, territory and media specifically set forth hereinbelow.

b. From the domestic television receipts referred to and defined in sub-Paragraph 13 of this agreement, a sum

equal to 40% of all said monies received by the Distributor.
The above terms and distribution fees shall prevail, except as
is otherwise specifically set forth hereinbelow and for the
times, territory and media specifically set forth hereinbelow.

c. From the foreign receipts including all territories throughout the world, other than the United States,
Alaska, and Hawaii as referred to in sub-Paragraph 13c of this
agreement a sum equal to 42-1/2% of all said net monies received
by Distributor (its being understood that Distributor employs
American Trading Association and/or another company or corporation as its foreign agent or agents and shall pay said agent
or agents from its 42-1/2% fee). The above terms and distribution fees shall prevail, except as is otherwise specifically
set forth hereinbelow.

It is agreed that Distributor will enter into an agreement for the theatrical distribution of the picture in Canada
with _____, herein called "Canadian Distributor,"
for a period of five (5) years wherein and whereby Canadian Distributor (subject to censorship clearance in all Provinces) to
pay an advance payment in the amount of Four Thousand Dollars
($4,000.00) (less Canadian taxes withheld) as an advance guar-
antee against the proceeds of distribution against the picture
in Canada, Canadian Distributor to receive a distribution fee
of 50% and Distributor to receive a distribution fee of 10%.

16.   <u>PRODUCER'S SHARE OF ADJUSTED GROSS RECEIPTS</u>.

The remaining adjusted gross receipts after deducting said distribution fees are hereinafter referred to as "Producer's share of the adjusted gross receipts." All of Producer's share of the adjusted gross receipts shall be retained by Distributor as its property until Distributor shall have reimbursed itself and shall have recouped therefrom, a sum equal to the total costs and charges expended and incurred by Distributor for the account of Producer, for the following items relating to the picture;

a.   <u>Advertising</u>. All sums expended or incurred by Distributor for advertising, publicity and exploitation purposes throughout the licensed territory, including but not limited to the conception and execution of advertising plans and campaigns, trade advertisements, novelties, records, recordings, personal appearances by actors or other production personnel in connection with or for the picture, trailers for theatrical and television exploitation, pressbooks, posters and other advertising material usually and customarily used in the motion picture industry, but no more than fifteen thousand dollars ($15,000.00) without Producer's consent for all said advertising, publicity and exploitation costs in connection with United States distribution, as defined above.

The revenue from trailers, if any, shall be included in the adjusted gross receipts from domestic theatrical gross receipts.

However, it is understood and agreed that the costs of advertising and/or exploitation at the theater level, whether for one theater or a saturation campaign for a group of theaters and whether shared partly by exhibitor or borne completely by Distributor as enumerated and deducted in Paragraph 14 hereof are in addition to the costs, charges and expenses enumerated hereinabove in this Paragraph 16.

    b. Cost of "Pool Prints." The cost of "pool prints," dupe negatives, and all sums actually expended or incurred by Distributor in processing said material throughout the licensed territory. All laboratory work shall be done at prevailing rates at a laboratory designated by Producer and approved by Distributor.

    c. Other Costs and Expenses. All sums expended or incurred by Distributor throughout the licensed territory in connection with any of the following: Cost of search of copyright or title records, or of obtaining copyrights in the Picture; costs of changing the titles of the Picture; insurance premiums paid or incurred upon any insurance carried on "pool prints" of the Picture; transportation, freight, shipping and storage charges in connection with said "pool prints," the amount of any music copyright and/or sound royalties paid or incurred in connection with the picture; all costs and expenses incurred by Distributor in connection with the preparation and making of trailers; the costs of import fees

and licenses and other similar requirements to secure the right

to import and distribute the Picture in any foreign country;

import, export, tariff, customs and other similar duties, all

costs and expenses incurred by Distributor in preparing any

foreign language version of the Picture for any foreign country,

including but not limited to, the cost of dubbing, cutting,

editing and subtitling; any and all expenses including reason-

able attorneys' fees paid or incurred by Distributor, its Fran-

chise Holders, its sub-Distributors and licensees in contesting

the imposition of any tax on Producer's share or in connection

with any litigation concerning title or rights in said Picture

or incidental to the assertion or maintenance of claims for

the infringement of or with the Picture or any part thereof or

other interference by third persons of or with the Picture or

any part thereof or any rights granted to Distributor hereunder.

   d. Advances. Under the provision of Paragraph 3

hereof, Producer agrees to advance and bear certain expenses

as therein provided. Under said paragraph, Distributor has the

right to advance such expenses if Producer fails to do so. If

Distributor does advance such expenses, the same may be deducted

and recouped from Producer's share of the adjusted gross receipts.

   Producer authorizes Distributor to undertake the payment

of the cost of any or all of the items specified in subdivisions

a, b, c and d of this paragraph. Distributor undertakes to

advance the cost of the said items for the account of Producer.
In any event, Producer agrees and hereby authorizes Distributor
to deduct all such costs and expenses which may be thus advanced
by Distributor from Producer's share of the adjusted gross receipts as hereinabove provided and Producer further agrees and
hereby authorizes Distributor, at its option, to assign to any
third person, firm or corporation, Distributor's right to receive the moneys thus advanced by Distributor, for account of
Producer, and the moneys which it may be entitled to deduct as
aforesaid in repayment of such advances.

 17. DISTRIBUTION OF NET PRODUCER'S SHARE.

  The balance remaining after Distributor shall have deducted and recouped the aforesaid amounts out of Producer's
share of the adjusted gross receipts shall be hereinafter referred to as "net Producer's share." Distributor shall account
for and remit to Producer, or as Producer may direct, the net
Producer's share in accordance with the provisions of Paragraph 18 hereof.

 18. DISTRIBUTOR'S PAYMENTS TO PRODUCER, REPORTS AND
  SETTLEMENT STATEMENTS.

  With respect to the net Producer's share of the gross
receipts of the picture as hereinbefore defined in Paragraph 17
hereof, Distributor agrees to furnish to Producer during the
first thirty-six (36) months from and after the first release
of the picture a monthly report showing both billings and

collections for each preceding month period. After the first thirty-six (36) months, such statement shall be furnished quarterly.

The said statements may be on a billings or on a collection basis, and Distributor shall have a right to change the method from time to time, but each statement shall specify whether it is on a billings or on a collection basis. In the event that the said statements shall be made on a billing basis, Distributor shall have the right in subsequent statements to make adjustments for uncollected bills. Each such statement shall include a statement in reasonable detail of the various items included in the computation of the net Producer's share, including gross receipts and fees and expenses deducted therefrom. Distributor shall accompany each such statement with a remittance to Producer, or as Producer may direct, of such sums as may be shown to be due to Producer under the terms of this agreement by such statement.

19. FOREIGN RECEIPTS.

Receipts derived from the picture from foreign territories (to wit: countries or territories other than the continental United States, Alaska and Hawaii) shall be included in the "gross receipts" and shall be available for disbursement, and shall be subject to recoupment by the Distributor, only upon and subject to the following provisions of this Paragraph 19, to wit:

a.   Such foreign receipts shall be included in the gross receipts, if paid in dollars in the United States to the Distributor or any of its subsidiaries;   and

b.   If received by the Distributor or any of its subsidiaries in foreign currency which is not "blocked" (as defined in sub-Paragraph 19c and is actually converted into United States funds and remitted to the United States, or could promptly and legally be so converted and remitted to the United States if so desired by the Distributor, the net proceeds of such conversion and remittance, in United States currency, shall be included in the gross receipts; and

c.   If received in a foreign currency which is subject to moratorium, embargo, banking or exchange restrictions, blocking or other restrictions against conversion or remittance to the United States in unrestricted United States funds, such funds (herein referred to as "blocked funds") shall be included in the gross receipts only as follows:

(1)   Where remittances in dollars are received from a country or territory in which a quota of remittances is authorized by its fiscal authorities for a fixed period, then that percentage of the receipts from said picture in the country or territory in question during the period fixed by the quota shall be included in the gross receipts which results from taking the ratio of the cost in blocked funds of remittances from such country or territory for such period which are actually

received by the Distributor in dollars in the United States,
to the total amount in blocked funds which became available to
the Distributor within such fixed period from such country or
territory and which would have been or could have been used for
remittances during such fixed period if no blocking were in
effect.

(2) Where remittances in dollars are received
from a country or territory under authorization granted by the
fiscal authorities from time to time for remittance of a portion
of the total blocked funds accumulated by the Distributor in
such country or territory, then the local currency of each particular remittance shall be considered as having come from the
oldest restricted currency accumulated by the Distributor in
the affected territory. At such time as the earlier accumula-
tions of blocked funds in such country or territory have been
exhausted, then and thereafter, all receipts from the picture
in such country or territory, up to the date to which the
blocked funds for the purchase of a particular remittance were
accumulated, shall be included in the gross receipts in accordance with the formula set forth in Subdivision (1) of this sub-
Paragraph c, and at the rate of exchange at which such remittance was received by the Distributor.

d. In any country or territory in which there are
blocked funds, as defined herein, Distributor may only deduct
and recoup in United States dollars that proportion of the

of the distribution fees measured by gross receipts derived from

such country or territory and that proportion of the expenses

incurred in connection with the derivation of such gross receipts

as the amount of the gross receipts derived from such country or

territory which has been converted and remitted in United States

funds to the United States bears to the total amount of gross

receipts derived from such country or territory. To the extent

that Distributor may not under the sentence just preceding de-

duct and recoup in United States dollars such distribution fees

and expenses, then Distributor must deduct and recoup the same

in the currency of the particular country or territory involved.

   e. Producer shall bear its proportionate part of

the entire cost and expense of converting and remitting foreign

currency to the United States in United States dollars.

  20. KEEPING OF RECORDS.

  Distributor agrees to maintain complete and accurate

books of account and records of the distribution of the picture.

Producer and/or its accountants and/or other representatives

may examine such books of account and records and take excerpts

therefrom at all reasonable times during business hours at Dis-

tributor's place of business in Los Angeles, California.

  21. FINALITY OF STATEMENTS.

  Any statement submitted to Producer by Distributor

hereunder shall be deemed conclusively true and accurate if

not disputed in writing within one (1) year after such statement shall have been delivered to Producer.

    22.   COPYRIGHT.

        Producer agrees to protect the Picture by copyright,
and Distributor shall in no event be liable therefor. The
United States copyright shall be taken in the name of Producer.
Distributor is hereby authorized to take such steps as Distributor may deem advisable to protect Distributor's rights and
those of Producer and to copyright the Picture in the United
States and elsewhere in the licensed territory at Producer's
sole cost and expense and for such purpose, Distributor is appointed the attorney-in-fact of Producer. Distributor shall
be under no liability of any kind in the event there shall be
a failure to secure any such copyright or a defect in any such
copyright.

    23.   ADVERTISING.

        Distributor is granted the exclusive and irrevocable
right to publicize, advertise and exploit the picture throughout the term hereof, and to cause or permit others so to do.
Distributor is granted complete discretion, except as herein
otherwise provided, as to the manner, mode and method of advertising, publicizing and exploiting the picture, the amounts to
be expended in connection therewith, the media to be employed,
the advertising agency to be designated, the type of advertising campaign to be utilized, and the time or times such exploitation is to become effective, and shall have the right from

time to time to change any campaigns, or elements thereof.

24. COMMERCIAL TIE-UPS.

Wherever Producer in its contracts with actors or other persons rendering services in connection with the Picture secures general or limited rights to utilize the name and/or likeness of such person or persons for the purpose of endorsing commercial products or for any commercial tie-ups, such rights shall be and are hereby automatically assigned solely and exclusively to Distributor for use throughout the licensed territory. Distributor shall have complete discretion as to the utilization of such rights so assigned to it and as to whether or not such rights shall be supplied to the owners or sponsors of the commercial products involved free or for a consideration, or whether or not any consideration so paid shall be payable in whole or in part to the person or persons whose name or names is or are utilized in that connection. Any proceeds from commercial tie-ups shall be treated, disposed of and charged as though they were proceeds from United States theatrical distribution.

25. TRAILERS.

It is agreed that so long as Distributor maintains an agreement or agreements with National Screen Service Corporation for the manufacture and distribution of trailers for the picture for use in the United States, said trailers shall be made and distributed by National Screen Service Corporation. Thereafter, or if such agreement or agreements are terminated, Distributor shall have the sole and exclusive right to make and enter into a similar agreement or agreements with another person, firm or corporation rendering the same or similar services. Distributor shall pay and bear the cost thereof of the charges of National Screen Service Corporation for the manufacture of accessories for the picture and shall in consequence thereof be entitled to any revenue therefrom.

26. ALLOCATION OF ADVERTISING COSTS.

If in any advertising, publicity or exploitation the picture is advertised with a group of other pictures, the cost of such advertising, publicity and exploitation shall be allocated between the picture and such other motion pictures with regard to the proportion that the space, emphasis and position used to advertise the picture bears to the total space, emphasis and position used for the entire group.

27. RIGHT TO ADVERTISE.

Subject to the limitations contained in this agreement, Producer gives and grants to Distributor the exclusive and irrevocable right for advertising, publicity and exploitation purposes.

a. To publish or cause or permit to be published in all languages and in such forms as Distributor may deem advisable, synopses, summaries, resumes and stories and any excerpts from the picture and any literary, dramatic or musical

material used in the picture or upon which the picture is based
(not exceeding, however, 7,500 words in length in newspapers,
magazines, trade periodicals, comic books, heralds, programs,
booklets, posters, lobby displays, pressbooks and any other
periodicals and in all other media of advertising and publicity
whatsoever.

b. To broadcast by radio, wire, television, or any
other means or method, or license or authorize others so to
broadcast, in any language, adaptations, versions or sketches
of the picture, or any parts or portions thereof, from sound
records or with living persons, or otherwise, and in connection
therewith the right to use part of, or excerpts from, or theme
of any literary, dramatic or musical material contained in the
picture or upon which the picture was based, and to use in connection therewith any other literary, dramatic or musical material.

c. To use the name and reproductions of the physical likeness and reproductions of the voice of any party rendering services in connection with the picture, including all of
the right, title and interest which the producer acquires, under
any contracts of employment or otherwise, for the purpose of
advertising or exploiting the picture in connection with any
product, commodity or service manufactured, distributed or licensed by Distributor, subject to the limitations imposed upon
Producer by such contracts of employment or otherwise

RELEASE BY DISTRIBUTOR.

Distributor shall have the right, but not the obligation, to include, at Distributor's expense, on the main and end titles of, and on advertising and publicity material for the picture, Distributor's trademark or emblem, together with the words, "Released by or through _____(Distributor)" or similar words.

28. CREDITS.

Producer agrees to deliver to Distributor a complete statement, in triplicate, setting forth the names of all persons to whom Producer is contractually obligated to accord credit on the screen or in any paid advertising, publicity or exploitation of the picture, hereinafter referred to as "credit," and to include in such statement excerpts from any such agreements defining or describing the form and nature of such required credits. Producer agrees that such statements shall be delivered to Distributor as early as possible and in no event shall such statement contain inconsistent requirements for credit.

Producer represents that it will not agree to accord any person screen or advertising credit except in customary fashion, and that it has not given screen or advertising credits of the kind or type not customary in the motion picture industry.

Distributor agrees to accord to the director, writer or writers and members of the case of the picture the credit described in Producer's statement. Producer hereby consents to

Distributor's according to any such person more prominent or
more extensive credit than that described in Producer's statement if the same will not constitute a violation of the provisions of any agreement between Producer and any person concerning credit; its being agreed, however, that Distributor shall
only be required to accord to such persons the credit required
by the terms of Producer's agreement with such person or persons,
as described in Producer's statement.

        Distributor shall be entitled to rely entirely upon
the Producer's statement, and if by reason of any improper or
insufficient credit, or no credit, and such person shall by
written notice notify Distributor that there has been a breach
of contract concerning credit, then at Distributor's election,
evidenced by written notice to Producer, Producer agrees at his
own cost and expense to defend, indemnify and hold Distributor
harmless against any such claim, action or proceeding, including any judgments that may be sustained against Distributor for
the breach charged. If Distributor fails to accord credit to
any person in accordance with Producer's statement and such person shall by reason thereof make claim or institute any action
or proceeding against Producer, then Distributor agrees to indemnify and hold Producer harmless of and from any loss, liability, cost or expense, including attorney's fees, arising out of
such claim, action or proceeding and at Producer's election,
evidenced by written notice to Distributor, agrees to come in

and defend such claim, action or proceeding in Producer's behalf.

If any person shall claim that Distributor has accorded
him improper or insufficient credit, or that Distributor shall
have improperly accorded him credit, and shall demand that Distributor either accord him certain credit and/or cease or re-
frain from according him credit, Distributor agrees immediately
to notify Producer thereof in writing or by telegraph. Producer
agrees that within seven (7) days after the receipt of such notice, Producer will notify Distributor in writing that Producer
does or does not consent to Distributor's compliance with the
demand of such person and shall give or withhold said consent
to the compliance by Distributor with the demand. If the Producer shall within such seven-(7)-day period fail to notify Distributor in such regard, Distributor, at Distributor's election,
may comply with the demand of such person and in the event that
Distributor does comply with such demand Distributor may recoup
all expenses reasonably incurred in complying with such demand
from any monies otherwise payable to Producer pursuant to this
agreement provided such demand is inconsistent with Producer's
statement, and in the event that Distributor does not comply
with such demand to the extent possible, Distributor agrees to
indemnify Producer of and from any loss, liability, cost or expense, including attorneys' fees, arising by reason of Distributor's so failing to comply with such demand. If Producer

notifies Distributor that Producer does not consent to Distributor's compliance with such demand, Distributor shall continue to accord or withhold credit in accordance with Producer's statement, subject to Producer's obligations with respect to such statement, as hereinabove set forth.

Distributor agrees to give Producer credit as Producer of the Picture on the screen and in all advertising paid or otherwise where Producer credit is given. Such credit shall be given in the following form: "_____ FILMS PRODUCTION."

29. PRODUCER'S WARRANTIES.

Producer hereby represents and warrants that:

a. It has the right to enter into this agreement, and print, sell, assign, transfer and convey to Distributor all the rights and licenses herein contained, and there are not and will not be outstanding any claims, liens, encumbrances or rights of any nature in or to the picture, or any part thereof, which can or will impair or interfere with the rights or licenses herein granted to Distributor.

b. It owns and controls the exclusive right to distribute, exhibit and otherwise exploit the picture in any manner and form whatsoever throughout the licensed territory.

c. Neither the picture nor any part thereof (including the sound synchronization therewith) or the exercise by any authorized party of any right granted to Distributor hereunder,

will violate or infringe upon the trademark, trade name, copyright, literary, dramatic, music, artistic, personal, private,
civil or property rights or rights of privacy or other right of
any party.

      d. Producer has not sold, assigned, trasferred,
or conveyed, and will not sell, assign, transfer, or convey,
to any party, any right, title or interest in and to such
picture or any part thereof, or the dramatic or literary material upon which it is based, adverse to or derogatory of the
rights granted to Distributor; and Producer will not, and will
not authorize any other party during the term hereof to produce,
distribute or exhibit any motion picture based in whole or in
part upon such literary or dramatic material.

      e. It owns or controls all motion picture rights
in and to the picture, and all literary, dramatic and musical
material contained therein, required for the full and complete
exercise and enjoyment of all rights granted to Distributor
hereunder, without any limitation on the part of any person,
firm or corporation whatsoever.

    30. INDEMNIFICATION.

Producer will, at its own expense, indemnify Distributor,
its assignees and licensees, and hold them harmless from any and
all loss, damage, liability or expense, including attorneys' fees,
as hereinbelow provided, resulting from any breach of any of the
warranties made herein by Producer. Distributor will give

Producer prompt written notice of the institution of any action
or the making of any claim alleging a breach of warranty hereunder. Producer shall then have the right, at its election, to
retain counsel to represent Distributor in said action. If Producer fails to retain counsel to represent Distributor in said
action, then Distributor may, at its election, be represented
by counsel retained by Distributor, and the reasonable cost of
such representation may be charged against Producer's share of
the adjusted gross receipts of the picture; its being understood that the right to make such charge shall in no wise limit
Producer's obligation to pay such cost to distributor, independently of such right to make such charge. If Producer does retain counsel to represent Distributor in said action, nevertheless Distributor shall have the right at its election to retain
additional counsel who will cooperate with the counsel retained
by Producer in defending said action, and, in said event, Producer shall bear and assume the entire attorneys' fees of the
additional counsel retained by Distributor.

In the event that any claim, action or proceeding is
brought or threatened based upon an alleged breach of any of
the foregoing warranties, Distributor's obligations hereunder
shall, at Distributor's option, be suspended until such claim,
action or proceeding has been finally settled or adjudicated in
favor of Producer and Distributor, and unless the same is finally
settled or adjudicated within eighteen (18) months from the first

notice to Distributor of such claim, action or proceeding, Distributor may terminate this agreement.

If any person maintains that the Picture or any part thereof infringes upon any copyright, right of privacy, or other right, Distributor may deposit in a special bank account in a bank in Los Angeles, California, designated by Producer, such part of the gross receipts of the Picture as Producer may then or thereafter become entitled to, as the parties hereto shall agree shall be sufficient to satisfy Producer's liability in connection with such claim, plus a reasonable amount for the expense of defending or contesting such claim. In the event the parties hereto do not agree as to the amount to be impounded, such dispute shall be submitted to arbitration. After the final determination of any suit or proceeding involving such claim or after any settlement of such claim, Distributor being hereby expressly authorized to make such settlement as it deems proper, Distributor shall pay to Producer any portion of Producer's share of the adjusted gross receipts as aforesaid which may have been impounded and which is not required for the payment of settlement of such suit, proceeding or claim or as an expense of defending the same. If Producer elects to be represented by its own counsel, the expenses thereof shall not be recouped from any portion of the gross receipts of the Picture. All loss, damage, liability or expense resulting from any breach of Producer's warranties hereunder shall be recouped by the

Distributor from Producer's share of the adjusted gross receipts
of the Picture. If Distributor shall settle or compromise any
suit or claim based upon any alleged breach by Producer of its
warranties hereunder (and Distributor is granted complete discretion and authority to settle and compromise such suits or
claims), then the cost thereof shall be charged to Producer.

Nothing contained herein shall limit the liability of
Producer or the right to Distributor resulting from any breach
of warranty by Producer in the event Producer's share of the
adjusted gross receipts of the Picture are insufficient to satisfy any liability in connection with such claim, plus a reasonable amount for expense of defending or contesting the same.

31.   ACTIONS AGAINST THIRD PERSONS.

If any person, firm or corporation other than Franchise
Holders, sub-Distributors and licensees of Distributor shall do
or perform any acts which Distributor believes constitute a copyright infringement of the picture or of any of the literary, dramatic or musical material contained in the picture, or constitute a plagiarism, or violate or infringe any rights of Producer or Distributor therein, or if any person, firm or corporation other than Franchise Holders, sub-Distributors and licensees
of Distributor shall do or perform any acts which Distributor
believes constitute an unauthorized or unlawful distribution,
exhibition or use thereof, then and in any such event, Distributor may institute such suits or proceedings as may be necessary

or appropriate to prevent such acts and conduct and to secure
damages and other relief by reason thereof, and generally to
secure full protection of the rights of the parties. Distributor may take such steps or institute such suits or proceedings
in its own name or in the name of the Producer or in the names
of the parties hereto jointly, and Distributor is hereby appointed and constituted the lawful Attorney-in-Fact of Producer
to do all acts and things permitted or contemplated by the terms
of this paragraph. Distributor shall be entitled to recoup,
from the gross receipts of the Picture, its reasonable costs
and expenses (including reasonable attorneys' fees) paid or
incurred in connection with the foregoing. Nothing herein contained shall be deemed a limitation or restriction of the indemnity provisions set forth in Paragraph 30 hereof.

32. FORCE MAJEURE.

Anything herein contained to the contrary notwithstanding, neither party shall be liable to the other in damages because of any failure to perform hereunder caused by any cause
beyond its control including, but not limited to fire, earth-
quake, flood, epidemic, accident, explosion, casualty, strike,
lockout, labor controversy, riot, civil disturbance, act of a
public enemy, embargo, war, act of God, any governmental ordinance or law, the issuance of any executive or judicial order,
any failure or delay in respect to any electrical or judicial
order, any failure or delay of any transportation agency, any

failure or delay in respect to any electrical or sound equipment or apparatus, or by any laboratory, any failure, without
fault, to obtain material, transportation, power, or any other
essential thing required in the conduct of its business or any
similar cause. This reduction shall apply only to Distributor's
fee and shall not affect the fees or commissions of Distributor's
franchise holders or sub-Distributors.

33.   SUB-DISTRIBUTORS.

In the event Distributor distributes the film through
franchise holders or sub-Distributors, then the Distributor's
share of gross receipts shall be reduced by the fees or commissions of said franchise holders or sub-Distributors, up to
and no more than one-half of Distributor's share of gross receipts.

34.   NO PARTNERSHIP.

Nothing herein contained shall constitute a partnership between or joint venture by the parties hereto, or constitute either party the agent of the other. Neither party
shall hold itself out contrary to the terms of this paragraph,
and neither party shall be or become liable by any representation, act or omission of the other contrary to the provisions
hereof. This agreement is not for the benefit of any third
party and shall not be deemed to give any right or remedy to
any such party whether referred to herein or not.

35. NO CONTINUING WAIVER.

No waiver by either party of any breach hereof shall be deemed a waiver of any preceding, continuing or succeeding breach of the same, or any other term hereof.

36. CONSTRUCTION.

This agreement shall be deemed made, and is to be construed and interpreted under the laws of the State of California.

37. NOTICES.

All written notices, payments, accountings and other data which Distributor is required or may desire to send or deliver to or serve upon Producer shall be delivered in person to an officer of Producer, or deposited in the United States mails, postage prepaid, registered, return receipt requested, or deposited in a telegraph or cable office with all charges prepaid or provided for, addressed to Producer at:

_____

_____

or such other address or addresses as Producer may designate from time to time in writing.

All written notices, payments, accountings and other data which Producer is required or may desire to send or deliver to or serve upon Distributor shall be delivered in person to an officer of Distributor, or deposited in the United States mails, postage prepaid, registered, return receipt requested,

or deposited in a telegraph or cable office with all charges
prepaid or provided for, addressed to Distributor at:

_____

_____

or such other address or addresses as Distributor may designate
from time to time in writing.

If any of said notices, etc., are by United States mail,
they shall be deemed served or made or delivered on the actual
date received, but in any event not later than five (5) days
from the date of deposit in the United States mail. If said
notices, etc., are sent by telegraph, they shall be deemed
served or made or delivered on the date received, but in any
event not later than two (2) days after the date of deposit in
the telegraph or cable office. Sundays and holidays shall be
excluded for the purpose of computing the period of time hereunder.

38. HEADINGS.

The headings of this agreement or any paragraphs hereof
are inserted only for the purpose of convenient reference, and
it is recognized that they may not accurately or adequately de-
scribe the contents of the paragraphs which they head. Such
heading shall not be deemed to limit, cover, or in any way affect the scope, meaning or intent of this agreement, or any
part hereof, nor shall they otherwise be given any legal effect.

IN WITNESS WHEREOF, the parties hereto have caused this agreement to be executed by their duly authorized officers as of the day and year above written.

DISTRIBUTOR: _____

By: _____
                                              , President

By: _____
                                          , Vice President

(Corporate Seal)

PRODUCER: _____

By: _____
                                              , President

By: _____
                                              , Secretary

(Corporate Seal)

PART IX

C O P Y R I G H T

    Here's a fast introduction to the field of copyright -
a little talk; extracts from the U.S. law; extracts from the
U.S, regulations; more discussion; a glamorous case involving
a mighty network, a mighty movie studio, and a great comedian;
a Copyright Office circular and a Copyright Office form.

PART IX

COPYRIGHT

The law of copyright covers the right to copy and to prevent others from copying literary, artistic and certain other material.

There are additional areas of law which concern the right to copy, such as the areas of patents, trademarks, trade secrets, unfair competition, etc.

Copyright Law is taught as a law school course in many, but not all, of the law schools.

Copyright Law is a specialty.

The information provided herein is not designed to make a layman reader into a copyright lawyer specialist. However, it is hoped that the following extracts will help the producer and businessman understand what their attorney is talking about.

You have probably seen copyright notices near the titles of motion pictures as credits flash on the screen. The notices may have three parts:

1. The word "Copyright" and the symbol "©".
2. The year in usually Roman letter numerals.
3. The name(s) of the copyright proprietor.

There may be additional words such as "All Rights Reserved," "International Copyright Secured."

Copyright is complicated, partly because it has state, national and international aspects and histories, partly because

there are treaties, conventions, statutes, regulations, cases,
studies, texts, etc.

For you, the reader, we have settled on elementary introductory materials: a few statutes in one chapter, a few regulations concerning the Copyright Office in another chapter, some
other information spread throughout this book. If you are interested in further copyright information, please see the bibliography.

U.S. COPYRIGHT ACT

COPYRIGHTS is the heading of Title 17, United States Codes. The statutes are brief and require only about 35 pages in the United States Codes.

The following extracts should be of interest to motion picture industry businessmen:

"*Section 1. Exclusive rights as to copyrighted works*

Any person entitled thereto, upon complying with the provisions of this title, shall have the exclusive right:

(a) To print, reprint, publish, copy, and vend the copyrighted work;
. . . .

(d) To perform or represent the copyrighted work publicly if it be a drama or, if it be a dramatic work and not reproduced in copies for sale, to vend any manuscript or any record whatsoever thereof; to make or to procure the making of any transcription or record thereof by or from which, in whole or in part, it may in any manner or by any method be exhibited, performed, represented, produced, or reproduced; and to exhibit, perform, represent, produce, or reproduce it in any manner or by any method whatsoever; and "

. . . .

"*Section 2. Rights of author or proprietor of unpublished work*

Nothing in this title shall be construed to annul or limit the right of the author or proprietor of an unpublished work, at common law or in equity, to prevent the copying, publication, or use of such unpublished work without his consent, and to obtain damages therefor."

. . . .

"Section 3. Protection of component parts of work copy-
righted; composite works or periodicals

The copyright provided by this title shall protect all
the copyrightable component parts of the work copyrighted, and
all matter therein in which copyright is already subsisting, but
without extending the duration or scope of such copyright. The
copyright upon composite works or periodicals shall give to the
proprietor thereof all the rights in respect thereto which he
would have if each part were individually copyrighted under this
title."

. . . .

"Section 5. Classification of works for registration

The application for registration shall specify to which
of the following classes the work in which copyright is claimed.
belongs:

(a) Books, including composite and cyclopedic
works, directories, gazetteers, and other compilations.

(b) Periodicals, including newspapers.

(c) Lectures, sermons, addresses (prepared for oral
delivery.

(d) Dramatic or dramatico-musical compositions.

(e) Musical compositions.

(f) Maps.

(g) Works of art; models or designs for works of
art.

(h) Reproductions of a work of art.

(i) Drawings or plastic works of a scientific or
technical character.

(j) Photographs.

(k) Prints and pictorial illustrations including
prints or labels used for articles or merchandise.

(l) Motion-picture photoplays.

(m) Motion pictures other than photoplays.

"The above specifications shall not be held to limit
the subject matter of copyright as defined in section 4 of
this title, nor shall any error in classification invalidate
or impair the copyright protection secured under this title."

. . . .

"*Section 7. Copyright on compilations of works in
public domain or of copyrighted works; subsisting copyrights
not affected*

Compilations or abridgments, adaptations, arrangements,
dramatizations, translations, or other versions of works in the
public domain or of copyrighted works when produced with the
consent of the proprietor of the copyright in such works, or
works republished with new matter, shall be regarded as new
works subject to copyright under the provisions of this title;
but the publication of any such new works shall not affect the
force or validity of any subsisting copyright upon the matter
employed or any part thereof, or be construed to imply an exclusive right to such use of the original works."

. . . .

"*Section 10. Publication of work with notice*

Any person entitled thereto by this title may secure
copyright for his work by publication thereof with the notice
of copyright required by this title; and such notice shall be
affixed to each copy thereof published or offered for sale in
the United States by authority of the copyright proprietor,
except in the case of books seeking ad interim protection under
section 22 of this title."

. . . .

"*Section 12. Works not reproduced for sale*

Copyright may also be had of the works of an author,
of which copies are not reproduced for sale, by the deposit,
with claim of copyright, of one complete copy of such work if
it be a lecture or similar production or a dramatic, musical
or dramatico-musical composition; of a title and description,
with one print taken from each scene or act, if the work be a
motion-picture photoplay; of a photographic print if the work
be a photograph; of a title and description, with not less
than two prints taken from different sections of a complete
motion picture, if the work be a motion picture other than a
photoplay; or of a photograph or other identifying reproduction thereof, if it be a work of art or a plastic work or
drawing. But the privilege of registration of copyright secured
hereunder shall not exempt the copyright proprietor from the

deposit of copies, under sections 13 and 14 of this title, where the work is later reproduced in copies for sale."

. . . .

"Section 11 (Omitted above). Registration of claim and issuance of certificate.

Such person may obtain registration of his claim to copyright by complying with the provisions of this title, including the deposit of copies, and upon such compliance the Register of Copyrights shall issue to him the certificates provided for in section 209 of this title."

. . . .

"Section 19. Notice; form

The notice of copyright required by section 10 of this title shall consist either of the word "Copyright" or the abbreviation "Copr.", accompanied by the name of the copyright proprietor, and if the work be a printed literary, musical, or dramatic work, the notice shall include also the year in which the copyright was secured by publication."

. . . .

"Section 20. Same; place of application of; one notice in each volume or number of newspaper or periodical

The notice of copyright shall be applied, in the case of a book or other printed publication, upon its title page or the page immediately following, or if a periodical either upon the title page or upon the first page of text of each separate number or under the title heading, or if a musical work either upon its title page or the first page of music. One notice of copyright in each volume or in each number of a newspaper or periodical shall suffice."

. . . .

"Section 26. Terms defined

In the interpretation and construction of this title "the date of publication" shall in the case of a work of which copies are reproduced for sale or distribution be held to be the earliest date when copies of the first authorized edition were placed on sale, sold, or publicly distributed by the proprietor of the copyright or under his authority, and the word

"author" shall include an employer in the case of works made
for hire."

. . . .

"Section 28.   Assignments and bequests

Copyright secured under this title or previous copyright
laws of the United States may be assigned, granted, or mortgaged
by an instrument in writing signed by the proprietor of the copyright, or may be bequeathed by will."

. . . .

"Section 30.   Same;   record

Every assignment of copyright shall be recorded in the
copyright office within three calendar months after its execution in the United States or within six calendar months after
its execution without the limits of the United States, in default of which it shall be void as against any subsequent purchaser or mortgagee for a valuable consideration, without notice,
whose assignment has been duly recorded."

. . . .

"Section 31.   Same;   certificate of record

The Register of Copyrights shall, upon payment of the
prescribed fee, record such assignment, and shall return it
to the sender with a certificate of record attached under seal
of the copyright office, and upon the payment of the fee prescribed by this title he shall furnish to any person requesting
the same a certified copy thereof under the said seal."

. . . .

"Section 32.   Same;   use of name of assignee in notice

When an assignment of the copyright in a specified book
or other work has been recorded the assignee may substitute his
name for that of the assignor in the statutory notice of copyright prescribed by this title."

. . . .

U.S. COPYRIGHT ACT

(Continued)

CHAPTER 2 - INFRINGEMENT PROCEEDINGS

Sec.

. . . .

U.S. COPYRIGHT ACT

(Continued)

CHAPTER 3 - COPYRIGHT OFFICE

. . . .

COPYRIGHT OFFICE REGULATIONS

The following pages contain extracts from Title 37,
Code of Federal Regulations.

CHAPTER II - COPYRIGHT OFFICE, LIBRARY OF CONGRESS

Part
  201   General provisions.
  202   Registration of claims to copyright.

  PART 201 - GENERAL PROVISIONS

Sec.
  201.1   Communications with the Copyright Office.
  201.2   Information given by the Copyright Office.
  201.3   Catalog of Copyright Entries.
  201.4   Assignments of copyright and other papers.
  201.5   Amendments to completed Copyright Office
            registrations and other records.
  201.6   Payment and refund of Copyright Office fees.
  201.7   Preparation of catalog card.
  201.8   Import statements.

     AUTHORITY: The provisions of this Part 201 issued
under sec. 207, 61 Stat. 666; 17 U.S.C. 207.

     SOURCE: The provisions of this Part 201 appear at
24 F.R. 4955, June 18, 1959, unless otherwise noted.

Section 201.1 Communications with the Copyright Office.

     Mail and other communications shall be addressed to the
Register of Copyrights, Library of Congress, Washington, D.C.
20540.

Section 201.3 Catalog of Copyright Entries.

     The subscription price for all parts of the complete
yearly Catalog of Copyright Entries, effective with Volume 20,
is $50.00. Each part of the Catalog is published in two semi-
annual numbers covering, respectively, the periods of January-

June and July-December.   The prices given in the list below are
for each semi-annual number; the price of an annual subscription
to any part is twice the price of the semi-annual number.   The
entire annual Catalog or any of its parts may be obtained, upon
payment of the established price, from the Superintendent of Documents, Government Printing Office, Washington, D.C., 20402, to
whom requests for copies should be addressed and to whom the remittance should be made payable.

> *Part 1 - Books and Pamphlets, Including Serials and*
> *Contributions to Periodicals, $7.50.*
> *Part 2 - Periodicals, $2.50.*
> *Parts 3-4 - Dramas and Works Prepared for Oral Delivery,*
> *$2.50.*
> *Part 5 - Music, $7.50.*
> *Part 6 - Maps and Atlases, $2.50.*
> *Parts 7-11A - Works of Art, Reproductions of Works of*
> *Art, Scientific and Technical Drawings,*
> *Photographic Works and Pictorial Illus-*
> *trations, $2.50.*
> *Part 11B - Commercial Prints and Labels, $2.50.*
> *Parts 12-13 - Motion Pictures and Filmstrips, $2.50.*

Section 201.4 Assignments of copyright and other papers.

Assignments of copyright and other papers relative to
copyrights will be recorded in the Copyright Office upon payment of the statutory fee. Examples of such papers include
powers of attorney, licenses to use a copyrighted work, agreement between authors and publishers covering a particular work
or works and the rights thereto, mortgages, certificates of
change of corporate title, wills, and decrees of distribution.
The original, signed instrument should be submitted for recordation, and is returned to the sender with a certificate
of record. Where the original instrument is not available, a
certified or other copy may be submitted, but it shall be accompanied by a statement that the original is not available."

. . . .

PART 202 - REGISTRATION OF CLAIMS TO COPYRIGHT

Section 202.1 Material not subject to copyright.

The following are examples of works not subject to copyright and applications for registration of such works cannot be
entertained:

(a) Words and short phrases such as names, titles,
and slogans; familiar symbols or designs; mere variations of
typographic ornamentation, lettering or coloring; mere listing
of ingredients or contents;

(b) Ideas, plans, methods, systems, or devices, as
distinguished from the particular manner in which they are expressed or described in a writing;

(c) Works designed for recording information, such
as, time cards, graph paper, account books, diaries, bank checks,
score cards, address books, report forms, order forms and the
like;

(d) Works consisting entirely of information that
is common property containing no original authorship, such as,
for example: Standard calendars, height and weight charts,
tape measures and rulers, schedules of sporting events, and
lists or tables taken from public documents or other common
sources.

Section 202.2 Copyright notice.

    (a) General.

        (1) With respect to a published work, copyright is secured, or the right to secure it is lost, at the date of publication, i.e., the date on which copies are first placed on sale, sold, or publicly distributed, depending upon the adequacy of the notice of copyright on the work at that time.

        (2) If publication occurs by distribution of copies or in some other manner, without the statutory notice or with an inadequate notice, the right to secure copyright is lost. In such cases, copyright cannot be secured by adding the notice to copies distributed at a later date.

        (3) Works first published abroad, other than works eligible for ad interim registration, must bear an adequate copyright notice at the time of their first publication in order to secure copyright under the law of the United States.

    (b) Defects in notice. Where the copyright notice does not meet the requirements of the law, the Copyright Office will reject an application for copyright registration. Common defects in the notice include, among others, the following:

        (1) The notice lacks one or more of the necessary elements (i.e., the word "Copyright," the abbreviation "Copr." or the symbol ©; the name of the copyright proprietor; or, when required, the year date of publication);

        (2) The elements of the notice are dispersed;

        (3) The notice is not in one of the positions prescribed by law;

        (4) The notice is in a foreign language;

        (5) The name in the notice is that of someone who had no authority to secure copyright in his name;

        (6) The year date in the copyright notice is later than the date of the year in which copyright was actually secured, including the following cases:

        (i) Where the year date in the notice is later than the date of actual publication;

        (ii) Where copyright was first secured by

registration of a work in unpublished form, and copies of the same work as later published without change in substance bear a copyright notice containing a year date later than the year of unpublished registration;

　　　(iii) Where a book or a periodical published abroad, for which ad interim copyright has been obtained, is later published in the United States without change in substance and contains a year date in the copyright notice later than the year of first publication abroad;

　　Provided, however, That in each of the three foregoing types of cases, if the copyright was actually secured not more than one year earlier than the year date in the notice, registration may be considered as a doubtful case.

　　(7) A notice is permanently covered so that it cannot be seen without tearing the work apart;

　　(8) A notice is illegible or so small that it cannot be read without the aid of a magnifying glass: *Provided, however,* That where the work itself requires magnification for its ordinary use (e.g., a microfilm, microcard or motion picture) a notice which will be readable when so magnified, will not constitute a reason for rejection of the claim;

　　(9) A notice is on a detachable tag and will eventually be detached and discarded when the work is put to use;

　　(10) A notice is on the wrapper or container which is not a part of the work and which will eventually be removed and discarded when the work is put in use;

　　(11) The notice is restricted or limited exclusively to an uncopyrightable element, either by virtue of its position on the work, by the use of asterisks, or by other means.

Section 202.3 Application forms.

　　(a) In general. Section 5 of title 17 of the U.S. Code provides thirteen classes (Class A through Class M) of works in which copyright may be claimed. Examples of certain works falling within these classes are given in Sections 202.4 to 202.15 inclusive, for the purpose of assisting persons, who desire to obtain registration of a claim to copyright, to select the correct application form.

(b) *Claims of copyright.*

(1) All works deposited for registration shall be accompanied by a "claim of copyright" in the form of a properly executed application, together with the statutory registration fee. The Office reserves the right to refuse to accept any application that is a carbon copy, illegible, defaced, or otherwise not in an acceptable condition for examination and recording.

(2) Where these separate elements are not received simultaneously, the Copyright Office holds the submitted elements for a reasonable time and, in default of the receipt of the missing element or elements after a request made therefor, the submitted item or items may be returned to the sender. Such action does not constitute a waiver of the right of the Register of Copyrights pursuant to section 14, title 17, U.S. Code, to demand compliance with the deposit provisions of that title.

(3) Applications for copyright registration covering published works should reflect the facts existing at the time of first publication, and should not include information concerning changes that have occurred between the time of publication and registration. The name given as copyright claimant in the copyright notice.

(4) Applications should be submitted by the copyright claimant, or by someone acting under his authority.

(5) All information requested by the Copyright Office application form should be given in the appropriate spaces provided. There should not be attached to the application any slips of paper or extra pages containing additional information, or a continuation of requested information.

(c) *Forms.* The Copyright Office supplies without charge the following forms for use when applying for the registration of a claim to copyright in a work and for the filing of a notice of use of musical compositions on mechanical instruments.

Form A - Published book manufactured in the United States of America (Class A).
Form A-B Ad Interim - Book or periodical in the English language manufactured and first published outside the United States of America (Classes A-B).
Form B - Periodical manufactured in the United States of America (Class B).

Form BB - Contribution to a periodical manufactured in the United States of America (Class B).

Form C - Lecture or similar production prepared for oral delivery (Class C).

Form D - Dramatic or dramatico-musical composition (Class D).

Form E - Musical composition the author of which is a citizen or domiciliary of the United States of America or which was published in the United States of America and which was not first published in the United States of America (Class E).

Form E Foreign - Musical composition the author of which is not a citizen or domiciliary of the United States of America and which was not first published in the United States of America (Class E).

Form F - May (Class F).

Form G - Work of art of a model or design for a work of art (Class G).

Form H - Reproduction of a work of art (Class H).

Form I - Drawing or plastic work of a scientific or technical character (Class I).

Form J - Photograph (Class J).

Form K - Print or pictorial illustration (Class K).

Form KK - Print or label used for an article of merchandise (Class K).

Form L-M - Motion picture (Classes L-M).

Form R - Renewal copyright.

Form U - Notice of use of copyrighted music on mechanical instruments.

Section 202.4 Books (Class A)

(a) *Subject matter and forms.* This class includes such published works as fiction and nonfiction, poems, compilations, composite works, directories, catalogs, annual publications, information in tabular form, and similar text matter, with or without illustrations, as books, either bound or in loose-leaf form, pamphlets, leaflets, cards, single pages or the like. Applications for registration of claims to copyright in published books manufactured in the United States of America are made on Form A; in books manufactured outside of the United States of America, except those subject to ad interim provisions of the copyright law, on Form A-B Foreign; and in books in the English language manufactured and first published outside the United States of America, and subject to the ad interim provisions of the copyright law, on Form A-B Ad Interim.

(b) *Ad interim registrations.*

(1) An American edition of an English-language

book or periodical identical in substance to that first published abroad will not be registered unless an ad interim registration is first made.

(2)   When a book or periodical has been registered
under the ad interim provisions, an American edition of the same
work, to be registrable, must be manufactured and published in
the United States within five years after the date of first
publication abroad.

(3)   Since by law ad interim copyright expires at
the end of the ad interim term unless an American edition is
published during that term, a renewal application covering a
work registered only under the ad interim provisions will be
rejected. Where both an ad interim and an American edition
have been registered, the registrability of the renewal application is governed by the date of the first publication abroad.

Section 202.5 Periodicals (Class B).

This class includes such works as newspapers, magazines,
reviews, bulletins, and serial publications, published at inter-
vals of less than a year. Applications for registration of
claims to copyright in published periodicals manufactured in
the United States of America are made on Form B; in periodicals,
or in contributions thereto, manufactured outside the United
States of America, except those subject to the ad interim provisions of the copyright law, on Form A-B Foreign; and in periodicals, or in contributions thereto, in the English language
manufactured and first published outside of the United States
of America, and subject to the ad interim provisions of the
copyright law, on Form A-B Ad Interim. Applications for registration of claims to copyright in contributions to periodicals
manufactured in the United States of America are made on Form
BB. Application for registration of claims to copyright in
contributions to periodicals, which contributions are prints
published in connection with the sale or advertisement of an
article or articles of merchandise, are made on Form KK.

*Section 202.6 Lectures or similar productions prepared for
            oral delivery (Class C).*

This class includes the scripts of unpublished works
prepared in the first instance for oral delivery, such as lectures, sermons, addresses, monologs, panel discussions, and
variety programs prepared for radio or television. The script
submitted for registration in Class C should consist of the
actual text of the work to be presented orally. Formats, outlines, brochures, synopses, or general descriptions of radio

and television programs are not registrable in unpublished form. When published with notice as prescribed by law, such works may be considered for registration as "books" in Class A.

Section 202.7 Dramatic and dramatico-musical compositions (Class D).

This class includes published or unpublished works dramatic in character such as the acting version of plays for the stage, motion pictures, radio, television and the like, operas, operettas, musical comedies and similar productions, and pantomimes. Choreographic works of a dramatic character, whether the story or theme be expressed by music and action combined or by actions alone, are subject to registration in Class D. However, descriptions of dance steps and other physical gestures, including ballroom and social dances or choreographic works which do not tell a story, develop a character or emotion, or otherwise convey a dramatic concept or idea, are not subject to registration in Class D.

Section 202.8. Musical compositions (Class E).

(a) This class includes published or unpublished musical compositions in the form of visible notation (other than dramatico-musical compositions), with or without words, as well as new versions of musical compositions, such as adaptations or arrangements, and editing when such editing is the writing of an author. The words of a song, when unaccompanied by music, are not registrable in Class E.

(b) A phonograph record or other sound recording is not considered a "copy" of the compositions recorded on it, and is not acceptable for copyright registration. Likewise, the Copyright Office does not register claims to exclusive rights in mechanical recordings themselves, or in the performances they reproduce.

. . . .

Section 202.15 Motion pictures (Classes L-M).

A single application Form L-M is available for registration of works in Classes L (Motion-Picture Photoplays) and M (Motion Pictures other than Photoplays).

(a) *Photoplays (Class L).* This class includes published or unpublished motion pictures that are dramatic in character and tell a connected story, such as feature films, filmed television plays, short subjects and animated cartoons having a plot.

        (b)   Other than photoplays (Class M).   This class includes published or unpublished nondramatic films such as newsreels, travelogs, training or promotional films, nature studies, and filmed television programs having no plot.

    . . . .

Section 202.17   Renewals.

        (a)   Claims to renewal copyright must be registered within the last (28th) year of the original copyright term.   The original term for a published work is computed from the date of first publication;   the term for a work originally registered in unpublished form is computed from the date of registration in the Copyright Office.   Unless the required application and fee are received in the Copyright Office during the prescribed period before the first term of copyright expires, copyright protection is lost permanently and the work enters the public domain.   The Copyright Office has no discretion to extend the renewal time limits.

        (b)   Renewal claims may be registered only in the names of persons falling within one of the classes of renewal claimants specified in the copyright law.   If the work was a new version of a previous work, renewal may be claimed only in the new matter.

Section 202.18   Notices of use.

        Notices of use of copyrighted musical compositions on mechanical instruments, required by section 1(e) of title 17, U.S. Code, will be recorded upon receipt of a properly executed Form U and upon payment of the prescribed fees.   Notices of intention to use will be received pursuant to section 101(e) of title 17, U.S. Code;   no special form is provided therefor."

    . . . .

COPYCAT

I

"How much may I steal without getting caught?" is
wondered by many writers and producers, and worries many businessmen.

One quickie producer said, "Let's take *HIGH NOON*, mix it
with *SHANE*, set it in New York in the 1920's, and get it indorsed
by some organization we will found ourselves as a classic. How
much can we steal from *HIGH NOON*, *SHANE*, and *STREETS OF NEW YORK*
without being sued?"

II

Jack Benny took the MGM movie *GAS LIGHT*, starring Charles
Boyer, Ingrid Bergman and Joseph Cotton. He burlesqued *GAS LIGHT*
with Jack Benny in a leading role.

Loew's Incorporated (MGM) sued Jack Benny and the Columbia Broadcasting System.

Judge James M. Carter of the United States District
Court for the Southern District of California, Central Divison,
held for Loew's (that there had been copyright infringement).

The United States Court of Appeals for the Ninth Circuit
affirmed the decision.

The Supreme Court of The United States split 4-4, thus
affirming the lower courts' decisions.

The opinion of the Supreme Court was brief: "Per Curiam.

The judgment is affirmed by an equally divided Court."

The opinion of the United States Court of Appeals is interesting for various reasons to various readers. It concerns mighty forces (movies versus television), star names (Benny, Bergman, Boyer, Cotton, in alphabetical order), mystery (who will win the case?), humor (the imagination of defense counsel), readability in its discussion of copyright, copying, fair use, and unfair use.

Extracts from *The Opinion of the United States Court of Appeals* are elsewhere in this book.

III

There is much copying. One of the values of copyrights in older motion pictures to studios is the right of studios to copy their own copyright features. Of course, the movie copyright owners of a movie based on a book or other copyright-protected source material are not allowed to infringe on the original source material.

There are very few lawsuits compared to infringements. Motion picture companies have efficient attorneys who try to stall plaintiffs to weariness. Part of the infringing defendants' strategy is to make infringement lawsuits so expensive for plaintiffs' attorneys that relatively few attorneys are willing to take movie infringement cases.

BENNY v. LOEW'S INCORPORATED

COLUMBIA BROADCASTING SYSTEM, INC. v. LOEW'S, INC.

U.S. Court of Appeals, Ninth Circuit (1956) 239 F
2d 532, 112 US PQ 11, 30 Copr. Decis. Bull. 73

. . . .

"McALLISTER, *Circuit Judge.* Patrick Hamilton, an English
author and a British subject, some time prior to December, 1938,
conceived and wrote an original play entitled, 'Gas Light.' It
was published and protected by copyright in February, 1939.
Shortly thereafter, it was publicly performed in England, first,
in Richmond, and later, in London. On December 5, 1941, it was
produced as a play in New York under the name, 'Angel Street,'
and had a successful run of 1,295 consecutive performances, extending over a period of more than 37 months.

"On October 7, 1942, the exclusive motion picture rights
for 'Gas Light' were acquired by Loew's, Inc., better known under its trade name of Metro-Goldwyn-Mayer.

"Loew's spent $2,458,000 in the production and distribu-
tion of the motion picture photoplay of 'Gas Light.' The actual
making of the film extended over a period of more than two and a
half years.

"In producing the motion picture, Loew's acquired the
services of three great artists in the cinema field, Charles
Boyer, Ingrid Bergman, and Joseph Cotton.

"The photoplay, 'Gas Light,' was exhibited in the United
States and fifty-six foreign countries. Approximately fifty-two
million persons paid admission to see it. The gross receipts in
rentals for the play amounted to $4,857,000.

"There is no question of the right of the dramatic work
to protection under the copyright laws of both Great Britain
and the United States.

"On October 14, 1945, Jack Benny, a successful performer
in the field of comedy, after securing Loew's consent to present
a parody of 'Gas Light' on radio, caused to be written, produced,
performed, and broadcast over a national radio network a fifteen-
minute burlesque of the play. In preparing the program, the
radio writers for Benny had access to the acting script of the
motion picture, 'Gas Light.'

"More than six years later, on January 27, 1952, the Columbia Broadcasting System caused to be written and produced a half-hour-long television show burlesquing 'Gas Light,' with Jack Benny in the leading role. It was broadcast over the Columbia Broadcasting System network and was 'sponsored' by the American Tobacco Company. Neither Mr. Benny nor the Columbia Broadcasting System nor the American Tobacco Company secured consent from Loew's or Mr. Hamilton to publish and broadcast the televison burlesque, or, as it is sometimes called, the parody.

"Immediately after the presentation of the television show, Loew's dispatched a telegram to the Columbia Broadcasting System, notifying that company that Loew's was the owner of the exclusive rights of production and recording of the play, 'Gas Light,' and adaptations thereof by means of talking films, sound tracks, and television; that Columbia had used substantial portions of the play in its television program; and that Loew's intended to enforce its rights against infringement. A short time thereafter, counsel for Columbia replied to the above telegram, informing Loew's that its burlesque appropriation of the play, 'Gas Light,' was a 'fair use' of the dramatic work, and that Columbia had the right to parody it as it did in the television show. Loew's, in turn, informed Columbia that the burlesque television show constituted an infringement of the copyright of 'Gas Light'; and when Columbia prepared for a similar presentation over several television channels, Loew's filed this action, and secured a temporary restraining order.

"Upon a trial of the issues, the district court found that the Benny television play was copied in substantial part from Loew's motion picture photoplay, 'Gas Light'; that the portion so copied was a substantial part of the copyrighted material in such photoplay; and that the Benny television presentation was an infringement of the copyrighted photoplay, 'Gas Light.' The court, accordingly, granted injunctive relief, restraining the showing of the television play, all of which appears in the able and comprehensive opinion by Judge James M. Carter, reported in 131 F. Supp. 165.

"On review, the chief contention advanced by appellants is that the burlesque presentation of 'Gas Light' was a 'fair use' of appellees' photoplay; that, although the play was copyrighted, and neither Benny, Columbia, nor the American Tobacco Company had received any consent on the part of the copyright owners to adapt the play in the way they did, nevertheless, they had the right to adapt the original copyrighted dramatic work of the author of the play and of the photoplay version as a burlesque, and to present, vend, and appropriate it thus, for their own profit.

"Appellees submit that the Copyright Act insures to the copyright owners the exclusive right to any lawful use of their property, whereby they may get a profit out of it. They further submit that there is no doctrine of fair use which justifies the appropriation of substantial copyrighted material of a dramatic work without the consent of the copyright owner, whether such appropriation is made for the purpose of pirating the work openly, or under the guise of a burlesque or a parody.

"In considering the law and its application to this case, the facts themselves are most important. The play is a remarkable dramatic production. As outlined by appellees and somewhat supplemented by the record, the play tells the story of a man who sets out upon a deliberate plan to drive his wife insane. He is motivated in this endeavor by the need of having access to a house which was inherited by his wife and in which they live. Some years prior, he had murdered the aunt of his wife for the sake of some valuable jewels which he had intended to steal, but in which he had been frustrated. His method of achieving his objective of finding the jewels without the wife's knowledge, and, at the same time, avoiding her suspicion, is to keep her attention diverted by inducing in her the belief that she is having hallucinations, suffering great lapses of memory, and gradually losing her mind. He does this by abstracting, without her knowledge, articles which he had entrusted to his wife, and by removing a portrait from the wall, making her believe that she had been responsible for the misplacement of the articles and the removal of the picture, of which she had lost all recollection. He fosters such a belief in her, in part, by causing the servants to bear witness that they did not remove the portrait. The suspense aroused by the picture is focused upon whether he will succeed in his scheme of finding the jewels and driving his wife insane. He fails, because of the intervention of a detective from Scotland Yard who, suspicious of the husband's conduct, has become interested in, and then obviously enamoured of, the heroine. The detective apprehends the husband at the climax of the plot, binds him to a chair in his own home to secure his arrest, and then reveals the truth, which he has learned, to the wife. At her request, she is given an opportunity to talk to the husband, who attempts once again, through his personal charm, to subdue her to his will. She, however, resists. In this scene, at her husband's request, she procures a knife, which he has kept nearby. The suspense is heightened by the question whether she will use the knife to cut her husband's bonds, as he has asked her to do, or whether she has come to a determination to kill him. She does neither, but contents herself with denouncing him, and turning him over to the police.

"A comparison of appellees' 'Gas Light' and the Columbia
telvision show discloses the following: The locale of Loew's
photoplay is in the early 1870's when the story begins. In the
burlesque television show, the story begins in 1871. The setting
is a gloomy old four-story Victorian house. The characters are
a murderer, his wife, a detective from Scotland Yard, and a maid.
The murderer has killed a woman ten years before in this house.
(In the Columbia television show, the time of the murder is fifteen years before.) Thereafter, the murderer marries the young
girl who has inherited the house from the murdered woman, so
that he can pursue his search for the jewels for which he had
committed the crime. All of the foregoing is the same in the
Columbia television show except that it does not mention that
the wife had inherited the house.

"In carrying out his objective, the husband follows the
above mentioned plan of driving his wife insane, so that she
may eventually be placed in an asylum. He leaves the house
nightly and then secretly returns through another entrance to
the attic to search for the jewels. In one of the incidents,
the husband questions, in the presence of the wife, the maid,
concerning the picture which has been removed from its place on
the wall, in spite of the wife's begging the husband not to hu-
miliate her before a servant. The maid denies having touched
the picture, and the husband uses this incident also to make
his wife believe that she has lost her mind. The husband is
finally caught by the Scotland Yard detective, who has deduced
that he is the murderer.

"During the entire play, except at the climax, the wife
is deeply in love with her husband and is grieved that he leaves
her alone each night. Because of the husband's machinations,
she fears that she is losing her mind and repeatedly begs for
the sympathy and understanding of her husband, who coldly repels
her. The detective from Scotland Yard, who has been noticing
the husband's suspicious actions and watching the house for some
time, calls on the wife when her husband is away and tells her
of his past and of the murder several years previously. In talking with the wife, the detective gets her to admit that she knows
it is her husband who is prowling in the attic and making the
mysterious noises there at night. Upon the return of the husband, the detective conceals himself in the house, but appears
as the husband commences to bully his wife. He then places the
husband under arrest, allows the wife to talk with him alone for
a few minutes while he waits outside the door, and then, at her
call, returns and takes him into custody. The foregoing is similar in both the photoplay and the television play.

"Title 17 U.S.C.A. Section 1, provides, among other

matters, that a copyright owner shall have the exclusive right
to make any other version of the copyrighted work; to dramatize
it, if it be a non-dramatic work; to convert it into a novel or
other nondramatic work, if it be a drama; to arrange or adapt
it, if it be a musical work; to perform the copyrighted work
publicly, if it be a drama; to make or to procure the making
of any transcription or record thereof, by or from which, in
whole or in part, it may in any manner or by any method be exhibited, performed, represented, produced, or reproduced; and
to exhibit, perfrom, represent, produce, or reproduce it in any
manner or by any method whatsoever.

"The district court found, as a fact, that appellants'
television play was copied by them, in substantial part, from
appellees' motion picture photoplay, 'Gas Light,' and that the
'part so copied was and is a substantial part of (appellants'
television) play, and of the copyrightable and copyrighted material in (appellees') motion picture photoplay.' The district
court found as facts '(1) that the locale and period of the
works are the same; (2) the main setting is the same; (3) the
characters are generally the same; (4) the story points are
practically identical; (5) the development of the story, the
treatment (except that defendants' treatment is burlesque), the
incidents, the sequences of events, the points of suspense, the
climax are almost identical and finally, (6) there has been a
detailed borrowing of much of the dialogue with some variation
in wording. There has been a substantial taking by defendants
from the plaintiffs' copyrighted property.' 131 F. Supp. 171.
Accordingly, the district court found that appellants were
guilty of infringement of appellees' photoplay, 'Gas Light.'

"The photoplay is an original dramatic work. It deals
with incidents familiar in life and fiction, but the grouping
of those incidents presents a novel arrangement of events; and
it is that originality which is protected by copyright.

"A comparison of the photoplay and the television play
indicates how much was copied. If the material taken by appellants from 'Gas Light' is eliminated, there are left only a few
gags, and some disconnected and incoherent dialogue. If the
television play were presented without appellants' contribution,
there would be left the plot, story, principal incidents, and
same sequence of events as in the photoplay.

"A review of the record, a comparison of the scripts of
appellees' photoplay and appellants' television play, and a viewing of the motion picture photoplay and the television play, as
projected upon the screen - all convince us that the findings
of fact of the district court that appellants copied the photo-

play in substantial part, and that the part so copied was a substantial part of the television play and of the material in appellees' photoplay, are clearly supported by the evidence.

"Appellants' chief defense is that the use which they
made of appellees' photoplay in their television play was a fair
use, by reason of the fact that the material which they appropri-
ated from the motion picture, 'Gas Light,' was used in the creation of a burlesque, and that by reason of such circumstance,
they are not guilty of infringement.

"The so-called doctrine of fair use of copyrighted
material appears in cases in federal courts having to do with
compilations, listings, digests, and the like, and is concerned
with the use made of prior compilations, listings, and digests.
In certain of these cases, it is held that a writer may be
guided by earlier copyrighted works, may consult original authorities, and may use those which he considers applicable in
support of his own original text; but even in such cases, it
is generally held that if he appropriates the fruits of another's
labors, without alteration, and without independent research,
he violates the rights of the copyright owner. In these instances, as has been said, there are certain to be considerable
resemblances, 'just as there must be between the work of two
persons compiling a directory, or a dictionary, or a guide for
railroad trains, or for automobile trips. In such cases the
question is whether the writer has availed himself of the earlier writer's work without doing any independent work himself.'
Chautauqua School of Nursing v. National School of Nursing, 2
Cir., 238 F. 151, 153. See also cases digested in 18 F. Dig.,
Copyrights, Section 55. But up to the time of the present controversy, no federal court, in any adjudication, has supposed
that there was a doctrine of fair use applicable to copying the
substance of a dramatic work, and presenting it, with few variations, as a burlesque. The fact that a serious dramatic work
is copied practically verbatim, and then presented with actors
walking on their hands or with other grotesqueries, does not
avoid infringment of the copyright. 'Counsel have not disclosed
a single authority, nor have we been able to find one, which
lends any support to the proposition that wholesale copying and
publication of copyrighted material can *ever* be fair use.' *Leon
v. Pacific Telephone & Telegraph Co.*, 9 Cir., 91 F.2d 484, 486.
(Emphasis supplied). Whether the audience is gripped with tense
emotion in viewing the original drama, or, on the other hand,
laughs at the burlesque, does not absolve the copier. Otherwise,
any individual or corporation could appropriate, in its entirety,
a serious and famous dramatic work, protected by copyright, merely by introducing comic devices of clownish garb, or movement,
or facial distortion of the actors, and presenting it as burlesque.

One person has the sole right to do this - the copyright owner,
inasmuch as, under Title 17 U.S.C.A. Section 1, he has the exclusive right to make any other version of the work that he desires. He can have it read or sung or danced or pantomimed or
burlesqued, because, in the language of the statute, he has the
sole right to 'exhibit, perform, represent, produce, or reproduce it in any manner or by any method whatsoever.'

"The fact that it has been Mr. Benny's custom to present
from time to time, his, or the Columbia Broadcasting System's
'version' of various dramatic works during the past twenty-five
years, is no defense to this action for infringement of copyright. Appellants cannot copy and present another's dramatic
work as they have in the instance before us, unless they receive
the consent of the copyright owner.

"An apparently alternative contention that the presentation of the burlesque was, in effect, literary or dramatic criticism and, therefore, not subject to an action for infringement
of copyright, would seem to be a parody upon the meaning of
criticism.

"The record in this case includes a beguiling dissertation on the history of the drama, of English literature, of
parody, and of burlesque, by Dr. Frank C. Baxter, a widely recognized and eminent authority in this field of study. Briefs
of appellants' counsel, too, disclose a wealth of literary ap-
preciation. However, there is only a single decisive point in
the case: One cannot copy the substance of another's work without infringing his copyright. A burlesque presentation of such
a copy is no defense to an action for infringement of copyright.
As was said by the district judge, a 'parodied or burlesque taking is to be treated no differently from any other appropriation;
that, as in all other cases of alleged taking, the issue becomes
first one of fact, i.e., what was taken and how substantial was
the taking; and if it is determined that there was a substantial taking, infringement exists.'   131 F. Supp. 183.

"The finding of the district court that appellants had
copied a substantial part of appellees' photoplay is clearly
supported by the evidence. The judgment is affirmed upon the
findings of fact and conclusions of law of the district court
and for the reasons set forth in the opinion of Judge James M.
Carter."

BOOK V

CHAPTER 106
COPYRIGHT OFFICE
THE LIBRARY OF CONGRESS
WASHINGTON, D.C. 20540

Cir. 45
Page 458

COPYRIGHT FOR MOTION PICTURES

What Is a "Motion Picture"?

In general, the term "motion picture" applies to complete photographic films ready for projection or exhibition. It does not include scenarios or synopses, and the Copyright Office cannot register works of this sort in unpublished form. Filmstrips and slide films are generally registrable as "photographs" on Form J.

The general idea, outline, or title of a motion picture or of a filmed series cannot be copyrighted. Registration of one film does not protect other films in a series or give any sort of "blanket" protection to the series as a whole.

Classes of Motion Pictures

The copyright law provides for two classes of motion pictures:

- Class L, *motion-picture photoplays,* for motion pictures that are dramatic in character and tell a connected story, such as feature films, filmed television plays, short subjects having a plot, and animated cartoons.

- Class M, *motion pictures other than photoplays,* for such films as newsreels, travelogs, training or promotional films, nature studies, and filmed television programs having no plot.

Application forms are furnished free by the Copyright Office upon request. The form for all motion pictures is designated Form L–M.

Published Motion Pictures

Copyright is secured on the date of first publication if all copies distributed bear notice of copyright. "Publication" generally means the sale, placing on sale, or public distribution of copies; in the case of motion pictures it may also include distribution to film exchanges, film distributors, exhibitors, or broadcasters under a lease or similar arrangement.

The copyright notice must consist of the word "Copyright," the abbreviation "Copr.," or the symbol ©, accompanied by the name of the copyright proprietor and the year date of publication. Example:

© John Doe 1969

(OVER)

The notice should preferably appear on the title frame or near it. The use of the symbol © with the name of the copyright owner and the year date may result in securing copyright in countries outside the United States under the provisions of the Universal Copyright Convention.

NOTE: Once a work has been published without the required copyright notice, the right to secure copyright protection for that film is permanently lost.

Promptly *after publication* the following items should be deposited in the Copyright Office:

- Two complete copies of the best edition of the motion picture then published. The "best" edition is usually the most valuable form of prints available—for example, color prints rather than black and white, or 35-mm. rather than 16-mm.;

- An application on Form L–M. Item 3 of this application *must* be checked to show whether the film is Class L or Class M. If the motion picture is part of a series, the application should list both the series and episode title;

- A description in the form of a continuity, press book, etc.; and

- The statutory registration fee of $6.

The copies (i.e., reels) of published motion pictures deposited in the Copyright Office are subject to retention by the Library of Congress under the provisions of section 213 of the copyright law. A contract, however, may be made with the Librarian for the return to the applicant of the deposited copies under certain conditions. For information regarding this contract, address the Exchange and Gift Division, Library of Congress, Washington, D.C. 20540. Contract forms will be supplied by the Copyright Office upon request.

Unpublished Motion Pictures

Copyright may also be secured for an unpublished motion picture (i.e., one not reproduced in copies for sale or public distribution), upon deposit in the Copyright Office of the following:

- One print (i.e., frame or blow-up) taken from each scene or act if the film is a photoplay, *or* at least two prints taken from different sections if the film is not a photoplay;

- An application on Form L–M. Item 3 of the application *must* be checked to show whether the film is Class L or Class M;

- The title and description of the film in the form of a continuity, press book, etc.; and

- The statutory registration fee of $6.

Registration of a claim prior to publication does not relieve the claimant of the duty of depositing, with an application and registration fee, two copies of the best edition of the published film after copies containing the statutory copyright notice have been placed on sale, sold, or publicly distributed.

A complete play with dialog and dramatic action, ready for filming, may be registered as a "dramatic composition." Ask for application Form D.

COPYRIGHT OFFICE REGISTRATION

On the next few pages you will find Copyright Office Circular 45 entitled *COPYRIGHT FOR MOTION PICTURES*, and an *APPLICATION FOR REGISTRATION OF A CLAIM TO COPYRIGHT IN A MOTION PICTURE* (Form L-M).

The registration applicant sends in Form L-M pages 1, 2, 3, 4. The Copyright Office keeps pages 1-2, and returns pages 3-4.

FORM L-M

CLASSES	REGISTRATION NO.
L-M	
	DO NOT WRITE HERE
	LP LU MP MU

Application for Registration of a Claim to Copyright
in a motion picture

Instructions: Make sure that all applicable spaces have been completed before you submit the form. The application must be **SIGNED** at line 10. For published works the application should not be submitted until after the date of publication given in line 5 (a), and should state the facts which existed on that date. For further information, see page 4.

Pages 1 and 2 should be typewritten or printed with pen and ink. Pages 3 and 4 should contain exactly the same information as pages 1 and 2, but may be carbon copies.

Mail all pages of the application to the **Register of Copyrights**, Library of Congress, Washington, D.C., 20540, together with:

(a) If unpublished, title and description, prints as described on page 4, and the registration fee of $6.

(b) If published, two complete copies, description, **and the** registration fee of $6.

Make your remittance payable to the Register of Copyrights.

1. Copyright Claimant(s) and Address(es): Give the name(s) and address(es) of the copyright owner(s). For published works the name(s) should ordinarily be the same as in the notice of copyright on the copies.

Name   *VILLA YORE PRODUCTIONS*

Address   *1422-1/2 North Cherokee, Hollywood, California 90028*

Name

Address

2. (a) Title: *"THE JOE YORE STORY"*
(Give the title of this particular motion picture as it appears on the copies)

(b) Series Title:
(If work is part of a series with a continuing title, also give series title)

3. (a) Nature of Work: (One of the following boxes **MUST** be checked. *For further information, see page 4.*)

   ☒ Photoplay   ☐ Motion picture other than a photoplay

(b) Description of Copies: *4 Reels*
(Give running time, footage, or number of reels)

(c) Number of Prints Deposited: (For unpublished works only)

4. Author: Citizenship and domicile information must be given. Where a work is made for hire, the employer is the author. The citizenship of organization formed under U.S. Federal or State law should be stated as U.S.A. If the copyright claim is based on new matter (see line 6) give information about the author of new matter.

Name   *Richard Bernstein*   Citizenship   *U.S.A.*
(Name of country)

Domiciled in U.S.A. ☒ Yes ☐ No   Address   *6633 Woodley, Van Nuys, California*

➤➤ **NOTE: Leave all spaces of line 5 blank unless your work has been PUBLISHED.** ◄◄

5. (a) Date of Publication: Give the complete date when copies of this particular work were first placed on sale, sold, or publicly distributed. The date when the motion picture was made or exhibited should not be confused with the date of publication. (NOTE: The full date (month, day, and year) must be given.

     2   5   70
     (Month)   (Day)   (Year)

(b) Place of Publication: Give the name of the country in which this particular motion picture was first published.

   U.S.A.

➤➤ **NOTE: Leave all spaces of line 6 blank unless the instructions below apply to your work.** ◄◄

6. Previous Registration or Publication: If a claim to copyright in any substantial part of this work was previously registered in the U.S. Copyright Office in unpublished form, or if a substantial part of the work was previously published anywhere, give requested information.

Was work previously registered? Yes _____ No _____ Date of registration _____ Registration number _____

Was work previously published? Yes _____ No _____ Date of publication _____ Registration number _____

If there any substantial **NEW MATTER** in this version? Yes _____ No _____ If your answer is "Yes," give a brief general statement of the nature of the **NEW MATTER** in this version. (New matter may consist of compilation, abridgment, editorial revision, and the like, as well as additional cinematographic work.)

EXAMINER

Complete all applicable spaces on next page

7. If registration fee is to be charged to a deposit account established in the Copyright Office, give name of account:

----

8. Name and address of person or organization to whom correspondence or refund, if any, should be sent:

Name ..... *VILLA YORE PRODUCTIONS* ..... Address ..... *1422-1/2 N. Cherokee*
Hollywood, California   90028

9. Send certificate to:

(Type or
print
name and
address)

Name ..... *VILLA YORE PRODUCTIONS* .....

Address ..... *1422-1/2 N. Cherokee* .....
(Number and street)

..... *Hollywood, California*   *90028* .....
(City)   (State)   (ZIP code)

10. **Certification:** (NOTE: Application not acceptable unless signed)

I CERTIFY that the statements made by me in this application are correct to the best of my knowledge.

☛ ....
(Signature of copyright claimant or duly authorized agent)

Application Forms

Copies of the following forms will be supplied by the Copyright Office without charge upon request.

Class A Form A—Published book manufactured in the United States of America.

Class A Form A–B Foreign—Book or periodical manufactured outside the United States of America (except works subject to
or B   the ad interim provisions of the copyright law).
         Form A–B Ad Interim—Book or periodical in the English language manufactured and first published outside the United
              States of America.

Class B Form B—Periodical manufactured in the United States of America.
         Form BB—Contribution to a periodical manufactured in the United States of America.

Class C Form C—Lecture or similar production prepared for oral delivery.

Class D Form D—Dramatic or dramatico-musical composition.

Class E Form E—Musical composition the author of which is a citizen or domiciliary of the United States of America or which
              was first published in the United States of America.
         Form E Foreign—Musical composition the author of which is not a citizen or domiciliary of the United States of
              America and which was not first published in the United States of America.

Class F Form F—Map.

Class G Form G—Work of art or a model or design for a work of art.

Class H Form H—Reproduction of a work of art.

Class I Form I—Drawing or plastic work of a scientific or technical character.

Class J Form J—Photograph.

Class K Form K—Print or pictorial illustration.
         Form KK—Print or label used for an article of merchandise.

Class L Form L–M—Motion Picture.
or M
         Form R—Renewal copyright.

         Form U—Notice of use of copyrighted music on mechanical instruments.

FOR COPYRIGHT OFFICE USE ONLY		
Application received	Prints received	One copy received
Two copies received		
Title and description received		
Fee received		
Renewal		

U.S. GOVERNMENT PRINTING OFFICE: 1965—O—791-331

Page 3

Certificate
Registration of a Claim to Copyright
in a motion picture

FORM L-M

CLASSES	REGISTRATION NO.
L-M	DO NOT WRITE HERE

This Is To Certify that the statements set forth on this certificate have been made a part of the records of the Copyright Office. In witness whereof the seal of the Copyright Office is hereto affixed.

Register of Copyrights
United States of America

1. Copyright Claimant(s) and Address(es):

Name _____ *VILLA YORE PRODUCTIONS* _____

Address _____ *1422-1/2 North Cherokee, Hollywood, California 90028* _____

Name _____

Address _____

2. (a) Title: _____ *"THE JOE YORE STORY"* _____
(Give the title of this particular motion picture as it appears on the copies)

(b) Series Title: _____
(If work is part of a series with a continuing title, give series title)

3. (a) Nature of Work:

☒ Photoplay   ☐ Motion picture other than a photoplay

(b) Description of Copies: _____ *4 Reels* _____
(Give running time, footage, or number of reels)

(c) Number of Prints Deposited: (For unpublished works only) _____

4. Author:

Name _____ *Richard Bernstein* _____ Citizenship _____ *U.S.A.* _____
(Name of country)

Domiciled in U.S.A. Yes ☒ No ☐ Address *6633 Woodley, Van Nuys, California* _____

5. (a) Date of Publication:

_____ 2 _____ 5 _____ 70 _____
(Month)   (Day)   (Year)

(b) Place of Publication:

_____ *U.S.A.* _____
(Name of country)

6. Previous Registration or Publication:

Was work previously registered? Yes _____ No _____ Date of registration _____ Registration number _____

Was work previously published? Yes _____ No _____ Date of publication _____ Registration number _____

Is there any substantial **NEW MATTER** in this version? Yes _____ No _____ If your answer is "Yes," give a brief general statement of the nature of the **NEW MATTER** in this version:

_____

EXAMINER

Complete all applicable spaces on next page

7. Deposit account:

---

8. Send correspondence to:

Name _____ *VILLA YORE PRODUCTIONS* _____   Address _____ *1422-1/2 North Cherokee*
Hollywood, California 90028

9. Send certificate to:

(Type or print name and address)

Name _____ *VILLA YORE PRODUCTIONS* _____

Address _____ *1422-1/2 North Cherokee* _____
(Number and street)

Hollywood, California   *90028*
(City)   (State)   (ZIP code)

Information concerning copyright in motion pictures

When To Use Form L–M. Form L–M is appropriate for unpublished and published motion pictures.

What Is a "Motion Picture"? The copyright law provides for two classes of motion pictures.

—*Photoplays* (Class L) include motion pictures that are dramatic in character and tell a connected story, such as feature films, filmed television plays, and animated cartoons.

—*Motion Pictures Other Than Photoplays* (Class M) include such films as newsreels, travelogues, promotional films, nature studies, and filmed television programs having no plot.

Unpublished Scenarios. The Copyright Office cannot make registration for an unpublished scenario, synopsis, format, or general description of a motion picture.

No "Blanket" Copyright. The general idea, outline, or title of a motion picture or of a filmed series cannot be copyrighted. Registration for a motion picture covers the copyrightable material in the film, but does not give any sort of "blanket" protection to the characters or situations portrayed, to future films in the series, or to the series as a whole.

Duration of Copyright. Statutory copyright begins on the date the work was first published, or, if the work was registered for copyright in unpublished form, copyright begins on the date of registration. In either case, copyright lasts for 28 years, and may be renewed for a second 28-year term.

Unpublished motion pictures

How To Register a Claim. To obtain copyright registration mail the following material to the Register of Copyrights, Library of Congress, Washington, D.C., 20540: (1) the title of the film; (2) a description (synopsis, press book, continuity, etc.); (3) for photoplays, one print (frame or blow-up) taken from each scene or act, and for other motion pictures, at least two prints taken from different sections of the film; (4) an application on Form L–M; and, (5) a fee of $6.

Procedure To Follow if Work Is Later Published. If the work is later reproduced in copies and published, it is necessary to make a second registration, following the procedure outlined below. To maintain copyright protection, all copies of the published work must contain a copyright notice in the required form and position.

Published motion pictures

What is "Publication"? Publication, generally, means the sale, placing on sale, or public distribution of copies. In the case of a motion picture, it may also include distribution to film exchanges, film distributors, exhibitors, or broadcasters under a lease or similar arrangement.

How To Secure Copyright in a Published Motion Picture:

1. *Produce copies with the copyright notice.*
2. *Publish the work.*
3. *Register the copyright claim* by sending to the Copyright Office: (1) two complete copies of the best edition of the motion picture; (2) a description (synopsis, press book, continuity, etc.); (3) an application on Form L–M; and, (4) a **fee of $6.**

The Copyright Notice. In order to secure and maintain copyright protection for a published work, it is essential that all copies published in the United States contain the statutory copy-

right notice. For motion pictures this notice should appear on or near the title frame, and should consist of the word "Copyright," the abbreviation "Copr.," or the symbol ©, accompanied by the name of the copyright owner and the year date of publication. Example: © John Doe 1966. Use of the symbol © may result in securing copyright in countries which are parties to the Universal Copyright Convention.

NOTE: If copies are published without the required notice, the right to secure copyright is lost and cannot be restored.

Return of Deposit Copies. The deposit copies (i.e., reels) of published motion pictures are subject to retention by the Library of Congress. However, it may be possible to enter into a contract with the Librarian for the return of the copies under certain conditions, and contract forms may be obtained on request. Information regarding the contract may be obtained from the Exchange and Gift Division, Library of Congress, Washington, D.C., 20540.

FOR COPYRIGHT OFFICE USE ONLY		
Application received	Prints received	One copy received
Two copies received		
Title and description received		
Fee received		

D E C I S I O N S

of

UNITED STATES COURTS INVOLVING COPYRIGHT

The United States Copyright Office, Library of Congress, Washington, D.C. publishes bi-annually *DECISIONS OF THE UNITED STATES COURTS INVOLVING COPYRIGHTS*.

The volumes since 1909 are for sale for under $50.00 total.

A "Cumulative Index 1909-1954" was published in 1954. This lists some of the hundreds of motion pictures involved in copyright litigation, and specifies the *DECISIONS* ... volume and page which contains the case.

While case opinions often are technical, many are readable and understandable by laymen.

The combination of glamorous movies, glamorous litigants, and interesting legal issues make these books excellent browsing for laymen.

Lawyers will appreciate the key numbers provided by West Publishers, the subject index of cases, and the concentration of a thousand (?) copyright cases in about a foot of shelf space.

COPYRIGHT SEARCH REQUEST

Date: _____

Fulton Brylawski, Esq.
224 East Capital Street
Washington, D.C.

RE: _____(Title)

By _____

Dear Mr. Brylawski:

Please make a copyright search of the above-mentioned property. Information we have which may be of assistance to you is:

1. Date of publication: _____

2. Where published: _____

3. Other pertinent information (if any): _____

_____

_____

We desire to know whether this property is in the public domain in the United States, in Canada, and world-wide, and if there is any impediment to our exhibiting a film(s) based upon the foregoing property in any media, anywhere, in perpetuity.

Kindly bill _____
for this search, and send a copy of your report to _____
_____ of our company.

Very truly yours,

(Producer): _____

By: _____

INVESTORS AND LENDERS SHOULD LEARN

ABOUT

THE UNIFORM COMMERCIAL CODE

Many states have adopted the Uniform Commercial Code or Commercial Code with no or few variations.

Persons who are willing to lend money (bankers, private lenders) or perform services on credit (laboratories, directors, stars, writers, producers), and persons who invest money (stockholders, limited partners, partners) and persons who are contingently liable (completion guaranty, insurers, guarantors) may be interested in benefiting from the provisions of the Uniform Commercial Code.

California has several forms approved by its Secretary of State:

Form UCC-1   Financing Statement
                 (Debtor, Secured Party, Property)

Form UCC-2   Financing Statement Change
                 (Continuation or Release or
                  Assignment or Termination or
                  Amendment or Other)

Form UCC-3   Request for Information or Copies
                 (Interested Party request Filing Officer to
                  give information about a Debtor)

Persons interested in learning about the producer or production company or other key men can send to the Secretary of State Form UCC-3, which says in part: "INFORMATION REQUEST, Filing Officer please furnish certificate showing whether there is on file any presently effective financing statement naming

the Debtor listed below and any statement of assignment thereof,

and if there is, giving the date and hour of filing of each such

statement and the names and addresses of each secured party

named therein."

Interested persons can get (buy) a copy of any and all

statements on file.

Lenders will want to file Financing Statements in order

to protect their rights in the copyright, the negative, prints,

physical objects and intangibles, rights to income, etc.

OFFICE OF THE

Secretary of State

UNIFORM COMMERCIAL CODE DIVISION
P. O. BOX 1738
SACRAMENTO, CALIFORNIA 95808

IMPORTANT NOTICE

Effective November 8, 1967, the fee for a financing statement certificate, issued pursuant to Section 9407 of the Commercial Code, will be five dollars ($5.00). This will be a fixed fee regardless of the number of effective filings reported in a certificate.

Each request for a financing statement certificate must be accompanied by a five-dollar ($5.00) remittance. Requests received without such a remittance will be returned.

The fee for copies of filed statements will remain the same at one dollar ($1.00) for the first **page** and fifty cents ($0.50) for each page thereafter.

Because it is difficult for a requestor to determine the total fee for copies of documents at the time the request is made, we will continue to extend limited credit for copy fees only. Failure to promptly pay balances due will cause credit privileges to be discontinued.

If copies of documents are requested along with a financing statement certificate, it is suggested that the remittance be in the form of a blank check. Upon computing the total fees for copies of documents and the certificate, the check will be completed for the proper amount.

A further reminder to the effect that when standard form UCC-3 is used to request a financing statement certificate, each request should relate to only one debtor name or trade name. Forms which reflect more than one name will be processed for only one of the names appearing thereon. All other names will be disregarded and the requestor advised to submit separate requests for each of the additional names.

FRANK M. JORDAN
Secretary of State

This **FINANCING STATEMENT** is presented for filing pursuant to the California Uniform Commercial Code

1. DEBTOR (LAST NAME FIRST)		1A. SOCIAL SECURITY OR FEDERAL TA
1B. MAILING ADDRESS	1C. CITY, STATE	1D. ZIP COD
1E. RESIDENCE ADDRESS (IF AN INDIVIDUAL AND DIFFERENT THAN 1B)	1F. CITY, STATE	1G. ZIP COD
2. ADDITIONAL DEBTOR (IF ANY) (LAST NAME FIRST)		2A. SOCIAL SECURITY OR FEDERAL TA
2B. MAILING ADDRESS	2C. CITY, STATE	2D. ZIP COD
2E. RESIDENCE ADDRESS (IF AN INDIVIDUAL AND DIFFERENT THAN 2B)	2F. CITY, STATE	2G. ZIP COD
3. DEBTOR(S) TRADE NAME OR STYLE (IF ANY)		3A. FEDERAL TAX NO.
4. ADDRESS OF DEBTOR(S) CHIEF PLACE OF BUSINESS (IF ANY)	4A. CITY, STATE	4B. ZIP COD

5. SECURED PARTY		5A. SOCIAL SECURITY NO., FEDERAL T OR BANK TRANSIT AND A.B.A. N
NAME		
MAILING ADDRESS		
CITY	STATE	ZIP CODE

6. ASSIGNEE OF SECURED PARTY (IF ANY)		6A. SOCIAL SECURITY NO., FEDERAL T OR BANK TRANSIT AND A.B.A. N
NAME		
MAILING ADDRESS		
CITY	STATE	ZIP CODE

7. This FINANCING STATEMENT covers the following types or items of property (if crops or timber, include description of real pr on which growing or to be grown)

7A. Maximum amount of indebtedness to be sec any one time (OPTIONAL).

$ _____

8. Check ☒ If Applicable	A ☐ Proceeds of collateral are also covered	B ☐ Products of collateral are also covered	C ☐ Proceeds of above described original collateral in which a security interest was perfected	D ☐ Collateral was brought into this State sub to security interest in another jurisdiction

9.

(Date) _____ 19____

By: _____
           SIGNATURE(S) OF DEBTOR(S)   (TITLE)

By: _____
           SIGNATURE(S) OF SECURED PARTY(IES)   (TITLE)

CODE: 1 2 3 4 5 6 7 8 9

10. This Space for Use of Filing Officer (Date, Time, File Number and Filing

11.   **Return Copy to**

NAME
ADDRESS
CITY, STATE
AND ZIP

(1) FILING OFFICER COPY
STANDARD FORM—FILING FEE $2.00   UNIFORM COMMERCIAL CODE—FORM UCC-1
Approved by the Secretary of State

This **STATEMENT** is presented for filing pursuant to the California Uniform Commercial Code

FILE NO. OF ORIG. FINANCING STATEMENT	1A. DATE OF FILING OF ORIG. FINANCING STATEMENT	1B. DATE OF ORIG. FINANCING STATEMENT	1C. PLACE OF FILING ORIG. FINANCING STATEMENT

DEBTOR (LAST NAME FIRST)		2A. SOCIAL SECURITY NO., FEDERAL TAX NO.

MAILING ADDRESS	2C. CITY, STATE	2D. ZIP CODE

ADDITIONAL DEBTOR (IF ANY) (LAST NAME FIRST)		3A. SOCIAL SECURITY OR FEDERAL TAX NO.

MAILING ADDRESS	3C. CITY, STATE	3D. ZIP CODE

SECURED PARTY

NAME

MAILING ADDRESS

CITY   STATE   ZIP CODE

4A. SOCIAL SECURITY NO., FEDERAL TAX NO. OR BANK TRANSIT AND A.B.A. NO.

ASSIGNEE OF SECURED PARTY (IF ANY)

NAME

MAILING ADDRESS

CITY   STATE   ZIP CODE

5A. SOCIAL SECURITY NO., FEDERAL TAX NO. OR BANK TRANSIT AND A.B.A. NO.

A ☐ CONTINUATION—The original Financing Statement between the foregoing Debtor and Secured Party bearing the file number and date shown above is continued. If collateral is crops or timber, check here ☐ and insert description of real property on which growing or to be grown in Item 7 below.

B ☐ RELEASE—From the collateral described in the Financing Statement bearing the file number shown above, the Secured Party releases the collateral described in Item 7 below.

C ☐ ASSIGNMENT—The Secured Party certifies that the Secured Party has assigned to the Assignee above named, all the Secured Party's rights under the Financing Statement bearing the file number shown above in the collateral described in Item 7 below.

D ☐ TERMINATION—The Secured Party certifies that the Secured Party no longer claims a security interest under the Financing Statement bearing the file number shown above.

E ☐ AMENDMENT—The Financing Statement bearing the file number shown above is amended as set forth in Item 7 below. (Signature of Debtor required on all amendments.)

F ☐ OTHER

(Date)_____19____

By:_____
SIGNATURE(S) OF DEBTOR(S)   (TITLE)

By:_____
SIGNATURE(S) OF SECURED PARTY(IES)   (TITLE)

Return Copy to

CODE
1
2
3
4
5
6
7
8
9

9. This Space for Use of Filing Officer
(Date, Time, Filing Office)

┌   ┐

└   ┘

NAME
ADDRESS AND
CITY STATE

FILING OFFICER COPY
STANDARD FORM—FILING FEE $_____   UNIFORM COMMERCIAL CODE—FORM UCC-2
Approved by the Secretary of State

REQUEST FOR INFORMATION OR COPIES. Present in Duplicate to Filing Officer

1. ☐ INFORMATION REQUEST. Filing officer please furnish certificate showing whether there is on file any presently effective filing statement naming the Debtor listed below and any statement of assignment thereof, and if there is, giving the date and
of filing of each such statement and the names and addresses of each secured party named therein.

1A. DEBTOR (LAST NAME FIRST)		1B. SOC. SEC. OR FED. TA
1C. MAILING ADDRESS	1D. CITY, STATE	1E. ZIP CODE
1F.		

Date_____19_____   Signature of Requesting Party_____

2. CERTIFICATE:

FILE NUMBER	DATE AND HOUR OF FILING	NAME(S) AND ADDRESS(ES) OF SECURED PARTY(IES) AND ASSIGNEE(S), IF ANY

The undersigned filing officer hereby certifies that the above listing is a record of all presently effective financing statemen
statements of assignment which name the above debtor and which are on file in my office as of _____19_____ at _____

_____19_____   _____
        (DATE)   (FILING OFFICER)

                                          By:_____

3. ☐ COPY REQUEST. Filing officer please furnish_____copy(ies) of each page of the following statements concerni
debtors listed below ☐ Financing Statement ☐ Amendments ☐ Statements of Assignment ☐ Continuation State
☐ Statement of Release ☐ Termination Statement ☐ All Statements on file.

FILE NUMBER	DATE OF FILING	NAME(S) AND MAILING ADDRESS(ES) OF DEBTOR(S)	DEBTORS SO OR FED. TA

Date_____19_____   Signature of Requesting Party_____

4. CERTIFICATE:

The undersigned filing officer hereby certifies that the attached copies are true and exact copies of all statements requested

_____19_____   _____
        (DATE)   (FILING OFFICER)

                                          By:_____

5.   **Mail Information or Copies to**

NAME
MAILING
ADDRESS
CITY, STATE
AND ZIP

UNIFORM COMMERCIAL CODE—FORM UCC-3

FORMS AND CONTRACTS

This book contains forms and contracts. Please don't
worship them. All forms can stand improvements. Contracts are
usually the result of a mixture of cleverness, bargaining power,
ability to write and weariness; all can be improved. Are the
contracts thorough, complete, up-to-date, usable, and should
they be copied as is? No. We disclaim all responsibility for
everything except that we are furnishing invaluable study
material.

How chicken can we get with our disclaimers?

We are proud of the fact that we are furnishing you
with educational material. But don't expect fairness in contracts. Each side tries to make as much money as it can.

PRODUCER - EMPLOYEE

EMPLOYMENT   AGREEMENT

     PRODUCER: _____

     EMPLOYEE: _____

       Address: _____

       City, State, Zip: _____

       Telephone No: _____

       Social Security No: _____

The parties hereto agree as follows:

     1.   Producer employs Employee, and Employee accepts
such employment, to render services in the role or capacity of
_____ and otherwise as Producer
may require, at such times and places as Producer may designate,
with respect to the motion picture photoplay (hereinafter the
"Photoplay") tentatively entitled "_____."

     2.   Employee's services commence on _____, 19____
and shall continue for such period as Producer may require.
Producer shall have the right, after lay-off or dismissal of Employee, to recall Employee for further services hereunder.

     3.   Provided Employee fully performs all services re-
quired by Producer and all other obligations hereunder, Producer
shall pay to Employee $_____ for each day in which Employee's
services are required by Producer, except for days of incidental
services as provided below. SUCH SUM SHALL BE PAYABLE ONLY OUT
OF THE FIRST NET PROCEEDS WHICH PRODUCER RECEIVES FROM EXPLOITA-
TION OF THE PHOTOPLAY. If such payment is made to Employee more
than six (6) months but less than one (1) year after completion
of photography for the Photoplay, Employee shall receive an additional sum equal to five per cent (5%) of the aforementioned
payments. If such payment is made to Employee more than one (1)
year after completion of photography for the Photoplay, Employee
shall receive an additional sum equal to ten per cent (10%) of
the aforementioned payments. The payments provided for in this
paragraph shall be full consideration for all services required

of Employee hereunder and for all rights acquired by Producer
hereunder. Payments shall be made to Employee at the address
hereinabove indicated, or at such other address as Employee
may designate to Producer.

STANDARD TERMS AND CONDITIONS

4.   Employee shall render such services as Producer
may designate with respect to the production of motion picture
photographs, still photographs and sound recordings, and shall
devote full diligence, efforts and abilities to render all services required in a competent, painstaking and artistic manner.

5.   The term "incidental services," as referred to in
Paragraph 3 above, shall include all still photography sittings,
wardrobe fittings, hairdressing, make-up, publicity interviews,
production conferences, services for the making of film trailers,
and all other similar or dissimilar services which are not
generally considered as work time in the motion picture industry.

6.   Employee agrees that no other commitment of any kind
shall interfere with Employee's rendering of all services required by Producer with full and complete diligence.

7.   Producer shall be entitled to all rights in and to
all performances, appearances and sounds by Employee and all
other results and proceeds of Employee's services, without
restriction or limitation. Without limiting the generality
of the foregoing, Producer shall be the sole and exclusive
owner of all rights throughout the world in perpetuity in and
to the Photoplay, all motion picture photographs, still photographs and sound recordings, such rights including (but not
limited to) the sole and exclusive rights to exhibit, advertise,
merchandise and exploit the Photoplay and all motion picture
photographs, still photographs and sound recordings, in any
fields and media now or hereafter known, without any limitation
whatsoever, and without any obligation to Employee other than
the payments set forth in Paragraph 3 hereof.

8.   Producer shall have the right in perpetuity (but
shall be under no obligation) to authorize others to use Employee's name, voice, likeness and biographical material concerning Employee in and in connection with the production,
exhibition, advertising, merchandising and exploitation, in any
fields and media now or hereafter known, of the Photoplay or
any rights therein, or any motion picture photographs, still
photographs or sound recordings.

9.   Employee agrees that the manner in which Employee

performs, appears, and sounds in the Photoplay, motion picture photographs, still photographs and sound recordings shall be determined by Producer in Producer's sole discretion. Employee understands and agrees that, as a material part of the consideration inducing Producer to enter into this Agreement, Employee will make no claim against Producer, any and all distributors and exhibitors, or the shareholders, directors, officers, employees, agents, successors, licensees and assigns of the foregoing, on grounds to the effect that the manner in which Employee performs, appears or sounds in the Photoplay, motion picture photographs, still photographs, still photographs or sound recordings as produced and exploited, in any fields or media, in any way violates standards of decency, morality or propriety or Employee's rights of privacy or publicity. In addition, Employee understands and agrees that Producer shall have no responsibility or obligation to Employee arising out of any claim, demand or action of any nature whatsoever made or taken against Employee with reference to Employee's participation in the production of the Photoplay, motion picture photographs, still photographs or sound recordings, whether such claim, demand or action be instituted by any federal, state or local governmental agency or authority, or by any private person, firm or corporation whatsoever. In particular, and without limiting the generality of the foregoing, Employee understands and agrees that Producer shall have no responsibility or obligation to Employee arising out of any claim, demand or action made or taken against Employee alleging the violation of standards of propriety, morality or decency, or alleging that the Photoplay, motion picture photographs, still photographs or sound recordings is or are lewd, obscene or pornographic.

10. Producer agrees to use its reasonable efforts to produce and release or distribute the Photoplay. In the event, however, that Producer is unable to complete production of the Photoplay, or to obtain its release or distribution, Producer shall have no obligation to Employee of any nature whatsoever.

11. Nothing herein contained shall be deemed to require Producer to utilize Employee's services hereunder, or the results and proceeds thereof, its being agreed that Producer shall have discharged all obligations to Employee by exercising the efforts hereinabove referred to in Paragraph 10 and by making the payments hereinabove referred to in Paragraph 3 upon the terms and conditions specified therein. Producer agrees that if Employee's services are not used in any manner whatsoever, that, for the purposes of computing payment under Paragraph 3, Employee shall be deemed to have been required to render services for one (1) day.

12.   Employee agrees to furnish at no cost or expense to Producer, all modern wardrobe and wearing apparel required by Producer for the portrayal of Employee's role in the Photoplay.

13.   In the event of any breach by Producer of any of its obligations under this Agreement, Employee's remedies shall be limited to the recovery of monetary damages, and shall not include injunctive or any other form of specific relief in connection with the Photoplay, motion picture photographs, still photographs or sound recordings.   In no event shall Employee have the right to rescind the grant to Producer of any rights herein contained and provided for.

14.   Employee agrees that the services to be rendered by Employee hereunder are of a special, unique, unusual, extraordinary and intellectual character, which gives them peculiar value, the loss of which cannot be reasonably or adequately compensated by damages in action at law.   If Employee shall violate any of the terms of this Agreement to be performed by Employee, Producer shall be entitled to equitable relief by way of injunction or to any other remedy, at law or in equity, which may be available to Producer.

15.   Producer may freely assign and/or lease and/or license its rights hereunder in full or in part, to any person, firm or corporation, and this Agreement may be assigned, leased or licensed by any assignee, lessee or licensee thereof.

16.   Employee agrees to execute any and all additional instruments and documents which Producer may reasonably deem necessary or desirable to evidence or establish its rights hereunder.

17.   No provision hereof shall be construed to violate any applicable law contrary to which the parties have no legal right to contract.   However, if any provision hereof shall be adjudged by a court to be void or unenforceable under the circumstances, the same shall in no way affect any other provision of this Agreement, the application of such provision in any other circumstances or the validity or enforceability of this Agreement.

18.   This Agreement constitutes the entire agreement between the parties, replacing all prior understandings.   There is no representation, warranty or undertaking except as herein specifically provided.   Employee acknowledges that Producer is relying on the rights granted herein in planning for the production, financing and distribution of the Photoplay.   Any amendments, waivers or terminations of this Agreement or any

provisions thereof must be in writing and signed by both parties. This Agreement shall be interpreted by the laws of the State of California.

   IN WITNESS WHEREOF, the parties have executed this Agreement this _____ day of _____, 19_____.

PRODUCER:

_____

By: _____

EMPLOYEE:

_____

MATERIAL SUBMISSION

CONTRIBUTOR - PRODUCER AGREEMENT

To: _____ (Producer)
    _____
    _____

Gentlemen:

I am submitting to you herewith the material described
on the following page or pages, which I request you to read and
evaluate, and you hereby agree to do so.

I warrant that I am sole owner and author of said material and that I have full right and authorization to submit it
to you upon all of the terms and conditions stated herein. I
will indemnify you from any and all claims that may be made a-
gainst you at any time, by any person, firm or corporation, in
connection with said material or any use thereof.

I agree that any part of said material which is not
novel, or is not original, or is not legally protectible under
the law of literary property, may be used by you without any
liability to me, and that nothing in this agreement shall be
deemed to place you in any different position from anyone else
with respect to such material by reason of my submission or
your use thereof.

I realize that you have access to and/or may create or
have created literary materials and ideas which may be similar
or identical to my material in theme, plot, idea, format, or
other respects. I understand that I will not be entitled to
any compensation because of the use by you of any such similar
or identical material.

You agree that if you use said material and provided
such material is novel and original, and is protectible under
the law of literary property, and has not been obtained by you
from another source, you will pay me the reasonable value thereof. If we are unable to agree as to the reasonable value, the
amount will be conclusively determined by a panel of three arbitrators, one to be selected by each of us and they to select a
third, all of whom shall be persons well acquainted with the
entertainment industry. Such arbitration shall be conducted

under the rules of the American Arbitration Association, except as may be otherwise herein provided. You agree that you will appoint an arbitrator within thirty (30) days after you have received written notice of my claim, and I shall do the same. The arbitrators' decision shall be controlled by the terms of this agreement, and I agree that the amount of any reward by said arbitrators may not exceed $1,000.00.

I agree that any claim arising in connection with the subject matter of this agreement must be brought within six months after your first use of the material in question, and that the provisions of the preceding paragraph shall apply to all such claims; provided, however, that notwithstanding the foregoing, no breach of this agreement by you or failure by you to perform the terms hereof, which breach or failure to perform would otherwise be deemed a material breach of this agreement, shall be considered a material breach of this agreement unless within ten (10) days after I acquire knowledge of such breach or failure to perform, or of facts sufficient to put me upon notice of any such breach or failure to perform, I serve written notice upon you of such breach or failure to perform and you do not cure said breach or failure to perform within a further period of ten (10) days after receipt by you of said written notice.

I have retained a copy of my material, and I release you from liability for loss or other damage to it.

I execute this agreement with the express understanding that you agree to read and evaluate my material in express reliance upon my agreements and warranties herein. This is the sole agreement between us, and there is no other agreement expressed or implied with respect to the subject matter of this agreement.

I understand that whenever the word "you" or "your" is used above, it refers to (1) you; (2) any company affilaited with you by way of common stock ownership or otherwise; (3) your subsidiaries; (4) subsidiaries of such affiliated companies; (5) any firm, person or corporation to whom you are leasing production facilities; (6) clients of any subsidiary or affiliated company of yours; and (7) the officers, agents, servants, employees, stockholders, clients, successors and assigns of you, and of all such persons, firms, and corporations referred to in (1) through (6) hereof.

((*NOTE TO READER FROM EDITOR: This agreement has been included only for educational purposes. The producer needs protection from litigation nuts. The writer who has agreed to this one-sided agreement may be able to sue successfully for infringement despite this agreement.*))

I have described my material in the space provided
below, and I hereby warrant that all of the important elements
of my material have been stated therein.

Dated: _____   Very truly yours,

STATE OF CALIFORNIA)
COUNTY OF LOS ANGELES) ss

                                         _____
        On _____,   Signature (to be notarized)
19___, before me _____
_____ personally ap-   _____
peared _____   Print Name
known to me as (or proved to me
on the oath of _____   _____
_____) to be the person   Address
whose name is subscribed to the
within instrument, and acknowl-   _____
edged that he executed said   City, State and Zip Code
instrument.
                                         _____
                                         Telephone Number

                                         _____
                                         Social Security Number

_____
Notary Public in and for said
     County and State.

AGREED: _____
        (Producer)

By: _____

RECEIPT OF COPY OF THIS AGREEMENT ACKNOWLEDGED THIS _____ DAY
OF _____, 19____.

                                         _____
                                         Signature

THE ABOVE FORM IS TO BE SIGNED IN THE PRESENCE OF A NOTARY. ALL
PAGES MUST BE COMPLETED AND SIGNED.

NOTE: The following information must be given for screenplays,
treatments, novels, short stories, plays and similar material.

TITLE OF MATERIAL: _____

FORM OF MATERIAL: (e.g., screenplay, treatment, novel, short
                          story, play)

                    _____

SUMMARY OF THEME AND PLOT OF MATERIAL SUBMITTED: _____

_____

_____

_____

_____

_____

_____

PRINCIPAL CHARACTERS: _____

_____

_____

Writers Guild of America Registration No. _____

_____

Signature: _____

_____

_____

NOTE: The following information must be given for television
and motion picture ideas, formats and similar material.

TITLE OF MATERIAL SUBMITTED: _____

_____

Circle each item in the classification that applies to your idea:

        ( ) Television   ( ) Motion Pictures

MOTION PICTURE SYNCHRONIZATION LICENSE

MOTION PICTURE SYNCHRONIZATION LICENSE made as of the 24th day of April, 1970, between and among:

    1. The undersigned SOUND TRACK "MASTER" OWNER, doing business as _____, at _____, (hereinafter referred to as "Owner");

    2. The undersigned MOTION PICTURE PRODUCER, doing business as _____, at _____, (hereinafter referred to as "Producer"); and

    3. The undersigned MOTION PICTURE DISTRIBUTOR, a California Corporation, at _____, (hereinafter referred to as "Distributor").

In consideration of the mutual covenants herein contained, the parties hereto agree as follows:

    1. <u>Representations and Warranties</u>.

    a. Producer represents to Owner and Distributor that it is the Producer of the motion picture entitled "_____," (hereinafter referred to as the "Photoplay"), and that it has assigned and set over all of its right, title and interest in and to the Photoplay to Distributor.

    b. Distributor represents to Owner and Producer that it is a California corporation in good standing, and is the owner of the motion picture Photoplay entitled "_____" by reason of its purchase from Producer.

    c. Owner represents to Producer and to Distributor that it owns all of the rights in the master recordings of the songs entitled "_____" and "_____" by the group known as _____, (hereinafter the "Master"), including but not limited to the right to synchronize and use said Master as part of the sound track of a motion picture, all rights under copyright and all necessary authorization from all artistic personnel performing services in connection with the production of the Master, and that it is authorized to enter into this agreement and grant the rights granted herein.

2.   Grant of License.

        Owner hereby grants to Producer as producer and to
Distributor as owner of the Photoplay the non-exclusive, irrevocable and perpetual right, license, privilege and authority
to use the Master as part of the sound track of the Photoplay,
as well as the non-exclusive irrevocable right, license, privilege and authority to publicly perform and authorize others to
publicly perform the Master as recorded in said sound track of
the Photoplay, and in radio, screen and television trailers for
the advertising and exploitation of the Photoplay, in all countries of the world. Nothing contained herein, however, shall
be construed to authorize Producer or Distributor to use the
Master for the production of phonograph records.

        3.   Concurrently with the execution of this agreement,
Producer has paid to Owner the sum of One Thousand Dollars
($1,000.00) as full consideration for all of the rights and li-
censes granted to Distributor and Producer hereunder.

        4.   Owner hereby advises Producer and Distributor it is
negotiating with Record Company, Inc. for Record Company, Inc.
to include the material recorded on the Master as part of a
phonograph record to be distributed by Record Company, Inc.
Owner recognizes that the distribution of the Photoplay will
substantially benefit the exploitation of a phonograph record
embodying the music recorded on the Master. Accordingly, Owner
agrees that in the event it licenses Record Company, Inc. or
any other record distributor to distribute a record which util-
izes the performance recorded on the Master, Owner shall pay to
Distributor twenty-five per cent (25%) of the net receipts received by Owner from such record distributor. Net receipts
shall mean the gross receipts after first deducting the artist's
share from the gross receipts. Said sum shall be paid by Owner
to Distributor within two weeks after Owner receives payment of
such sums, and shall be accompanied by copies of the royalty
statements received by Owner from the record distributor. Distributor shall be and hereby is authorized to notify Record
Company, Inc. or such other record distributor of its 25% in--
terest in the net receipts from the sale of records embodying
the Master, and to direct Record Company, Inc. or such other
record distributor to pay such sum directly to Distributor.

        Nothing contained herein shall in any way require
Owner to take any action against Record Company, Inc. or such
other record distributor to require payment of royalties, its
being understood that Distributor's only right is to receive
twenty-five per cent (25%) of the net monies actually received
from time to time by Owner from Record Company, Inc. or such

other record distributor.

5.   Notwithstanding that the rights and licenses granted by Owner to Producer and Distributor hereunder are non-exclusive, Owner agrees that it will not authorize the use of the Master in the sound track of any other motion picture for a period of three (3) years after the date of this agreement.

6.   Owner hereby grants to Distributor the right to advertise and publicize the musical compositions included in the Master and those persons performing services in connection with the production of the Master. The form and placement of such advertising and publicity shall be at the sole discretion of Distributor.

IN WITNESS WHEREOF, the parties have executed this agreement at Los Angeles, California, on the date first above written.

SOUND TRACK "MASTER" OWNER

By: _____

MOTION PICTURE PRODUCER

By: _____

MOTION PICTURE DISTRIBUTOR

By: _____

PRODUCER - STAR AGREEMENT

AGREEMENT made this _____ day of _____, 19____
between _____, a California corporation
(hereinafter called "Producer"), and _____
(hereinafter called "Star").

IT IS AGREED:

I

The Producer hereby engages Star to act, play and perform the role of _____ in a full length motion picture tentatively entitled "_____,"
(hereinafter called the "Photoplay").

II

The term of employment shall begin on or about _____,
197_, and shall continue until completion of the Photoplay and
recordation of the said role, including retakes, added scenes,
transparencies, process shots, trick shots, sound track, trailers,
and foreign versions of the Photoplay.

III

As full compensation for Star's services, Producer shall
pay Star a minimum of thirty thousand dollars ($30,000), payable
as follows:

A. Sixteen thousand dollars ($16,000) payable eight
thousand dollars ($8,000) per week for two weeks' work, and pro

rata thereafter.

        B.   Fourteen thousand dollars ($14,000), which shall be deferred until Producer has paid in full the following:

        1.   A first lien loan against the Photoplay in favor of _____ Trust Company, a New York corporation, or its assignee;

        2.   A second lien loan in favor of a person or persons to be designated by Producer; and,

        3.   A third lien loan in favor of a laboratory to be selected by Producer.

        In this connection, Producer represents and warrants that the aggregate of the said three lien loans shall not exceed the sum of two hundred thousand dollars ($200,000).

        The Producer has informed the Star that, during the production of the Photoplay, it will incur obligations to other persons, which obligations shall also be deferred until payment of the aforesaid three lien loans, and Star agrees with Producer that the deferred compensation payable to Star shall be paid immediately following the aforesaid two hundred thousand dollars ($200,000), and before payment of any other deferments.

        C.   As additional compensation for Star's services, Producer does hereby assign and convey to Star a sum equal to twenty per cent (20%) of one hundred per cent (100%) of the Producer's share of the adjusted gross receipts of the Photoplay, as that term is defined in the distribution agreement between

Producer and Distributor, portions of which are attached hereto
as Exhibit A, after Producer has recovered the negative cost of
the Photoplay. The twenty per cent (20%) paid to Artist as described above is not reduced by any percentages given to others.

IV

The Producer shall have the unlimited right to release
and to rerun the Photoplay on television without paying Star
any additional compensation for such television release or re-
runs, except that, in the event television release or rerun
compensation becomes payable to Star under the terms of the Producer-Screen Actors Guild Codified Basic Agreement of 19____,
or any subsequent agreement with or requirement of the Screen
Actors Guild, Inc., Star shall be paid the minimum compensation
prescribed, which payment or payments shall be made not later
than the latest date permitted therein.

V

The Star grants to the Producer, without additional consideration therefor, the exclusive right and license to use and
simulate the Star's name, photograph, likeness, silhouette, and
voice-in, and in connection with the Photoplay, and in connection with advertising, exploiting, and exhibiting the Photoplay.

VI

The rights and licenses granted to the Producer in this
Agreement shall extend throughout the world, and, irrespective
of the expiration or termination of the term of this Agreement,

shall continue so long as the Producer fulfills its obligations under this paragraph.

VII

In addition to Star's services hereunder, the Producer shall be entitled to and shall own all the results and proceeds of such services (including all rights throughout the world of production, manufacture, recordation, reproduction, exhibition in any and all media, whether now or hereafter known, and by any art of method, and, in addition thereto, all copyrights, trade-marks and patents) whether such results and/or proceeds consist of literary, dramatic, musical, vocal, motion picture, mechani-cal or any other form of work, theme, idea, composition, crea-tion or product; and Star hereby assigns and transfers to the Producer all the foregoing and all rights of every kind and character in and to the same, without reservation, condition or limitation; and, specifically and without in any way limiting the generality of the foregoing language, Star expressly gives and grants to the Producer all rights of every kind and charac-ter in and to any and all acts, portrayals, poses and plays, and in and to all literary, dramatic, and/or musical material of any and all kinds, which the Star may write, compose, sug-gest, direct, produce, or furnish to the Producer for use here-under, but only in connection with the production, exhibition, and exploitation of the Photoplay.

VIII

The services of the Star hereunder shall be exclusive to the Producer during the term of this Agreement.

IX

The Star agrees that, during the term of this Agreement, and at all times during the production, exhibition and distribution of the Photoplay to be produced hereunder, the Star will conduct _____self with due regard to public morals and conventions, and will not do anything which will tend to degrade ___ (him, her) in society or bring (him, her) into public disrepute, contempt, scorn or ridicule, or that will tend to shock, insult, or offend the community or any substantial group thereof, or public morals or decency, or prejudice the Producer. In the event of any breach of the terms or provisions of this paragraph, the Producer, in addition to any other right or remedy, may terminate this Agreement and may refuse to give Star screen credit.

X

On condition that Star keeps and performs all of the covenants and conditions by (him, her) to be kept and/or performed pursuant to this Agreement, the Producer agrees to give Star the following screen credit billing on all positive prints of the Photoplay.

A. The Star shall have sole position billing over the title of the Photoplay, with the size of the lettering of

Star's name to be equal in size and type with the title of the
Photoplay. No other performer shall receive billing to exceed
90% of size and type of title.

      B.   Title cards shall be in the following order:

      1.   "_____ (Distributor) presents
_____" or similar wording using Distributor's
name.

      2.   "_____ (Star) starring in
_____," with Star's names to
be 100% of size and type of title.

      3.   "A _____ (Producer) - _____
(Star) Production," with the names of Producer and Star to be
of equal size.

      4.   "_____," (Name of the
Picture).

Nothing herein contained shall be construed so as to
prevent so-called "Teasers" or special advertising, publicity
or exploitation without mentioning Star's name therein or as
to prevent so-called "Trailer" or other advertising on the
screen without mentioning Star's name. No casual or inadver-
tent failure by us to comply with the provisions of this paragraph shall be deemed to constitute a breach of this Agreement
by us.

XI

Producer may assign or transfer this Agreement, or all

or any part thereof, to any person, firm or corporation.

IN WITNESS WHEREOF, the parties hereto have executed
this Agreement the day and year first above written.

PRODUCER: _____

       By: _____

STAR & ARTIST: _____

       By: _____

       Each of the undersigned individuals guarantees
performance of all of the obligations of the Producer under the
foregoing agreement.

                 _____

                 _____

                 _____

ACTOR-ADVISOR LETTER AGREEMENT

Gentlemen:

I desire to obtain your advice, counsel and direction in the development and enhancement of my artistic and theatrical career. The nature and extent of the success or failure of my career cannot be pre-determined and it is therefore my desire that your compensation be determined in such manner as will permit you to accept the risk of failure and likewise benefit to the extent of my success. In view of the foregoing we have agreed as follows:

1.   I do hereby engage you as my personal manager for a period of thirty-six (36) months commencing , and continuing to and including ; provided, however, this agreement and all of the terms and provisions hereof shall be automatically extended for an additional thirty-six (36) month period from and after , unless I have given you a written notice of termination on or before .
As and when requested by me during and throughout the term hereof you agree to perform for me one or more of the services as follows: Advise and counsel in the selection of literary, artistic and musical material; advise and counsel in any and all matters pertaining to publicity, public relations and advertising; advise and counsel with relation to the adoption of proper format for presentation of my artistic talents and in the determination of proper style, mood, setting, business and characterization in keeping with my talents; advise, counsel and direct in the selection of artistic talent to assist, accompany or embellish my artistic presentation; advise and counsel with regard to general practices in the entertainment and amusement industries and with respect to such matters of which you may have knowledge concerning compensation and privileges extended for similar artistic values; advise and counsel concerning the selection of theatrical agencies and persons, firms and corporations.

2.   I hereby irrevocably appoint you as my true and lawful attorney and in my name and behalf::

(a)   To approve and permit any and all publicity advertising;

(b)   To approve and permit the use of my name, photograph, likeness, voice, sound effects, caricatures, literary, artistic and musical materials for purposes of advertising and publicity and in the

promotion and advertising of any and all products
and services;

(c)   To sign, make, execute, acknowledge and deliver
any and all contracts and agreements for my professional services, talents and/or artistic
literary and musical materials;

(d)   To collect and receive sums as well as endorse my
name upon and cash any and all checks payable to
me for my services, talents and literary and
artistic materials and retain therefrom all sums
owing to you;

(e)   To engage, as well as discharge and/or direct for
me, and in my name, theatrical agents and employment agencies as well as other persons, firms and
corporations who may be retained to obtain contracts, engagements or employment for me.

The authority herein granted to you is coupled with an interest
and shall be irrevocable during the term hereof.

3.   I agree to at all times devote myself to my career and to
do all things necessary and desirable to promote my
career and earnings therefrom. I shall at all times engage proper theatrical agencies to obtain engagements and employment for me and I agree that I
shall not engage any theatrical or employment agency of which you may
disapprove. It is clearly understood that you are not an employment
agent or theatrical agent; that you have not offered or attempted or
promised to obtain employment or engagements for me, that you are not obligated, authorized, or expected to do so.

4.   This Agreement shall not be construed to create a partnership between us. It is specifically understood that you
are acting hereunder as an independent contractor and you may appoint or
engage any and all other persons, firms and corporations throughout the
world in your discretion to perform any or all of the services which you
have agreed to perform hereunder. Your services hereunder are not exclusive and you shall at all times be free to perform the same or similar
services for others as well as engage in any and all other business
activities. You shall only be required to render reasonable services as
and when reasonably requested by me. Due to the difficulty which we may
have in determining the amount of services to which I may be entitled, it
is agreed that you shall not be deemed to be in default hereunder until
and unless I shall first deliver to you a written notice describing the
exact service which I require on your part and then only in the event that
you shall thereafter fail for a period of fifteen (15) consecutive days to
commence the rendition of the particular service required. You shall not
be required to travel or to meet with me at any particular place or places
except in your discretion and following arrangements for costs and expenses of such travel.

5.   In full compensation for your services hereunder, I agree to pay to you, as and when received by me, a sum equal to fifteen (15%) per cent of my earnings; for each week which I earn Fifteen Hundred Dollars ($1500.00) or more, I agree to pay to you, as and when received by me, a sum equal to twenty (20%) per cent of my earnings. "Earnings" as used herein shall mean all compensation, sums and other things of value which I may receive as a result of my activities in and throughout the entertainment, amusement, musical recording and publishing industries, including any and all sums resulting from the use of my artistic talents and the results and proceeds thereof, and without in any manner limiting the foregoing; the matters upon which your compensation shall be computed shall include any and all of my activities in connection with matters as follows: motion pictures, television, radio, music, literary, theatrical engagements, personal appearances, public appearances in places of amusement and entertainment, records and recordings, publications, and the use of my name, likeness and talents for purposes of advertising and trade. I likewise agree to pay you a similar sum following the expiration of the term hereof upon and with respect to any and all engagements, contracts and agreements entered into during the term hereof relating to any of the foregoing, and upon any and all extensions, renewals and substitutions thereof.

6.   In the event of any dispute under or relating to the terms of this Agreement it is agreed that the same shall be submitted to arbitration to the American Arbitration Association in Los Angeles, California, in accordance with the rules promulgated by the said Association. Any judgment rendered as a result of said arbitration may be entered by any court having jurisdiction thereof, and the prevailing parties in any such arbitration shall be entitled to recover any and all reasonable attorney's fees and other costs incurred in connection with such arbitration.

7.   This Agreement shall be deemed to be executed in the State of California and shall be contrued in accordance with the laws of said State. In the event any provisions hereof shall for any reason be illegal or unenforceable then, and in any such event, the same shall not affect the validity of the remaining portions and provisions hereof.

This Agreement is the only Agreement between us and there is not other or collateral Agreement (oral or written) between us and in any manner relating to the subject matter hereof. I agree to execute such other and further instruments as may be necessary to carry this Agreement into effect.

     If the foregoing meets with your approval please indicate your acceptance and agreement by signing in the space hereinbelow provided.

                           Very truly yours,

                                       _____

ACCEPTED AND AGREED TO:

_____

WRITERS - REPRESENTATIVE CONTRACT

THIS CONTRACT AND AGREEMENT made and entered into by and
between _____ and _____, hereinafter jointly
called WRITERS, and _____, hereinafter called
REPRESENTATIVE, WITNESSETH:

WHEREAS, WRITERS and REPRESENTATIVE are jointly desirous
of causing to be produced and distributed a motion picture and
related productions, based upon an original script, entitled
_____, written by WRITERS, for the
mutual benefit of WRITERS and REPRESENTATIVE, for the considerations, and upon the terms, provisions and conditions hereinafter
set forth:

IT IS THEREFORE AGREED BY AND BETWEEN WRITERS AND
REPRESENTATIVE AS FOLLOWS:

1. WRITERS hereby give limited power of attorney to
REPRESENTATIVE, to represent WRITERS for the term hereinafter
set forth, for all right, title and interest of WRITERS throughout the world, to the sole and exclusive motion picture, television and recording rights and copyrights thereto, excluding
script publication rights and copyrights of a presently unpublished script written by WRITERS.

2. During the term of this agreement, the REPRESENTA-
TIVE shall have the right to represent WRITERS in connection
with:

a. The exclusive right to produce and distribute, or cause to be produced and distributed, in all languages, a motion picture, based upon the subject matter, including the screen play, adaptations, titles, and themes which may be made for such motion picture and televised motion picture versions of the subject matter, or any part or portion thereof; and

b. The exclusive right to mechanically reproduce and license the reproduction of spoken words of the subject matter on records, tapes and/or other devices.

3. WRITERS represent as follows:

a. No prior assignment, license or agreement has been made by WRITERS with respect to the subject matter, or any portion thereof, or in conflict with this agreement, and so far as is authorized and protected by the law of privacy, WRITERS are the sole owners of all right, title and interest in and to the subject matter, and are fully authorized to make this assignment.

b. Copyright registration has been effected by or through WRITERS.

4. This AGREEMENT may be cancelled at the option of WRITERS, upon thirty (30) days written notice to REPRESENTATIVE at the address below his signature, in the event that no firm commitment containing MINIMUM REQUIREMENTS set forth in Paragraph 8 has been made in writing, by or through REPRESENTATIVE, within five (5) months from the date of this AGREEMENT, for the

production and distribution of said motion picture, which commitment shall provide for the actual commencement of production of
said motion picture within one (1) year from the date of such
written commitment for such production and distribution of said
motion picture, and for completion of such production within a
reasonable time after the commencement of such production, and
default under such commitment shall likewise be cause for cancellation of this agreement by WRITERS upon written notice to
REPRESENTATIVE. Upon completion of the production and distribution of said motion picture, this agreement shall be irrevocable by WRITERS.

5. WRITERS agree to pay REPRESENTATIVE payment of ten
percent (10%) of monies realized by WRITERS in sale of said
script for motion picture production, stage play adaptations,
television production and recording of spoken words therein contained, and all other related productions. WRITERS agree to
make said payment to REPRESENTATIVE directly upon receipt of
monies earned.

6. This AGREEMENT shall bind the parties hereto, their
heirs, executors, successors, representatives and assigns.

7. WRITERS and REPRESENTATIVE each agree to further
execute all necessary instruments as shall be reasonably required to further effectuate and implement the purposes of
this AGREEMENT.

8. The MINIMUM REQUIREMENTS, referred to in Paragraph 4,

which any agreement for the sale of motion picture rights must
have before it will approved, include:

      a. Minimum net payment to be received by WRITERS
simultaneous with execution of the agreement: $10,000.00.

      b. Percentage of budget: Minimum percentage of
budget for script and music rights: 10%.

      c. Percentage of profit for WRITERS: Minimum
percentage of producer's gross receipts from distributor: 10%.

      d. WRITERS may audit PRODUCER, and may audit
DISTRIBUTOR as PRODUCER'S representatives.

      9. REPRESENTATIVE is not authorized to negotiate any
deals for any rights until after the completion of a contract
for the motion picture rights. REPRESENTATIVE is not authorized to execute any contracts on behalf of WRITERS or to receive any money on behalf of WRITERS. He is merely authorized
to solicit such contracts; commission shall be due only on
gross receipts actually received.

      10. This AGREEMENT does not cover any copyright or
other rights concerning music. These rights are owned by the
following music publisher: _____.

      11. REPRESENTATIVE shall:

      a. Bear all of his own expenses, and shall not be
reimbursed.

      b. Use his best efforts to effectuate his tasks.

      c. Make informal written reports no less than once

a month to WRITERS listing each contract by person, company
represented, summary of conversations or result.

        d. Shall not assign the rights to receive money
under this contract to anyone, shall keep both WRITERS equally
notified by sending carbon copies of all communications to
either WRITER also to the other WRITER.

        WITNESS OUR HANDS on or about the _____ day of _____
_____, 19____.

Writer's Name:

Address:

City, State & Zip:

Phone:

Writer's Name:

Address:

City, State & Zip:

Phone:

Representative:

Address:

City, State & Zip:

Phone:

THEATRICAL MOTION PICTURE
ARTISTS' MANAGER CONTRACT
(AGENCY CONTRACT)

THIS AGREEMENT, made and entered into at.., by and between

...., an artists' manager, hereinafter called the "Agent", and

(please type or print)

...., hereinafter called the "Actor",

(please type or print)

WITNESSETH :

(1) The Actor employs the Agent as his agent in theatrical motion pictures as defined in the Regulations, Amended Rule 16(f), and the Agent accepts such employment. This contract is limited to theatrical motion pictures and to contracts of the Actor as an actor in such pictures, and any reference herein to contracts or employment whereby the Actor renders his services refer to contracts or employment in theatrical motion pictures unless otherwise specifically stated.

(2) The term of this contract shall be for a period of ...., commencing

...., 19.............

(3) (a) The Actor agrees to pay to the Agent as commissions a sum equal to................................per cent of all moneys or other consideration received by the Actor, directly or indirectly, under contracts of employment (or in connection with his employment under said employment contracts) entered into during the term specified in Paragraph (2) or in existence when this agency contract is entered into except to such extent as the Actor may be obligated to pay commissions on such existing employment contract to another agent. Commissions shall be payable when and as such moneys or other consideration are received by the Actor, or by anyone else for or on the Actor's behalf.

(b) No commissions shall be payable on any of the following:

(i) Separate amounts paid to Actor not as compensation but for travel or living expenses incurred by Actor;

(ii) Separate amounts paid to Actor not as compensation but as reimbursement for necessary expenditures actually incurred by Actor in connection with Actor's employment, such as for damage to or loss of wardrobe, special hairdress, etc.;

(iii) Amounts paid to Actor as penalties for violations by Producer of any of the provisions of the SAG collective bargaining contracts, such as meal period violations, rest period violations, penalties or interest on delinquent payments;

(iv) Sums payable to Actors for the release on free television of theatrical motion pictures produced after January 31, 1960, under the provisions of the applicable collective bargaining agreement providing for such payment; however, if an Actor's individual theatrical motion picture employment contract provides for compensation in the event motion pictures made for theatrical exhibition are exhibited over free television, in excess of the minimum compensation payable under the Basic Contract in effect at the time the employment contract was executed, commissions shall be payable on such compensation.

(c) Any moneys or other consideration received by the Actor, or by anyone for or on his behalf, in connection with any termination of any contract of the Actor by virtue of which the Agent would otherwise be entitled to receive commission, or in connection with the settlement of any such contract, or any litigation arising out of any such contract, shall also be moneys in connection with which the Agent is entitled to the aforesaid percentage; provided, however, that in such event the Actor shall be entitled to deduct attorney's fees, expenses and court costs before computing the amount upon which the Agent is entitled to his percentage. The Actor shall also be entitled to deduct reasonable legal expenses in connection with the collection of moneys or other consideration due the Actor arising out of an employment contract in theatrical motion pictures before computing the amount upon which the Agent is entitled to his percentage.

(d) The aforesaid percentage shall be payable by the Actor to the Agent during the term of this contract and thereafter only where specifically provided herein and in the Regulations.

(e) The Agent shall be entitled to the aforesaid percentage after the expiration of the term specified in Paragraph (2), for so long a period thereafter as the Actor continues to receive moneys or other consideration under or upon employment contracts entered into by the Actor during the term specified in Paragraph (2) hereof, including moneys or other consideration received by the Actor under the extended term of any such employment contract, resulting from the exercise of an option or options under such an employment contract, extending the term of such employment contract, whether such options be exercised prior to or after the expiration of the term specified in Paragraph (2), subject, however, to the applicable limitations set forth in the Regulations.

(f) If during the period the Agent is entitled to commissions a contract of employment of the Actor be terminated before the expiration of the term thereof, as said term has been extended by the exercise of options therein contained, by joint action of the Actor and employer, or by the action of either of them, other than on account of act of God, illness, or the like, and the Actor enters into a new contract of employment with said employer within a period of sixty (60) days, such new contract shall be deemed to be in substitution of the contract terminated as aforesaid, subject, however, to the applicable limitations set forth in the Regulations. No contract entered into after said sixty (60) day period shall be deemed to be in substitution of the contract terminated as aforesaid. Contracts of substitution have the same effect as contracts for which they were substituted, provided, however, any increase or additional salary, bonus or other compensation payable to the actor thereunder over and above the amounts payable under the contract of employment which was terminated shall be deemed an adjustment and, unless the Agent shall have a valid agency contract in effect at the time of such adjustment, the Agent shall not be entitled to any commissions on any such additional or increased amounts. In no event may a contract of substitution with an employer extend the period of time during which the Agent is entitled to commission beyond the period that the Agent would have been entitled to commission had no substitution taken place. A change in form of an employer for the purpose of evading this provision or a change in the corporate form of an employer resulting from reorganization or the like shall not preclude the application of these provisions.

(g) So long as the Agent receives commissions from the Actor, the Agent shall be obliged to service the Actor and perform the obligations of this agency contract with respect to the services of the Actor on which such commissions are based, unless the Agent is relieved therefrom under express provisions of the Regulations.

(h) The Agent has no right to receive money unless the Actor receives the same, or unless the same is received for or on his behalf, and then only in the above percentage when and as received. Money paid pursuant to legal process to the Actor's creditors, or by virtue of assignment or direction of the Actor, and deductions from the Actor's compensation made pursuant to law in the nature of a collection or tax at the source, such as Social Security, Old Age Pension taxes, State Disability taxes or income taxes shall be treated as compensation received for or on the Actor's behalf.

(4) Should the Agent, during the term specified in Paragraph (2), negotiate a contract of employment for the Actor and secure for the Actor a bona fide offer of employment, which offer is communicated by the Agent to the Actor in reasonable detail and in writing, which offer the Actor declines, and if, within

sixty (60) days after the date upon which the Agent gives such written information to the Actor, the Actor accepts said offer of employment on substantially the same terms, then the Actor shall be required to pay commissions to the Agent upon such contract of employment. If an agent employed under a prior agency contract is entitled to collect commissions under the foregoing circumstances, the Agent with whom this contract is executed waives his commission to the extent that the prior agent is entitled to collect the same.

(5) (a) The Agent may represent other persons who render services in theatrical motion pictures, or in other branches of the entertainment industry.

(b) Unless and until prohibited by the Actor, the Agent may make known the fact that he is the sole and exclusive representative of the Actor in theatrical motion pictures. However, it is expressly understood that even though the Agent has not breached the contract the Actor may at any time with or without discharging the Agent, and regardless of whether he has legal grounds for discharge of the Agent, by written notice to the Agent prohibit him from rendering further services for the Actor or from holding himself out as the Actor's Agent, and such action shall not give Agent any rights or remedies against Actor, the Agent's rights under this paragraph continuing only as long as Actor consents thereto but this does not apply to the Agent's right to commissions. In the event of any such written notice to the Agent the 91-day period set forth in Paragraph (6) of this agency contract is suspended and extended by the period of time that the Agent is prohibited from rendering services for the Actor.

(6) If during any period of ninety-one (91) days immediately preceding the giving of the notice of termination hereinafter mentioned in this paragraph the Actor fails to be employed and receive or be entitled to receive compensation in an amount equal to his past customary theatrical motion picture salary for fifteen (15) days' employment (one week's employment is deemed to be the equivalent of 5 or 6 days depending on whether the Actor is deemed to be on a 5 or 6 day week under the provisions of the SAG collective bargaining agreement governing working conditions in theatrical motion pictures), whether such employment or compensation is from the motion picture industry or any other branch of the entertainment industry in which the Agent may be authorized by written contract to represent the Actor, then either the Actor or the Agent may terminate the employment of the Agent hereunder by written notice to the other party, subject to the definitions and qualifications hereinafter in this paragraph set forth:

(a) The Actor's past customary theatrical motion picture salary for fifteen (15) days' employment is determined as follows:

Take the last day the Actor has worked in theatrical motion pictures during the year immediately preceding the 91-day period; count back 91 days from said date; take the Actor's total gross basic salary from theatrical motion pictures during such 91 days; divide such gross basic salary by the number of days the Actor has been employed in theatrical motion pictures during such 91-day period; multiply by 15; the result is the Actor's "past customary theatrical motion picture salary for fifteen (15) days employment".

(b) In making the computation of what the Actor has received during either 91-day period, overtime, extra pay for work on Saturdays, Sundays and holidays and the like do not count. In each case it is the Actor's basic salary which is the determining factor.

(c) In making the computation of what the Actor has received during the 91-day period which is the basis of termination, additional compensation for reuse of television motion pictures, theatrical use of television motion pictures, use or reuse of television filmed commercials, and release of theatrical film for television do not count unless the employment from which such compensation resulted was within such 91-day period.

(d) Saturdays, Sundays and holidays are included in counting days elapsed during both 91-day periods.

(e) If the Actor has not been employed in theatrical motion pictures during the year immediately preceding the 91-day period which is the basis of termination, then the requirement of this paragraph for termination shall be deemed to be failure to receive during the ninety-one (91) days immediately preceding notice of termination, fifteen (15) days employment in motion pictures or any other branch of the entertainment industry in which the Agent may be authorized by written contract to represent the Actor.

(f) The 91-day period which is the basis of termination shall be extended by the amount of employment the Actor would have received from calls for his services in theatrical motion pictures and at or near the Actor's usual places of employment at a salary and from an employer commensurate with the Actor's prestige, which calls are actually received by the Agent and reported in writing to the Actor, when the Actor is in such a locality (away from his usual place of employment) that he cannot return in response to such a call, or when the Actor is unable to respond to such a call by reason of physical or mental incapacity, or by reason of another engagement in a field in which the Actor is not represented by the Agent; provided, however, that if the Actor is rendering services in another engagement in a field in which the Agent is authorized to represent the Actor, then the time spent in such engagement shall not be added to the 91-day period. The 91-day period which is the basis of termination shall also be extended for any period of time which the Actor has declared himself to be unavailable and has so notified the Agent in writing, or has confirmed in writing a written communication from the Agent to such effect.

(g) If at any time during the term of any agency contract between a member of SAG and an agent the production of theatrical motion pictures in general (as distinguished from production at one or more studios) should be suspended, thereupon the 91-day period herein mentioned shall be extended by the period of such general suspension of theatrical motion picture production.

(h) The Actor may not exercise the right of termination if at the time he attempts to do so he is under a written contract or contracts, which guarantee the Actor employment in theatrical motion pictures for at least his customary theatrical motion picture salary for a period of time during a period of 182 days immediately after the expiration of the 91-day period in question, which employment when added to the number of days the Actor has been employed in theatrical motion pictures during the period of ninety-one (91) days in question shall equal forty-five (45) days' employment.

(i) If the Agent is authorized to represent the Actor on the legitimate stage, and the Actor accepts an engagement on the legitimate stage, and the compensation received from such engagement is not commensurate with the Actor's customary theatrical motion picture salary, the 91-day period which is the basis of termination shall be extended by the length of such stage engagement including rehearsals, and the money earned by the Actor on such stage engagement shall not count in making the computation of money earned during such 91-day period. Regardless of whether or not the Agent is authorized to represent the Actor on the legitimate stage, if the Actor accepts an engagement on the legitimate stage under a run of the play contract, the 91-day period which is the basis of termination shall be extended by the length of such run of the play contract including rehearsals.

(j) If the Actor is under a contract or contracts for the rendition of his services in a theatrical motion picture or pictures during the succeeding period of 182 days after the expiration of the 91-day period in question, at a guaranteed compensation for such services of Twenty Thousand Dollars ($20,000.00) or more (even though for less than forty-five (45) days), then the Actor may not exercise the right of termination. If the Actor is under an employment contract which provides that any part of the Actor's guaranteed compensation shall be deferred or if said compensation is spread over a period prior or subsequent to the time of the actual performance of the Actor's services under said employment contract, then for the purpose of determining the Actor's right to terminate under the provisions of this subparagraph the guaranteed compensation shall be deemed to have been paid to the Actor during the period of the actual performance of Actor's services under said employment contract.

(k) In the event the Agent has given the Actor notice in writing of a bona fide offer of employment (and there is in fact such an offer) in theatrical motion pictures and at or near the Actor's usual place of employment at a salary and from an employer commensurate with the Actor's prestige, which notice sets forth the terms of the proposed employment in detail, and the Actor refuses such proffered employment, then the period of guaranteed employment specified in said offer and the compensation which would have been received thereunder shall be deemed as time worked or compensation received by the Actor, as the case may be, in computing amounts of money earned or time worked with reference to the right of the Actor to terminate under the provisions of this paragraph, subject, however, to Subparagraph (n) hereof.

(1) Periods of lay-off, absence or leave of absence under a term contract shall not be deemed to be periods of unemployment hereunder, unless under said contract the Actor has the right to do other theatrical motion picture work during such period.

(m) No termination under this Paragraph (6) shall deprive the Agent of the right to receive commissions or compensation on moneys earned or received by the Actor prior to the date of termination, or earned or received by the Actor after the date of termination of the Agent's employment, on contracts for the Actor's services entered into by the Actor prior to the effective date of any such termination.

(n) In addition to the right of termination given by the first paragraph of this Paragraph (6), the Actor shall have the right of termination, beginning with the 77th day of the 91-day period, whenever it becomes apparent that the Agent will be unable to procure the required employment pursuant to this Paragraph (6) during such 91-day period. In considering whether it has become so apparent, the possibility that after the Actor exercises the right of termination, the Agent might preclude exercise of the right by compliance with Subparagraphs (f), (h), (i), (j) or (k) shall be disregarded. In considering whether or not the right has accrued, it shall be presumed that any employment the Actor would secure in the balance of the 91-day period would be by the day at his customary theatrical motion picture salary. To illustrate: If the Actor has had no employment for seventy-seven (77) days, Actor may terminate on the 77th day since only fourteen (14) days remain and Agent cannot obtain fifteen (15) days employment for the Actor in such period. If Actor received one (1) day's employment at his customary theatrical motion picture salary in seventy-eight (78) days, Actor may terminate on the 78th day since only thirteen (13) days remain and Agent cannot obtain fourteen (14) days employment for Actor in such period. However, if Actor received one (1) day's employment at twice his customary theatrical motion picture salary in seventy-eight (78) days he may not terminate on the 78th day, but may terminate on the 79th day if he receives no employment on such day.

Anything herein to the contrary notwithstanding:

(i) If the Agent submits to the Actor a bona fide offer of employment in writing (defined as in Paragraph (6), Subparagraph (k)) after the right of termination has accrued under Paragraph (6) but the Actor has not yet terminated the agency contract, and if the Actor thereafter terminates the agency contract pursuant to Paragraph (6) and thereafter accepts the offer within sixty (60) days of the date of submission of the offer to the Actor by the Agent, the Actor shall pay the Agent commission on the compensation received by the Actor pursuant to such employment.

(ii) If the Agent submits to the Actor a bona fide offer of employment in writing (defined as in Paragraph (6), Subparagraph (k)) during the period after the lapse of seventy-seven (77) days above set forth, which guarantees fifteen (15) days or more of work, the Actor and the Agent may by separate written agreement start the 91-day period above mentioned all over again, if they so choose, without consent of SAG, provided that such is done contemporaneously with the execution of the contract of employment pursuant to said offer.

(7) Amended Rule 16(f) of the Screen Actors Guild, Inc., which contains regulations governing the relations of its members to artists' managers, is hereby referred to and by this reference hereby incorporated herein and made a part of this contract. The provisions of said Rule are herein sometimes referred to as the "Regulations" and the Screen Actors Guild, Inc., is herein sometimes referred to as "SAG".

1
2
3
4
5
6
7
8
9
10
11
12
13
14
15
16
17
18
19
20
21
22
23
24
25
26
27
28
29
30
31
32
33
34
35
36
37
38
39
40
41
42
43
44
45
46
47
48
49
50

(8) The Agent agrees that the following person only shall personally supervise the Actor's business during the term of this contract. (*This italicized provision is a note from SAG to the Actor, and is not a part of the contract. If the Actor is executing this contract in reliance on the fact that a particular person is connected with the Agent, then the Actor should require that only such person's name be inserted in the space following. If the Actor is not executing this contract in reliance on such fact, then the Agent may insert only one name.*)

....

The person above named shall be available at all reasonable times for consultation with the Actor at the city named in Paragraph (9) or its environs during reasonable business hours, subject to absence of the person from the office occasioned by his agency activities outside of the office at the studios and elsewhere, and subject further to reasonable absences due to illness or reasonable vacation periods. The Agent upon request of the Actor and on reasonable notice shall assign such person to conduct negotiations for the Actor at such city or its environs and such persons shall do so; it being understood that sub-agents employed by the Agent who are not named herein may handle agency matters for the Actor or may aid the above named person in handling agency matters for the Actor. In the event the person above named shall cease to be active in the affairs of the Agent by reason of death, disability, retirement or any other reason, the Actor shall have the right to terminate this contract upon written notice to the Agent. The rights of the parties in such case are governed by Sections XI and XII of the Regulations.

(9) The Agent agrees to maintain telephone service and an office open during all reasonable business hours (emergencies such as sudden illness or death excepted) within the city of...

...., or its environs, throughout the term of this agreement and that some representative of the Agent will be present at such office during such business hours. This contract is void unless the blank in this paragraph is filled in with the name of a city at which the Agent does maintain an office to render services to Actors in the theatrical motion picture business.

(10) Any controversy under this contract, or under any contract executed in renewal or extension hereof or in substitution herefore or alleged to have been so executed, or as to the existence, execution or validity hereof or thereof, or the right of either party to avoid this or any such contract or alleged contract on any grounds, or the construction, performance, nonperformance, operation, breach, continuance or termination of this or any such contract, shall be submitted to arbitration in accordance with the arbitration provisions in the Regulations regardless of whether either party has terminated or purported to terminate this or any such contract or alleged contract. Under this contract the Agent undertakes to endeavor to secure employment for the Actor. This provision is inserted in this contract pursuant to a rule of the SAG, a bona fide labor union, which Rule regulates the relations of its members to artists' managers. Reasonable written notice shall be given to the Labor Commissioner of the State of California of the time and place of any arbitration hearing hereunder. The Labor Commissioner of the State of California, or his authorized representative, has the right to attend all arbitration hearings. The clauses relating to the Labor Commissioner of the State of California shall not be applicable to cases not falling under the provisions of Section 1700.45 of the Labor Code of the State of California.

(11) Both parties hereto state and agree that they are bound by the Regulations and by all of the modifications heretofore or hereafter made thereto pursuant to the Basic Contract and by all waivers granted by SAG pursuant to said Basic Contract or to the Regulations.

(12) (a) Anything herein to the contrary notwithstanding, if the Regulations should be held invalid, all references thereto in this contract shall be eliminated; all limitations of the Regulations on any of the provisions of this contract shall be released, and the portions of this contract including, but not limited to

1 Paragraphs (8) and (10) which depend upon reference to the Regulations shall be deleted, and the provisions
2 of this contract otherwise shall remain valid and enforceable.

3   (b) Likewise, if any portion of the Regulations should be held invalid, such holding shall not affect the
4 validity of remaining portions of the Regulations or of this contract; and if the portion of the Regulations
5 so held invalid should be a portion specifically referred to in this contract, then such reference shall be
6 eliminated herefrom in the same manner and with like force and effect as herein provided in the event the
7 Regulations are held invalid; and the provisions of this contract otherwise shall remain valid and enforceable.

Whether or not the Agent is the Actor's agent at the time this contract is executed, it is understood that in executing this contract each party has independent access to the Regulations and has relied exclusively upon his own knowledge thereof.

IN WITNESS WHEREOF, the parties hereto have executed this agreement the..day of

...., 19..............

....
                                                    Actor

....
                                                    Agent

By..

This artists' manager and/or agency is licensed by the Labor Commissioner of the State of California.
This artists' manager and/or agency is franchised by the Screen Actors Guild, Inc.
This form of contract has been approved by the Labor Commissioner of the State of California on July 15, 1968.
This form of contract has been approved by the Screen Actors Guild, Inc.
(The foregoing references to California may be deleted or appropriate substitutions made in other states.)

AMERICAN FEDERATION OF TELEVISION AND RADIO ARTISTS

STANDARD AFTRA EXCLUSIVE AGENCY CONTRACT
UNDER RULE 12-B

THIS AGREEMENT, made and entered into at.., by and between

...., hereinafter called the "AGENT," and

...., hereinafter called the "ARTIST."

WITNESSETH:

1. The Artist employs the Agent as his sole and exclusive Agent in the transcription, radio broadcasting and television industries (hereinafter referred to as the "broadcasting industries") within the scope of the regulations (Rule 12-B) of the American Federation of Television and Radio Artists (hereinafter called AFTRA), and agrees not to employ any other person or persons to act for him in like capacity during the term hereof, and the Agent accepts such employment. This contract is limited to the broadcasting industries and to contracts of the Artist as an artist in such fields and any reference hereinafter to contracts or employment whereby the Artist renders his services, refers to contracts or employment in the broadcasting industries, except as otherwise provided herein.

2. The Artist agrees that prior to any engagement or employment in the broadcasting industries, he will become a member of AFTRA in good standing and remain such a member for the duration of such engagement or employment. The Artist warrants that he has the right to make this contract and that he is not under any other agency contract in the broadcasting fields. The Agent warrants that he is and will remain a duly franchised agent of AFTRA for the duration of this contract. This paragraph is for the benefit of AFTRA and AFTRA members as well as for the benefit of the parties to this agreement.

3. The term of this contract shall be for a period of..., commencing the........................ day of.., 195.........

NOTE—The term may not be in excess of three years.

4. (a) The Artist agrees to pay to the Agent a sum equal to...per cent (not more than 10%) of all moneys or other consideration received by the Artist, directly or indirectly, under contracts of employment entered into during the term specified herein as provided in the Regulations. Commissions shall be payable when and as such moneys or other consideration are received by the Artist or by anyone else for or on the Artist's behalf.

(b) Any moneys or other consideration received by the Artist or by anyone for or on his behalf, in connection with any termination of any contract of the Artist on which the Agent would otherwise be entitled to receive commission, or in connection with the settlement of any such contract, or any litigation arising out of such contract, shall also be moneys in connection with which the Agent is entitled to the aforesaid commissions; provided, however, that in such event the Artist shall be entitled to deduct arbitration fees, attorney's fees, expenses and court costs before computing the amount upon which the Agent is entitled to his commissions.

(c) Such commissions shall be payable by the Artist to the Agent, as aforesaid, during the term of this contract and thereafter only where specifically provided herein.

(d) The agent shall be entitled to the aforesaid commissions after the expiration of the term specified herein, for so long a period thereafter as the Artist continues to receive moneys or other consideration under or upon employment contracts entered into by the Artist during the term specified herein, including moneys or other consideration received by the Artist under the extended term of such employment contracts, resulting from the exercise of an option or options given an employer under such employment contracts, extending the term of such employment contracts, whether such options be exercised prior to or after the expiration of the term specified herein.

(e) If after the expiration of the term of this agreement and during the period the Agent is entitled to commissions, a contract of employment of the Artist be terminated before the expiration thereof, as said contract may have been extended by the exercise of options therein contained, by joint action of the Artist and employer, or by the action of either of them, other than on account of an Act of God, illness or the like and the Artist enters into a new contract of employment with said employer within a period of sixty (60) days, such new contract shall be deemed to be in substitution of the contract terminated as aforesaid. In computing the said sixty (60) day period, each day between June 15th and September 15th shall be counted as three-fifths (3/5) of a day only. No contract entered into after said sixty (60) day period shall be deemed to be in substitution of the contract terminated as aforesaid. Contracts of substitution have the same effect as contracts for which they were substituted; provided, however, that any increase or additional salary, bonus or other compensation payable to the Artist (either under such contract of substitution or otherwise) over and above the amounts payable under the contract of employment entered into prior to the expiration of the term of this agreement shall be deemed an adjustment and unless the Agent shall have a valid Agency contract in effect at the time of such adjustment the Agent shall not be entitled to any commissions on any such adjustment. In no event may a contract of substitution with an employer entered into after the expiration of the term of this agreement, extend the period of time during which the Agent is entitled to commission beyond the period that the Agent would have been entitled to commission had no substitution taken place, except to the extent, if necessary, for the Agent to receive the same total amount of commission he would have received had no such substitution taken place; provided, however, that in no event shall the Agent receive more than the above percentages as commissions on the Artist's adjusted compensation under the contract of substitution. A change in form of an employer for the purpose of evading this provision, or a change in the corporate form of an employer resulting from reorganization or like, shall not exclude the application of these provisions.

(f) So long as the Agent receives commissions from the Artist, the Agent shall be obligated to service the Artist and perform the obligations of this contract with respect to the services of the Artist on which such commissions are based, subject to AFTRA's Regulations Governing Agents.

(g) The Agent has no right to receive money unless the Artist receives the same, or unless the same is received for or on his behalf, and then only proportionate in the above percentages when and as received. Money paid pursuant to legal process to the Artist's creditors, or by virtue of assignment or direction of the Artist, and deductions from the Artist's compensation made pursuant to law in the nature of a collection or tax at the source, such as Social Security or Old Age Pension taxes, or income taxes withheld at the source, shall be treated as compensation received for or on the Artist's behalf.

5. Should the Agent, during the term or terms specified herein negotiate a contract of employment for the Artist and secure for the Artist a bona fide offer of employment, which offer is communicated by the Agent to the Artist in reasonable detail and in writing, which offer the Artist declines, and if, after the expiration of the term of this agreement and within ninety (90) days after the date upon which the Agent gives such written information to the Artist, the Artist accepts said offer of employment on substantially the same terms, then the Artist shall be required to pay commissions to the Agent upon such contract of employment. If an Agent previously employed under a prior agency contract is entitled to collect commissions under the foregoing circumstances, the Agent with whom the present contract is executed waives his commission to the extent that the prior agent is entitled to collect the same.

6. (a) If during any period of ninety-one (91) days immediately preceding the giving of the notice of termination hereinafter mentioned in this paragraph, the Artist fails to be employed and receive, or be entitled to receive, compensation for fifteen (15) days' employment, whether such employment is from fields under AFTRA's jurisdiction or any other branch of the entertainment industry in which the Agent may be authorized by written contract to represent the Artist, then either the Artist or the Agent may terminate the employment of the Agent hereunder by written notice to the other party. (1) For purposes of computing the fifteen (15) days' employment required hereunder, each separate original radio broadcast, whether live or recorded, and each transcribed program, shall be considered a day's employment, but a rebroadcast, whether recorded or live, or an off-the-line recording, or a prior recording or time spent in rehearsal for any employment in the radio broadcasting or transcription industry, shall not be considered such employment. (2) During the months of June, July and August, each day's employment in the radio broadcasting industry, shall, for purposes of computing fifteen (15) days' employment under this sub-paragraph "(a)" and for no other purpose, be deemed one and one-half (1½) days' employment. (3) For the purposes of computing the fifteen (15) days' employment required hereunder, each separate television broadcast (including the rehearsal time) shall be considered two and one-half (2½) days' employment. However, any days spent in rehearsal over three days inclusive of the day of the telecast, and any days of exclusivity over three days inclusive of the day of telecast, will automatically extend the ninety-one (91) day period by such overage. (4) During the months of June, July and August, each day's employment in the television broadcasting field shall, for the purpose of computing fifteen (15) days' employment under this sub-paragraph "(a)" and for no other purpose, be deemed three and three-quarters (3¾) days' employment. (5) Each master phonograph record recorded by the Artist shall be one (1) day's employment.

(b) The ninety-one (91) day period which is the basis of termination shall be suspended during any period of time which the artist has declared himself to be unavailable or has so notified the agent in writing or has confirmed in writing a written communication from the agent to such effect. The said ninety-one (91) day period which is the basis of termination shall also be suspended (1) during the period of time in which the artist is unable to respond to a call for his services by reason of physical or mental incapacity or (2) for such days as the artist may be employed in a field in which the artist is not represented by the agent.

(c) In the event that the Agent has given the Artist notice in writing of a bona fide offer of employment as an Artist in the entertainment industry and at or near the Artist's usual places of employment at a salary and from an employer commensurate with the Artist's prestige (and there is in fact such an offer), which notice sets forth the terms of the proposed employment in detail and the Artist refuses or negligently fails to accept such proffered employment, then the period of guaranteed employment specified in said offer, and the compensation which would have been received thereunder shall be deemed as time worked or compensation received by the Artist in computing the money earned or time worked with reference to the right of the Artist to terminate under the provisions of this paragraph.

(d) No termination under paragraph 6 shall deprive the Agent of the right to receive commissions or compensation on moneys earned or received by the Artist prior to the date of termination, or earned or received by the Artist after the date of termination of the Agent's employment on contracts for the Artist's services entered into by the Artist prior to the effective date of any such termination and during the term or terms specified herein, or commission or compensation to which the Agent is entitled pursuant to paragraphs 4(e) and 5 hereof.

(e) The Artist may not exercise the right of termination if at the time he attempts to do so, either:

(1) the Artist is actually working under written contract or contracts which guarantee the Artist employment in the broadcasting industries for at least one program each week for a period of not less than thirteen (13) consecutive weeks. For the purposes of this sub-paragraph a "program" shall be either (i) a regional network program of one-half (½) hour length or more; (ii) a national network program of one-quarter (¼) hour length or more; or (iii) a program or programs the aggregate weekly compensation for which equals or exceeds the Artist's customary compensation for either (i) or (ii), or

(2) the Artist is under such written contract, as described in the preceding sub-paragraph "(1)" or in sub-paragraph "(5)" below, and such contract begins within forty-five (45) days after the time the Artist attempts to exercise the right of termination, or

(3) where the artist attempts to exercise the right of termination during the months of August or September, and the artist is under such written contract as described in the preceding sub-paragraph "(1)" or in sub-paragraph "(5)" below and such contract begins not later than the following October 15th, or

(4) if during any period of ninety-one (91) days immediately preceding the giving of notice of termination herein referred to, the artist has received, or has been entitled to receive, compensation in an amount equal to not less than thirteen (13) times his past customary compensation for a national network program of one-half (½) hour's length, whether such employment or compensation is from the broadcasting industries or any other branch of the entertainment industry in which the agent may be authorized by written contract to represent the Artist.

(5) The Artist is actually working under written contract or contracts which guarantee the Artist either (a) employment in the television broadcasting field for at least one (1) program every other week in a cycle of thirteen (13) consecutive weeks where the program is telecast on an alternate week basis, or (b) employment for at least eight (8) programs in a cycle of thirty-nine (39) consecutive weeks, where the program is telecast on a monthly basis or once every four (4) weeks.

In the cases referred to in sub-paragraphs (1), (2), (3) and (5) above, the ninety-one (91) day period begins upon the termination of the contract referred to in such sub-paragraphs; and for the purpose of such sub-paragraphs any local program which under any applicable AFTRA collective bargaining agreement is the equivalent of a regional or national network program, shall be considered a regional or national network program as the case may be.

(f) Where the Artist is under a contract or contracts for the rendition of his services in the entertainment industry in any field in which the agent is authorized to act for the artist, during the succeeding period of One hundred and eighty-two (182) days after the expiration of the ninety-one (91) day period in question, at a guaranteed compensation for such services of Twenty-five Thousand ($25,000.00) Dollars or more, or where the Artist is under a contract or contracts for the rendition of his services during said 182 day period in the radio, phonograph recording and/or television fields at a guaranteed compensation for such services of Twenty thousand dollars ($20,000.00) or more, then the artist may not exercise the right of termination.

(g) Periods of layoff or leave of absence under a term contract shall not be deemed to be periods of unemployment hereunder, unless under said contract the Artist has the right during such period to do other work in the radio or television field or in any other branch of the entertainment industry in which the Agent may be authorized by written contract to represent the Artist. A "term contract" as used herein means a contract under which the Artist is guaranteed employment in the broadcasting industries for at least one program each week for a period of not less than thirteen (13) consecutive weeks, and also includes any "term contract" as defined in the Regulations of the Screen Actors Guild, Inc. in respect to the motion picture industry, under which the Artist is working. Also, a "term contract" as used herein relating to the television field means a contract under which the Artist is guaranteed employment in the television field as set forth in sub-paragraph (e) (5) above.

(h) Where the Artist has a contract of employment in the broadcasting industries and either the said contract of employment, or any engagement or engagements thereunder, are cancelled by the employer pursuant to any provision of said contract which does not violate any rule or regulation of AFTRA, the Artist shall be deemed to have been employed and to have received compensation for the purposes of paragraph 6(a) for any such cancelled broadcasts, with the following limitation—where a contract providing for more than one program has been so cancelled, the Artist shall not be deemed to have been employed or to have received compensation under such contract, with respect to more than one such program on and after the effective date of cancellation of such contract.

(i) For the purposes of this paragraph 6, where the Artist does not perform a broadcast for which he has been employed but nevertheless is compensated therefor, the same shall be considered employment hereunder.

(j) If at any time during the original or extended term of this contract, broadcasting over a majority of both the radio stations as well as a majority of the television broadcasting stations shall be suspended, the ninety-one (91) days period mentioned in this paragraph 6 shall be extended for the period of such suspension.

7. The Agent may represent other persons. The Agent shall not be required to devote his entire time and attention to the business of the Artist. The Agent may make known the fact that he is the sole and exclusive representative of the Artist in the broadcasting industries. In the event of a termination of this contract, even by the fault of the Artist, the Agent has no rights or remedies under the preceding sentence.

8. The Agent agrees that the following persons, and the following persons only, namely

(HERE INSERT NOT MORE THAN FOUR NAMES)

shall personally supervise the Artist's business during the term of this contract. One of such persons shall be available at all reasonable times for consultation with the Artist at the city or cities named herein. The Agent, upon request of the Artist, shall assign any one of such persons who may be available (and at least one of them always shall be available upon reasonable notice from the Artist), to engage in efforts or handle any negotiations for the Artist at such city or its environs and such person shall do so. Employees of the Agent who have signed the AFTRA covenant and who are not named herein may handle agency matters for the Artist or may aid any of the named persons in handling agency matters for the Artist.

9. In order to provide continuity of management, the name or names of not more than four (4) persons connected with the Agent must be written in the following space, and this contract is not valid unless this is done:

(HERE INSERT NOT MORE THAN FOUR NAMES)

In the event three (3) or four (4) persons are so named, at least two (2) of such persons must remain active in the Agency throughout the term of this contract. In the event only one (1) or two (2) persons are so named, at least one (1) such person must remain active in the Agency throughout the term of this contract. If the required number of persons does not remain active with the Agency, the Artist may terminate this contract in accordance with Section XXIII of AFTRA's Regulations Governing Agents.

10. The Artist hereby grants to the Agent the right to use the name, portraits and pictures of the Artist to advertise and publicize the Artist in connection with Agent's representation of the Artist hereunder.

11. The Agent agrees:

(a) To make no deductions whatsoever from any applicable minimums established by AFTRA under any collective bargaining agreement.

(b) At the request of the Artist, to counsel and advise him in matters which concern the professional interests of the Artist in the broadcasting industries.

(c) The Agent will be truthful in his statements to the Artist.

(d) The Agent will not make any binding engagement or other commitment on behalf of the Artist, without the approval of the Artist, and without first informing the Artist of the terms and conditions (including compensation) of such engagement.

(e) The Agent's relationship to the Artist shall be that of a fiduciary. The Agent, when instructed in writing by the Artist not to give out information with reference to the Artist's affairs, will not disclose such information.

(f) That the Agent is equipped, and will continue to be equipped, to represent the interests of the Artist ably and diligently in the broadcasting industry throughout the term of this contract, and that he will so represent the Artist.

(g) To use all reasonable efforts to assist the Artist in procuring employment for the services of the Artist in the broadcasting industries.

(h) The Agent agrees that the Agent will maintain an office and telephone open during all reasonable business hours (emergencies such as sudden illness or death excepted) within the city of.. or its environs, throughout the term of this agreement, and that some representative of the Agent will be present at such office during such business hours. This contract is void unless the blank in this paragraph is filled in with the name of a city at which the Agent does maintain an office for the radio broadcasting and television agency business.

(i) At the written request of the Artist, given to the Agent not oftener than once every four (4) weeks, the Agent shall give the Artist information in writing, stating what efforts the Agent has rendered on behalf of the Artist within a reasonable time preceding the date of such request.

(j) The Agent will not charge or collect any commissions on compensation received by the Artist for services rendered by the Artist in a package show in which the Agent is interested, where prohibited by Section VIII of AFTRA's Regulations.

12. This contract is subject to AFTRA's Regulations Governing Agents (Rule 12-B). Any controversy under this contract, or under any contract executed in renewal or extension hereof or in substitution herefor or alleged to have been so executed, or as to the existence, execution or validity hereof or thereof, or the right of either party to avoid this or any such contract or alleged contract on any grounds, or the construction, performance, nonperformance, operation, breach, continuance or termination of this or any such contract, shall be submitted to arbitration in accordance with the arbitration provisions in the regulations regardless of whether either party has terminated or purported to terminate this or any such contract or alleged contract. Under this contract the Agent undertakes to endeavor to secure employment for the Artist.

(FOR CALIFORNIA ONLY)

This provision is inserted in this contract pursuant to a rule of AFTRA, a bona fide labor union, which Rule regulates the relations of its members to agencies or artists managers. Reasonable written notice shall be given to the Labor Commissioner of the State of California of the time and place of any arbitration hearing hereunder. The Labor Commissioner of the State of California, or his authorized representative, has the right to attend all arbitration hearings. The clauses relating to the Labor Commissioner of the State of California shall not be applicable to cases not falling under the provisions of Section 1647.5 of the Labor Code of the State of California.

Nothing in this contract nor in AFTRA's Regulations Governing Agents (Rule 12-B) shall be construed so as to abridge or limit any rights, powers or duties of the Labor Commissioner of the State of California.

WHETHER OR NOT THE AGENT IS THE ACTOR'S AGENT AT THE TIME THIS AGENCY CONTRACT IS EXECUTED, IT IS UNDERSTOOD THAT IN EXECUTING THIS CONTRACT EACH PARTY HAS INDEPENDENT ACCESS TO THE REGULATIONS AND HAS RELIED AND WILL RELY EXCLUSIVELY UPON HIS OWN KNOWLEDGE THEREOF.

IN WITNESS WHEREOF, the parties hereto have executed this agreement the............day of................................., 19 ....

....
ARTIST

....
AGENT

NOTE: This contract must be signed at least in triplicate. One copy must be promptly delivered by the Agent to AFTRA, one copy must be promptly delivered by the Agent to the Artist, and one copy must be retained by the Agent. If AFTRA has an office in the city where the contract is executed, AFTRA's copy of the contract must be delivered to that office within 15 days of execution; or at the Agent's option, to AFTRA's main office in New York City within 30 days of execution.

This agency or artists manager is licensed by the Labor Commissioner of the State of California.

This agency or artists manager is franchised by the American Federation of Television and Radio Artists.

This form of contract has been approved by the Labor Commissioner of the State of California on July 21, 1953, and by the American Federation of Television and Radio Artists.

(The foregoing references to California may be deleted or appropriate substitutions made in other states.)

PART XII

SHORTER FORMS AND CONTRACTS

THAT HAVE BEEN USED

Signing contracts scares some people who are not afraid of signing forms. Well, this may come as a shock - but often forms are contracts.

The elements of a contract are two or more parties, a meeting of the minds as to what they want, the subject matter and the consideration. The subject matter states who will do what act; the consideration states who will pay how much and when. If you look at so-called forms, you will probably find most or all of these elements.

Again we wish to state that the forms are included here for education; you may wish to tailor-make your forms to suit your purposes.

HOllywood

Contract for Lease of Equipment

Cameras for Motion Pictures and Television

DAILY RATE

WEEKLY RATE

RENT BEGINS

RENT ENDS

Leased To:

_____ Phone _____

Address _____ Prod. No. _____ Order No. _____

Quantity	Article	Number	Quantity	Article	N
	Mitchell Camera			Geared Head	
	Arriflex camera (35mm) (16mm)			Adapter Plate	
	Eclair Camera			Sound motor (220) (110)	
	Eyemo camera			96 v. multi duty motor	
	Camera case			Wild Motor	
	Accessory case			Hi-Speed Motor	
	Lens Hole Cover			Motor Batteries & Case	
	Motor door			Jumper (Y) (Tri)	
	Crank (Tripod & camera)			Battery charger	
	15 MM. Lens			Line up finder	
	18 MM. Lens			Reducing lens	
	20 MM. Lens			Friction Head	
	25 MM. Lens			Standard tripod	
	28 MM. Lens			Sawed-off Tripod	
	30 MM. Lens			Baby Tripod	
	35 MM. Lens			Hi-Hat	
	40 MM. Lens			Barney & case	
	50 MM. Lens			Changing bag	
	75 MM. Lens			Periscope Extension	
	90 MM. Lens			Tilt plate	
	100 MM. Lens			Triangle	
	150 MM. Lens			Blimp, incl. matte box	
	Finder Reducing Lens			Slate	
	Finder Enlarging lens			Camera dolly	
	Diffusion			Glass filters	
	Pola screen			Camera tape	
	Matte Box			Gelatin filters	
	Wide Angle Matte Box				
	Pan handle			Magazines, 1000'-400'-200'	
	Inside filter holders & box			Magazine cases	
	Finder & Brkt.				
	Follow-focus unit				
	SOM lens				
	Aux. lenses				

TRANSF. FROM _____ FIN.,

TRANSF. TO NEW START _____

Notations: _____

_____

I hereby lease the above listed equipment subject to the terms set forth on the reverse side of t sheet and which conditions are made a part of this contract.

For _____

Dated _____ By _____

EQUIPMENT

RENTAL CONDITIONS AND TERMS

1.   Lessee acknowledges that he has examined and tested the equipment listed herein and that the same is in good workable mechanical condition and accepts the same as is, and without any rental reductions or claim therefor. Lessee acknowledges that this equipment is leased without warranty or guarantee of any kind, express or implied, and that lessor assumes no responsibility implied in fact or in law for the performance or non-performance of said equipment. Lessee agrees to return all equipment not in workable condition for exchange, at lessee's own cost and expense.

2.   This equipment, or any part thereof, may not be removed from the County of Los Angeles, State of California, without the prior consent of the lessor endorsed hereon. Lessee agrees to return all equipment to lessor's office, at lessee's expense. Pickup and delivery charges are extra.

3.   Upon termination of the lease period or upon the breach of any provision hereof, or in the event any legal process is levied upon the equipment herein described or upon any use of equipment in derogation or violation of lessor's superior title and ownership, lessor or his agents shall be at liberty at any time thereafter to remove said equipment without liability for damage caused by any such entry for such purpose and without prejudice to lessor's right to receive rent due or accrued to and including date of removal of said equipment.

4.   The terms of payment are based upon credit information at time of rental. Should there be any change in such information lessee agrees that lessor is privileged to revise the terms of payment without further notice. All past-due accounts bear interest at the rate of eight per cent (8%) per annum, and if lessor places the account in the hands of an attorney for collection, lessee agrees to pay reasonable attorney's fees and all court costs which may accrue.

5.   Full additional day's rental at daily rate will be charged for equipment returned to lessor's place of business later than 9:30 A.M. When on daily schedule, daily rate will be charged for Sundays and holidays if equipment is used. Daily rate will be charged for a full day or any portion thereof.

6.   Lessee specifically agrees that the value of leased equipment in the event of any loss or damage during rental period is as per list posted in lessor's office.

7.   This contract expresses the entire agreement between the parties and any change must be in writing.

RIGHT OF PRIVACY RELEASE

_____ (Producer)
_____
_____

Gentlemen:

1.   I hereby agree to your filming my appearance and participation in your film and/or television program to be presented in theatres and institutions and to be telecast over the facilities of television broadcast stations throughout the world, herein called the Movie.

2.   I acknowledge that you are and will be the sole owner of all rights in and to the Movie, and the film thereof, for all purposes in the entertainment industry. You shall have the right, among other things, to telecast and exhibit the Movie one or more times, on a sustaining or commercial basis, over any station on a network or syndicated basis, and in any theater or other institution.

3.   I understand that I shall receive no compensation for my appearance in and participation in the Movie.

4.   You shall have the right to use and license others to use my name, portrait, picture and biographical material to publicize and advertise the Movie, but not as an endorsement of any product or service.

5.   I agree to hold you and any third parties harmless against any liability, loss or damage (including reasonable attorney's fees) caused by or arising from the telecast or exhibition of my appearance in the Movie, or any utterance made by me or material furnished by me in connection with my participation therein.

6.   I am over 21.

Very truly yours,

_____
Signature of participant

Address: _____

_____

Date: _____

R E L E A S E

AUTHORIZATION TO REPRODUCE PHYSICAL LIKENESS

For good and valuable consideration, the receipt of which from _____ is acknowledged, I hereby expressly grant to said _____ _____ and to its employees, agents, and assigns, the right to photograph me and use my picture, silhouette and other reproductions of my physical likeness (as the same may appear in any still camera photograph and/or motion picture film), in and in connection with the exhibition, theatrically, on television or otherwise, of any motion picture or motion pictures in which the same may be used or incorporated, and also in the advertising, exploiting and/or publicizing of any such motion picture, but not limited to television or theatrical motion pictures.

I hereby certify and represent that I have read the foregoing and fully understand the meaning and effect thereof and, intending to be legally bound, I have hereunto set my hand this _____ day of _____, 19_____.

_____

WITNESS:

_____

PURCHASE OF ALL RIGHTS - UNPUBLISHED WORK

( ) Story

( ) Screenplay

( ) Story and Screenplay

_____

TO: _____ (Producer)

_____

_____

_____ :

     The following, when accepted by you, will constitute my agreement with you for the acquisition by you of all rights in and to a story (hereinafter referred to as "the work"), now entitled "_____."

    1. I warrant and represent that I am the sole and exclusive author, creator, and owner of the work; that I have full power and authority to enter into this agreement; that the use by you or your licensees or assigns of the work and the title hereof will not violate the copyright or any other right of any person, firm or corporation whatsoever, including any rights of privacy; that the work has not been published or copyrighted; that the work has not been publicly performed by radio, television, motion pictures, or in any other manner; that I have not licensed or otherwise authorized the publication, performance, or other use of the work in any manner; that the work is not in the public domain; that I have not granted any rights or entered into any agreements, the performance of which would in any way prevent, limit or restrict the performance of any of the terms of this agreement; and that I have no knowledge of any claims by any person, firm or corporation, which, if sustained, would be contrary to my warranties and representations herein contained.

    2. I do hereby grant and transfer to you the work, the title and theme thereof, the ideas, formats, characters, characterizations and all other material therein contained, sequel

rights therein and thereto, the right to use the work as the basis of one or more series of television programs, radio programs, and motion pictures and all now or hereafter existing rights of every kind and character whatsoever pertaining to the work, whether or not said rights are now known, recognized or contemplated, and the complete and unconditional and unencumbered title in and to the work for all purposes whatsoever. To evidence my grant and transfer to you hereunder, I am executing concurrently herewith an "Assignment of all Rights" attached hereto as "Exhibit A."

3. I grant to you, your licensees and assigns, and to any exhibitor of a motion picture based on the work, the right to use and permit others to use my name and likeness for the purpose of advertising and publicizing said picture, said exhibitor and said exhibitor's products and services, provided that any such use of my name and likeness may not be as an endorsement or testimonial.

4. You may make any changes in, deletions from, or additions to, the work which you in your sole discretion may consider necessary or desirable for your purposes. You are under no obligation to me to broadcast all or any part of the work. I do not offer to make such revisions, changes or modifications as are or will be necessary with respect to the work.

5. As full compensation for the work and all rights therein and thereto granted to you hereunder, and for any warranties, representations and agreements herein contained, and upon condition that I perform all of the terms, covenants, and conditions of this agreement upon my part to be kept, observed, or performed, you agree to pay me the sum of _____ ($_____) within ten (10) days from the date I deliver the work to you.

6. You shall have the right to assign this agreement, the work, and any or all of the rights granted to you herein to any other person, firm or corporation.

7. This agreement is entire and all negotiations and understandings have been merged herein. This agreement may be amended only by an instrument in writing executed by one of your officers and myself.

If the foregoing is in accordance with your understanding of my agreement with you, please so indicate on the line provided below.

Very truly yours,

_____
Writer

ACCEPTED AND AGREED TO: Producer

By: _____

WRITER COLLABORATION AGREEMENT

PRODUCER: _____

We, the undersigned writers, hereby agree to col-

laborate with each other, as a team of writers, in the event of

our employment by _____ (Producer) to write a story

and a teleplay for their production now entitled "_____

_____."

WRITERS: _____

_____

EMPLOYED WRITER
CERTIFICATE OF AUTHORSHIP

     I hereby certify that I wrote (or collaborated in the writing of) as an employee of _____ (herein referred to as "said Producer") the _____ tentatively entitled "_____" (referred to herein as "said material"). I further certify that said material was written by me in the regular course of my employment and that said Producer is the author and owner thereof and is entitled to the copyright therein (if said material is copyrightable) and all renewals thereof and all rights of any kind or nature therein, with the right to make such changes therein and uses thereof as said Producer may from time to time determine as such author and owner.

DATED: _____

                       _____

Minor Contract
Parental Indemnity Letter

_____(Date)

TO: _____ (Producer)

    _____

    _____

Gentlemen:

    As a material part of the consideration inducing you to enter into an employment agreement dated _____ with _____ (herein referred to as "said Minor") re: _____, Production # _____, concurrently with the execution thereof, I do irrevocably become surety for and guarantee to you, your successors and assigns, the full, prompt and faithful discharge by said minor of each and all of the provisions, and conditions of said agreement. In particular, without limiting the generality of the foregoing I hereby irrevocably guarantee and warrant that said minor will not disaffirm or disavow said agreement on the ground that he is a minor at the date of the execution thereof, or on any similar grounds whatsoever. In the event of breach of said agreement by said minor or if the same is disaffirmed for the reasons stated above, I also agree to indemnify you, your successors and assigns, against any and all loss, cost, damages and expenses of any kind or nature, including attorney's fees, that may be suffered or incurred by you as a result of such breach or disaffirmance, or that may be incurred by you in enforcing said agreement against said minor by reason of his failure to perform in accordance therewith.

    In connection with the foregoing, I agree that no waiver, modification, amendment, extension or renewal of agreement in substitution of the aforesaid employment agreement shall be applicable as well to any modification, amendment, extension or substitution of said agreement, and to said agreement as modified by any waiver.

Very truly yours,

_____
(Parent or Guardian of
said minor)

PHOTOGRAPHER-CUSTOMER COPYRIGHT AGREEMENT

The undersigned PHOTOGRAPHER and the undersigned CUSTOMER agree that all copyrights in the photographs taken of CUSTOMER in _____ (date) belong to CUSTOMER.

PHOTOGRAPHER acknowledges receipt of $_____ as payment in full.

CUSTOMER authorizes PHOTOGRAPHER to make more copies of the negatives for sale by PHOTOGRAPHER to any of the persons photographed and to make copies during 1970 only for usage by publications. PHOTOGRAPHER need not give CUSTOMER any proceeds from such sale. PHOTOGRAPHER must, however, clear his right-of-privacy clearances with the individual persons shown in the respective photographs before he sells any photograph to any publication.

Date: _____

PHOTOGRAPHER: _____
       Address:
  City & State:
     Telephone:

CUSTOMER   : _____
       Address:
  City & State:
     Telephone:

MUSIC DEPARTMENT PAYROLL

DATE: _____   PRODUCTION _____

DATE OF CALL: _____   TYPE OF CALL: _____

INSTRUMENT	NAME	RATE	AMOUNT	HOURS WORKED
VIOLINS				
VIOLAS				
CELLOS				
BASS				
FLUTES				
OBOE				
CLARINETS				
BASSOON				
HORNS				
TRUMPETS				
TROMBONES				
DRUMS				
PIANO				
HARP				
CONTRACTOR				

APPROVED: _____

AGREEMENT OF LIMITED PARTNERSHIP

1. This is an agreement entered into this _____ day

of _____, 19____, at _____,

_____.

2. The names of the parties:

    a. Partner #1 _____

       Doing business as _____

       Address: _____

       City, State, Zip: _____

       PHONE: _____

       SOC. SECURITY NO: _____

    b. Partner #2 _____

       Address: _____

       City, State, Zip: _____

       PHONE: _____

       SOC. SECURITY NO: _____

3. The undersigned hereby desire to and do form a limited partnership under the Uniform Limited Partnership Act as set forth and amended in Title 2, Chapter 2, of the California Corporations Code.

4. Super Duper Productions Project #7 shall be the name of the partnership.

5. The character of the partnership shall be the processing of the four projects named below, but the production of only

one of the projects.

      a. _____, a potential 1/2 hour
television syndication.

      b. _____, a 1-hour musical
comedy special for syndication.

      c. A sexploitation film on the boards tentatively
entitled "_____."

      d. A murder mystery motion picture film, "_____
_____."

    6. Super Duper Productions, at _____
_____, shall be the location of
the principal place of business.

    7. The names and places of residence of the General and
Limited Partner(s) are:

      a. General Partner: _____

                                  _____

                                  _____

      b. Limited Partner: _____

                                  _____

                                  _____

    8. The partnership shall continue for _____ years.

    9. The amount of cash contributed by each Limited Part-
ner is as follows: _____, $_____.

    10. Each Limited Partner may make additional contribu-
tions to the capital of the partnership as may from time to time

be agreed upon by the General Partner(s) and the Limited Partner concerned.

11. Each Limited Partner may make such withdrawals from his capital account as may from time to time be agreed upon by the General Partner(s) and the Limited Partner concerned, and may withdraw from the partnership upon giving ninety (90) days' notice in writing to all other Partners.

12. By reason of their contributions the Limited Partner(s) shall receive the following percentages of the net profits of the partnership:

NAME OF LIMITED PARTNER	PERCENTAGE OF THE NET PROFITS
_____	_____
_____	_____

13. In the event of the retirement, expulsion, bankruptcy, death or insanity of a General Partner, the remaining Partner(s) shall have the right to continue the business of the partnership under the same name by themselves, or in conjunction with any other person or persons they select.

14. A Limited Partner has the right to substitute an assignee as contributor in his place.

15. The General Partners have the right to admit additional partners.

16. No Limited Partner has the right of priority over other Limited Partner(s) as to contributions or as to compensation by way of income.

17. No _Limited_ Partner has the right to demand and receive property other than cash in return for his contribution.

18. The money provided by the Limited Partner(s) may be used as pre-production money.

19. The General Partner hereby informs the Limited Partner(s) that this is a show business matter; that everyone hopes that every show business project will make money; that as a practical matter many projects peter out because of a variety of reasons. Therefore, a Partner may make money, or may lose money, or both.

IN WITNESS WHEREOF we have hereunto set our hands this day.

GENERAL PARTNER: _____.

LIMITED PARTNER: _____.

DISTRIBUTION SHIPPING ROOM FORM

INSPECTION & SHIPPING CARD

THEATRE	CITY	STATE	PRT.#	# REELS	ACCOUNT		DATE IN	REL.#

	SHIP DATE	PLAY DATE	DUE BACK	DATE BACK	REEL CONDITION 1 2 3 4 5 6 7	INSP. DATE

DISTRIBUTION SHIPPING ROOM FORM

DAILY RECEIVING & INSPECTION

ACCOUNT:

DATE:

Received FROM	TITLE	EP. No.	PRT No.	CARRIER	BILL No.	CDN'S	PIECES NORFC	S'pln'cted	DIC'abs'd	AL'n'DroP	By	(REMARKS)

(Additional Remarks.)

ARTISTS' WEEKLY TIME SHEET

ARTIST'S NAME _____

W/E _____

PRODUCTION # _____

EXEMPTIONS _____

DATE	MAKEUP IN	MAKEUP OUT	TRAVEL LV	TRAVEL ARR	ON SET	MEALS	DISMISSED SET	DISMISSED STUDIO	TOTAL HOURS	WEEKLY TIME T.T. WORK	WEEKLY TIME MU-WB	TIME OVER 8 HRS T.T. WEEK	TIME OVER 8 HRS MU-WB	REMARKS

SALARY _____ PER WEEK _____ CTEE _____

REGULAR PAY _____

OVERTIME _____

MAKEUP _____

WARDROBE _____

TRAVEL TIME _____

S.U.I. _____

F.I.C.A. _____

W/H _____

M.P.R.F. _____

P.C.C. _____

PENSION _____

NET PAY _____

(HOURS) (DAYS) _____

O.T. HOURS _____

O.T. HOURS _____

O.T. HOURS _____

O.T. HOURS _____

O.T. HOURS _____

_____ % TO PCC _____ % MPRF

TOTAL: _____

APPROVED _____ ARTIST

FORM 134

CALL SHEET

DATE

PICTURE

DIRECTOR

SET

LOCATION

NAME	TIME CALLED	SCENES, WARDROBE

SIGNED

CONTINUITY BREAKDOWN

TITLE: _____

B. D. PAGE No. _____

PROD. NO. _____ DIRECTOR _____

SEQUENCE _____

SET _____

DAY OR NIGHT _____

SCENE No. _____

SCRIPT PAGES _____

SYNOPSIS: _____

CAST	COS. No.	ATMOSPHERE	PROPS

BITS

SPECIAL EFFECTS

VEHICLES AND LIVESTOCK

SOUND

MUSIC

SPECIAL NOTE: _____

TIME

WEEKLY REPORT OF CONTRIBUTIONS
SCREEN ACTORS GUILD-PRODUCERS PENSION AND WELFARE PLANS

Send 1 copy with payment to ——➤ 7755 Sunset Blvd., Hollywood, Calif. 90046—Phone 876-2770

Employer _____

Street Address _____

City and State _____

Name of Picture: _____

Check type of Motion Picture

TELEVISION MOTION PICTURE ☐
THEATRICAL MOTION PICTURE ☐
INDUSTRIAL or EDUCATIONAL ☐

WEEK ENDING _____

List only the Actors employed during the above indicated week WHO WORKED UNDER S.A.G. JURISDICTION and for whom contributions are due the Pension and Welfare Plans.

SOCIAL SECURITY NUMBER	NAME OF ACTOR			CODE: KIND OF EARNINGS (S) Current Service (R) Residual or Reuse (D) Deferred Comp. (see below)	GROSS COMPENSATION
	LAST	FIRST	INITIAL		

Total Gross Compensation Subject to Contributions . . . . $_____

Employer's Contribution @ 6½% of Compensation . . . . $_____
Actors employed in Theatrical Motion Pictures and TV Motion Pictures, including re-runs thereof, made on and after July 1, 1967

Employer's Contribution @ 5% of Compensation . . . . $_____
For Re-Runs of TV Motion Pictures made before July 1, 1967, Industrial & Educ. Films, and N.Y. Extra Player employment

Make Check payable to:
SCREEN ACTORS GUILD-PRODUCERS PENSION and WELFARE PLANS: Check Numbered _____

The filing by Producer of this report shall be deemed an acceptance by Producer of the Pension & Welfare Fund provisions of the applicable collective bargaining contract of Screen Actors Guild, Inc., and an agreement by Producer to be bound thereby and by the Pension & Welfare Plans established thereunder.

I certify that the information contained herein is correct, and that all compensation subject to contribution earned by Actors in our Employ during the period covered has been reported herein.

Signature _____

NOTE—"Deferred Comp." is compensation paid in a year other than the year in which services were rendered. Attach a brief explanation of such payments

Title _____

Date _____

EMPLOYMENT OF DAY PLAYER

Company_____   Date_____

Date Employment Starts_____   Name_____

Part_____   Address_____

Production Title_____   Telephone No._____

Production Number_____   Social Security No._____

Daily Rate_____   Legal Resident of What State_____

Weekly Conversion Rate_____   Citizen of U.S._____

Married_____   Quota No._____

Date of Birth_____   Date of Entry U.S._____

The employment is subject to all of the provisions and conditions applicable to the employment of DAY PLAYERS contained or provided for in the Producer-Screen Actors Guild Codified Basic Agreement of 1967 as the same may be supplemented and/or amended.

The Player (does) (does not) hereby authorize the Producer to deduct from the compensation hereinabove specified an amount equal to _____ per cent of each installment of compensation due the Player hereunder, and to pay the amount so deducted to the Motion Picture and Television Relief Fund of America, Inc.

PRODUCER_____   PLAYER_____

By_____

STANDARD SCREEN ACTORS GUILD EMPLOYMENT
CONTRACT FOR TELEVISION COMMERCIALS

Date_____, 19____

Between_____, Producer, and_____,
Player.

Producer engages Player and Player agrees to perform services for Producer in television commercials as follows:

Date of Engagement_____

Time and Place of Engagement_____

For_____ and_____
        (Advertising Agency)   (Advertiser)

Address_____   NO. OF

PRODUCT_____   COMMERCIALS_____

CLASSIFICATION: ( ) On Camera   ( ) Off Camera

( ) Actor   ( ) Singer-5 or more
( ) Announcer (Commercial)   ( ) Singer-Signature-solo or duo
( ) Announcer (Program opening and closing,   ( ) Singer-Signature-3 or 4
           standard lead-ins and lead-outs)   ( ) Singer-Signature-5 or more
( ) Singer-solo or duo   ( ) Stunt Player
( ) Singer-3 or 4   ( ) Puppeteers

	Daily Base Pay (On-Camera Players)	Session Fee (Off-Camera Players)
Compensation	_____	_____

CHECK: Commercial is Dealer ☐;   Seasonal ☐;   Test ☐
        Flight Insurance ($5) Payable ☐.   _____
        If wardrobe to be furnished by Producer ☐;   by Player ☐
        No. of garments _____   Wardrobe Fee at $2.50 ☐
                                at 5.00 ☐
                                at 7.50 ☐   _____

                                        Total _____

The standard provisions printed on the reverse side hereof are a part of this contract. If this contract provides for compensation at minimum SAG scale, no additions, changes or alterations may be made in this form other than those which are more favorable to the Player than herein provided.

If this contract provides for compensation above mimimum SAG scale, additions may be agreed to between Producer and Player which do not conflict with the provisions of the SAG Commercials Contract; provided that such additional provisions are separately set forth under "Special Provisions" hereof and signed by the Player.

Until Player shall otherwise direct in writing, Player authorizes Producer to make all payments to which Player may be entitled hereunder as follows:

☐ To Player at _____
                              (Address)

☐ To Player c/o _____ at _____
                                              (Address)

This contract is subject to all of the terms and conditions of the SAG Commercials Contract.

Producer _____   Player _____

By _____   Social Security No. _____

Player hereby certifies that he is 21 years of age or over. (If under 21 years of age this contract must be signed below by a parent or guardian.)

I, the undersigned, hereby state that I am the_____ of the above
                                   (Mother, Father, Guardian)

named Player and do hereby consent and give my permission to this agreement.

_____
        (Signature of Parent or Guardian)

STANDARD SCREEN ACTORS GUILD EMPLOYMENT
CONTRACT FOR TELEVISION COMMERCIALS

STANDARD PROVISIONS

1. RIGHT TO CONTRACT

Player states that to the best of his knowledge, he has not authorized the use of his name, likeness or identifiable voice in any commercial advertising any competitive product or service during the term of permissible use of commercial(s) hereunder and that he is free to enter into this contract and to grant the rights and uses herein set forth.

2. EXCLUSIVITY

Player states that since accepting employment in the commercial(s) covered by this contract, he has not accepted employment in nor authorized the use of his name or likeness or identifiable voice in any commercial(s) advertising any competitive product or service and that he will not hereafter, during the term of permissible use of the commercial(s) for which he is employed hereunder, accept employment in or authorize the use of his name or likeness or identifiable voice in any commercial(s) advertising any competitive product or service.

3. OTHER USES (Strike "a" or "b" if such rights not granted by Player)

(a) Foreign Use

Producer shall have the right to the foreign use of the commercial(s) produced hereunder, for which Producer agrees to pay Player not less than the additional compensation provided for in the SAG Commercials Contract. Producer agrees to notify SAG in writing promptly of any such foreign use.

(b) Theatrical & Industrial Use

Producer shall have the right to the commercial(s) produced hereunder for theatrical and industrial use as defined and for the period permitted in the SAG Commercials Contract, for which Producer shall pay Player not less than the additional compensation therein provided.

4. ARBITRATION

All disputes and controversies of every kind and nature arising out of or in connection with this contract shall be subject to arbitration as provided in Section 40 of the SAG Commercials Contract.

5. PRODUCER'S RIGHTS

Player acknowledges that player has no right, title or interest of any kind or nature whatsoever in or to the commercial(s). A role owned or created by the Producer belongs to the Producer and not to the player.

6. SPECIAL PROVISIONS FOR OVERSCALE PLAYERS

STANDARD SCREEN ACTORS GUILD EMPLOYMENT
CONTRACT FOR INDUSTRIAL FILMS
DAILY OR WEEKLY EMPLOYMENT

Date _____, 19_____

Between _____, Producer, and _____,

Player whose address is: _____

and telephone number is: _____

and Social Security Number is: _____.

Producer engages Player and Player agrees to perform services for Producer in industrial films as follows:

Working Title of Film(s): _____

Role: _____

Term of Employment: _____ Guaranty: _____ day(s) or _____ week(s)
                         (Starting date)

	DAY PLAYERS	WEEKLY PLAYERS
Compensation: _____	$_____ per day	$_____ per week

Form 139 is continued on Page 539.

STANDARD SCREEN ACTORS GUILD EMPLOYMENT
CONTRACT FOR INDUSTRIAL FILMS
DAILY OR WEEKLY EMPLOYMENT

RESIDUALS:

a) Additional compensation for Theatrical Exhibition only (payable at time of exhibition):

100% of total applicable salary

b) Additional compensation for Television Rights (payable at time of exhibition):

TV Run	Percentage of Total Applicable Salary
1st	40%
2nd	30%
3rd, 4th, 5th	25% each
6th & all subsequent	25%

c) Additional compensation for both Theatrical and Television Rights may be acquired at the following rates *if paid at time of original employment*

Effective date:	7/21/68	7/21/69	7/21/70	4/21/71
Percentage of Total Applicable Salary:	150%	160%	165%	175%

CHECK if wardrobe to be furnished by Player ☐

Wardrobe Fee for each 3 day period:

Up to 2 outfits   Men $2.50 ☐   Each additional outfit $2.50 ☐

Women $5.00 ☐   (If female dress costume) $5.00 ☐

This employment is subject to all provisions of the 1968 Industrial Contract and, except as expressly modified therein, is also subject to the Producer-Screen Actors Guild Codified Basic Agreement of 1967.

PRODUCER_____   PLAYER

BY_____

LOCATION PERSONNEL AND REQUIREMENTS

Prod. No. _____   Title _____   Director _____

Date _____   Set _____   Location _____

Prod. Scene No. _____

Transp. Plate No. _____

No.	STAFF	No. Days Incl. T.T.	No.	CAST	No. Days Incl. T.T.	No.	STUDIO EXTRAS	No. Days Incl. T.T.	No.	LOC. EXTRAS	No. Days Incl. T.T.	No.	STUDIO CREW	No. Days Incl. T.T.	No.	LOC. CREW	No. Days Incl. T.T.
	Producer						Extras			BITS @			Head Prop. Man			Head Prop. Man	
	Director						Stand-ins			Bits			Ass't Prop. Men			Ass't Prop. Men	
	2nd Unit Director						Stock Players			Extras			Head Grip			Head Grip	
	Writer						Stunt Men			Extras-Racial			2nd Grip			2nd Grip	
	Ass't Prod. Mgr.						Doubles			Stand-ins			Grips			Grips	
	Ass't Director						Singers			Riders			Gaffer			Gaffer	
	2nd Ass't Directors						Dancers			Riders-Racial			Best Boy			Best Boy	
	Art Director						Musicians			Stunt Men			Electricians			Electricians	
	Cutter						Minors			Doubles			Prop Shop Men			Prop Shop Men	
	Script Clerk						Teachers			Swimmers			Powder Men			Powder Men	
	1st Cameraman						Swimmers			Divers			Painter			Painter	
	Opr. Cameramen						Divers			Minors			Nurserymen			Nurserymen	
	Ass't Cameraman									Teachers			S. B. Laborer			S. B. Laborer	
	Tech. Director												Carpenter Fore.			Laborers	
	Tech. Technician												Carpenters			Carpenter Fore.	
	Tech. Assistant												Transportation Fore.			Carpenters	
	Tech. Loader												Boom Operator			Transportation Fore.	
	Still Cameraman												Boom Crew			Boom Operator	
	Sound Mixer		BITS @										P. A. Operator			Boom Crew	
	Sound Boom Opr.												Dream Operator			P. A. Operator	
	Sound Cableman												Generator Men			Dream Operator	
	Sound Recorder												Policemen			Generator Men	
	Makeup Men												Firemen			Policemen	
	Hair Dressers												Forestrymen			Firemen	
	Body Makeup												Camera Mech.			Forestrymen	
	Wardrobe Men												Garage Mech.			Camera Mech.	
	Wardrobe Women												Watchmen			Garage Mech.	
	Doctors												Plaster and Staff			Watchmen	
	Dialogue Dir.												Livestock Sup't.			Plaster and Staff	
	Technical Dir.												Veterinarian			Livestock Sup't.	
	Musical Adv.												S.P.C.A.			Veterinarian	
	Loc. Auditor												Wranglers			S.P.C.A.	
	Loc. Timekeeper												Draperymen			Wranglers	
	Publicity Dept.												Projectionist			Draperymen	
	Secretaries												Swing Gang			Projectionist	
													Laborers			Swing Gang	
																Doctors	

LOCATION REMARKS

WEATHER

FILM SHIPPING

CARE OF TECH. FILM

LOCATION FEES

HOTELS AND MEALS

FILM DAILIES

1. METHOD OF TRANSPORTATION TO STUDIO — AIR ☐   TRAIN ☐   AUTO ☐

2. RUSHES SHOWN — NONE ☐   LOCATION SITE ☐   LOCAL CITY ☐

TRANSPORTATION

No.	STUDIO	No. DAYS INCL. T.T.	AVER. MILES	@ PER HR.	No.	LOCATION	@ PER HR.	No. DAYS INCL. T.T.	AVER. MILES	@ PER HR.
	7 Pass. Cars					7 Pass. Cars				
	Convertible					Convertible				
	5 Pass. Cars					5 Pass. Cars				
	Camera Car					Camera Car				
	Blue Goose					Blue Goose				
	Insert Car					Insert Car				
	Stretchout					Station Wagon				
	Station Wagon					Sta. Wagon Sound				
	Sta. Wagon Sound					Staff Bus				
	Staff Bus					Crew Bus				
	Crew Bus					Extras Bus				
	Extras Bus					Grip Truck				
	Grip Truck					Elect. Truck				
	Elect. Truck					Prop. Truck				
	Prop. Truck					Boom Truck				
	Boom Truck					Horse Truck				
	Horse Truck					Horse Trailer				
	Horse Trailer					Wardrobe Truck				
	Wardrobe Truck					Nursery Truck				
	Nursery Truck					Weapons Carrier				
	Weapons Carrier					Jeep				
	Jeep					Set Dress. Truck				
	Sanitary Unit					Water Wagon				
	Dress Rm. Trailer					Const. Truck				
	Const. Truck					Const. Car				
	Const. Car					Const. Bus				
	Const. Bus					Ambulance				
	Water Wagon					Highway Patrol				
	Hot Food Truck					Set Striking Car				
	Set Dress. Truck					Set Striking Truck				
						Set Striking Bus				
						Road Scraper				
						Road Caterpillar				

ACTION PROPS

STUDIO	@	LOCATION	@
Cast Horses		Cast Horses	
Horses		Double Horses	
Trick Horses		Horses	
Double Horses		Trick Horses	
Cattle		Cattle	
Cattle (Horns)		Cattle (Horns)	
Wagons		Wagons	
Animals		Animals	

HOTEL	ROOMS	MEALS
Staff		
Cast		
Bits and Extras		
Crew		
Drivers		
Loc. Personnel		
Misc.		
Total		

SPEC. WARDROBE

SPEC. MAKE-UP

LOCATION OFFICE	TRAIN AND PLANE SCHEDULES	WARDROBE SPACE AND RACKS	WATER WAGON AND PUMP
LOCATION PERMITS	PLANE INSURANCE	MAKEUP ROOM AND TABLES	LONG HOSE
BANKING FACILITIES	WEATHER REPORTS	CHEMICAL TOILETS	P. A. SYSTEM
LOCAL UNION LABOR	WEATHER PROTECTION	SALAMANDERS	WALKIE TALKIE
CHILD LABOR LAWS	SPECIAL CLEANING (COSTUMES)	DIRECTION SIGNALS SLOW SIGNS	TRACKS FOR PLAYBACK
SOCIAL SECURITY NUMBERS	FIRST AID	TABLES AND BENCHES	UNDER CRANKING FACILITIES
TIME CARDS ON CREW	FIRE PROTECTION	BOOM OR DOLLY TRACK	SPECIAL CAMERA MOUNTS
IDENTIFICATION CARDS	ROOM AND MEALS	GENERATOR FLATS	RUSHES (PROJECTION ROOM)
SHIP FILM AND REPORTS	DARK ROOM	ELECTRICAL HOOKUP	GLASS OR MATTE SHOT
FILM CRATES AND LABELS	SCHOOL ROOM	WORK LIGHTS	STILL PICTURES FOR MATCHING
INSURANCE AND TAXES	DRESSING ROOM	OFFICE AND MEDICAL SUPPLIES	LETTER TO CREW
PORTABLE PROJECTION BOOTH	CONSTRUCTION MATERIALS	CAMERA BOOM No.	SNOW
PLANE FOR AIR SHOTS	ALDIS LAMP (Light Signal Gun)		

FORM 143

LOCATION CONTRACTS

HOTELS

BANK

TRANSPORTATION

ANIMALS

ACTORS

LOCATIONS

BOOK V

FORM 144

Page 544

SHIPPING CONFIRMATION

DISTRIBUTOR: _____

WEEK OF: _____

SHIP DATE	TITLE	PRT. #	THEATRE	CITY & STATE	PLAY DATE	DUE BACK	SHIP VIA:	WAYBILL NUMBER	SHIP #	REMARKS

PLEASE DO NOT WRITE IN SPACE BELOW.   USE ADDITIONAL SHEET IF NECESSARY.

TOTAL SHIPMENTS THIS PERIOD: _____ PER ABOVE, AT $ _____ EA. _____ TOTAL $ _____

REPAIR TIME OR ADDITIONAL LABOR PER ATTACHED _____ AT $ _____

SUPPLIES; REEL BANDS, _____ PER ATTACHED AT $ _____ EA.

LEADERS: _____ PER ATTACHED AT $ _____ EA.

OTHER: _____

TOTAL _____

PREVIEW INTERVIEW CARD

This Picture is still in unfinished form and is brought to you for your opinion before final editing.   Your answers to the following questions will be greatly appreciated.

1. Did you like the Picture?_____

_____

2. Would you recommend this picture to your friends?

_____

3. Was the action entirely clear?   If not, where was it

confusing? _____

_____

4 Which sequence would you suggest cutting or shorten-

ing? _____

_____

5. Do you enjoy this kind of picture? _____

_____

6. Do you like the title of the picture? _____

_____

7. Other comments? _____

_____

Please check your age group:

12 to 17	☐	31 to 45	☐
18 to 30	☐	Over 45	☐
Male	☐	Female	☐

Date _____

Name_____

ARTIST DAILY TIME CARD
THIS SIDE FOR PRODUCTION CALLS ONLY

					IN/OUT	
DO NOT USE SPACE BELOW	STUDIO	USE THIS SPACE UPON FIRST ENTERING STUDIO PREMISES AND AGAIN ON LEAVING FOR THE DAY.			IN	
					OUT	
	MAKE-UP	CALL		PROD.	IN	
		DISMISS		APP'D.	OUT	
	WARD-ROBE	CALL .		PROD.	IN	
		DISMISS		APP'D.	OUT	
	SET CALL	CALL:	MADE UP AND READY ON SET		IN	
		FIRST MEAL PERIOD	½ HOUR ACTUAL TIME 1 HOUR	DISMISSED FROM SET		
				RETURNED TO SET		
		SECOND MEAL PERIOD	½ HOUR ACTUAL TIME 1 HOUR	DISMISSED FROM SET		
				RETURNED TO SET		
		THIRD MEAL PERIOD	½ HOUR ACTUAL TIME 1 HOUR	DISMISSED FROM SET		
				RETURNED TO SET		
		DISMISSED FROM SET			OUT	

CERTIFIED CORRECT		LOCATION TRAVEL TIME	LV.
			ARR.
ARTIST'S SIGNATURE			LV.
			ARR.
APPROVED BY ASST. DIRECTOR			LV.
			ARR.

LABORATORY–CASH CUSTOMER PARTIAL AGREEMENT

CONDITIONS

All orders placed with this Company, by and for the account of the Customer, are subject to the following conditions:

LIMITATIONS OF LIABILITY OF LABORATORY

This Company respectfully points out that as its prices are never proportionate to the value of the negatives and positives entrusted to it, Customer's films are received, developed, printed, and stored by this Company only at Customer's risk, and this Company does not accept responsibility for any loss of or damage to such films from any cause whatsoever. Customer should, therefore, insure all films delivered to this Company against all risks. In no event shall this Company be liable for the loss or damage of any films delivered to it by or for the account Customer for any amount in excess of the replacement value of the raw film involved.

This Company will exercise reasonable care and will exert its best efforts to produce high quality work hereunder, but does not make any warranty nor does it assume any responsibility as to the character or quality of the material or service to be furnished or provided by it hereunder nor as to the results of any of its undertakings hereunder. Without limiting the foregoing in any particular, this Company shall not be liable for loss of any kind whatsoever due to delays or failure in performance caused directly or indirectly by acts of God, strikes, fire, failure of transportation agencies, public enemy, the elements, war, insurrection, shortages of labor or material, government regulation, damage or accident to machinery or equipment, electric power failure, injury or damage to, or loss of, films delivered to this Company by Customer, or any other cause.

LABORATORY LIEN ON FILMS

Films delivered to this Company are accepted upon the express condition that this Company holds a lien thereon for the general balance from time to time due this Company from the Customer, whether in respect to processing, printing or otherwise.

The Customer agrees that if the Company shall enforce its rights under said lien, either the Company or any other party acquiring ownership of such films at private or public sale shall have, and is hereby granted, a license under the underlying contracts and literary material of such films, to distribute, exhibit, televise and otherwise exploit such films for its own account.

The Company will store negatives of films during the time of production and release printing and for a reasonable period thereafter. However, Customer acknowledges that Company is not a warehouse and that it is not economically feasible for, nor is it a proper function of the Laboratory to provide storage for negatives or master positives which are used only occasionally for libraries, re-runs, etc., and, therefore, it will be necessary to charge 10¢ per can of film per month for all material left with the Company beyond the primary production and release period.

Customer agrees that failure to pay said incidental charge for storage and keeping shall give the Company a lien on the film for such charges and the right to sell the film to satisfy said lien and costs of sale pursuant to California law.

REMOVAL OF LEFT-OVER FILMS

The Customer agrees to remove from this Company's premises all negative and positive cut-out, trims, and unused films in connection with each motion picture produced by Customer within 90 days after the completion of said picture, or within 90 days after the last photographic work thereon in case production on said picture is terminated, and further agrees that upon Customer's failure to do so this Company may make such disposition of said cut-out, trims and unused films as it sees fit.

LABORATORY WARRANTY

Should a print be found defective, or labeled or shipped in error, ___ will promptly replace or repair such defective print and/or correct an error in shipment at its expense provided the defective print is returned and written notice of such imperfection and/or error in labeling or shipment is given this Company within ten days after its arrival at destination. But in no event shall this Company be liable for any consequential damages.

INFORMATION FROM LABORATORY

This Company will endeavor to keep its customers advised concerning the condition of the negative films received from them for processing but it shall not be held responsible for failure to do so.

SHIPPING CHARGES AND TAXES

All prices are f.o.b. Hollywood, California, and are subject to any applicable state and local taxes.

In the absence of any other instructions from the Customer, this Company will make all shipments via Railway Express, subject to the Express Company's minimum of $50.00 insurance per shipment.

MINIMUM AND SPECIAL PRICES

The per foot prices specified herein on the regular schedules are predicated upon a production basis and are calculated so as to give the Customer the best price possible on volume footage orders. Processing and operations on short lengths of film create special conditions which necessitate the establishment of minimum and/or additional charges.

All prices are subject to any fluctuation in cost of raw film and labor, retroactive to effective date thereof and are subject to change without notice.

STANDARD SYNCHRONIZATION LEADERS

Negatives must be provided with standard leaders bearing clear and proper synchronization marks. Any errors in synchronization shall be the responsibility of the Customer.

CUSTOMER LIABILITY

Customer hereby assumes, as far as Company is concerned, all liability under the copyright laws and under any and all other statutes arising out of the performance by Company of any services for the account of Customer, and agrees to indemnify and hold Company free and harmless of all suits, claims, damages, and other liability and expense which may arise either directly or indirectly out or by reason of services performed by Company for Customer.

OWNERSHIP OF FILMS

Customer represents that it is the sole owner or has the complete right and authority to make positive prints, video tapes or other reproductions thereof of all motion picture material (negative, fine grains, positive prints or video tape) delivered to Company. Customer warrants that processing of such material by Company will not violate any copyright, patent, common law right, contract right or any other right of any person, firm or corporation. Customer will indemnify Company and company officers, agents and employees, and will hold Company harmless from any loss or damage arising from breach of the representation or warranty, including reasonable counsel fees.

OLD NEGATIVES

Old or shrunken negatives, or those showing any unusual photographic or physical condition, are accepted for printing with the understanding that a charge will be made for lost time and/or materials whether or not a satisfactory print is ultimately produced.

TERMS OF PAYMENT

Customer agrees to make payment to the Company by the 10th of the month following billing date. Interest will be charged at legal rates on all bills not paid when due. If Company institutes any legal action to collect any sums due Company by Customer, Customer agrees to pay Company for all costs of suit including reasonable attorney's fees.

ADJUSTMENTS

All claims for adjustment must be made to Company within 30 days from date of invoice.

Customer hereby agrees that all laboratory work performed or services rendered for the account of Customer shall be governed by the above terms and conditions; these terms and conditions can only be modified by an instrument in writing. Any question as to the validity and construction of th above terms and conditions shall be governed by the laws of the State of California.

PART XIII

QUERY: Is there no Part XIII because one of the

          editors is superstitious?

ANSWER: Yes.

PART XIV

PRODUCTION BUDGETS AND COSTS FORMS

INTRODUCTION

A producer and a distributor agreed on a script, on the
theory of the distributor's distributing the picture and guaran-
teeing the bank loan.

Distributor: "How much do you want to make the picture
for?"

Producer: "I can make it for $100,000 or for a million.
Which do you want?"

Distributor: "About $600,000."

Producer: "OK. I'll have a budget prepared."

The producer had a friend who was familiar with budgets.
The two prepared a budget for $600,000. They went to the dis-
tributor.

Producer: "We have a $600,000 budget. It's tight.
There's no fat, no waste."

Distributor: "Cut it to $400,000."

Producer: "OK."

This part of the book contains a form entitled *PICTURE
BUDGET DETAIL* which can be used to prepare a budget. Suggestion -
use a pencil, not ink.

The pre-production work was begun. At the end of the
first week after the signing of the Producer-Distributor contract

money had been spent.   To keep track of money spent and to compare money spent with the budget, the Producer had his bookkeeper
prepare a *SUMMARY OF DETAIL BUDGET AND COST REPORT*.

When the money man saw how unrealistic the budget was,
when compared to expenses, the money man screamed at the Producer.   The Producer promised to do better in the future.

Each week the money man knew the BUDGET, the CHARGES
THIS WEEK, and TOTAL TO DATE from the just-mentioned *SUMMARY OF
DETAIL BUDGET AND COST REPORT*.   The money man wondered about the
ESTIMATED COST TO COMPLETE, ESTIMATED TOTAL COST, OVER-OR-UNDER
BUDGET, and other information.

To record that information in convenient form, the bookkeeper prepared *SUMMARY PRODUCTION COSTS* each week.

The money man wished that all three forms used the identical sequence of expenses and identical number systems.   The
Producer agreed with the money man.

PICTURE BUDGET DETAIL

TITLE _____   PICTURE NO. _____

DATE PREPARED _____ , 19 _____

ACCOUNT NUMBER	DESCRIPTION			TOTAL		TOTALS		TOTALS	
1	Story								
2	Continuity and Treatment								
3	Producer								
4	Director								
5	Cast								
6	Bits								
7	Extras								
	Sub Total								
8	Production Staff Salaries								
9	Production Operating Staff								
10	Set Designing								
11	Set Operation Expenses								
12	Cutting - Film - Laboratory								
13	Music								
14	Sound								
15	Transportation - Studio								
16	Location								
17	Studio Rental								
18	Tests and Retakes								
19	Publicity								
20	Miscellaneous								
21	Insurance - Taxes - Licenses and Fees								
22	General Overhead								
	Sub Total								
	Grand Total								

Approved _____ Producer

Prepared From _____ Page Script Dated _____

_____ Day Shooting Scheduled at _____ Studio

Director _____

Budget by _____

_____

TITLE _____   PICTURE NO. _____

DATE PREPARED _____

ACCOUNT NUMBER	DESCRIPTION	DAYS, WKS, OR QUANTITY	RATE		TOTALS	
1	STORY –					
	A. STORY PURCHASE					
	B. TITLE PURCHASE					
	TOTAL STORY					
2	CONTINUITY AND TREATMENT					
	A. WRITERS					
	B. STENOGRAPHER					
	C. MIMEOGRAPH EXPENSE					
	D. RESEARCH EXPENSE					
	TOTAL CONTINUITY AND TREATMENT					
3	PRODUCER					
	A. PRODUCER					
	B. ASST. PRODUCER					
	C. SECRETARIES					
	TOTAL PRODUCER					
4	DIRECTOR					
	A. DIRECTOR					
	B. SECRETARIES					
	C. PENSION CONTRIBUTIONS					
	TOTAL DIRECTORS					

TITLE _____   PICTURE NO. _____

DATE PREPARED _____

ACCOUNT NUMBER	DESCRIPTION	DAYS, WKS. OR QUANTITY	RATE	TOTALS	
8	PRODUCTION STAFF SALARIES				
	A. PRODUCTION MANAGER				
	B. UNIT MANAGER				
	C. 1st ASST. DIRECTOR				
	SEVERANCE				
	D. 2nd ASST. DIRECTOR				
	SEVERANCE				
	E. EXTRA ASST. DIRECTORS				
	F. SECRETARIES				
	G. DIALOGUE CLERK				
	H. SCRIPT CLERK				
	U. DANCE DIRECTOR				
	J. CASTING DIRECTOR & STAFF				
	K. TECHNICAL ADVISOR				
	L. FIRST AID				
	M. LOCATION AUDITOR				
	TOTAL PRODUCTION STAFF				
9	PRODUCTION OPERATING STAFF				
	A. CAMERAMEN				
	1. 1st CAMERAMAN				
	2. CAMERA OPERATORS				
	3. FOCUS ASST. CAMERAMEN				
	4. ASST. CAMERAMEN				
	5. CAMERA MECHANICS				
	6. COLOR DIRECTOR				
	7. STILL MAN				
	8. STILL GAFFER				
	9. PROCESS CAMERAMAN				
	10. ASST. PROCESS CAMERAMAN				
	11. EXTRA CAMERA OPERATORS				
	12. EXTRA CAMERA ASSISTANTS				
	13. O.T. CAMERA CREW 43-48 HOURS				
	TOTAL ACCT. 9-A				

TITLE _____   PICTURE NO. _____

DATE PREPARED _____

ACCOUNT NUMBER	DESCRIPTION	DAYS, WKS. OR QUANTITY	RATE	TOTALS	
9	PRODUCTION OPERATING STAFF (Contd.)				
	B. SOUND DEPT.				
	1. MIXER				
	2. RECORDER				
	3. BOOM MAN				
	4. CABLEMAN				
	5. CABLE BOOM MAN				
	6. P.A. SYSTEM OPERATOR				
	7. DREAM OPERATOR				
	8. SOUND MAINTENANCE				
	TOTAL ACCT. 9-B				
	C. WARDROBE DEPT.				
	1. WARDROBE DESIGNER				
	2. WARDROBE BUYER				
	3. 1ST WARDROBE GIRL				
	4. 2ND WARDROBE GIRL				
	5. 1ST WARDROBE MAN				
	6. 2ND WARDROBE MAN				
	7. TAILOR				
	8. SEAMSTRESS				
	9. EXTRA HELP				
	TOTAL ACCT. 9-C				
	D. MAKE-UP AND HAIRDRESSING				
	1. HEAD MAKE-UP MAN				
	2. 2ND MAKE-UP MAN				
	3. HEAD HAIRDRESSER				
	4. 2ND HAIRDRESSER				
	5. BODY MAKE-UP GIRL				
	6. EXTRA HELP				
	TOTAL ACCT. 9-D				

TITLE _____   PICTURE NO. _____

DATE PREPARED _____

ACCOUNT NUMBER	DESCRIPTION	DAYS, WKS. OR QUANTITY	RATE	TOTALS
	PRODUCTION OPERATING STAFF (Contd.)			
	E. GRIP DEPT.			
	1. 1ST GRIP			
	2. BEST BOY			
	3. SET OPERATION GRIPS			
	4. EXTRA LABOR			
	5. CAMERA BOOM OPERATORS			
	6. CRAB DOLLY GRIP			
	TOTAL ACCT. 9-E			
	F. PROPERTY			
	1. HEAD POOPERTY MAN			
	2. 2ND PROPERTY MAN			
	3. 3RD PROPERTY MAN			
	4. OUTSIDE HELP			
	5. EXTRA HELP			
	TOTAL ACCT. 9-F			
	G. SET DRESSING DEPT.			
	1. HEAD SET DRESSER			
	2. ASST. SET DRESSER			
	3. SWING GANG			
	4. DRAPERY MAN			
	5. ASST. DRAPERY MAN			
	6. NURSERY MAN			
	7. EXTRA LABOR			
	TOTAL ACCT. 9-G			
	H. ELECTRICAL DEPT.			
	1. GAFFER			
	2. BEST BOY			
	3. ELECTRICAL OPERATING LABOR			
	4. GENERATOR OPERATOR			
	5. ELECTRICAL MAINTENANCE MAN			
	6. RIGGING & STRIKING CREW			
	7. WIND MACHINE OPERATOR			
	TOTAL ACCT. 9-H			

TITLE _____ PICTURE NO. _____

DATE PREPARED _____

ACCOUNT NUMBER	DESCRIPTION	DAYS, WKS. OR QUANTITY	RATE		TOTALS	
9	**PRODUCTION OPERATING STAFF (Contd.)**					
	I. LABOR DEPT.					
	1. STANDBY LABORER					
	2. ASST. LABORERS					
	TOTAL ACCT. 9-I					
	J. SPECIAL EFFECTS					
	1. HEAD SPECIAL EFFECTS MAN					
	2. ASST. SPECIAL EFFECTS MAN					
	3. PLUMBER					
	TOTAL ACCT. 9-J					
	K. SET STANDBY OPERATORS					
	1. CARPENTER					
	TOTAL ACCT. 9-K					
	L. SET STANDBY PAINTERS					
	1. PAINTER					
	TOTAL ACCT. 9-L					
	M. SET WATCHMAN					
	1. WATCHMEN					
	TOTAL ACCT. 9-M					
	N. WRANGLERS					
	1. S.P.C.A. MAN					
	2. HEAD WRANGLER					
	3. WRANGLERS					
	O. MISCELLANEOUS					
	GRAND TOTAL SET OPERATING SALARIES					

TITLE _____ PICTURE NO. _____

DATE PREPARED _____

ACCOUNT NUMBER	DESCRIPTION	TIME		RATE			TOTAL
10	**SET CONSTRUCTION**						
	A. Art Director						
	B. Asst. Art Director						
	C. Sketch Artist						
	D. Draftsman						
	E. Set Supervisor						
	F. Material & Supplies						
	G. Construction Supervisor						
	H. Miscellaneous						
		LABOR		MATERIAL			
	1						
	2						
	3						
	4						
	5						
	6						
	7						
	8						
	9						
	10						
	11						
	12						
	13						
	14						
	15						
	16						
	17						
	18						
	19						
	20						
	21						
	22						
	23						
	24						
	25						
	26						
	27						
	28						
	29						
	30						
	31						
	32						
	33						
	34						
	35						
	36						
	37						
	38						
	39						
	Rigging Labor Grip						
	Striking						
	Backings						
	Greens						
	TOTAL SETS						

TITLE _____

PICTURE NO. _____

DATE PREPARED _____

ACCOUNT NUMBER	DESCRIPTION	DAYS, WKS. OR QUANTITY	RATE		TOTALS	
11	SET OPERATION EXPENSES					
	A. Camera Equipment Rentals					
	B. Camera Equipment Purchases					
	C. Camera Car Rentals					
	D. Camera Crane Rentals					
	E. Wardrobe Purchased					
	F. Wardrobe Rentals					
	G. Wardrobe Maintenance					
	H. Grip Equipment Rented					
	I. Prop Equipment Rented					
	J. Props Purchased					
	JJ. Prop Man's Petty Cash Exp.					
	K. Props Rented					
	L. Props - Loss & Damaged					
	M. Set Dressing Rentals					
	N. Set Dressing Purchased					
	O. Draperies Purchased & Rented					
	P. Nursery - Purchased & Rented					
	Q. Process Equipment Rentals					
	R. Make-up Purchases					
	S. Hairdressing Purchases & Rentals					
	T. Electrical Equipment Rentals					
	U. Electrical Equipment Purchased					
	V. Electrical Power					
	W. Rentals on Picture Cars - Trucks - Planes - Wagons - Livestock, etc.					
	X. Miscellaneous Rentals & Purchases					
	Y. Generator Rental - Gas & Oil -					
	Z. Special Effect Purchases & Rentals					
	Total Set Operation Expense					

TITLE _____   PICTURE NO. _____

                                        DATE PREPARED _____

ACCOUNT NUMBER	DESCRIPTION	DAYS, WKS, OR QUANTITY	RATE	TOTALS
12	CUTTING FILM LABORATORY			
	A. EDITOR			
	B. ASST. CUTTER			
	C. SOUND CUTTER			
	D. MUSIC CUTTER			
	E. NEGATIVE CUTTER			
	TOTAL LABOR			
	F. NEGATIVE ACTION RAW STOCK			
	G. NEGATIVE SOUND RAW STOCK			
	GG. TAPE RENTAL			
	H. DEVELOP ACTION			
	HH. DEVELOP SOUND			
	I. PRINT ACTION			
	II. PRINT SOUND			
	J. MAGNASTRIPE - PRODUCTION			
	JJ. MAGNASTRIPE - SCORE & DUBBING			
	K. COLOR SCENE PILOT STRIPS			
	KK. 16MM COLOR PRINTS (FROM CCO)			
	KKK. INTER-NEGATIVE			
	L. SEPARATION MASTERS			
	LL. INTER-POSITIVE			
	M. ANSWER PRINT			
	MM. COMPOSITE PRINT			
	N. FINE GRAIN PRINT			
	NN. PANCHROMATIC (FG)			
	NNN. 16MM PRINTS			
	O. FADES-DISSOLVES-DUPES & FINE GRAIN			
	OO. REPRINTS			
	P. TITLES, MAIN & END			
	Q. CUTTING ROOM RENTAL			
	R. CODING			

TITLE			PICTURE NO.	

DATE PREPARED

ACCOUNT NUMBER	DESCRIPTION	DAYS, WKS. OR QUANTITY	RATE	TOTALS
12	CUTTING FILM LABORATORY (Contd.)			
	R. PROJECTION			
	S. MOVIOLA RENTALS			
	T. REELS & LEADER			
	U. CUTTING ROOM SUPPLIES			
	V. STOCK SHOTS			
	W. PROCESS PLATES			
	X. SALES TAX			
	XX. CODING			
	LABORATORY SUB-TOTAL			
	TOTAL CUTTING FILM LABORATORY			

TITLE _____   PICTURE NO. _____

DATE PREPARED _____

ACCOUNT NUMBER	DESCRIPTION	DAYS, WKS. OR QUANTITY	RATE		TOTALS	
13	MUSIC					
	A. Music Supervisor					
	B. Director					
	C. Composer					
	D. Musicians					
	E. Singers					
	F. Arrangers					
	G. Copyists					
	H. Royalties					
	I. Purchases					
	J. Miscellaneous					
	K. Instrument Rental & Cartage					
	L. Librarian					
	Total Music					
14	SOUND					
	A. Royalties					
	B. Dubbing Room Rental					
	C. Pre-Score Equipment Rentals					
	D. Scoring Equipment Rentals					
	E. Labor for Dubbing & Etc.					
	F. Sound Equipment Rentals					
	G. Miscellaneous					
	H. Transfer Time					
	Total Sound					
15	TRANSPORTATION STUDIO					
	A. Labor					
	B. Car Rentals					
	C. Truck Rentals					
	D. Bus Rentals					
	E. Car Allowance					
	F. Miscellaneous					
	G. Gas & Oil, - Generator - Mileage					
	H. Wranglers Cars					
	I. Livestock Transportation					
	Total Transportation					

TITLE _____   PICTURE NO. _____

DATE PREPARED _____

ACCOUNT NUMBER	DESCRIPTION	DAYS, WKS. OR QUANTITY	RATE	TOTALS	
16	**LOCATION**				
	A. TRAVELING				
	B. HOTEL				
	C. MEALS				
	D. LOCATION SITES RENTAL				
	E. SPECIAL EQUIPMENT				
	F. CAR RENTALS				
	G. BUS RENTALS				
	H. TRUCK RENTALS				
	I. SUNDRY EMPLOYEES				
	J. LOCATION OFFICE RENTAL				
	K. GRATUITIES				
	L. MISCELLANEOUS				
	M. SCOUTING & PRE-PRODUCTION				
	N. POLICE SERVICES & PERMITS				
	O. CONTACT MAN				
	TOTAL LOCATION				
17	**STUDIO RENTALS**				
	A. STAGE SPACE				
	B. STREET RENTALS				
	C. TEST				
	D. VACATION ALLOWANCE (STUDIO)				
	E. SURCHARGE ON RENTALS & STUDIO CHARGES				
	F. MISCELLANEOUS EXPENSES				
	G. DRESSING ROOMS - PORTABLE				
	H. OFFICE RENTALS				
	TOTAL STUDIO RENTALS				
18	**TESTS & RETAKES**				
	A. TESTS PRIOR TO PRODUCTION				
	B. TESTS DURING PRODUCTION				
	C. RETAKES AFTER PRINCIPAL PHOTOGRAPHY				
	D. PRE-PRODUCTION EXPENSE OR SHOOTING				
	TOTAL TESTS & RETAKES				

TITLE _____

PICTURE NO. _____

DATE PREPARED _____

ACCOUNT NUMBER	DESCRIPTION	DAYS, WKS. OR QUANTITY	RATE	TOTALS
19	**PUBLICITY**			
	A. ADVERTISING			
	B. UNIT PUBLICITY MAN			
	C. ENTERTAINMENT			
	D. TRADE AND NEWSPAPER SUBSCRIPTIONS			
	E. PUBLICITY STILLS SALARIES			
	F. PUBLICITY STILLS SUPPLIES EQUIPMENT			
	G. PUBLICITY STILLS LAB. CHARGES			
	H. STILL GALLERY RENTAL & EXPENSE			
	I. Trailer			
	J. PRESS PREVIEW EXPENSE			
	K. SUPPLIES, POSTAGE AND EXPRESS			
	L. MISCELLANEOUS			
	TOTAL PUBLICITY			
20	**MISCELLANEOUS**			
	A. VACATION ALLOWANCE			
	B. RETROACTIVE WAGE CONTINGENCY			
	C. SUNDRY UNCLASSIFIED EXPENSE			
	D. COSTS IN SUSPENSE			
	E. SET COFFEE			
	F. WATER & ICE			
	TOTAL MISCELLANEOUS			
21	**INSURANCE, TAXES, LICENSE AND FEES**			
	A. CAST INSURANCE			
	B. NEGATIVE INSURANCE			
	C. LIFE INSURANCE			
	D. MISCELLANEOUS INSURANCE			
	E. COMPENSATION & PUBLIC LIABILITY INS.		%	
	F. SOCIAL SECURITY TAX		%	
	G. PERSONAL PROPERTY TAX			
	H. MISCL. TAXES AND LICENSES			
	I. CODE CERTIFICATE - MPPA			
	J. CITY TAX AND LICENSE			
	K. UNEMPLOYMENT TAX		%	
	L. PENSION PLAN CONTRIBUTION ACTORS|DIRECTORS|WRITERS		%	
	M. HEALTH & WELFARE CONTRIBUTION			
	N. PENSION PLAN — CRAFTS		%	
	TOTAL A/C 21			

TITLE _____

PICTURE NO. _____

DATE PREPARED _____

ACCOUNT NUMBER	DESCRIPTION	DAYS, WKS. OR QUANTITY	RATE	TOTALS
22	GENERAL OVERHEAD			
	A. FLAT CHARGE			
	B. CORPORATE OVERHEAD EXPENSE			
	C. CASTING OFFICE SALARIES			
	D. ENTERTAINMENT - EXECUTIVES			
	E. TRAVEL EXPENSE - EXECUTIVES			
	F. OFFICE RENTAL AND EXPENSE			
	G. AUDITOR			
	H. TIMEKEEPER			
	I. SECRETARIES			
	J. PUBLIC RELATIONS HEAD			
	K. PUBLIC RELATIONS SECRETARY			
	L. LEGAL FEES			
	M. OFFICE SUPPLIES			
	N. POSTAGE - TELEPHONE & TELEGRAPH			
	O. CUSTOMS BROKERAGE			
	P. CONTINGENCY			
	Q. GENERAL OFFICE O.H.			
	R. FILM SHIPPING			
	TOTAL GENERAL OVERHEAD			
	GRAND TOTAL			

SUMMARY OF DETAIL BUDGET AND COST REPORT

WEEKLY NEGATIVE COST REPORT

DIRECTOR_____

EST. FINISH DATE_____

EST. NO. OF DAYS_____

NEGATIVE FOOTAGE_____

PRODUCTION:_____

WEEK ENDING_____

STARTED_____

FINISHED_____

CAMERA DAYS TO DATE_____

NEG. ACCT.	CLASSIFICATION	BUDGET		CHARGES THIS WEEK		TOTAL TO DATE	
1	STORY, PRODUCER, DIRECTOR & CAST						
2	PRODUCTION STAFF						
3	PRODUCTION OPERATIONS SALARIES						
4	SET DESIGNING						
5	SET CONSTRUCTION						
6	SET OPERATIONS EXPENSE						
7	SPECIAL EFFECTS						
8	CUTTING FILM AND LABORATORY						
9	MUSIC AND ROYALTIES						
10	SOUND						
11	TRANSPORTATION						
12	LOCATION						
13	STUDIO CHARGES						
14	TESTS						
15	GENERAL OVERHEAD						
16	MISCELLANEOUS						
17	PUBLICITY						
	TOTALS						

1—Story, Producer, Director & Cast

WEEK ENDING_____19

		BUDGET		CHARGES THIS WEEK		TOTAL TO DATE
A	STORY					
B	CONTINUITY AND TREATMENT					
C	PRODUCER'S SALARY					
D	DIRECTOR'S SALARY					
E	STAR'S SALARY					
F	CAST SALARIES					
G	ASSISTANTS TO PRODUCER					
H	PRODUCER'S AND DIRECTOR'S SECRETARIES					
I	ARTISTS' PERSONAL ATTENDANTS					
J						
	TOTAL					

2—Production Staff

A	PRODUCTION OFFICE SALARIES					
B	ASSISTANT DIRECTORS					
C	LOCATION AND UNIT MANAGERS					
D	CASTING OFFICE SALARIES					
E	SCRIPT CLERKS					
F	DIALOGUE AND TECHNICAL DIRECTORS					
G	SPECIAL EFFECTS DIRECTORS					
H	DANCE DIRECTORS					
I	FIRST AID					
J	WELFARE WORKERS					
K						
	TOTAL					

3—Production Operations Salaries

A	EXTRA TALENT					
B	CAMERAMEN					
C	SOUND CREW					
D	WARDROBE DESIGNER AND STAFF					
E	GRIPS					
F	PROPERTY MEN					
G	DRAPERS					
H	MAKEUP AND HAIRDRESSING					
I	SWING GANG					
J	ELECTRICIANS					
K	STANDBY LABOR					
L	WRANGLERS					
M	STRIKING LABOR					
N	SPECIAL EFFECTS LABOR AND PROP. MAKERS					
O	SOCIAL SECURITY TAXES					
P	INSURANCE-COMPENSATION PUBLIC LIABILITY					
Q	SET WATCHMEN					
R	SET DRESSER AND OUTSIDE MAN					
	TOTAL					

4—Set Designing

WEEK ENDING_____ 19 ___

		BUDGET		CHARGES THIS WEEK		TOTAL TO DATE	
A	ART SUPERVISION						
B	ARTISTS AND DRAFTSMEN						
C	SPECIAL SKETCH ARTISTS						
D	SUPPLIES AND EXPENSE						
E	SET MODELS						
F							
	TOTAL						

5—Set Construction

		BUDGET		CHARGES THIS WEEK		TOTAL TO DATE	
A	LABOR						
B	MATERIALS						
C	RENTAL OF STANDING SETS						
D	LIGHT SCAFFOLDING - LABOR AND MATERIALS						
E	EXPENSES						
F	SUPERVISION-CONSTRUCTION BOSS						
G	GREENS - LABOR AND MATERIALS						
H	MINIATURES - FOREGROUND AND BACKGROUND						
I	BACKINGS						
	TOTAL						

6—Set Operations Expense

		BUDGET		CHARGES THIS WEEK		TOTAL TO DATE	
A	CAMERA RENTALS						
B	CAMERA PURCHASES AND EXPENSE						
C	WARDROBE RENTALS						
D	WARDROBE PURCHASES AND EXPENSE						
E	GRIP EQUIPMENT RENTALS						
F	GRIP EQUIPMENT PURCHASES AND EXPENSE						
G	PROP RENTALS						
H	PROP PURCHASES AND EXPENSE						
I	SET DRESSING RENTALS						
J	SET DRESSING PURCHASES AND EXPENSE						
K	DRAPERY RENTALS						
L	DRAPERY PURCHASES AND EXPENSE						
M	WIG AND HAIR GOODS RENTALS						
N	MAKEUP AND WIG PURCHASES AND EXPENSE						
O	ELECTRICAL EQUIPMENT RENTALS						
P	ELECTRICAL POWER						
Q	ELECTRICAL GLOBES AND SUPPLIES						
R	SET OPERATIONS MATERIALS						
S	LIVE AND ROLLING STOCK						
T	MISCELLANEOUS						
	TOTAL						

7—Special Effects

			BUDGET		CHARGES THIS WEEK		TOTAL TO DA`
	A	TRANSPARENCY PROCESS					
	B	MATTE AND OTHER PROCESSES					
	C	MONTAGE					
	D	MINIATURE EXPENSE - LABOR					
	E	STOCK SHOTS - PURCHASES					
	F	BACKGROUNDS - PURCHASES					
	G	SPECIAL EFFECTS MATERIALS AND RENTALS					
	H						
		TOTAL					

8—Cutting Film and Laboratory

	A	SOUND, MUSIC, AND ASSISTANT CUTTERS					
	B	RAW STOCK - ACTION					
	C	RAW STOCK - SOUND					
	D	RAW STOCK DEVELOPED					
	E	PRINT ACTION					
	F	PRINT SOUND					
	G	FINEGRAINS, DUPES, FADES AND DISSOLVES					
	H	CUTTING ROOM SUPPLIES					
	I	CUTTING CONTINUITY					
	J	TITLES AND INSERTS					
	K	COMPOSITE PRINTS					
		TOTAL					

9—Music and Royalties

	A	DIRECTOR AND CONDUCTOR					
	B	MUSICIANS' SALARIES					
	C	STANDBY LABOR					
	D	SINGERS AND COMMENTATORS					
	E	ARRANGERS					
	F	COPYING AND SUPPLIES					
	G	LICENSES AND ROYALTIES					
	H	RENTAL OF INSTRUMENTS					
	I	WAXES					
	J						
		TOTAL					

10—Sound

	A	PRERECORDING AND SCORING FACILITIES					
	B	RERECORDING FACILITIES					
	C	ROYALTIES					
	D	PURCHASES AND EXPENSE					
	E	WILD LINES AND SOUND EFFECTS					
	F	SOUND EQUIPMENT RENTALS					
	G	MISCELLANEOUS					
		TOTAL					

11—Transportation

WEEK ENDING _____ 19 ___

			BUDGET		CHARGES THIS WEEK		TOTAL TO DATE	
A	AUTOS AND TRUCKS	STUDIO						
B	AUTOS AND TRUCKS	OUTSIDE						
C	CAMERA CAR RENTALS							
D	BUSSES							
E	MISCELLANEOUS - MESSENGERS - ETC.							
F	PERSONAL CARS							
G								
	TOTAL							

12—Location

A	SEARCH AND RENTALS						
B	HOTEL AND MEALS						
C	FARES AND INCIDENTALS						
D							
	TOTAL						

13—Studio Charges

% OF						
VACATION FUND						
TOTAL						

14—Tests

A						

15—General Overhead

WEEK ENDING_____19 __

			BUDGET		CHARGES THIS WEEK		TOTAL TO DAT
	A	ACCOUNTING DEPARTMENT AND CLERICAL					
	B	PAYROLL DEPARTMENT					
	C	STATIONERY AND SUPPLIES					
	D	POSTAGE · TELEPHONE · TELEGRAPH					
	E	RENTAL OF OFFICE EQUIPMENT					
	F	REPAIRS TO OFFICE EQUIPMENT					
	G	ALTERATION TO OFFICE, ETC.					
	H	STATE AND COUNTY TAXES					
	I	LEGAL					
	J	MIMEOGRAPHING					
	K	INTEREST					
		TOTAL					

16—Miscellaneous

			BUDGET		CHARGES THIS WEEK		TOTAL TO DAT
	A	RESEARCH					
	B	CAST INSURANCE					
	C	NEGATIVE INSURANCE					
	D	LIFE INSURANCE					
	E	MISCELLANEOUS INSURANCE					
	F	SUNDRY UNCLASSIFIED					
	G	TRAVEL EXPENSE · EXECUTIVES					
	H	ENTERTAINMENT EXPENSE · EXECUTIVES					
	I	NEW YORK EXPENSE					
	J	PREVIEW					
	K	JOHNSTON OFFICE CERTIFICATE					
	L	EXECUTIVE EXPENSE					
		TOTAL					

17—Publicity

			BUDGET		CHARGES THIS WEEK		TOTAL TO DAT
	A	SALARIES					
	B	SUPPLIES					
	C	STILLS					
	D	TRADE AND NEWSPAPER SUBSCRIPTIONS					
	E	ENTERTAINMENT					
	F	MISCELLANEOUS					
	G	ADVERTISING					
	H	TRAILER					
	I						
		TOTAL					

SUMMARY PRODUCTION COSTS

PRODUCTION
NUMBER   TITLE   DATE

PRODUCER   ASSOCIATE
PRODUCER   DIRECTOR

CAST
DATE   WRITER   CAMERAMAN
STARTED   SCHEDULED   FINISH
         FINISH DATE   DATE

ACCT. No.	CLASSIFICATION	BUDGET	COST TO DATE	ESTIMATED COST TO COMPLETE	ESTIMATED TOTAL COST	OVER OR (UNDER) BUDGET
01	Story					
02	Supervisors					
03	Cast					
04	Direction					
	Total Above the Line Costs					
05	Director's Staff					
06	Camera					
07	Set Operations					
08	Set Construction Cost					
09	Set Design					
10	Set Dressings					
11	Special Effects					
12	Process					
13	Miniature					
14	Draperies					
15	Props					
16	Live Stock — Handlers and Eqpt.					
17	Locations					
18	Transportation					
19	Lighting					
20	Wardrobe					
21	Make-up and Hairdressing					
22	Film and Laboratory					
23	Sound Recording					
24	Sound Royalties					
25	Sound Dubbing and Scoring					
26	Film Editing					
27	Titles and Inserts					
28	Music					
29	Studio Rentals					
30	Tests and Pre-production					
31	Studio General					
	Total Below the Line Costs					
	Total Direct Cost					
0 - 000	Contingency					
	General Studio Overhead					
	TOTAL COST					

Remarks:

Film Budgeted   Feet Film Shot   Feet

Signed   Signed

           Producer   Production Dept.

Production No._____

Date_____

PRODUCTION COST STATEMENT

	BUDGET	COST TO DATE		
01-000 STORY				
01-001 Writers				
01-002 Rights Purchased				
01-003 Rights Developed in Studio				
01-004 Stenographic and Mimeograph				
01-300 Miscellaneous				
TOTAL				

	BUDGET	COST TO DATE		
02-000 SUPERVISION				
02-001 Producer and Assistants				
02-002 Production Manager				
TOTAL				

	BUDGET	COST TO DATE		
03-000 CAST				
03-001 Stars and Leads				
03-002 Supporting Cast				
03-003 Day Players				
03-004 Extra Talent — Stand-ins — Doubles				
03-005 Silent Musicians				
03-006 Commissions				
03-300 Miscellaneous				
TOTAL				

	BUDGET	COST TO DATE		
04-000 DIRECTION				
04-001 Director				
04-002 Dialogue, Technical and Dance Directors				
TOTAL				

	BUDGET	COST TO DATE		
05-000 DIRECTOR'S STAFF				
05-001 Assistant Directors				
05-002 Script Supervisors				
05-300 Miscellaneous				
TOTAL				

	BUDGET	COST TO DATE		
06-000 CAMERA				
06-001 Cameraman — Still — Assistant — Loader				
06-200 Rentals				
06-300 Miscellaneous				
TOTAL				

Production No._____

Date _____

PRODUCTION COST STATEMENT

03-000 CAST		BUDGET		COST TO DATE		
03-001 Stars and Leads						
CHARACTER	PLAYER					
	SUB-TOTAL					
03-002 SUPPORTING CAST						
CHARACTER	PLAYER					
	SUB-TOTAL					
03-003 Day Players						
03-004 Extra Talent — Stand-ins — Doubles						
03-005 Silent Musicians						
03-006 Commissions						
03-300 Miscellaneous						
	TOTAL					

Production No._____

Date_____

PRODUCTION COST STATEMENT

		BUDGET		COST TO DATE		
07-000	**SET OPERATIONS**					
07-001	Company Grips					
07-002	Company Prop Men					
07-003	Set Operations — Stand-by Labor					
07-004	Set Maintenance					
07-005	Green Work — Maintenance					
07-100	Material and Supplies					
07-200	Rentals					
07-300	Miscellaneous					
	TOTAL					

08-000	**SET CONSTRUCTION COSTS**					
08-001	Construction Labor					
08-002	Striking					
08-003	Scaffolds					
08-004	Backing					
08-005	Green Work					
08-100	Material and Supplies					
08-200	Rentals					
08-300	Miscellaneous					
	TOTAL					

09-000	**SET DESIGN**					
09-001	Unit Art Directors					
09-002	Assistant Art Directors					
09-003	Sketch Artists					
09-004	Model Makers					
09-005	Draftsmen					
09-006	Set Supervisor					
09-100	Material and Supplies					
09-300	Miscellaneous					
	TOTAL					

10-000	**SET DRESSINGS**					
10-001	Set Dressers and Swing Gang					
10-005	Loss and Damage					
10-006	Set Dressings Constructed					
10-010	Set Dressings Purchased					
10-110	Set Dressings Rental Contract					
10-200	Rentals — Outside					
10-300	Miscellaneous					
	TOTAL					

PRODUCTION COST STATEMENT

Production No._____

Date_____

11-000 SPECIAL EFFECTS	BUDGET		COST TO DATE			
11--001 Labor						
11-100 Materials						
11-200 Rentals						
11-300 Miscellaneous						
TOTAL						

12-000 PROCESS						
12-001 Backgrounds Made						
12-011 Labor Operating						
12-016 Plates						
12-200 Rentals						
12-300 Miscellaneous						
TOTAL						

13-000 MINIATURE						
13-001 Labor						
13-013 Matte Shots						
13-015 Contract						
13-100 Material						
13-200 Rentals						
13-300 Miscellaneous						
TOTAL						

14-000 DRAPERIES						
14-001 Drapery — Labor						
14-100 Material						
14-200 Rentals						
14-300 Miscellaneous						
TOTAL						

15-000 PROPS						
15-001 Labor — Swing Gang						
15-005 Loss and Damage						
15-006 Props Constructed						
15-010 Props Purchased						
15-011 Props — Inserts Made						
15-200 Rentals						
15-300 Miscellaneous						
TOTAL						

Production No._____

PRODUCTION COST STATEMENT

Date_____

		BUDGET		COST TO DATE			
16-000	LIVE STOCK — Handlers and Equipment						
16-003	Operators and Animal Handlers						
16-006	Equipment Constructed						
16-010	Animals and Wagons						
16-200	Rentals						
16-300	Miscellaneous						
	TOTAL						

		BUDGET		COST TO DATE			
17-000	LOCATIONS						
17-001	Sundry Employees						
17-002	Hotel and Meals						
17-012	Traveling						
17-200	Rentals						
17-300	Miscellaneous						
17-310	Surcharge						
	TOTAL						

		BUDGET		COST TO DATE			
18-000	TRANSPORTATION						
18-001	Labor						
18-100	Material and Supplies						
18-200	Rentals						
18-300	Miscellaneous						
	TOTAL						

		BUDGET		COST TO DATE			
19-000	LIGHTING						
19-001	Rigging and Striking						
19-002	Operating						
19-100	Material and Supplies						
19-110	Globe Insurance						
19-150	Electric Current						
19-200	Rentals						
19-300	Miscellaneous						
	TOTAL						

		BUDGET		COST TO DATE			
20-000	WARDROBE						
20-001	Designer						
20-003	Wardrobe Men						
20-005	Wardrobe Women						
20-100	Wardrobe Purchased						
20-200	Rentals						
20-300	Miscellaneous						
	TOTAL						

PRODUCTION COST STATEMENT

Production No._____

Date_____

		BUDGET	COST TO DATE	
21-000	MAKE-UP AND HAIRDRESSING			
21-001	Make-up Men and Women			
21-002	Hairdressers			
21-100	Materials and Supplies			
21-200	Rentals			
21-300	Miscellaneous			
	TOTAL			
22-000	FILM AND LABORATORY			
22-010	Negative Raw Stock			
22-011	Positive Raw Stock			
22-160	Laboratory Charges			
22-170	Still Laboratory Charges			
22-300	Miscellaneous			
22-012	Tape and Transfers			
	TOTAL			
23-000	SOUND RECORDING			
23-001	Recording Crew			
23-200	Rentals			
23-300	Miscellaneous			
	TOTAL			
24-000	SOUND ROYALTIES			
24-001	Domestic			
24-002	Foreign			
	TOTAL			
25-000	SOUND DUBBING AND SCORING			
25-011	Labor — Operating			
25-110	Rent — Dubbing and Scoring Room			
25-200	Rentals			
25-300	Miscellaneous			
	TOTAL			
26-000	FILM EDITING			
26-001	Film Editors and Assistants			
26-011	Projectionist			
26-110	Rental — Cutting Room			
26-200	Rental — Equipment			
26-300	Miscellaneous			
	TOTAL			

BIBLIOGRAPHY

(Business)

ACADEMY AWARDS ILLUSTRATED, Osborne, Robert, Marvin Miller
         Enterprises, 1965.
ACADEMY PLAYERS' DIRECTORY, Academy of Motion Picture Arts
         and Sciences, Published 3 times annually.
ACQUIRING AND USING MUSIC, 8th Annual Program on Legal Aspects
         of the Entertainment Industry, Beverly Hills Bar
         Association and USC School of Law.
AMERICAN MOTION PICTURE PRODUCTION IN FOREIGN COUNTRIES, 5th
         Annual Program on Legal Aspects of the Entertainment
         Industry, Beverly Hills Bar Association and USC School
         of Law.
ANATOMY OF A MOTION PICTURE, Griffith, Richard, St. Martin's
         Press, 1959.
A TREE IS A TREE, Vidor, King, Harcourt, Brace and Co., 1953
BASHFUL BILLIONAIRE, *(Howard Hughes)*, Gerber, Albert G., Dell,
         1967.
CARPETBAGGERS, THE, Robbins, Harold, Trident Press, 1961,
         Pocket Books, 1962.
CHAPLIN v. CHAPLIN, Sullivan, Ed, Marvin Miller Enterprises,
         1965.
CLASSICS OF THE FOREIGN FILM, Tyler, Parker, Citadel Press,
         1962.
CLASSICS OF THE SILENT SCREEN, Franklin, Joe, Citadel Press,
         1959.
COLLECTIVE BARGAINING AGREEMENTS, 7th Annual Program on Legal
         Aspects of the Entertainment Industry, Beverly Hills
         Bar Association and USC School of Law.
COLLIER QUICK AND EASY GUIDE TO TV WRITING, Lowther, George,
         Collier Books, 1963.
COPYRIGHT AND INTELLECTUAL PROPERTY, Marke, Julius J., Fund
         for the Advancement of Education, 1967.
CREATIVE FILMMAKING, Smallman, Kirk, Collier Books, 1969.
CURRENT INDUSTRY DEVELOPMENTS, 12th Annual Program on Legal
         Aspects of the Entertainment Industry, Beverly Hills
         Bar Association and USC School of Law, 1966.
CZAR, Wiseman, Thomas, Avon, 1965.
DISNEY VERSION, THE, Schickel, Richard, Avon Discus Books,
         1968.
DRAT! (W. C. Fields), Darien Books, 1968, Signet Books, 1969.
ENTERTAINMENT, PUBLISHING, AND THE ARTS, VOL. 1, Books, Maga-
         zines, Newspapers, Plays, Motion Pictures, Liney,
         Alexander, Clark Boardman Company, 1967.

BIBLIOGRAPHY

(Business)

ENTERTAINMENT, PUBLISHING AND THE ARTS, VOLUME 2,
        Television, Radio, Music, Records, Art, Photographs,
        Advertising, Publicity, Commercial Photography.
        Linder, Alexander, Clark Boardman, 1967.
FAME, Annual Audit of Personalities of Screen and Television,
        Quigley Publishing Company, Annual.
FILM, Manvell, Roger, Pelican, 1944.
FILM, A MONTAGE, MacCann, Richard Dyer, Dutton Paperback,
        1966.
FILM DAILY YEARBOOK OF MOTION PICTURES, Film Daily, Annual.
FILM 67-68, National Society of Film Critics, Schickel,
        Richard and Simon, John, Simon and Schuster, 1968,
        Annual.
FILM, THE (Its Economic, Social and Artistic Problems),
        Holbein Publishing Company, 1948.
FILM WORLD, Montagu, Ivor, Pelican Books, 1964.
FILMS OF CECIL B. DeMILLE, Ringold, Gene, and Bodeen, DeWitt,
        Citadel Press, 1969.
FINANCING A THEATRICAL PRODUCTION, Taubman, Joseph, Federal
        Legal Publications, 1964.
GLOSSARY OF MOTION PICTURE TERMINOLOGY, Jordan, Thurston C.,
        Jr., Pacific Coast Publishers, 1968.
GUIDE TO FILMMAKING, Pincus, Edward, Signet Books, 1969.
HARLOW, An Intimate Biography, Shulman, Irving, Bernard Geis
        Associates, 1964.
HOLLYWOOD BABYLON, Anger, Kenneth, Associated Professional
        Services, Inc., 1965.
HOLLYWOOD CONFIDENTIAL, Hirsch, Paul, Pyramid Books, 1967.
HOLLYWOOD, THE DREAM FACTORY, Powdermaker, Hortense, Little
        Brown and Company, 1950.
HOLLYWOOD UNCENSORED, Hirsch, Phil, Pyramid Books, 1965.
I.E. AN AUTOBIOGRAPHY, Rooney, Mickey, Bantam, 1966, G.P.
        Putnam, 1965.
INTERNATIONAL FILM GUIDE 1969, Cowie, Peter, A.S. Barnes and
        Company, Inc., 1969, Annual.
KING, THE, Cooper, Morton, Signet Books, 1967.
LA DOLCE VITA, Fellini, Frederico, Ballantine Books, 1961.
LARRY EDMUNDS BOOKSHOP CINEMA LIST '65-1966, Lubouski, G.
        and Larry Edmunds Bookshop, 1965, Irregular Series.
LEGAL ASPECTS OF THE ENTERTAINMENT INDUSTRY, Beverly Hills
        Bar Association and USC Law Center, Annual.
LITERARY PROPERTY, Wincor, Richard, Charles N. Potter, Inc.,
        Publisher, 1967.

BIBLIOGRAPHY

(Business)

LIVELIEST ART, THE (A Panoramic History of the Movies). The
        Macmillan Company, 1957. Mentor Books, 1957.
MAN AND THE MOVIES. Robinson, W.R. Pelican, 1967.
MARKETING OF MOTION PICTURES. Musun, Chris. Chris Musun Com-
        pany, 1969.
MERELY COLOSSAL. Mayer, Arthur. Simon and Schuster, 1953.
MOTION PICTURE THEATRE MANAGEMENT. Franklin, Harold B. George
        H. Doran Company, 1927.
MOVIES, CENSORSHIP AND LAW. Carmen, Ira H. University of
        Michigan Press, 1966.
MOVIES, THE. Griffith, Richard and Mayer, Arthur. Simon and
        Schuster, 1957.
MR. LAUREL AND MR. HARDY. McCabe, John. Signet Books, 1961.
MUSIC INDUSTRY BOOK, THE. Hurst, Walter E. and Hale, William
        Storm. 7 Arts Press, Inc., 1963.
MY AUTOBIOGRAPHY. Chaplin, Charles. Pocketbooks, Simon and
        Schuster, Inc., 1964.
MY LIFE WITH CHAPLIN. Chaplin, Lita Grey. Dell, 1966. Ber-
        nard Geis Associates, 1966.
NEW AMERICAN CINEMA. Battcock, Gregory. Dutton Paperback,
        1967.
PEOPLE WHO MAKE MOVIES. Taylor, Theodore. Doubleday and Com-
        pany, 1967. Avon Camelot Books, 1968.
PERSONAL SERVICE CONTRACTS. 4th Annual Program on Legal Aspects
        of the Entertainment Industry. Beverly Hills Bar Associ-
        ation and USC School of Law, 1958.
PICTORIAL HISTORY OF THE SILENT SCREEN. Blum, Daniel. Grosset
        and Dunlap, 1953.
PICTURE. Ross, Lillian. Avon Discus Books, 1952.
PRODUCTION FINANCING. 14th Annual Program on Legal Aspects of
        the Entertainment Industry. USC Law Center, 1968.
PUBLISHER'S OFFICE MANUAL, THE. Hurst, Walter E. and Hale,
        William Storm. 7 Arts Press, Inc., 1966.
RECORD INDUSTRY BOOK, THE. Hurst, Walter E. and Hale, William
        Storm. 7 Arts Press, Inc., 1961.
SINATRA, Twentieth Century Romantic. Shaw, Arnold. Holt, Rine-
        hart and Winston, 1968. Pocket Books, 1969.
SKOURAS, King of Fox Studios. Curti, Carlos. Holloway House,
        1967.
STUDIO, THE. The Guild. Holloway House, 1969.
SUBSIDIARY RIGHTS AND RESIDUALS. Taubman, Joseph. Federal
        Legal Press, 1968.

BIBLIOGRAPHY

(Business)

TECHNIQUE OF DOCUMENTARY FILM PRODUCTION. Baddeley, W. Hugh.
        Hastings House, 1963.
*TELEVISION BUSINESS, THE (Accounting Problems of a Growth
            Industry)*. Ogden, Warde B. Ronald Press, 1961.
TELL IT TO LOUELLA. Parsons, Louella. G. P. Putnam and Sons,
        1961. Lancer Books, 1966.
TORTS AND TAXES. 10th Annual Program on Legal Aspects of the
        Entertainment Industry. Beverly Hills Bar Association
        and USC School of Law.
U.S. MASTER PRODUCERS & BRITISH MUSIC SCENE BOOK. Hurst, Walter
        E. and Hale, William Storm. 7 Arts Press, Inc., 1968.
VALENTINO. Shulman, Irving. Trident Press, 1967. Pocket Books,
        1968.
VALENTINO. Steiger, Brad and Mank, Chaw. MacFadden Books, 1966.
WESTERN FILM AND TV ANNUAL. Speed, F. Maurice. MacDonald, Lon-
        don, Annual.
WESTERNS. Warman, Eric and Vallance, Tom. Golden Pleasure
        Books, Annual.
YES I CAN (Sammy Davis, Jr.). Davis, Sammy Jr., and Boyar,
        Jane and Burt, 1965.

BIBLIOGRAPHY

(Legal)

AMERICAN JURISPRUDENCE. See General Index Volumes for heading, "Moving Pictures." Bancroft Whitney Company. Annual Pocket Parts.

AMERICAN JURISPRUDENCE LEGAL FORMS ANNOTATED. See General Index Volume heading, "Motion Pictures," "Theaters, Shows and Exhibitions," "Literary Property and Copyright." Bancroft-Whitney. Pocket Parts Each Year or Two Years.

AMERICAN JURISPRUDENCE PLEADING AND PRACTICE FORMS ANNOTATED. See General Index heading of "Literary Property and Copyright." Bancroft-Whitney. Pocket Parts Each Year or Two Years.

ANTI-TRUST IN THE MOTION PICTURE INDUSTRY (Economic and Legal Analysis). Conant, Michael. University of California Press, 1960.

BENDER'S FORM OF INTERROGATORIES. Matthew Bender and Company. Pocket Parts. In General Index, see heading, "Literary Property and Copyright."

BULLETIN OF THE COPYRIGHT SOCIETY OF THE U.S.A. Copyright Society of the U.S.A. 6 issues annually.

COPINGER and SKONE JAMES on COPYRIGHT. Skone James, F.E. and E.P. Sweet and Maxwell, London, 1965.

COPYRIGHT (Monthly Review). United International Bureaux for the Protection of Intellectual Property (BIRPI). BIRPI, Geneva, Switzerland. Monthly.

COPYRIGHT AND RELATED TOPICS. Los Angeles Copyright Society and UCLA School of Law. University of California Press, 1964.

COPYRIGHT DECISIONS. Copyright Office, Library of Congress. Published every 2 years.

COPYRIGHT ENACTMENTS (Laws Passed in the United States Since 1783). Copyright Office Bulletin No. 3. Copyright Office, Library of Congress, 1963.

COPYRIGHT HANDBOOK, THE (For Fine and Applied Arts). Walls, Howard. Watson-Guptill Publication.

COPYRIGHT IN THE U.S.S.R. and OTHER EUROPEAN COUNTRIES OR TERRITORIES UNDER COMMUNIST GOVERNMENT. Selective Bibliography with Digest and Practice.

COPYRIGHT LAW SYMPOSIUM. American Society of Composers, Authors and Publishers. Columbia University Press. Annual.

COPYRIGHT LAW (Basic and Related Materials). Rothenberg, Stanley. Clark Boardman Company, Ltd., 1956.

COPYRIGHT LAW REVISION STUDIES. Copyright Office. 1958, 1959.

COPYRIGHT PROBLEMS ANALYZED. Federal Bar Association of N.Y., N.J. and Connecticut. Commerce Clearing House. 1951, 1953, 1966.

BIBLIOGRAPHY

(Legal)

COPYRIGHT THOUGHT IN CONTINENTAL EUROPE. Kase, Francis J.
        Fred B. Rothman and Company, 1967.
*COPYRIGHT (Unfair Competition, and Other Topics Bearing on the
        Protection of Literary, Musical, and Artistic Works).*
        Kaplan, Benjamin and Brown, Ralph S., Jr. Foundation
        Press.
COPYRIGHTS. Title 17, U.S.C., FEDERAL CODE ANNOTATED. Bobbs-
        Merrill Company. Bound volume and Annual pocket parts.
COPYRIGHTS. Title 17, United States Code Annotated. West Pub-
        lishing Company. Annual Pocket Parts.
CORPUS JURISPRUDENCE. See General Index Volume heading, "Motion
        Pictures." West Publishing Company. Annual Pocket
        Parts.
HOWELL'S COPYRIGHT LAW. Latman, Alan. BNA, Inc. 1962.
INTRODUCTION TO SOVIET COPYRIGHT LAW. No. 8 of Law in Eastern
        Europe Series. Levitsky, Serge L. A.W. Sythoff-Leyden,
        1964.
LAW OF COPYRIGHT UNDER THE UNIVERSAL CONVENTION. Bogsch, Arpad.
        R.R. Bowker Company, 1968.
LAW OF LITERARY PROPERTY. Wittenberg, Philip. World Publishing
        Company, 1956.
LEGAL PROTECTION OF LITERATURE, ART AND MUSIC. Clark Boardman
        Company, 1960.
MODERN FEDERAL PRACTICE DIGEST. See headings, "Copyright,"
        "Literary Property." West Publishing. Annual Pocket
        Parts.
MOTION PICTURE LAW DIGEST. Hartman, Dennis. Dennis Hartman,
        1947.
MUSIC INDUSTRY BOOK, THE. Hurst, Walter E. and Hale, William
        Storm. 7 Arts Press, Inc. 1963.
NIMMER ON COPYRIGHT. Nimmer, Melvin. Matthew Bender, 1963.
        (Brought up to date annually with replacement or addi-
        tional pages).
PROOF OF FACTS. (American Jurisprudence Proof of Facts Anno-
        tated). Bancroft-Whitney Company. In General Index
        Volume see heading, "Motion Pictures As Evidence."
PROTECTION OF LITERARY PROPERTY. Wittenberg, Philip. The
        Writer, Inc., 1968.
PUBLISHER'S OFFICE MANUAL, THE. Hurst, Walter E. and Hale,
        William Storm. 7 Arts Press, Inc., 1966.
*PUBLISHING, ENTERTAINMENT, ADVERTISING and OTHER FIELDS LAW
        QUARTERLY.* Callaghan and Company. Published Quarterly.
QUESTION OF COPYRIGHT. Putnam, George Haven. Knickerbocker
        Press, 1891.

BIBLIOGRAPHY

(Legal)

RADIO AND TELEVISION RIGHTS. Warner, Harry P. Matthew Bender
    and Company, 1953.

RADIO AND THE LAW. Moser, J.G. and Lavine, Richard A. Parker
    and Company, 1947.

RECORD INDUSTRY BOOK, THE. Hurst, Walter E. and Hale, William
    Storm. 7 Arts Press, Inc., 1961.

TRIALS, VOLUME 9 (American Jurisprudence Trials). Bancroft-
    Whitney, 1965. "Copyright Infringement Litigation,"
    by Arthur H. Seidel, pp 293-426.

TRIALS, VOLUME 10 (American Jurisprudence Trials Series).
    Bancroft-Whitney Company, 1965. "Obscenity Litigation,"
    by O. John Rogge, pp 1-254.

UNHURRIED VIEW OF COPYRIGHT, AN. Kaplan, Benjamin. Columbia
    University Press, 1967.

UNITED STATES COPYRIGHT LAW DIGEST. Martindale-Hubbell Law Di-
    rectory, Volume V. Annual.

UNITED STATES MASTER PRODUCERS and BRITISH MUSIC SCENE BOOK.
    Hurst, Walter E. and Hale, William Storm. 7 Arts Press,
    1968.

*WHAT THE GENERAL PRACTITIONER SHOULD KNOW ABOUT TRADEMARKS AND
    COPYRIGHTS.* Seidel, Arthur H. American Law Institute
    and the American Bar Association, 1967.

WORKING RULES AND JOB DESCRIPTIONS

NABET has published an excellent book "Working Rules And Job Descriptions", prepared with William E. Hines. The book shows job categories, duties, requirements, employments. There is an excellent series of job descriptions, duties, requirements, supervision, etc. It is must reading for anyone planning to make an intelligent movie budget and should be in every film producer's and film course library.

NABET is the National Association of Broadcast Employers and Technicians, AFL-CIO. Hollywood Local 531, Association of Film Craftsmen, it is at 1800 N. Argyle Avenue, Suite 501, Hollywood, California 90028.

Persons interested in learning the availability of this and other books written by William E. Hines, can inquire at the above address.

The following glossary is designed to be helpful from the business or legal standpoints. Technical terms are used because they appear in contracts or cases.

ADVERTISING - Advertising, centered on stars and stories, is channeled to two classes of buyers: exhibitors and the general public. Advertising directed toward exhibitors is found chiefly in trade journals and in direct mail announcements. Advertising to the general public is placed in film trailers, in newspapers, in magazines and on billboards. Public appearances of stars, in person and on other media of communication, such as radio and television, are used to sell their films.

ANSWER PRINT - The first projection print of a newly completed film. It is submitted by the laboratory for the approval or comments of the producer. As a result of the examination of the answer print the grading of various scenes may be changed or the color balance may be altered in subsequent prints or other corrections may be made.

AUTHORS LEAGUE OF AMERICA, INC. - The Authors League of America Inc. was founded in 1912 by writers including Book Tarkington, Arthur Train, and Jack London. The organization concerned itself primarily with problems of novelists and magazine writers. It wanted to protect the new and inexperienced authors from the greediness of publishers, and to protect experienced authors from the inexperienced. It taught members values of underlying rights in material. The Authors League of America, Inc. gave birth to various offspring, some of which have left home.

BLANKET DEAL - A master agreement is a licensing agreement covering the exhibition of features in a number of theatres, usually comprising a circuit.

BLIND SELLING - Blind selling is a practice whereby a distributor licenses a feature before the exhibitor is afforded an opportunity to view it.

BLOCK BOOKINGS - Block booking is the licensing of films only in groups and not singly. Exhibitors are forced to rent the lesser quality films if they want those with popular stars.

BOOKING AGENTS - Exhibitors combined by employing booking agents to bargain for films for a group. By virtue of the large numbers of theatres represented by a booking agent, the booking agent has more economic power to buy on better terms than the individual theatres have. Also, by buying intelligently for a theatre-client, the booking agent can save the theatre owner the time and trouble of having to buy intelligently. The booking agent is in a position to collect box office figures from clients who play films early, and can then decide to buy or not buy for his other clients. He need not rely on the distributors phoney box office figures.

CARTRIDGE - A lightproof metal or plastic container for a role or reel of film permitting daylight loading.

CASTING COUCH - A sexploitation picture set prop without any sexploitation picture.

CLEARANCE - A clearance is the period of time, usually stipulated in license contracts, which must elapse between runs of the same feature within a particular area or in specified theatres.

DIRECTOR - The NABET definition includes: The Director is directly responsible to the producer and shall be responsible for directing the production activities of the cast and crew as creatively and efficiently as possible in order to get the necessary photographic coverage of the best dramatic results obtainable.

DISTRIBUTORS - The distributors are the wholesalers in the motion picture industry. They sell the exhibitor the right to use a positive print of a film for a fixed number of weeks.

DUPE - To print a duplicate negative from a master negative, usually via a duping positive.

DUPE NEGATIVE - Negative which is taken from an original negative, usually via a duping print.

DUPING PRINT - Special print of low contrast made from a negative for the purpose of making a dupe negative.

EDMUNDS, LARRY CINEMA & THEATRE BOOK SHOP - 6658 Hollywood Boulevard, Hollywood, California 90028 is one of the best film bookshops in the world. Its catalog costs $1.00.

EXCHANGES - Exchanges are the wholesale offices in major cities that negotiate licenses with, and deliver films to, the theatres in that area of the country.

FILM RENTAL - Film rental is usually computed on one of the following bases:
(1) a flat amount.
(2) a percentage of the theater's gross revenue on the film.
(3) a guaranteed minimum plus a percentage of gross revenues.
(4) a sliding scale of percentages which increased as gross admissions on the film increased.
(5) the entire theater box office less a flat rental paid to the theater.

(6)   the entire box office less a sliding rental paid to the theater.

FOREIGN FILM SUBSIDIES - Various subsidies are given by
countries, government agencies, banks. Some subsidies are based on
money spent in the country. Other subsidies are available only to
citizens of, and corporations incorporated in, the country giving
the subsidy. Producers should not expect governments to pay promptly.

FRANCHISE - A franchise is a licensing agreement, or series of
licensing agreements, entered into as part of the same transaction,
in effect for more than one motion picture season and covering the
exhibition of features released by one distributor during the entire
period of the agreement.

GAFFER - The Gaffer (Chief Electrician) "is directly responsible
to the Director of Photography and shall be responsible for supervising the operation of the lighting crew as efficiently as practicable
in order to expedite lighting the set in the manner directed and for
the balance desired by the Director of Photography".
Quote from NABET's WORKING RULES AND JOB DESCRIPTIONS.

GRIP - "The Key Grip is directly responsible to the Director
of Photography and to the Gaffer during lighting procedures, when a
Gaffer is employed on a production. The Key Grip shall be responsible
for setting all reflectors and for supervising the operation of the
Grip crew as efficiently as practicable in order to prepare the set
and expedite lighting procedure involving the Grip crew". This
definition is in NABET's WORKING RULES AND JOB DESCRIPTIONS. For
expansion on the topic, see William Hines' book.

IATSE - INTERNATIONAL ALLIANCE OF THEATRICAL STAGE EMPLOYEES.
This union fought hard to raise wages and improve working conditions
for its members. Many of its members work irregularly, sometimes
one day weekly, sometimes fifteen days monthly. The daily wage is
high, but because days of employment income are followed by days of
unemployment, the annual amounts earned are not high. IATSE has
been blamed for forcing up wages so high that producers of individual
motion pictures prefer to shoot elsewhere or with NABET crews or
with non-union crews.

ICEBOX ELEMENT - "The thought and discussion that a good film
ought to provoke when the family returns home from the theater for
a midnight snack." King, Vidor, A Tree Is A Tree.

INTER-NEGATIVE - A negative that is made for the purpose of
running off release prints. It is made either from a reversal
master or a print, preferably a special duping print. An inter-
negative is also made as one stage in making opticals (mixes, fades,
wipes, overlays, etc.).

LOCATION - STUDIO ZONE LOCATION is a point within a ten mile radius from the intersections of Sunset and Vine Streets, Hollywood, California. NEARBY LOCATION is defined as outside the Studio Zone but where overnight lodging is not required for the Employee(s). DISTANT LOCATION is defined as outside the Studio Zone and where the Employee(s) is required to remain away and be lodged overnight. These definitions are in the NABET STANDARD MOTION PICTURE BASIC AGREEMENT.

MAGAZINE - a metal receptacle for a cartridge.

MANUFACTURING - Manufacturing, in the industry, is called production. The producer assembles a studio, story, actors and technicians, and after making a film, will license the negative or a number of positive prints to distributor(s), or market it through his own integrated distribution department.

MASTER AGREEMENT - A master agreement is a licensing agreement or "Blanket Deal" covering the exhibition of features in a number of theatres, usually comprising a circuit.

MOTION PICTURE ASSOCIATION OF AMERICA, INC. (MPAA). - Formerly called The Motion Picture Producers and Distributors of America, Inc. Created a censorship branch - Production Code Administration (PCA), created an advertising (dis)approval branch - Advertising Code Administration (ACA).

MOTION PICTURE EXPORT ASSOCIATION - Source of information concerning foreign countries' production (subsidies), distribution, exhibition.

MOTION PICTURE HEALTH AND WELFARE FUND - 6912 Hollywood Boulevard, Hollywood, California 90028.

MOTION PICTURE INDUSTRY PENSION PLAN - 7423 Beverly Boulevard, Los Angeles, California 90036.

MOVEOVER - A moveover is the privilege given a licensee to move a picture from one theatre to another as a continuation of the run at the licensee's first theatre.

MOVIOLA - A one-man projection machine used by the film editor that allows him to run the film at various speeds back and forth, and view it immediately through a magnifying glass.

NABET - National Association of Broadcasting Employees and Technicians, AFL-CIO. NABET and IATSE are bitter opponents. IATSE is at this time better entrenched in studios; NABET as an out has constructive ideas and methods which save producers money in the production of pictures. NABET represents film personnel in

Hollywood and elsewhere. Hollywood Local 531 is at 1800 North
Argyle Avenue, Suite 501, Hollywood, California 90028. NABET
cooperated with the gathering of information for this book;
IATSE did not.

NEGATIVE - The film before or after it has been exposed in a
camera before or after it is processed so that it carries an image
with the original tone inverted. "Positive" prints are made from
negative prints. 1. Raw stock. 2. Exposed film. 3. Processed film.

OPTICALS - Fades, mixes, wipes, superimpositions added during
the process of printing a film.

OVERAGE AND UNDERAGE - Refer to the practice of using excess
film rental earned in one circuit theatre to fulfill a rental
commitment defaulted by another.

POSITIVE PRINT - Print from a negative. Normal print for
projection.

PRODUCTION BANK ACCOUNT - A special bank account set up for the
specific purpose of paying expenses of a specific production. The
funds are, by agreement between the Producer and the Bank and/or the
Distributor, usable only for items of negative cost of the Picture.
The account frequently requires two signatures, one being that of
the Producer, the other being that of the Bank or Distributor.
Possibly private backers may insist on the right to have a representative sign on the account, too.

RELEASE-PRINT - Projection print of a finished film.

REVERSAL FILM - A type of filmstock which after exposure and
processing produces a positive image instead of a negative.

ROAD SHOW - A road show is a public exhibition of a feature
in a limited number of theatres, in advance of its general release,
at admission prices higher than those customarily charged in
first-run theatres in those areas.

ROUGH CUT - First assembly of a film in which the selected
takes are joined in sequence, but the finer points of editing have
not yet been carried out.

RUNS - Runs are successive exhibitions of a feature in a given
area, first-run being the first exhibition in that area, second-run
being the next, etc.

RUSHES - Film that has just been exposed by a film camera;
prints of scenes exactly as they were shot in the camera before
any cutting or editing.

SCREENPLAY - The written form of the story that is to be filmed, specifying dialogue, settings, physical descriptions of the characters and their actions, and sometimes camera angles.

SNEAK PREVIEW - The only method of market testing that approaches a scientific survey is the sneak preview of an individual film. At the preview the audience is questioned about its reactions. The producers then may delete parts of the film or make small additions to it.

SOURCE MATERIAL - Defined in agreements as all material upon which a motion picture or teleplay is based other than the story. . . including other material upon which the story was based.

UNDERAGE AND OVERAGE - Refer to the practice of using excess film rental earned in one circuit theatre to fulfill a rental commitment defaulted by another.

WORK PRINT - A preliminary, rough version of the film used for initial, critical screenings and by the various sound and photographic effects personnel in their work. The print of film, silent and sound, with which an editor works to shape the picture. It is usually composed of dailies intercut and in its final form provides the guide for negative cutting.

WORKING RULES and JOB DESCRIPTIONS - A booklet prepared by William Hines for Hollywood Local 531, Association of Film Craftsmen, as a part of the Standard Motion Picture Basic Agreement of NABET. Mr. Hines may, at the time you read this, have expaned into a book this excellent source of information listing duties and providing job descriptions of over sixty film occupations.

WRITERS GUILD OF AMERICA, WEST, INC. - This guild is a successor to the Screen Writers Guild, which was formed by the motion picture writers as an administrative unit and member guild of The Authors League of America, Inc. The Writers Guild of America, West, is a California corporation, while the Writers Guild of America, East, is a New York corporation. These corporations negotiate agreements concerning theatrical motion pictures and film television, free-lance writing in live television and radio, continuity and newswriting by network staff writers.

ZONES - Zones are the areas into which a city is divided for purposes of granting exclusive rights to runs.

ZOOM SHOT - A shot in which a special lens is attached to the camera, enabling the operator to change rapidly from a wide-angle shot to a tight close-up without moving the camera.

INDEX

I   THE RECORD INDUSTRY BOOK   IV   THE U.S. MASTER PRODUCERS & BRITISH MUSIC SCENE BOOK
II   THE MUSIC INDUSTRY BOOK   V   THE MOVIE INDUSTRY BOOK
III   THE PUBLISHERS OFFICE MANUAL   VI   THE MANAGERS', ENTERTAINERS' & AGENTS' BOOK

I   THE RECORD INDUSTRY BOOK

II   THE MUSIC INDUSTRY BOOK

III THE PUBLISHERS OFFICE MANUAL

IV   THE U.S. MASTER PRODUCERS & BRITISH MUSIC SCENE BOOK

V   THE MOVIE INDUSTRY BOOK

VI   THE MANAGERS', ENTERTAINERS' & AGENTS' BOOK

I   THE RECORD INDUSTRY BOOK   IV   THE U.S. MASTER PRODUCERS & BRITISH MUSIC SCENE BOOK
II   THE MUSIC INDUSTRY BOOK   V   THE MOVIE INDUSTRY BOOK
III THE PUBLISHERS OFFICE MANUAL   VI   THE MANAGERS', ENTERTAINERS' & AGENTS' BOOK

771   INDEX   Page 5

I   THE RECORD INDUSTRY BOOK
II   THE MUSIC INDUSTRY BOOK
III   THE PUBLISHERS OFFICE MANUAL

IV   THE U.S. MASTER PRODUCERS & BRITISH MUSIC SCENE BOOK
V   THE MOVIE INDUSTRY BOOK
VI   THE MANAGERS', ENTERTAINERS' & AGENTS' BOOK

I	THE RECORD INDUSTRY BOOK	IV	THE U.S. MASTER PRODUCERS & BRITISH MUSIC SCENE BOOK
II	THE MUSIC INDUSTRY BOOK	V	THE MOVIE INDUSTRY BOOK
III	THE PUBLISHERS OFFICE MANUAL	VI	THE MANAGERS', ENTERTAINERS' & AGENTS' BOOK

771   INDEX   Page 9

I	THE RECORD INDUSTRY BOOK	IV	THE U.S. MASTER PRODUCERS & BRITISH MUSIC SCENE BOOK
II	THE MUSIC INDUSTRY BOOK	V	THE MOVIE INDUSTRY BOOK
III	THE PUBLISHERS OFFICE MANUAL	VI	THE MANAGERS', ENTERTAINERS' & AGENTS' BOOK

I	THE RECORD INDUSTRY BOOK	IV	THE U.S. MASTER PRODUCERS & BRITISH MUSIC SCENE BOOK
II	THE MUSIC INDUSTRY BOOK	V	THE MOVIE INDUSTRY BOOK
III	THE PUBLISHERS OFFICE MANUAL	VI	THE MANAGERS', ENTERTAINERS' & AGENTS' BOOK

I	THE RECORD INDUSTRY BOOK	IV	THE U.S. MASTER PRODUCERS & BRITISH MUSIC SCENE BOOK
II	THE MUSIC INDUSTRY BOOK	V	THE MOVIE INDUSTRY BOOK
III	THE PUBLISHERS OFFICE MANUAL	VI	THE MANAGERS', ENTERTAINERS' & AGENTS' BOOK

I	THE RECORD INDUSTRY BOOK
II	THE MUSIC INDUSTRY BOOK
III	THE PUBLISHERS OFFICE MANUAL
IV	THE U.S. MASTER PRODUCERS & BRITISH MUSIC SCENE BOOK
V	THE MOVIE INDUSTRY BOOK
VI	THE MANAGERS', ENTERTAINERS' & AGENTS' BOOK

I   THE RECORD INDUSTRY BOOK
II   THE MUSIC INDUSTRY BOOK
III   THE PUBLISHERS OFFICE MANUAL

IV   THE U.S. MASTER PRODUCERS & BRITISH MUSIC SCENE BOOK
V   THE MOVIE INDUSTRY BOOK
VI   THE MANAGERS', ENTERTAINERS' & AGENTS' BOOK

771   INDEX   Page 22

I   THE RECORD INDUSTRY BOOK   IV   THE U.S. MASTER PRODUCERS & BRITISH MUSIC SCENE BOOK

II   THE MUSIC INDUSTRY BOOK   V   THE MOVIE INDUSTRY BOOK

III   THE PUBLISHERS OFFICE MANUAL   VI   THE MANAGERS', ENTERTAINERS' & AGENTS' BOOK

TABLE OF FORMS

For the convenience of the reader looking for an applicable form, this table lists forms in this book and in other books of The Entertainment Industry series:

I = The Record Industry Book

II = The Music Industry Book

III = The Publishers Office Manual

IV = The U.S. Master Producers & British Music Scene Book

V = The Movie Industry Book

VI = The Managers', Entertainers' & Agents' Book

* * * * * * * * * * * * * *

I	THE RECORD INDUSTRY BOOK	IV	THE U.S. MASTER PRODUCERS & BRITISH MUSIC SCENE BOOK
II	THE MUSIC INDUSTRY BOOK	V	THE MOVIE INDUSTRY BOOK
III	THE PUBLISHERS OFFICE MANUAL	VI	THE MANAGERS', ENTERTAINERS' & AGENTS' BOOK

I	THE RECORD INDUSTRY BOOK	IV	THE U.S. MASTER PRODUCERS & BRITISH MUSIC SCENE BOOK
II	THE MUSIC INDUSTRY BOOK	V	THE MOVIE INDUSTRY BOOK
III	THE PUBLISHERS OFFICE MANUAL	VI	THE MANAGERS', ENTERTAINERS' & AGENTS' BOOK

INDEX — FORMS

I	THE RECORD INDUSTRY BOOK	IV	THE U.S. MASTER PRODUCERS & BRITISH MUSIC SCENE BOOK
II	THE MUSIC INDUSTRY BOOK	V	THE MOVIE INDUSTRY BOOK
III	THE PUBLISHERS OFFICE MANUAL	VI	THE MANAGERS', ENTERTAINERS' & AGENTS' BOOK

I	THE RECORD INDUSTRY BOOK	IV	THE U.S. MASTER PRODUCERS & BRITISH MUSIC SCENE BOOK
II	THE MUSIC INDUSTRY BOOK	V	THE MOVIE INDUSTRY BOOK
III	THE PUBLISHERS OFFICE MANUAL	VI	THE MANAGERS', ENTERTAINERS' & AGENTS' BOOK

I   THE RECORD INDUSTRY BOOK   IV   THE U.S. MASTER PRODUCERS & BRITISH MUSIC SCENE BOOK
II   THE MUSIC INDUSTRY BOOK   V   THE MOVIE INDUSTRY BOOK
III   THE PUBLISHERS OFFICE MANUAL   VI   THE MANAGERS', ENTERTAINERS' & AGENTS' BOOK

WE PROUDLY REPRINT <u>ANOTHER ENTIRE REVIEW</u> OF *THE PUBLISHER'S OFFICE MANUAL*.

This review is by *THE LIBRARY JOURNAL*.

"HURST, Walter E., & HALE, William Storm, *The Publisher's Office Manual:* (How to Do Your Paperwork in the Music Publishing Industry). (Entertainment Industry Series, Volume 3). 1000 pp. 7 Arts Pr., 6605 Hollywood Boulevard, Suite 215, Hollywood, California 90028.

"This weighty tome (typewritten and reproduced by offset) owes something of its bulk to the fact that each page is printed only on one side - - - the blanks may be used for notes, but many are adorned with what the authors call 'pearls' (short for pearls of wisdom) in red type and often illustrated. Like its predecessors in the series, *The Record Industry Book* and *The Music Industry Book*, the volume is set up with occasionally interrupted pagination, with a view to future editions and additions. The points the authors make often take the form of stories, or are perhaps presented in funny paper style. Mr. Hurst, an attorney specializing in the entertainment field and a teacher at the University of California, and Mr. Hale, carefully unidentified under a pseudonym, are not given to stuffiness. In fact they have their little joke wherever they can get it in. But it should be pointed out that their field is strictly pops; in it they speak a special and sometimes mysterious language. Libraries interested in this field will certainly want the series, for the authors spell out the answers to many questions, even reproducing forms for contracts, copyright registration certificates, publisher's clearance forms, and so on." *Philip L. Miller, Formerly Chief, Music Div., New York P.L.*

— —

TO: 7 ARTS PRESS, INC.
          6605 Hollywood Boulevard, Suite 215
          Hollywood, California 90028

FROM: _____
                          (Name or Firm)

          _____
                (Street Address, City, State & Zip Code)

Please send me, for the enclosed payment in full:

_____	Copies of *THE RECORD INDUSTRY BOOK*	at $25.00 each
_____	Copies of *THE MUSIC INDUSTRY BOOK*	at $25.00 each
_____	Copies of *THE PUBLISHER'S OFFICE MANUAL*	at $25.00 each
_____	Copies of *THE U.S. MASTER PRODUCER'S BOOK*	at $25.00 each
_____	Copies of *THE MOVIE INDUSTRY BOOK*	at $25.00 each

California residents please add sales tax of $1.25 per book.

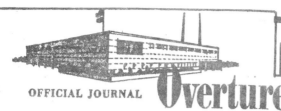

OFFICIAL JOURNAL **Overture**

DON MORRIS, Editor

MUSICIANS MUTUAL PROTECTIVE ASSN., LOCAL 47, A. F. of M.
817 N. VINE STREET, LOS ANGELES 38, CALIF.

THE RECORDING INDUSTRY

By Rene J. Hall

In my over thirty years as sideman, leader, aranger, recording consultant, independent master producer, and now member of the Board of Directors of Local 47, I have often wished that our field had a reference book which could answer our questions—just as electricians and engineers and various mechanics have reference books in their fields to supply answers to their professional problems.

Quite recently, I was presented with a copy of such a book, written by an attorney friend of mine who is an expert in the field of recordings. He knows what makes it .ick, and quotes book, chapter and verse in one big volume.

Having found this book to be of invaluable assistance to me in the field of independent master producing, I would like to take this opportunity to recommend it to the many musicians, who, like myself, are either already in or are desirous of entering this particular field of endeavor.

Everything is covered here, from fascinating case histories of artists, publishers, and songs, to the financing, big and small, of record companies, record sessions and independent record productions; how they are started and run. The book is packed, too, with explanatory charts and illustrations, sample contracts dealing with musicians, artists, distributors, etc., etc., etc., including foreign rights.

Although the cost of this book is less than one-half of a record date, it will both make and save a lot of money for anyone armed with its vast store of business knowledge. A musician may suggest to the owners of the clubs in which he plays or to his regular employers, that they finance master producing sessions at scale for playing and arranging, and thus have a chance at record exposure and royalties.

In my honest opinion this book is a real must for anyone engaged in or thinking of entering the business, a book that you will not only read with interest but that you will keep for research and answers that come up.

In the course of conduct of my daily business, I'm asked many questions by both beginners and professionals of many years standing, the answers to which were to be found within the pages of his highly informative book.

I wish that I could have had this book thirty years ago. Now, I have one copy of the book at home for reading and one available at my office for reference.

Walter E. Hurst writes with scholarly knowledge; w . compassion for people in the industry, with wit and good humor and sugar-coats the lessons that we must all learn.

There are many of us in he business who would have saved much work, money, and heartbreak if they had had, "THE RECORD INDUSTRY" (How to Make Money In the Record Industry) by Walter E. Hurst, published by 7 Arts Press, 1775 Las Palmas, Hollywood 28, California. ($25.00); to guide them.

ORDER FROM:

7 ARTS PRESS, INC.
6430 SUNSET BLVD.
SUITE 1223
HOLLYWOOD, CALIF. 90028

Phone: 469-1095

THE Hollywood REPORTER

NEW BOOKS

The complex and highly competitive recording business is given an exhaustive treatment by Walter E. Hurst, Hollywood attorney and advocate-at-law who has specilized in this field, and William Storm Hale (a non de plume to protect his identity) in a book tentatively titled "The Record Industry" ("How to Make Money In the Record Industry"), to be published by 7 Arts Press of Hollywood next month at $25 a copy. It's a big book, covering all angles and operations from songwriter, singer, publisher and disc firm down to the retail store; going into detail about contracts, distribution and promotion; citing artists who have made money; telling what artists should know about personal managers, disc jockeys, payola, the music trade press; the law of the recording field, Congressional investigation, etc. All in all, the book presents an almost overwhelming array of information, sprinkled with illustrations, charts and tabulations, sample forms, etc., that should prove invaluable to anyone in the record business or planning to enter the field.

NIGHT LIFE IN CHICAGO

Sid Ascher

THE RECORD INDUSTRY BOOK: Just finished reading a most fascinating book—"The Record Industry Book" (How To Make Money in The Record Industry) Volume One. This to me is truly wonderful. If you are already in the record business; if you want to go into the business; if you are a song writer or publisher, or a recording artist, this book is "must" reading. It is really an encyclopedia of the recording industry and should be in every library in the nation. For information on how you may purchase a copy write to 7 Arts Press, 6365 Selma Avenue, Hollywood 28, California.

DAILY VARIETY DAILY

WHAT'S THE SCORE?

By JOHN G. HOUSER

★ ★ ★

WORDS AND MUSIC: "THE RECORD INDUSTRY." AUTHORS Walter E. Hurst and William Storm Hale have contributed a massive, monumental and authoritative work that is as comprehensive a study of an intricate industry as it is possible to reveal. The material included in the invaluable work is a compendium and a textbook for neophyte and journeyman in all facets of the disk biz. It will be classed (as is Blackstone and Gray's Anatomy in the legal and medical professions) as the supreme authority for those in the recording industry. The price, $25, will be an investment many times recovered if the purchaser makes use of the lessons to be learned (the easy way). Authors have made "the lessons" an exciting panorama of case histories from artist to copyright and promotion to payola. Published by 7 Arts Press, the book should be at the right hand of every a&r man, musician, songwriter and publisher . . .

JOE YORE

Age Range:	22-40ish
Hair:	Dark Brown
Weight:	140 lbs.
Height:	5' 8"
Eyes:	Hazel
Phone:	

662-4529

SAG - AFTRA - ARTIST